THE BEST INNOVATIVE WRITING

First published 2009 by &NOW Books, an imprint of Lake Forest College Press.

Directors
Robert Archambeau
Davis Schneiderman

Associate Director
Joshua Corey

Box A-16
Lake Forest College
555 N. Sheridan Road
Lake Forest, IL 60045

lakeforest.edu/andnow

Lake Forest College Press, based at Chicago's National Liberal Arts College, publishes in the broad spaces of Chicago studies. Our imprint, &NOW Books, publishes innovative and conceptual literature, and serves as the publishing arm of the &NOW writers' conference and organization.

Cover Image:
"Royalty"
Maria Tomasula
oil on panel
32" x 36"
2008
private collection, United States

ISBN-13: 978-0-9823156-0-6
ISBN-10: 0-9823156-0-0

Book design by Emma Therieau

Printed in the United States

ACKNOWLEDGEMENTS

This volume would not have been possible without the work of numerous editors, contributors, research assistants, and friends. We would like to specifically acknowledge the following students in the Spring 2009 course "Book Editing" at Lake Forest College, who read and evaluated nominations of possible contributors. They served as assistant editors on the present volume:

Suzanne Block
Edward Brown
Alexandra Burrage
Katie Danklefsen
Ryann Freeman
Victoria Henson
Kristin Kojzarek
Nick Leland
Nathaniel Sullivan
Caitlyn Ulbert

Their instructor and Associate Editor for this volume, the inimitable **Eckhard Gerdes**, helped steer this unruly ship in its initial phases, and Associate Editor **Scott McFarland** helped do the same in its final moments before press. To both, we are indebted.

Additional thanks goes to three outstanding student Assistant Editors at Lake Forest College. **Sarah Spoto**, as a member of the 2009 Lake Forest College Richter Scholars Program, devoted countless hours to shaping and organizing submissions. **Edward Brown**, a member of the Spring 2009 course, continued his service in summer 2009 in reading and evaluating manuscripts, as well as assembling contributor information. Finally, **Emily Snowberg** worked tirelessly on administrative matters, preparing and coordinating the contracts, spreadsheets, and supporting documents necessary for a venture of this complexity.

The Visual Communications Department at Lake Forest College deserves a gold star and a bottle of champagne. Director of Visual Communications **Leslie Taylor** manages every crisis with the same pragmatic optimism; and our book designer, **Emma Therieau,** keeps everything looking better than we could have imagined.

Finally, this book is only as good as the work of its contributors, and in this regard, you hold in your hand an embarassement of riches.

Table of Contents

Note: Many contributions to this collection are portions of longer works. Contributions with separate names (chapter titles, individual poems, etc) are noted here and in the main section of this collection only by their *individual* titles, but information about their provenance can be found at the end of the book (Previous Publication Credits), where the titles of longer works appear. Conversely, contributions from a longer work with *no independent title* are listed in this table of contents and the book proper as "From," followed by the name of work, with full information also appearing at the close of the book.

STEVE TOMASULA

And Now &NOW: a foreword

It was the best of times, it was the worst of times. It was the middle-of-the-road of times. Never before had there been so much mediocrity. And greatness. Call our moment the fill-in-the-blank of times, and that might come closest. That is, ours is the most exciting of times, at least for literature, for never before has there been such a variety of authors, ways to write, things to write with or upon, or ways to publish. The consequences for literature have been seismic: unlike earlier times when the choice for poets was between lyric and epic, or prose authors were novelists and/or short story writers; unlike a time when it was easy to distinguish between poetry and prose (and readers thought it important enough to care), the plethora of forms that make up today's literary landscape are staggering, ranging from the traditional, neo-sonnet to (computer) code poetry or sound mashups that explore the most basic units of language. The authors bringing these forms into existence come from so many class, ethnic, and experiential backgrounds, and write out of so many differing authorial, theoretical/philosophical or aesthetic positions (including the no-theory theory) as to make the landscape of earlier generations seem flat. This galaxy of authors explores an equally dizzying range of writing surfaces and tools, ranging from page to stage, of course, but now the page is just as likely to be made of pixels, the stage a hologram cave, or the space in front of a subway surveillance camera.

Similar statements can be made for all of the arts. So why is it that a survey of most bookstores, course syllabi, prize winners, book reviews and other prominent markers reveal a much narrower literary spectrum? Why is there such variety in what counts as contemporary visual art, for example—art made of genetic code, earthen dams, as well as traditional painting and video—while what counts as a novel, for example, continues to be defined by criteria readers from an earlier time would recognize? Why is it, William Gass asks, that the dominant form of the 21st century novel is the 19th century novel?

There's no need here to detail the momentous social and material changes in the world outside of literature: e.g., two (postmodern) wars (war being that traditional marker between literary periods); the feminist revolution; the bio-tech revolution (and its accompanying shift in what it means to be human); global warming; an African-American president; the demise of newspapers; You-Tube, Kindle—the Napsterization of everything—and an attendant cut-paste-and-burn, sampling mentality....

It probably isn't necessary, either, to rehearse the consolidation of book publishing and selling that constitutes mainstream literature: the 40 New York houses that made up mainstream publishing 20 years ago are now owned by one of five global conglomerates, where literary publishing lives on as one investment among many in entertainment portfolios (which may also include cable-TV, merchandizing, theme parks, etc.). Independent bookstores that would have once sold the publications of those independent publishers have largely been replaced by one or two chain stores that focus on the great bulge in the demographic curve. And so, as with Hollywood movies, so with New York novels: if it won't sell at the mall, it won't be produced. The result has been a literary climate where bestseller lists are the barometers of literary value.

That is, though there are more books published now than ever, it has not been an easy time for artists whose medium is words. Or as composer Morton Feldman once put it, "To me, it seems as though the artist is fighting a heavy sea in a rowboat, while alongside him a pleasure line takes all these people to the same place." Indeed, considering the gulf between change in the world that authors and books live within and the conservatism of the world of books (best-seller lists, commercial reviews, chain-store shelves, or what most people consider a poem or a novel), we might wonder, as did Robbe-Grillet, why the forms of literature should remain "fixed, when everything around it" is "in evolution—even revolution."

Yet, it's important to note that there have always been rowboats as well as ocean liners: works of art and literature that strive to reflect (or emerge from) changes in the world and how we think of it, and those that (consciously or unconsciously) maintain an even keel, the status quo. While institutions such as chain bookstores and commercial publishers tend to limit the definition of what counts as a novel or poem, there has always been literature that tends to keep these definitions unresolved.

&NOW began as a festival of authors and literature that in some way fell into this more responsive, harder to characterize, literary tradition. In the past, writing like this might have gone by a variety of names: experimental, conceptual, avant-garde, surfiction, fusion, radical, slip-stream, language writing, avant-pop, postmodern, self-conscious, innovative, alternative, anti- or new literature. But in an age of virulent cross-pollination and rapid mutation, even these categories blur into something post-all-of-that.

At the same time, the works that make up the body of &NOW share much with all-of-that: literature conceived more as an art form than as a craft or product can be thought of as a literature whose aesthetic often shares an ethos with contemporary thought, a literature that takes its own medium as part of its subject matter, or works against the assumptions of the status quo, especially literature conceived in commercial terms. These contemporary works often make their points by employing a variety of linguistic games, slippages, puzzles, parodies, talking animals, historical disjunctions, discursive juxtapositions, appropriations, collage techniques, and other rhetorical strategies and constraints, even those of realism. If commercial, mainstream literature is the equivalent of a 19th century still-life, literature as a contemporary art form would be the equivalent of the art video or indie song that uses all sound as its medium. If mainstream literature can be characterized, as Don DeLillo once referred to it, as "around-the-house-and-in-the-yard" literature, that is, "well-behaved" literature, in the words of Robert Stone, a "kind of social realism…the educated American's alternative to religious revivalism" with its "penitential tone…insistence on seriousness… dislike of 'elitism'…obsessive pursuit of 'authenticy' and Narodnik romance with the land and ordinary people" (13), the stories and poems collected here in *The &NOW AWARDS* can be thought of as a kind of literature that is as invested in its own medium—language—as it is engaged with the world: a literature that is more interested in using form, like its counterpart in the visual arts, to work through ideas rather than to create a transparent, illusionistic window on the world. These are works of writing that manage to, like its counterpart, entertain, say something relevant, and maybe even say something true. They do so in surprising ways.

&NOW began in 2004 as a festival of literature(s) that seemed to share these family resemblances: a celebration of poems, short stories, novels, hybrid and electronic writing aware that its aesthetic lineage was not necessarily the same of other, more conventional authors and literary works, even if there might be an affinity or crossover between the two. The ampersand of the title serves as a reminder that all writing—be it in print, on screen, or skywriting—is always a form, with a material component, a fact that is often ignored by more transparent writing that strives to be the dream a reader gets lost in, or a lyric outpouring of the poet's soul. In the case of &NOW, it is a form that links its own unnamed tradition(s) to an ongoing moment: ours.

Continuously held every other year since 2004, the festival has continued to grow, and the anthology you hold in your hands is one outcome of this fact. Unlike most other "Best Of" anthologies, *The &NOW Awards* makes no claim to being an overview of all the literature published in a year, or even representing the "finest" of the small, large or medium press. How can one pick one poem to be "best of show" when it's getting harder and harder to say, exactly, what a poem is, where its boundaries begin or end? To do so seems to assume a belles-lettres aesthetic, and a publishing model that is going the way of printed newspapers, that is, the dodo bird. Rather, like other indie art forms, the works gathered here, and represented in the festival, tend to confound the idea of "best" by making it secondary to "interesting." What they have to say is put on an equal footing with *how* they say it—the traditional difference between "literature" and "writing"—with preference given to those works whose "how" keeps the definitions and categories from arriving at the same destination as Morton Feldman's ocean liner. Primarily, &NOW, both its anthology and the festival itself, is a celebration of authors having fun with language.

A snapshot of literature at our moment as it lives out at sea.

PAUL D. MILLER AKA DJ SPOOKY

The Future Is Here

I'm just happy to be alive in this era. It's truly exciting to travel around just checking out how strange it all is. I'd say this is going to be a century of hyper-acceleration, and I just get a kick out of seeing it. One of my favorite phrases comes from William Gibson: "The future is already here, it's just unevenly distributed."

So what is rhythm science and how do we measure its effects? A blip on the radar? A database sweep? A streamed numerical sequence? In a short space, my narrative has switched formats and functions, time and place—all were kind of like fonts—something to be used for a moment to highlight a certain mode of expression, and, of course, utterly pliable. As I sit here and type on my laptop, even the basic format of the words I write still mirrors some of the early developments in graphical user interface-based texts still echoes not only in how I write, but how I think about the temporal placement of the words and ideas I'm thinking about. It is a worldview that definitely ain't linear. The likes of Alan Kay, Douglas Engelbert, and Ivan Sutherland pioneered graphical user interfaces more than three decades ago, allowing users to interact with the icons and objects on the monitor's surface. But what they accomplished was even more profound than that, their work lets us move into the screen world itself. Context becomes metatext, and the enframing process, as folks as diverse as Iannis Xenakis, Kool Keith a.k.a. Dr Octagon or Eminem can tell you, like media philosopher Freidrich Kittler, "Aesthetics begins as 'pattern recognition.'"

We're probably the first generation to grow up in a completely electronic environment. I always think about the first time John Cage went into an "anechoic chamber," a place where there is literally "no sound" and he heard two weird rhythm patterns: one high frequency and one low frequency. The low frequency pattern was the sound of his blood circulating in his veins, and the high frequency was the sound of his nervous system. These days we'd be able to emulate and precisely take the sound of someone's "operating system"—wetware and hardware—and simulate them from the ground up. Once you get their basic credit information and various electronic representations of that person, who needs the real thing anymore? That's one of the oppositions I explore: my art critiques live and non-live. The two are utterly mutually conditioning, and this cycle will only intensify throughout the twenty-first century.

Repetition and Claude Shannon? Repetition and James Snead? As has been well documented by folks such as Tricia Rose and Sherry Turkle (whose book *The Second Self* is itself a digital era update on Du Bois's double consciousness) the sense here is one of prolonging the formal implications of the expressive act. Move into the frame, get the picture, re-invent your name. Movement, flow, flux: the nomad takes on the sedentary qualities of the urban dweller. Movement on the screen becomes an omnipresent quality. Absolute time becomes dream machine flicker. The eyes move. The body becomes symbol and synecdoche, sign and signification.

Sometimes stories work better.

First Story: One of the more intriguing parties I've been to was a few years ago just outside of Reykjavik. The mostly Icelandic crowd was rocking out. People were on glaciers, on the snow, in the cold, and the sound and light systems were also outside, scattered on the ice fields. It was dark, a surreal, gray dawn. The crowd was into hard techno and trance. In Iceland, there is a mix of cultures—Scandinavian, Inuit, and European—and they are also just a really open and friendly people, a fishing culture, a small island. When I got back from that party, I cut all my hair off, leaving green, foot long dreads on the floor.

Second Story: I was living at the Gas Station on Avenue B in Alphabet City on Manhattan's Lower East Side. I used to throw after-hours parties, we'd just leave the door open, and homeless people, crazy people would come through. For one party we put up these TVs, and every TV had static, and they were hanging from these industrial chains on the ceiling. People were coming in off the street, I had no idea who the fuck they were, but they would jump onto the TVs and swing around. The televisions were the only light in the room, and there was crazy music, and then you'd look out and see the melted metal and burned up sculptures. But that was a different time.

Third Story: It was one of those strange evenings that are becoming more and more quotidian in the twenty-first century. It was the middle of summer and a concert of Iron Maiden and Queensryche—two towering icons of seventies and eighties arena rock that some call heavy metal, and others just call plain old rock and roll—had just finished. I was sitting in the back of a taxi in a traffic jam caused by crowds exiting Madison Square Garden, summer heat adding layers and layers of "body noise" to the heady mix of the people swirling through the stalled cars and pointillist rendered signs blinking down on the snarled currents of humanity flowing through New York's center, I decided to simply let my mind float and go nowhere fast. I was presented with something that contemporary America seems to have in abundance, and that other countries are struggling to catch up with—a trend I like to call "demographic nostalgia." Each part of the crowd reflected their appreciation of the bands they had come to see. Stuck in the traffic their migration from the arena was causing, I was given a great point of view on the migratory patterns of the gathered concert-goers. They left the Garden and moved from the finely tuned precision of rows and seat numbers into clumps and clusters of people held together only by fashion and previous social and geographic allegiance like so many particles of gas drawn together by electro-chemical valences and atomic mass. The rules of the "real" world were asserting themselves and the crowd heeded the call of natural selection, twenty-first-century style.

Fourth Story: I was in Tokyo and doing a show with an old Japanese friend of mine, Dj Krush, and some new folks on the block, Anticon, young white kids from Middle America. They were doing a collaboration with Krush, a piece called "Song for John Walker"—the suburban kid who joined the Taliban. Needless to say, the backstage vibe was all about dialogue and we were all just kicking it. Krush's wife walked in and handed him a samurai sword before his set, and everyone in the room was… um… kind of silent. In a moment like that, the strangeness (strange-mess) of global culture, hip-hop, and of operating as a Dj on a global level crystallized before my eyes. We all sat there and paused for a second. It really felt like a still from a video art installation. Krush doesn't speak English, and we have communicated mostly with beats over the years. The show was a benefit for Afghani war orphans at Tokyo's Liquid Room in the Shinjuku district, and well… you just had to feel the oddity of being in a room with some white Americans talking about a lawyer's kid who read Malcolm X and defected to a terrorist organization and a Japanese kid who prayed with his family and was into Shinto Buddhism chants before he went on stage to do turntable tricks. A scene like that doesn't fit into any normal categorization of hip-hop that normal America wants, and it never will. That's the joy of being able to see how this stuff is unfolding in a real way across the globe. It's almost exactly a social approximation of the way web culture collapses distinctions between geography and expression, and it's almost as if the main issues of the day are all about how people are adjusting to the peculiarity of being in a simultaneous yet unevenly distributed world.

—

CHRISTIAN BÖK

The Xenotext Experiment

Introduction

"The Xenotext Experiment" is a literary exercise that explores the aesthetic potential of genetics in the modern milieu—doing so in order to make literal the renowned aphorism of William S. Burroughs, who has declared that "the word is now a virus" (49). In this experiment, I propose to address some of the sociological implications of biotechnology by manufacturing a "xenotext"—a beautiful, anomalous poem, whose "alien words" might subsist, like a harmless parasite, inside the cell of another life-form.

Thinkers as diverse as Pak Wong (a cybernetic expert), Eduardo Kac (a multimedia artist), and Paul Davies (an astronomic expert) have already begun to speculate that even now scientists might store data by encoding textual information into genetic nucleotides, thereby creating "messages" made from DNA—messages that we can then implant, like genes, inside cells, where such messages persist, undamaged and unaltered, through myriad cycles of mitosis, all the while preserved for later recovery and decoding.

Wong, for example, has enciphered the lyrics to "It's a Small World After All," storing this text as a strand of DNA inside *Deinococcus radiodurans*—a bacterium resistant to inhospitable environments. Wong argues that, in a world of fragile media with limited space for storage, DNA might permit us to preserve our cultural heritage against planetary disasters: "organisms [...] on Earth for hundreds of millions of years represent excellent candidates for protecting critical information for future generations" (98).

Kac has also used a genetic process of encipherment in his artwork called *Genesis*—a project intended to show that "biological processes are now writerly" (254). Kac encodes a short verse from the Bible into a strand of DNA, which he then inserts into a microbe, exposing the germ to doses of mutagenic radiation. Kac suggests that, by "editing" such a text through mutation, we can foster an unguided, aleatory message in a more innovative form, rather than accept the dominant, biblical passage in its last inherited form.

Davies has gone so far as to propose an extravagant speculation, suggesting that, instead of sustaining a radio beacon through many millenia or instead of projecting a large vessel across vast distances, aliens wishing to communicate with us might have already encoded messages in DNA, sending out legions of small, cheap envoys—self-maintaining, self-replicating machines that perpetuate their data over eons in the face of unknown hazards: "fortunately, such machines already exist"—and "they are called living cells" (30).

These three thinkers have all suggested the degree to which the biochemistry of living things has become a potential substrate for inscription. Not simply a "code" that governs both the development of an organism and the maintenance of its function, the genome can now become a "vector" for, heretofore unimagined, modes of artistic innovation and cultural expression. In the future, genetics might lend a possible, literary dimension to biology, granting every geneticist the power to become a poet in the medium of life.

Proposal

Stuart Kauffman (a MacArthur Fellow, who is now the iCore Chair for the Institute of Biocomplexity and Informatics at the University of Calgary) has agreed to lend me the expertise of his lab during its free time so that I might compose an example of such "living poetry." I propose to encode a short verse into a sequence of DNA in order to implant it into a bacterium, after which I plan to document the progress of this experiment for publication. I also plan to make related artwork for subsequent exhibition.

I plan to compose my own text in such a way that, when translated into a gene and then integrated into the cell, the text nevertheless gets "expressed" by the organism, which, in response to this grafted, genetic sequence, begins to manufacture a viable, benign protein—a protein that, according to the original, chemical alphabet, is itself another text. I hope, in effect, to engineer a primitive bacterium so that it becomes not only a durable archive for storing a poem, but also a useable machine for writing a poem.

I foresee producing a poetic manual that showcases the text of the poem, followed by an artfully designed monograph about the experiment, including, for example, the chemical alphabet for the cipher, the genetic sequence for the poetry, the schematics for the protein, and even a photograph of the microbe, complete with other apparati, such as charts, graphs, images, and essays, all outlining our results. I also want to include (at the end the book) a slide with a sample of the germ for scientific inspection by the public.

I do foresee enlarging charts and photos from this exercise so that I can display them in a gallery—but I also plan to create other works of conceptual art inspired by the structure of the encoded, genetic poem itself. I plan, for example, to submit the gene to DNA 11 (www.dna11.com), a company that makes giclée prints of abstract artworks produced through DNA-fingerprinting, and I also hope to build a colourful sculpture of the gene itself out of dozens of Molymod Molecular Kits (www.molymod.com).

I expect that the poem is going to be concise, probably about fifty words in length (so that the encoded, genetic text can easily fit into the genome without compromising the function of the organism itself). I have yet to determine what the poem might say under the biochemical constraints of this experiment, but I do expect that the work is going to address the relationship between language and genetics, doing so, self-reflexively and self-analytically. I want to convey the beauty of both the poetic text and its biotic form.

Rationale

Stuart Kauffman is a renowned theorist, who has argued that the complex, but orderly, structure of every living system arises spontaneously out of underlying principles of self-organization—principles no less important than the laws of selective evolution. First trained as a specialist in the humanities (with the intention of becoming a poet), he has instead gone on to pursue a career in the study of genetics. We believe that our overlapping territories of interest make us ideally matched to undertake this project.

My own artistic activity testifies to the fact that I have always regarded my poetry as a "conceptual experiment," reminiscent of work done in think tanks, where scientists might indulge in hypothetical speculations, putting into play the propriety of reasoning itself. Just as the "pataphysics" of Alfred Jarry, for example might intermix technical concepts with aesthetic conceits so as to create an archive of "imaginary solutions" (22), so also does my own artwork strive to create such a hybrid fusion of science and poetics.

We hope that our unorthodox experiment might serve to integrate two mutually isolated domains of research—domains that might not have, otherwise, had any reason to interact, except under the innovative conditions of this artistic exercise. Our collaboration allows us to explore the aesthetic potential of a "literary genetics," even as the project affords us an opportunity to refine methods for the biological encryption of data—methods that might be applied to domains as varied as cryptography, epidemiology, and agrobusiness.

We foresee that, if science can perfect the process for implanting lengthy, texual information into a germ, we might not only provide a secure method for transmitting secretive documents, but we might also "watermark" cells so as to track the movement of either microbial diseases or botanical products. We believe that, with such a burgeoning technology, books of the future may no longer take on the form of codices, scrolls, or tablets, but instead they may become integrated into the very life of their readers.

Conclusion

"The Xenotext Experiment" strives to "infect" the language of genetics with the "poetic vectors" of its own discourse, doing so in order to extend poetry itself beyond the formal limits of the book. I foresee that, as poetry adapts to the millenial condition of such innovative technology, a poem might soon resemble a weird genre of science-fiction, and a poet might become a breed of technician working in a linguistic laboratory. I hope that my project might, in fact, provoke debates about the future of science and poetics.

Even though this whimsical, aesthetic endeavour might accent some of the ironies in the ominous conceit of the poet, Christopher Dewdney, who has argued that "language may be regarded as a psychic parasite which has genetically earmarked a section of the cortex for its own accommodation" (59)—my attempt to build a literary parasite in the form of a "word-germ" has only the most miniscule, most negligible, chance whatsoever of producing any dangerous contagion (despite the alarmism of critics outside of biology).

My project merely highlights the degree to which the modern, social milieu has now taken for granted that the discursive structures of epidemiology (as seen, for example, in such notions as "viral marketing" or "viral computing") might apply to the transmission of ideas throughout our culture. If the poet plays "host" to the "germ" of the word, then the poet may have to invent a more innovative vocabulary to describe this "epidemic" called language. I feel that my project goes some way toward fulfilling this function.

I also believe, moreover, that such a poem might begin to demonstrate that, through the use of nanoscopic, biological emissaries, we might begin to transmit messages across stellar distances or even epochal intervals—so that, unlike any other cultural artifact so far produced (except perhaps for the Pioneer probes or the Voyager probes), such a poem, stored inside the genome of a bacterium, might conceivably outlast terrestrial civilization itself, persisting like a secret message in a bottle flung at random into a giant ocean.

I believe that, in the end, my own project draws concerted attention to the sublimity of language itself, teaching us about the wonders of science in a manner that might seem more engaging to a layperson untrained in biochemistry. I hope that my poem might urge readers to reconsider the aesthetic potential of science, causing them to recognize that, buried within the building blocks of life, there really does exist an innate beauty, if not a hidden poetry—a literal message that we might read, if only we deign to look for it.

Bibliography:

Burroughs, William S. *The Ticket That Exploded.* New York: Grove Press, 1967.

Davies, Paul. "Do We Have to Spell It Out." *New Scientist* 2459 (07 Aug 04): 30-31.

Dewdney, Christopher. *The Immaculate Perception.* Toronto: House of Anansi Press, 1986.

Jarry, Alfred. *Exploits and Opinions of Doctor Faustroll, Pataphysician.* Trans. Simon Watson Taylor. Boston: Exact Change, 1996.

Kac, Eduardo. "Genesis." *Telepresence & Bio Art: Networking Humans, Rabbits, and Robots.* Ann Arbor: University of Michigan Press, 2005. 249-263.

Wong, Pak Chung, et al. "Organic Data Memory Using the DNA Approach." *Communications of the ACM.* Vol 46.1 (Jan 2003): 95-98.

LANCE OLSEN

News Feed | Status Updates | Photos | Posted Items | Live Feed

...Kami has kitchen faucets that turn in new and disturbing directions. Wayde is wondering what the police are up to across the street. Maeko is making caution do 500 jumping jacks. Nico is in New Jersey. Safa is spoiling the birds with warm bathwater this morning. Peter is playing Viva Piñata. Chloe is white quiet. Roger is preparing for the robust theater of subtexts that is the Michelson Christmas Eve dinner. Heather is happy. Sara will pay Mother Earth to quit with the fucking snow already. Dixon is trying to convince his dog that the cats in the neighborhood aren't out to get her, even though he may be wrong about this. Freya is back from France. Sanjay is running out of time. Calista has 391 different attitudes and colors, allegedly. Ripley is revising. Shaun is should-ing all over himself. Jack is killing time the old-fashioned way—with a pistol. Elin is not sure whether she prefers Splenda or Nutrasweet. Vicki is feeling vomitous this morning. Tori is laughing at the name of Amish towns with her coworkers: Intercourse, Dildo, Blue Ball. Dennis is knee-deep in teleology. Anna is going running despite what the weather has in mind. David Pederson is packing. Daniel soothes crying babies—until he walks out of the room and they start crying again. Abbie believes there should be a word (Anglo-Saxonish in rootage, naturally) meaning "nostalgic for the land of colors." Ramiro got a rock in his eye this morning. Van is still burping up Thai food. Lucian does not want anyone to take seriously the joke he is playing on his Zionist friend. Melisa is off to perform miracles in the kitchen. Percy is telling you something personal here. Tom is gratefully taking his pills. Dixon's Chihuahua is resisting his peanut-butter-flavored toothpaste. Jacques decides if he can't make his nurses laugh, he will make them cry. Trish needs a title. Heather is very happy. Wanda feels like every day she's pressured a little bit more into obtaining a Gmail account. Jacob just got older. Ruby realizes with shame how long it's been since she's washed her hair. Staci is in Santa Cruz. Luis is in Laredo. Pamela is still in her pajamas. Cathy wants the coughing to stop. Bree believes it's always a mistake reading your ex's blog—seriously: get over it, you wienie. Bill believes snarkishness is the new warm-and-fuzzies. Brandon invented three new cookies last night. Sara is going to the courthouse today for jury duty. Mia would like to have lunch with Marcus Aurelius. Rusti has just been ravished. Luke is basking in the effulgence of his own laziness. Layla is not going to lie: there's something a little weird about reading scriptures while sitting in the bathtub. Cooper is worried about his cat. Wanda wonders what part of "no plastic toys from China, please" the grandparents don't understand. Gabriel is playing games that aren't, in fact, games. Ella remains baffled by the 80's. Cameron is in Katmandu. Donald is rocking Doctor Octoroc's 8-Bit Jesus. Vinny is in Vancouver. Steve: well, hey, lookee there: more snow. Lilly loves price adjustments. Lonny is in London. Liam suddenly wishes he could own a Lotus Evora. Doug had a dream last night that involved him climbing a tree in stilettos; he will take this as a sign that he should recycle more. Wayde is wondering what the fuck just happened. Knute cannot bend his left knee. Kami is remembering wistfully how much fun it was to shoot pumpkins in the desert on her birthday. Aimee is, to the best of her knowledge. Paige invites everyone over to pick plums. Ron is runner-up. Ramiro's eye is feeling better—note to self: snowballs bad: next time: duck. Wesley is concerned that Facebook is like 100,000 phone calls from people you hardly know anymore. Thelma thinks the snow is good luck. Peter is playing Rock Band 2. Seth plans to eat half a sheep's head at Hilde's tonight. Ryan is fairly sure hell just froze over. Rusti would like to clarify that she still wants attention, & that she still doesn't care whether it's good attention or bad attention. Trish needs to take a short break from being productive. Penny is feeling prepositional. Sara is afraid she just had not one, not two, but THREE donuts. Ava made it to the other side! Peter is playing Burnout Revenge. Sam doesn't understand the motives of mudslides. Freya is frightened there are stains out there that her arsenal of cleansers cannot tackle. Cindy talked to the Secret Service on Kailua Beach. Sandii: Thank God for Nicole, thought Space Ghost—finally someone paler than I in this universe. Winona wonders how to do a Lacan seminar when she's so excited about seeing Oasis this evening. Simon is lost in the ravaged landscape of Shostakovich. Paul is arriving in Toronto at 8 p.m.—people of earth, be warned. Benjamin is delighted there's a healthfood book called "What Would Jesus Eat?" David Pederson is is-ing. Sanjay is cleaning his gas oven while thinking of Sylvia. Frank is always sunny in Philadelphia. Emma just overheard this line over a Pumpkin Spice Latte at Starbucks: "Her Hitler hairdo is making me feel ill." Cooper's cat Kairos is hairballing again. Daniel knows he should go upstairs and check on the girls. Nico is ignoring 65 Facebook requests because he is frightened by things like the lil' green patch. Ella is decreasing her chances of death. Aaron is acting in Akron. Ripley finally sent off his novel manuscript and there was much rejoicing. Debbi is drunk in Dublin. Hank is horrified he just found a music file for Hoobastank on his computer. Daniel is amazed that his amazing daughters are amazingly older than they were 5 minutes ago. Rhonda is sad that today is her last as a redhead. Winona is asking herself when a vowel followed by a double consonant and a "y" is ever irregular. Heather feels just really, really blessed. Dennis wishes the local weatherman would show some pessimism. Peter is playing Battlefield: Bad Company. Kaden is somewhere between continents. Thurston has a theory that there are only two responses to life: love or fear. Owen is out of ideas. Alex is obviously a confused, sad little person with confused, sad little dreams who is NEVER drinking again. Penelope is so pleased that the power is still on and there is chicken soup for lunch. Virginia is sitting vigil with a dying family member. Polly sometimes finds interesting artifacts in her desk drawers. Freya wonders why these comments are supposed to be written in the third person. Sara wants a goiter for Christmas. David Pederson is heading to Omaha because Madison isn't quite cold enough. Rita is peeling red tape off her life. Brenda is researching broken ribs (not hers). Ethan is hating on Damien Hirst. Olivia Snerk may attempt to make her way through the blizzard this afternoon. Genkei has been granted a four-hour reprieve. Kami is seriously and unapologetically addicted to Josh Groban's Christmas CD. Gabriel is about to embark on Phase II of his love-handles augmentation procedure. Lena is so oh-Q-Tip-how-I've-missed-you! Peter is playing NBA 2K9. Jim just finished updating his Facebook status. Jeff loves jet lag and irony. Bob is in Berlin. Sandra is in Stockholm. Vicki's sinus infection meds are making her crave Bruce Willis movies. Myla wonders when her son will figure out that bobbing for apples isn't going to be easy with no front teeth. Jacques is fading away. Sara thinks: snowpocalypse! Ruby does not appreciate being awakened at 7 a.m. by a bailiff ringing the doorbell to deliver the second eviction notice—we heard you the first time, asshole. Ripley is almost positive he just got cold-called by a phonesex company; that's the official story, anyway. Rhonda is now a blond. Rusti wants you to be her little spider monkey. Trish is officially resuming productivity. Sara wonders what's more depressing: that she gained 2 lbs in the last 2 days or she just wasted 10 min of her life watching Fergie vids on youtube. Mia would like to have dinner with Brad Pitt, Heraclitus, and Sextus Empiricus. Lily has learned that hockey pants are called "breezers," but remains afraid to ask why. Aaron has email access again & feels both festive and anxious. Liam would not accept a poultice of mud and urine no matter how allergic to bee stings he is. Jacques was the noodle man, but now he is running out of noodles. Colin: wouldn't it be great to awaken surrounded by Italian & Japanese selvedge jeans in a 1950's sun-shot Prague? Tom is sitting with his left index finger up in the air to stop the bleeding. Wallace just heard the animals say: "We got the funk." Winona is Bachelarding: "If I were asked to name the chief benefit of the house, I should say: the house shelters daydreaming." Cooper: the hairballs are, for want of a better word, polychromatic. Tia believes in torture, not as a political tool, but as a lifestyle choice. Sam is asking Santa to help the Lakers beat the Celtics. Pauline is pigging in Peoria. Wes is watching some boring author boring everyone with her boring personality and her boring presentation on Book TV. Polly is: Ew, ew ew: I just found an alien hair in my library book! Herman got out of work the hard way: by flying down his front steps onto his back. Alex is: poke me if you think I'm, well, vaguely more feminine than masculine. Peter is playing Sonic Unleashed. Sara was dismissed—probably her shifty eyes. Trish is trying to figure out why her @tab variable is not working correctly. Elina is eating snow from a cup with a spoon. Alisha: If I were a Disney princess, these presents would wrap themselves—and sing while they did it. Tori: Dear Coworker: I love you to death, but your frog-noise text-message notification is making my brain melt. Kirby has cancelled the holidays—sorry, kids. Roger was enlightened once, but was able to see his way past it. Sofie suspects this year has really been all about next year. Anna's gallbladder scar is twinging. A. J. feels unplowed. Sara can't fit into her pants anymore. Peter is playing Castle Crashers. Chris is creating something with legs. Cameron just had his jacket stolen—keys, phone, wallet GONE! Ava has evidence there was a bunny party in her yard last night. Virginia is trying to get used to the sound of oxygen for her lover. Rhonda is now a bluehead. Daniel wonders why he buys toys for his kids when they can be entertained so well by a pair of socks. Nina thinks knight errantry is H=O=T. Luke is confident he is really the ghost of a lethargic butler. Dallas didn't think she'd ever do it, but she did and now she feels better. Heather can't begin to describe how totally, enthusiastically joyful she is. Jack would pay not an insubstantial amount of $$$ for people to stop talking about the fucking snow and what they're eating. Wayde doesn't know what the hell that was. Jim wonders if a narwhal could take a panda in a fight. Jan is beating herself up so that Nisa doesn't do it for her. Benjamin is like: KFC for dinner ... damn you, clever product placement on The Wire! Daniel wants to go to bed but must do Santa's work instead. Tori: all I want for Christmas is a top of the line nose-hair trimmer. Randy Chang is contemplating an article title: "In Praise of Candied Bacon." Anna is afraid she may have just come down with a weird rash. Wayde is waiting for the dream life to begin. Sam was there, but currently is here. Sara must—stop—eating. Peter is playing Left 4 Dead. Vicki is now friends with Advil® Liqui-Gels®. Sara did not just send you a gift. Fred is not on fire, but thanks for asking...

MATIAS VIEGENER

25 Random Things About Me Too, 60-65

25 Random Things About Me Too, 60

1. Once I stayed overnight at my boss's house, and when I went to the bathroom I found the toilet unflushed.
2. I didn't say anything, but I flushed before I used the toilet and again afterward.
3. Yesterday I flew in a hot air balloon with Susan Silton and fourteen other people. The best part was lying in the basket as the balloon inflates and you slowly lift upright, as if the hand of God is picking you up.
4. We flew over Del Mar, California. It's very clean, with almost no people. Big houses, palm trees, swimming pools, and eucalyptus trees.
5. Some plants look better from above than below.
6. As a kid I remember being fascinated with Learned Hand, an American judge who is the lower court judge most quoted by the Supreme Court.
7. These are the great protestant names, like Cotton Mather, the son of Increase Mather, the president of Harvard in the 17th century. Cotton Mather was a Puritan minister who wrote in support of the judges of the Salem witch trials.
8. The only thing keeping you aloft in a balloon is hot air, nylon and a few steel cables.
9. It's better if you stop thinking and just look out.
10. Sometimes I go into the men's room to find a toilet filled with wads and wads of toilet paper, and in some way this fills me with more repulsion than finding it full of shit, which is no doubt what is beneath all that paper.
11. I see the horror of someone so disgusted by what their bodies produce they bury it in an avalanche of white paper, yet seem to forget to flush it.
12. The scariest time in a balloon is when you climb higher than any building you know. Then you realize you're flying in the sky only held up by a few cords.
13. Sometimes I get the word dryad and dyad confused. Dryads are tree nymphs and dyads are a pair of something, but maybe dryads come in dyads too.
14. To see the shit of your boss is unspeakable.
15. An apotropaic gesture is a set of words or rituals to warding off evil. Knocking on wood, or saying "you're not going to kill me" to a mugger.
16. Once I went to the Rose Bowl flea market with Millie Wilson and we met Barbara Kruger there. She made sure we understood that she was just there from a sort of anthropological perspective, not to shop.
17. We were there to shop.
18. The tetragrammaton is the unspeakable Hebrew name of God, transliterated into four letters as YHWH, and pronounced as Yahweh.
19. It is blasphemous to speak the name of God.
20. One day when I was a teenager my father disappeared. He had gone to meet a friend of a friend at the airport and never came home. Over the next days we found out that it was a woman, a lawyer, and they had met before in Europe, and he was staying in her hotel in the city.
21. I remember my mother, brother and I very rationally planning what we should do, which at that point involved driving to Washington DC to get a divorce. I can't remember where that came from, but I think it was from my head, not my mother's.
22. After a week or so when my father finally came home late one night, he was hungry so I made him eggs and sausage. I remember throwing the plate down and saying there's your eggs!
23. It's not windy on a balloon ride, because you are being pushed along with the wind.
24. Later my parents got a king-size bed instead of their two twin beds. In my mind the big bed is American while the small ones are European.
25. Actually they just pushed the two twin beds together.

25 Random Things About Me Too, 61

1. Years ago I drove down to Derrida's classes at UC Irvine. He always wore white shoes, which made him seem kind of like a dandy.
2. People said UCI flew him around California in a helicopter, something between an emergency nurse and an important doctor.
3. There's too much life, too much work in my life.
4. No space for the random, which requires a bit of leisure to observe.
5. At that point Derrida was moving from his lectures on cannibalism and eating the other to those on the friend and the enemy.
6. A hot air balloon is so fat, bloated, but also thin, just a membrane.
7. And the world is so fat! It's really big, really really.
8. One of my earliest memories is at South Beach. The tide was coming in, so we gathered our toys and left. When I got home I realized we forgot my Barrel of Monkeys, a styrofoam barrel with plastic monkeys you could connect in a chain.
9. We went back to the beach the next day, and there were my monkeys in a different place, washed away by the tide but then washed up again. The Lord giveth and the Lord taketh away.
10. My father assures me we did not arrive in America on a propeller plane. He says it was a jet, a de Havilland Comet 4. He sent me a picture of it.
11. I reject this. It does not fit my narrative desire.
12. I was a Derridean pretty much before I was anything else, but eventually I became disenchanted with him.
13. Or more precisely I couldn't stand the Derrideans. It was a bit like the difference between Christ and the Christians.
14. I have many memories, at different parts of my childhood and later, of being in airplanes. It seemed like a big thing.
15. When I was a kid and went to the beach, I remember I thought sandbars were a kind of miracle. Out there, land past the water, sort of, and sometimes you had to pass through water over your head, and then you're standing again.
16. Actually I have even more memories of airports, some of them very wrenching.
17. There's something about the machinery and the people coming and going, a site of anguish, rupture, and reunion.
18. I always get sentimental at the end of the school year.
19. Today we had graduation reviews. All the MFA's work is so much better than it was when they started. Is it something the teachers did?
20. My brother and I got sent to a Lutheran church to decide if we believed in God, but after two or three years I guess we decided we didn't. I'm glad it happened now because otherwise I really wouldn't understand Christians.
21. I kind of like the random thing.
22. Maybe anybody's writing would get better after two years of working on it.
23. The MFA thing is a sort of self-fulfilling prophecy. Poof, you're a writer
24. Probably a lot of people today don't remember mimeographs, those ditto sheets they'd hand out in school, faint purple ink and smelling like acetone. They also called those machines "spirit duplicators."
25. Christine Wertheim and I decided that maybe we at CalArts are at least doing more than nothing. We're definitely not doing everything, but maybe we're doing something.

25 Random Things About Me Too, 62

1. When my leg falls asleep and I can't quite walk on it, it feels like my body is something other to me.
2. I'm not made for durational projects.
3. I'm weak.
4. When my leg falls asleep I am reminded of my mother's left leg, which was amputated six years before she died.
5. Allen Ginsberg wrote Kaddish for his mother's death.
6. The actual Kaddish was never spoken by mourners but only by the rabbi.
7. Another meeting with a curator.
8. I won't tell you more.
9. I looked it up and I was surprised to find the the traditional Kaddish is more about god's name and never mentions the dead nor even death.
10. That's not the kind of Kaddish I would write for my mother either.
11. My name means "gift of God." My parents picked it because it worked in both Spanish and German (and Portuguese, and Finnish) but it doesn't much exist in English.
12. In German it is usually spelled Matthias, which is the adaptation of the Greek name Matthaios (same as Matthew), which was an adaptation of the Hebrew Mattiyahu, gift of Yahweh, or God.
13. The Germans are big into modernizing archaic spellings of things. At least they were, once.
14. I remember one of the most horrible academics I studied with was Anne Bergren, who taught a class on the pre-Socratic roots of Post-Structuralist thought. After a semester of reading mostly Derrida, I realized that what she wanted was not a paper written the way Derrida would write, but an academic paper that put Derrida's ideas into a scholarly argument. She wanted me to prove something.
15. This was a big crisis for me.
16. Plop, plop, fizz, fizz. Oh what a relief it is.
17. LACMA, MOCA, LACE, MOMA, MALBA, MAMBO. All these museums or art spaces known by their acronyms. It's like baby talk.
18. But it's very serious baby talk, or pidgin: a simplified language developed between two groups who don't understand each other. Don't worry, I'll make time.
19. I was driving home last night and on the radio I heard the father of a two-year-old boy who died eighteen years ago by drowning. The family brought his body home in a wooden chest and kept him there to mourn for three days before his funeral.
20. It was the day after CalArts graduation reviews and I was still thinking about all the pain in the student work. The cruelty of families, of children, of lovers.
21. I started sobbing and had to pull the car over.
22. Pidgin is the Chinese alteration of the English word "business."
23. Eventually we all live through terrible things, or we die from them.
24. Flowers are restful to look at. They have neither emotions nor conflicts.
    —*Sigmund Freud*
25. For the most part the flowers I like are the irregular ones, not the daisies or the carnations. I like orchids, for example, pansies and calla lilies, the furthest from a lump shaped rose or anything shaped like a dinner roll.

25 Random Things About Me Too, 63

1. The flowers I like look like p's and q's, or k's, instead of the normal ones like o's or asterisks.
2. I have an ongoing struggle with Kathy Acker's Wikipedia page. Readers come along with some regularity and edit her biography, and the one thing they most often put in is that she worked as a prostitute in her twenties.
3. I like flowers that look like tears or hats or babies in a cradle, that suckle to their stems like piglets. I like the flowers that look like question marks, the ones that flap in the wind almost like mistakes.
4. My mother's ashes stayed in their cheap container for two years after her death. We knew we wanted to scatter them in the woods by the house, but my father, brother and I were never there together.
5. Finally just before he moved away to remarry, he and my brother impetuously scattered them and then called me to say they did it. I was unspeakably angry that I wasn't there.
6. So now and then I go to Wikipedia and remove the mentions of Kathy working as a prostitute. She didn't. She worked as an erotic dancer or a stripper, and then for only a year or so.
7. I sat with my anger for a few weeks and first wouldn't speak to either my brother or my father.
8. But finally I forgave them. Ashes are nothing, and that's their point. Nothing is left of us when we are gone.
9. One of my fantasies of teaching is that my students become so absorbed in their discussion they don't need me. After I ask a few questions they start talking so intensely that I can sink under the table. For the rest of the class I sit under the table and just listen to them be brilliant.
10. Kathy's experience as a stripper and the stories she heard from the women she worked with, stories of sexual abuse, rape and prostitution, were formative to her understanding of gender in America.
11. My mother made my cry as a child when she said that she wanted to cremated when she died and would be happy if a little plant grew from her ashes.
12. Don't worry, I'll make time.
13. There's something about the role of artists at CalArts... nowhere else would you gather to listen to artists expound on politics, like after 9/11.
14. Imagine gathering at the feet of political scientists to hear about art.
15. I know guys who call their penises their peter, or their little winkie. Maybe it's not that bad, until you realize they don't quite mean it as a joke.
16. And then there are words like boo-boo or ouchie. If I had a cut I would probably just say cut, or burn, or bruise. But of course I love those words too, the way boo-boo kind of naturally leads to bon-bon.
17. For a minute I saw myself as an animal looking in the window from outside would see me, as a species dedicated to activities that have no measurable relationship to their own survival.
18. Today is the ten-year anniversary of my mother's death.
19. About the only thing I can say for sure is that by now it's clear that she is dead and I am alive.
20. Kathy would not have minded being called a prostitute, but I remove it from the record because the record should be factual.
21. My mother died the day after Mother's Day, which was the last day I talked to her. I was planting apple trees at a house in the Los Padres mountains.
22. It was on a cordless phone and I was really planting apple trees while I talked to her.

23. She called me actually, thinking she had dialed my brother, who called her earlier. So the last time we talked she first called me by my brother's name, Valentin.
24. The stories the prostitutes told her echoed through Kathy's work for the rest of her life.
25. It's nice that I can still hear my mother's voice. I like that. I hear it over the telephone though, not live.

25 Random Things About Me Too, 64

1. What is my mother like as a dead person? Is she wiser?
2. Last week I videotaped a set of interviews for the writing job at CalArts. The writers were interesting but I kept wishing I could turn the camera on the committee, to capture us in unknowingness.
3. My first shopping mall was the Staten Island Mall, which was then "anchored" by a Sears and Macy's, sort of sensible and fancy, by our standards.
4. The announcer on the classical radio station has a voice inside his voice; he sort of swallows his words as if his voice is not really his.
5. Something else is there.
6. My mother had the capacity to reflect, but even more she had the power of cognition and connection.
7. It's hard to imagine how those powers work for dead people.
8. I'm admiring the bulging upper arm of a student. The muscles are plump but his skin is speckled like a plucked chicken.
9. We were dazzled by the mall thing, and I remember thinking what an improvement it was on 34th St., which was anchored by Macy's and B. Altman's with crummy old New York stores like Korvettes, A&S and Gimbels, where Lucy and Ethel shopped.
10. Miranda Mellis says "the monster is the message."
11. I admired the B. Altman and the Lord & Taylor logos and tried to style my handwriting after them.
12. My mother heard voices in her head. I mean she had bad memories, not voices telling her what to do.
13. Cough syrup is so powerful! Either that or I am so weak.
14. Pineapples are sweeter on the bottom than on the top. The sugar sinks.
15. On really sensitive microphones even the noise of someone moving the cable gets recorded; even the wind on the cable can be audible.
16. I'd like to do a project in which I dangle a good microphone cable out the window with the mike muted, to see what ambient noise it would pick up.
17. Peggy turns in circles before she she lies down to sleep, a kind of landing pattern.
18. There's a certain attentiveness you feel when you work a video camera. I see how the camera registers things. I don't just see as me, but as the camera.
19. How are writers and poets going to narrate the bailout?
20. Cristina Garcia says "you're reading it in English but hearing it in Spanish."
21. So no, death did not make my mother wiser, only quieter.
22. Henry James said the words are like irritants, what the oyster uses to make the pearl.
23. In a different light I can look healthy or unhealthy.
24. For a time when I was in college my mother was very interested in the question of prostitution. Once she and my father were in Times Square and they met a prostitute and took her to dinner and talked to her.
25. Kathy Acker and I once went to pet cemetery in the desert. We loved it. She noticed how much more people loved their animals than each other.

25 Random Things About Me Too, 65

1. I've been looking at the sex ads online and and I'm struck by both the variety of people's pleasures and their monotony, the slavish repetition.
2. This is a the problem of genre.
3. Walking outdoors, I will grab a leaf of whatever plant I pass and crush it to see what it smells like.
4. I just poked a lymph node in my neck which is swollen from my cold, and I realized that maybe homeopathic medicine does work. You give a tiny amount of poison to stimulate your body to respond to the disease.
5. This is a realization best made while high on cough syrup.
6. In the sex ads there a kind of arcana or lore as encoded as medieval scholasticism.
7. When she was a girl, being raised by her grandmother and very poor, my mother and her aunt would work as cleaners in a bordello owned by another aunt with more money.
8. She told me she liked the women there, and they were always very kind to her.
9. Why is no one talking about poor people?
10. Random things are what irritate, what makes the oyster make the pearl.
11. The newspaper is filled with stories about the great recession, but no one seems to be complaining, or depressed.
12. This must be a very upbeat downturn.
13. In general we have a bias in favor of certainty, or things we believe exist.
14. This is my problem with a certain amount of conceptual art, its favoring of that which exists over that which does not.
15. An exercise for guys. Look at your body: imagine your shoulders narrowing and your breasts coming forward. How does it feel?
16. Democracy is a concept. I have never actually lived in a full democracy.
17. All democracies so far are partial.
18. Never since ancient Greece and Rome has there been such a robust public display of phalluses.
19. Allegory is like camp. It's either intentional (on the part of the writer or artist) or a product of reading.
20. Therefore anything can be allegorical.
21. The gloryhole: now there is a word to behold.
22. As my mother aged, she began to dislike her body. Once I remember she came to the desert with me and my boyfriend and after we had to drag her into the jacuzzi she said it was "not aesthetical" for people to have to see an older person's body like this.
23. Reading sex ads online, I think that the misspellings often make them sexier, up to a point.
24. I often think of more things after I finish working on random things for the day than while I am thinking of random things for that day.
25. The phenomenon of including cock shots rather than a picture of yourself when you're looking to give a blow job has always interested me.

PETER O'LEARY

{ O. Eu. H.}

The soul's delved spectacle. That network. Its
secret society. Roots beeted with blood it radiates around,
in a platinum of darkness. A redness suspected but
esoteric to you. Coral-hard tendrils, fragile-looking
but living, so flexible—a slow-motion yoga of inversion. Porphyry taproots
the system alludes to quaff minerals out of the earth
the soul sucks likewise for itself, competitively.

Otherwise nothing is red.

Some metaphors for the inner world:
a landscape
sheets of rain wave over;
a forest
a forest of darkness
a tree
whose arborescence is a space ship's
—rocket-exhaust root-cloud—
a grassy field
with interdependent root-structure
roots
"roots & leaves themselves alone"
caves
caverns
cathedrals
with impressive vaults, decaying tombs a whole 20th century's worth of light pours
over achronical, embalmed
an illuminated manuscript stylometrically illegible
except to initiated readers
a semi-private room decorated in frescoes
of a mildly mythological import
an animal
a dove
any wingèd thing
a unicorn
a lover
a thirsty hart drinking from a source
for me, some of Thoreau, some of Emerson
Whitman & Dickinson
Ronald Johnson's *ARK*
a light
but a light sphered in adamantine blackness
viruses expand vibrantly over.

When Eurydice turned from Orpheus she was
already root, already crimson-redolent with the earthiness of sleep. The point here
is that she was real, however
unbearably
imagined.

YURIY TARNAWSKY

about the mininovel

Traditionally speaking, and simplifying things a bit, you could say there are two types of fiction—the novel and the short story, or long and short prose texts, each dealing with characters and events but each accomplishing their goal (that of impacting the reader) in a different way.

In a novel, the events tell us who the characters are and what they are capable of doing. After we read a novel we know much more about the characters than what we have been told. Not only do we know the story of their life but can also predict how they might behave in new untold situations. It is the described events that create the character for us. They are the case studies which show us how the characters behave and thus the engine that generates the characters. The goal of the novel is to describe the characters so fully that we would know them as if they were ourselves. It is accomplished through a description of a great number of events which requires a long text.

A short story is something quite different. Its goal is to describe an event, or a critical situation, and its impact on one or more characters. Here the characters are the objects of the events and the goal is to show what mark the latter leave on the former. After reading a short story, we know what impact the described event, or situation, might have on characters such as those in the text. We feel the pain, joy, sorrow, elation, boredom, etc. the characters feel as if we were they. This is a simpler task than building up characters and typically it can be accomplished through relatively short texts.

A mininovel is a blend of the two types—a short text which has an impact like that of a long one; having read a mininovel the reader feels as if he has read a much longer text. This is accomplished by inserting carefully crafted lacunae in the text and requiring the reader to fill them in. In other words, in a mininovel the reader becomes a co-creator of the work together with its author—in effect a co-author.

The lacunae may be said to constitute negative text which forces the reader's imagination to fill in the information missing in the text. Devices other than lacunae may be used to engage the reader's imagination in interpreting the work. These may be evocative names, unusual or unrealistic real-life situations, dreams, and so forth. But crafting the lacunae carefully seems to be the most effective, and indispensable, technique. It appears, then, that a mininovel must be a relatively short work consisting of a number of still shorter unconnected passages which the reader must link up in a unique way. The better is the reader's imagination, the finer will be the result of the reading.

In this, the mininovel is like poetry.

YURIY TARNAWSKY

Screaming (a mininovel)

1. the church

As Roark crossed the street and continued walking along the sidewalk, in this block flanked on the right by a tall iron fence overgrown with ivy, he heard a loud noise coming from the building on the other side and immediately labeled it as a scream of a large group of people united in an uncontrolled, limitless feeling of despair. Intrigued, his heart beating with excitement, he stopped without turning his head in the direction of the building, his ear cocked so that it could best catch the sounds coming from it, and listened. The noise lasted another six or seven seconds, abruptly stopped, and then started up again to last about the same amount of time, in other words some ten seconds.

Even while keeping his head straight while listening, by shifting his eyes right, Roark saw that the building the noise was coming from was a church and when silence followed the third wave of screaming he turned his head right and saw the top of the tall brown stone walls punctuated at regular intervals by the narrow ogival arches of the windows, the gray slate roof reaching desperately upward, and the small, rudimentary spires, undeveloped like limbs of thalidomide babies, on the background of the darkening evening sky, the color of brown-tinted car window glass.

He recalled then he had seen the facade of the church as he was crossing the street which was readily visible from that side, since the fence in front of it was much shorter than on the side, but had not paid any attention to it, being absorbed in his thoughts. He had not seen the church before, having never been in that part of town.

An uncontrollable urge whose nature was unknown to him, like an invisible thread, jerked him and he quickly turned around, walked back to the corner of the street he had just crossed, turned left, and headed toward the gate in the fence opposite the main door of the church. He had to see what was going on inside.

The screaming resumed as Roark closed the front gate and was walking toward the church and he quickened his step, afraid it would stop before he had a chance to get inside. The door was wide and tall, appropriately bright red like a badly inflamed throat, and to Roark's relief opened obligingly before him; he was afraid it was locked.

The first scream ended and the second one began when Roark entered the church. It was brightly lit, so that Roark had to squint, and he realized he hadn't seen the light from the outside because the windows in the church were all boarded up. The church was also stripped bare of all religious trappings, its space completely empty. Roark remembered then he hadn't seen any crosses on the outside of the church—the facade or the roof—which had surprised him although he hadn't become aware of it at the time. The building had obviously been acquired by some secular entity and was used for non-religious purposes.

Before him, stretched out on their backs on the floor, each on his/her own mat of the type used by the yoga crowd, lay some fifty to sixty people, their heads turned toward the wall against which the altar once stood and their feet toward him. They were arranged more or less in rows, but in front of them, like the leader of a band or a military formation, lay a man, clearly the lead person of the group. The scream filled the vast space of the church, stopped for a brief period, and then was repeated for the third time. No direction came from the man in front—the group was obviously adept at what it was doing.

The screaming then stopped and everyone got up as if on command. The session was over. The man in charge was dressed in a pair of overalls soiled with brown dirt, and the same kind of dirt was visible on his hands and face, especially the forehead.

Next to the man's mat on the floor lay a big shovel, its tip likewise caked with dirt, which the man picked up as he was getting ready to leave. All of this made Roark think of a grave digger and he was puzzled. Did the man rush in straight from his grave-digger's job and had no time to change? But then why the shovel? At the same time Roark tried to figure out what the group was. He remembered hearing about a school of therapy called "the primal scream." Was this what the group was practicing? But he hadn't heard about that approach for years and thought it had gone out of style. He didn't know what to think.

2. a conversation

Just then a woman detached herself from the group and came up to Roark. She had lain in the center, a few rows in, was middle aged, short, heavy, missed her left arm, and had a white string tied diagonally across her pasty, fat face. It had cut itself into her flesh like into a soft package, pushing it out of shape. She was dressed in an old, faded, navy blue sweat suit with the left sleeve tucked inside it. The following conversation took place between her and Roark.

WOMAN *(looking up at Roark since he is much taller, her head tilted to one side, the weight of her body shifted onto that foot and her voice brimming with goodwill and curiosity)*: Have you been coming here long?

ROARK *(not in the least startled)*: No, it's my first time here.

WOMAN *(pushing on, as if not caring about the answer)*: Did you enjoy the screaming?

ROARK: Oh, yes. I was enthused by it. It really had meaning for me. It projected good energy.

WOMAN *(tilting her head the other way and shifting the weight of her body onto the other foot)*: Have you ever screamed?

ROARK *(understands what she means)*: No, but I plan to.

WOMAN: Roger'll sign you up. Talk to him. *(Without a pause.)* What's your name?

ROARK: Rilke.

WOMAN *(visibly intrigued, tilting her head and shifting her weight to the other side again)*: Rilke? That's wonderful. What's your first name?

ROARK: Rilke's my first name. My last name is Roark.

WOMAN: Oh, what an interesting name... both of them.... *(Without a pause again.)* Were your parents crazy about Rilke? Like, was he their favorite poet?

ROARK: My father was fond of him. He came from Switzerland, the place where Rilke died... Val-Mont. *(Without a pause in turn, copying the woman.)* What's YOUR name?

WOMAN *(quickly)*: Alba.

ROARK: Alma? That's wonderful. It means "soul" in Spanish.

WOMAN: No, Alba... for the duchess of Alba that Goya painted. My father came from Spain, the place where Goya was born... Fuendetodos. *(Without a pause again.)* I didn't know Alma means "soul" in Spanish. My father didn't teach me the language.

ROARK *(giving up on the topic, eager to get to what interests him):* Is Roger a grave digger?

WOMAN *(turning her head around for an instant and looking at the leader who is just disappearing in one of the doors)*: No, he's a stock broker.

ROARK *(incredulous)*: A stock broker?... Really? Why is he all covered with dirt and has that shovel?

WOMAN *(laughing)*: Oh, that's for screaming. It helps you to scream better when you have the right objects near you. *(Without a pause, as so many times before.)* Do you know what I use to help me scream?

ROARK: No.

WOMAN *(beaming with joy)*: A fetus! *(Turning away from Roark.)* I'll show you....

She runs to her mat, picks up an object standing on the floor next to it, and in a few seconds is back with Roark. She shows him a glass jar filled with bluish liquid in which there floats a gray shape with ill-defined appendages like a botched poached egg. Roark looks at it with curiosity. He comes to the conclusion that the string tied over the woman's face is also a screaming aid. In the bright light the liquid in the jar sends off flashes like a beautiful blue eye.

3. rilke

Roark's dream.

Roark is walking up a garden path covered with sand. It crunches rhythmically under his feet. The ground slopes up—it is in Switzerland. Up ahead on the left grow bushes. Under one of them lies a human figure twisting on the ground. The person—it is a man—seems to be struggling with someone. Roark looks closer to see who the man's adversary is but there isn't anyone there—the man is struggling with himself. And it isn't just a game—he is obviously desperate and seems to be fighting for his life.

Roark passes the man and sees the latter is dressed in a tight-fitting black suit and has a well formed head with black, closely cropped hair and a trimmed beard. He realizes it is Rilke. He doesn't dare to stop and look but walks on. It would be impolite to stare at someone in such a situation, especially a man of Rilke's stature.

Roark walks on and soon reaches the crest of the hill. It is actually the peak of a very tall mountain. It is craggy. Down below shimmers the sea. Ships and boats can be seen on it. The latter are mostly sailboats. Roark knows Geneva, which is in Switzerland, is on a lake, and in the dream the lake has turned into a sea. He is not aware of this discrepancy. He is elated by the sight and he stretches his arms out to the sides and fills his chest with air. It is fresh and invigorating. Roark laughs. Time to go back!

Roark remembers Rilke under the bush. As he nears the spot he sees a black shape, all still, lying on the ground. Roark's heart beats faster. He is concerned something might have happened to Rilke. He is afraid he may have died. He rushes up to the bush and looks down. Rilke looks dead. He is like a suit thrown down on the ground in great haste. The phrase "irrelevant Rilke" passes through Roark's mind but he forgets it immediately. He worries about Rilke. The man is lying face down. Roark squats down beside him and turns him over. Rilke doesn't stir—he is definitely dead. His eyes are open and their irises have disappeared under his forehead. The sight is ghastly. Roark is frightened and disgusted at the same time. He quickly stands up, shooting up like a geyser. He then notices rose petals strewn all over the ground around Rilke. They are pink. The bush under which Rilke lies is a rosebush. It looks as if Rilke had struggled with the rosebush rather than himself and had lost. The rosebush has killed him. Roark feels pain in his left hand. He opens it and looks. There is a wound in it like in Christ's hand after he was taken off the cross. Blood flows from it. Roark then realizes he is clutching something in his right hand. He wants to see what it is and looks at it. It is a dagger. It is old-fashioned, with an ornate handle and a rhomboid blade. He doesn't know what to do with it.

Alba's dream.

Alba is in her kitchen, cooking. There is a big old-fashioned stove there, pots and pans are all around, and the windows are high up under the ceiling and are small. It seems to be in a basement of an old house—the walls are very thick. The air is full of steam and the smell of cooking. It is not pleasant. Then a tall male figure, all in black, comes into the kitchen. It is Rilke. He comes up to the stove, stands next to Alba, and starts stirring in the pot in front of him. Alba looks into the pot and sees it is full of little round gray things in a broth or thin sauce. They're fetuses. Rilke is cooking a fetus stew! Alba is aghast—who would eat it?! She can't believe Rilke would do anything like that. He stirs the stew vigorously however. He then turns to her and says it won't be enough. Alba forgets about her aversion and agrees with Rilke there won't be enough stew. What are they to do? Rilke suggests they chop off his left arm and add it to the stew. Alba sees no other solution. He says for her to help him get out of his clothes. She unbuttons his tight jacket and takes it off. Then they jointly take off his shirt. She still has two arms like she used to. A long serrated knife finds itself in Alba's hand. She starts sawing away with it at Rilke's arm at the shoulder. Rilke doesn't protest in any way. He doesn't seem to feel any pain. Alba saws through his flesh. She hits the bone. It shows in the wound. It is white and shines like mother of pearl. Alba can see the bone move in the joint.

4. the apartment

Following is a description of Roark's and Alba's apartment after they got married.

It is one very large room in a former factory building with windows along the entire outside wall. In the middle of it stands a toilet bowl without a seat. An old black quilt lies in a heap next to it. You can cover yourself with it when you use the toilet if you so desire. A large, old-fashioned sink with two basins is attached in the center of the wall opposite to the one with the windows. It is used for washing up as well as for doing dishes. On the left of it stands a refrigerator and on the right a gas stove. Both are old and white. On the right side of the stove stand two gray industrial style metal cupboards used for storing dishes, food, and clothes. In the corner of the room beyond the metal cupboards, at an angle of forty-five degrees, stands a large red tent which serves as the bedroom. It is chock full of pillows, quilts, sleeping bags, and other bed clothing. Mingled in among them is an old-fashioned rotary type black telephone. A wire is stretched above the tent from one wall to the next on which there hang clothes, both on hangers and merely draped over. In the opposite corner, also at an angle of forty-five degrees, that is, like a mirror image of the tent, stands a cube, about six feet on each side, with old, rusty pipes forming each of its twelve edges. It is called "the screaming cube" and screaming sessions are conducted in it. On the wall next to it, attached with scotch tape, hangs a full-size, high-quality reproduction of Edward Munch's famous lithograph "The Scream." In the very corner behind the cube stands a beautiful old grandfather clock, an heirloom from Roark's family, built by Roark's paternal grandfather upon the completion of his apprenticeship and admission to the rank of master clock maker, in Switzerland. A roughly twenty-foot long wooden industrial work bench, badly beaten up and stained with oil in places, stands in the middle of the room. It serves as a table. Piled up on it are dishes, kitchen utensils, books, papers, toilet articles, clothes, and so on. There are no chairs next to it nor anywhere else in the apartment. Four very bright fluorescent lamps arranged in a row high up on the ceiling illuminate the room. The walls in the room are painted white. The paint is old and peels in places. The floor is wooden, badly scuffed up, and stained with oil in places like the table.

The windowsills are all taken up with flowerpots, empty bottles, figurines of various sorts, and so on. On one of them stand glass jars containing fetuses. There are seven of them, three with the liquid tinged pink and four blue, for female and male respectively. The windows have rusty metal frames, the color of dried blood. Their small panes are dusty. Outside stretches a monotonous urban landscape of single-storied buildings with flat roofs, a smoggy sky above them.

5. screaming

Roark and Alba are sitting in the screaming cube in a position similar to the lotus position, looking each other in the eyes and screaming. This is an advanced position, used only by expert screamers. The screaming has nothing to do with either "primal scream" therapy or the practice of shattering glass for show-off purposes which so fascinated Lorca and Günther Grass. Rather, its foundation lies in the writings—a single article in German of a couple dozen pages titled "*Zur Theorie und Praxis des Geschreis*," that is, "Toward a Theory and Practice of Screaming"—by the obscure late nineteenth century Austrian mystic and inventor of Ruthenian background K. Ryk. It maintains that screaming, when performed properly, may have profound effects on the surroundings as well as the very person of the screamer with metaphysical consequences.

The combined scream of Roark and Alba is truly ear-shattering, reminiscent of the wailing of a siren, but also calming like an ostinato note in a musical composition, for instance one of Bach's keyboard pieces played on the organ. Because of its first quality one would expect that the neighbors above, below, and on both sides of Roark's and Alba's apartment would react to the screaming by knocking on the floor, ceiling, or the walls in indignation. This is not true however because all of Roark's and Alba's neighbors have moved out long time ago, unable to prevent the couple from exercising their rights to self-expression. It is for the same reason the owners of the building—a partnership of a few Japanese individuals—have not been able to evict them.

As the screaming goes on, a sound comes out of the mouth of the figure in Munch's lithograph—at first faint and hesitant, at times stopping altogether, but gradually growing louder and louder, more and more sure of itself, until finally uniting with the screams of Roark and Alba into one, as strong and as confident as they, perfectly matched with them as the third voice in a perfectly matched trio of singers, the united scream conveying a boundless feeling of despair that lies at its core as the sound of a perfectly matched trio of singers conveys the beauty that lies at the core of its singing, continuing unchanged from then on, powerful, steady, with no end in sight. The hands of the grandfather clock tremble, hesitate, stop, then move back in short, tentative movements, until finally they spin madly in the counterclockwise direction. A red and blue light, like vapor, appears in the room, growing denser and denser with time, coalescing toward the center, until it forms a bright pink ball that settles over the toilet bowl, hiding it completely. The fetuses in the jar stir shyly, then move more and more boldly, spinning and tumbling, swimming as much as they are able in their cramped spaces, looking like a team of world class athletes in the sport of synchronized underwater swimming recently admitted to the Olympics.

6. the final scene

It is evening, early spring. Roark is standing on the bank of a huge river, his back turned to the world. On the other side the sun is setting. There is no one around. Roark is screaming. The river is high, its banks overflowing with the spring flood. It flows right to left, fast, almost like a train moving, carrying huge floats of ice together with objects of various type on them, such as houses, barns, sheds, outhouses, trucks, cars, farm machinery, furniture, bedding, household articles, and so on. For some reason among the latter there appear very frequently grandfather clocks which are usually standing up. Occasionally a solitary human figure can be seen floating by—a middle-aged woman standing at the edge of a float, staring blank-eyed into distance, as if through a window, a young man lying face down, his head cradled in his hands, an old man frozen still in his rocking chair.

The earth is flat and perfectly bare, without a trace of plant life on it. It is a rich brown however, and looks fluffy, so it is probably very fertile and will eventually sprout lush vegetation. Apparently it has been a very hard winter until recently. The sky above is also brown, tinged by the light reflecting from below. It is very low—so low Roark has to stand with his head bent down. It stretches flat all the way to the horizon where there is only a thin opening left between it and the earth like the slot in a pinball machine. Someone on the other side is feeding shiny new quarters of light into it one by one, over and over again.

JESSICA BERGER

Teddi with an 'I'

I'm switching from *Vogue* to *British Vogue*. From faux-blonde to deep chestnut. From *GQ* to *Men's Vogue*. From *People* to *US Weekly*. From E!Online to Perez Hilton. From "Wheel of Fortune" to "Jeopardy!". From Oprah to Tyra. From "Golden Girls" reruns to "Living Single" reruns. From Pop Tarts to Frosted Flakes. From Garnier to John Frieda. From Lever to Dove. From Gwen Stefani to Lady GaGa. From Zac Posen to Zac Efron. From Courtney Love to Amy Winehouse. From nothing to anti-wrinkle cream. From Grande Mocha Lattes to Red Bull. From regular Coca-Cola to Diet Cherry Coke. From Skittles to M&Ms. From Krispy Kreme back to Dunkin Donuts. From Chipotle to Cosi. From Basquiat to Jeff Koons. From Diane Arbus to Sally Mann. From Fafi to Banksy. From Dunnys to Mongers. From Altoids to Tic Tacs. From "Passions" to "One Life to Live". From Diesels to Pumas. From green to orange. From white to black. From contacts all the time to glasses sometimes. From loose fit to straight leg. From Marc Jacobs to Proenza Schouler. From "America's Next Top Model" to "Project Runway". From *Godfather* to *Godfather II*. From Dance Dance Revolution to Singstar. From Grand Theft Auto back to Legend of Zelda. From Burger King to Wendy's. From briefs to boxers. From too many cigarettes to too much gum. From Gin & Tonic to Rum & Coke. From Natalie Portman to Keira Knightley. From "OC" DVDs to "Gossip Girl" DVDs. From Duran Duran to Tears for Fears. From secretly crying while listening to U2 to secretly crying while listening to Coldplay. From Dell to Apple. From Abercrombie to French Connection. From American Eagle to Urban Outfitters. From California Rolls to Dragon Rolls. From Greek Town to Chinatown. From Big Bowl to Wildfire. From Livejournal to Blogger. From Jim Jarmusch to Derek Jarman. From Ricky Gervais to Steve Coogan. From Girls Aloud to Danity Kane. From Anne Rice to Stephanie Meyer. From ironic vinyl to ironic cassettes. From the 80's to the 60's. From Victorian England to Revolutionary France. From Speed Racer to Rocky & Bullwinkle. From Lizzie McGuire to Hannah Montana. From "Sealab 2021" to "Aqua Teen Hunger Force". From Häagen-Dazs to Ben & Jerry's. From trucker hats to newsboy hats. From solids to stripes. From gas guzzlers to hybrids. From apathetic to environmentalist. From democrat to independent. From California to Florida. From Asia to South America. From "Abbey Road" to "Hard Day's Night". From John Lennon to Sean Lennon. From boys with looks to boys with cash. From scruffy to clean cut. From Kanye West to Lil Wayne. From going out to staying in. From wintergreen to cinnamon. From Miami to Las Vegas. From the Oscars to the Golden Globes. From "The Soup" to "Best Week Ever". From chocolate chip cookie dough to peach. From Marilyn Monroe to Scarlett Johansson. From Britney back to Madonna. From Stanley Kubrick to David Lynch. From Lindsay's *Freaky Friday* to Jodie's *Freaky Friday.* From "Queer as Folk" to "Entourage". From Macy's to Bloomingdales. From dairy to soy. From bananas to grapefruits. From Saint to anyone else. From PJ Harvey to Alison Goldfrapp. From Tobey Maguire to Christian Bale. From Superman to Batman. From Nightcrawler to Gambit. From Poison Ivy to Harley Quinn. From *Goldeneye* to *From Russia With Love*. From Starbucks to Caribou. From atheist to agnostic. From Crest to Colgate. From plain water to flavored water. From summer to winter. From IKEA to Crate & Barrel. From Burberry London to Calvin Klein Euphoria. From Internet Explorer to Mozilla Firefox. From Body Shop to Kiehl's. From pore strips to exfoliating masks. From homosexual to 10% bisexual. From solitaire to spider solitaire. From Trivial Pursuit to Scene It. From Monopoly to Scrabble. From "Next Generation" to "Voyager". From *Christmas Vacation* to *It's a Wonderful Life*. From Sudoku to Crosswords. From astrology to numerology. From AM/FM to satellite. From Cingular to US Cellular. From grocery shopping on Sunday to grocery shopping on Wednesday. From gummi worms to peach-o's. From Donkey Kong to Ms. Pac-Man. From *Crossroads* to *Glitter.* From public transportation to biking. From Amazon to Amazon Marketplace. From Borders to Barnes & Noble. From Jane Green to Plum Sykes. From Chuck Palahniuk to Miranda July. From Sylvia Plath to Virginia Woolf. From laughing at people who read romance novels to laughing at people who read manga. From Hotmail to Gmail. From Easy Mac to Ramen Noodles. From Daniel Craig to Clive Owen. From ironic to post-ironic. From Jack Sparrow to Ichabod Crane. From Pixar to classic Disney. From worrying about heart attacks to worrying about brain tumors. From vampires to zombies. From margaritas to mai-tais. From Smirnoff to Absolut. From Trojan to Durex. From Baileys to white Russians. From French fries to onion rings. From samurais to ninjas. From Visa to American Express. From Aston-Martin to Ferrari. From Italians to Irishmen. From feigning interest in football to feigning interest in soccer. From Baby Spice to Posh Spice. From the Field Museum to the Shedd Aquarium. From velociraptor to Godzilla. From teacup Chihuahua to Pomeranian. From post-apocalyptic to dystopian. From saying I loved *Man Who Fell to Earth* to saying I loved *I Am Curious...* From pretending I could watch *Sweet Movie* to pretending I could watch *Salo.* From Harry Potter to Narnia. From Heineken to Guinness. From Nietzsche to Kierkegaard. From *Pillow Talk* to *Lover Come Back.* From *Rocky Horror* to *Army of Darkness.* From creepy crush on James Spader to creepy crush on Alan Rickman. From Dasani to Aquafina. From hating Marilyn Manson to reluctantly liking Marilyn Manson. From Ancient Egypt to Ancient Rome. From tan to pale. From yoga to jogging. From wanting to play the guitar to wanting to play the drums. From ear buds to headphones. From Franz Ferdinand to Arctic Monkeys. From "Girls Next Door" to "A Shot at Love". From *Return of the Jedi* to *Empire Strikes Back.* From "Law & Order" to "Law & Order: SVU". From Guitar Hero to Rock Band. From weekly psychoanalysis to monthly psychoanalysis. From Yoplait to Dannon. From talking with my older sister to talking with my younger sister. From pepperoni to pineapple. From Conan to SNL reruns. From Ding Dongs to Ho Hos. From stable to seasonally depressed.

BLAKE BUTLER

Insomnia Door

1. Every moment that I sleep I've fought for with my entire body.
2. God still insists on waking me up every other hour.
3. Every other every other hour I am compelled to stumble to the restroom.
4. I believe I have the same size bladder I did at age eight.
5. If it's not the matter of a small bladder, there's a chance I have prostate cancer.
6. I should probably see a doctor.
7. At age 27 I weigh eighty pounds less than I did the year I got my learner's.
8. I experienced fat terror from age ten to almost seventeen.
9. Husky is the preferred term for fat kids but still not something you want to hear.
10 Once at a car show with my parents an MC called me on stage to play along in his joke routine. He asked the question 'What do you do for fun?' and as he leaned down so I could speak into the microphone, he whispered a suggestion: 'Eat.'
11. I said 'Eat' into the microphone.
12. The audience cackled wildly.
13. Afterwards my mother asked me why I'd said it. I said I didn't know.
14. Afterwards also the MC gave me a free T-shirt: 'The Heartbeat of America: Today's Chevy Truck.'
15. The shirt was XXL.
16. I slept in it for years.
17. I slept so much better as a fat child.
18. Better sleep then often the result of having eaten an entire box of cereal before bed.
19. Perhaps surprisingly, the cereal in question was most often Crispix or Rice Chex, and 2%, not skim or whole.
20. I imagine this procedure is still effective for inducing drowsiness at age 27, though my stomach's no longer up for it.
21. I still get big kicks though from buying sub par synthetic sugar cereals such as Waffle-O's and Mini-Swirlz.
22. Bad sugar fuels fucked dreams.
23. Constantly recurring dream as a very young child in which I lay paralyzed in my bed, an enormous boulder lodged in the ceiling and rolling toward me in slow motion.
24. Always waking with the boulder just inches from my face.
25. Further research revealing this state was most likely hypnopompia: an intermediate consciousness occurring during waking.
26. Consciousness in which hallucination and sensing a presence are common.
27. What presence; when what where; who what this thing lodged in my ceiling.
28. Also associated with this phenomenon: alien abduction, telepathy, apparition and prophetic vision.
29. Often having slept with my head hung in the hallway so as to see my parents in the living room, fearing the presence.
30. Even just my mother's voice a comfort.
31. Though often also: sleep walking; sleep terror; talking in sleep; sleep sound.
32. More active maybe in my sleep than I often am in waking.
33. Perhaps infused within my blood.
34. A cousin once having woken with the front door to his house wide open, knowing he'd gone out.

35. If the walker commits a criminal offense while asleep, the defence of automatism may be available.
36. [List item 36 deleted for fear of repercussion.]
37. My sleep speech probably more exactly what I mean.
38. The dream me a clearer me.
39. Last night the real you having moved the dream me from my sofa to my bed.
40. Last night the real me having thrown a candy bar in frustration.
41. Never again, if anything, taking my fury out on candy.
42. Candy my one irrefutable, perfect lover.
43. Whose breasts and brains will never malform.
44. Who would wait forever by my deathbed, regardless.
45. Candy marriage still not legal in 50 of 50 American states.
46. Also not legally possible: marriage to one's dream self.
47. The becoming of one's dream self.
48. Willful confinement to the hypnopompic state.
49. The boulder above me, still proceeding.
50. My mom forever just down the hall.

STEPHANIE STRICKLAND

From *Huracan's Harp*

142

technicians in blue collarless jumpsuits trained
at DeVry or State or where exactly penetrate my body

so fully open to their target beams mediated by non-
diaphanous machines from Siemens or GE a hardware

almost old school though not so old as robbery of graves
anatomy artist charts note bio-parts futures actively

traded today too new school stem cell deals having not gone
down yet even they passé the aim the blood brain barrier

mania to replace that wet vision engine map flesh out of
flesh for this technicians in white three-quarter

coats trained at MIT Harvard or Somewhere Institutes
visit the splayed plasticized donated Bodies exhibit

with a somewhat antiquarian interest (offensive as it
is to fundamentalists of all stripes who avow

'the body's' importance near death if not in life—
whitecoats know better dialing mindset on the hiPod)

136

the opening hands of clock time V ← see
already say fly! migration virtual event
lightcone ten-ten plot digitized spot pixels
far from steeple bells their wave≈≈sound≈≈

or *not* master-church slave-monk obedient
cipher scriptor in a cell executing tone
by rope (1010 is 10 in binary a semi-
extraneous sidebar (inline) here)

87

Algorithm Recipe

Ingredients	**Instructions**
instructions	map a metaphor or more to computational processes (not to compositional capiche) twiddle (de dee) tweak (de dum) execute/run repeat till well (enough) done oh will this one halt

35

minimum somethings consist altogether of

4	corners
4	faces
6	edges
12	angles
1	insideness
1	outsideness
1	concavity
1	convexity
2	poles of spinnability
32	features

behavioral potential

axial rotation
orbital travel

expansion-contraction
torque (axial twist)

inside-outing (involuting-evoluting)
precession (axial tilt)

interprecessionings among plural systems
self-steering of a system (precessionally done)

some **powers** are only otherness-viewable
some only multi-otherness-realizable

"…not until a six
otherness appears remotely, approaches, and associates
with the fivefold system can the latter learn
from the newcomer of its remote
witnessing that the fivefold
system has indeed
been *rotating*
axially…"

MEGAN MILKS

Slug

Patty will ask her date to walk her to the door. Patty will play I'm Frightened and Scared to be Alone in the Deep Dark Night. Of course he will accompany her, despite the drizzle. He will be happy to. Delighted. Then Patty will push him up against the door so that he's straddling the doorknob, so it's pressing into his asscrack, and shove his shoulders back, hard, and suck his tongue, hard, and rub his crotch, hard, and push his arms up and over his head and hold them there so that he is her prisoner. It is a good thing she wore her bitch boots tonight. It is a good thing she dressed prepared. She will take out her pocketknife and flip up the knife part and she will tickle him with the blade, slowly, deliberately, while he is still clothed, and she will increase pressure as she moves the knife down from his sternum to his pelvis. His stomach will retract involuntarily. She will press into it more. The flat side of the blade. This is foreplay, pre-foreplay. She will unlock the door, swing it wide, and step back, return to I'm Frightened and squeak, It Looks Like There Could Be a Burglar. Won't You Please Check? I'm So Scared. He will play along, say It Would Be My Pleasure to Check for the Burglar. Stay Behind Me. Stay Close. And he will grab her wrist firmly and push her behind him, stroking her wrist suggestively. It will be nice.

Patty's date works hard to clear his throat. The first try is phlegmy and meager, a throat-clearing that has miserably failed. He tries again, succeeds, changes the car radio to smooth jazz. Unbearable. Patty uncrosses, then recrosses her legs, begins to clench and unclench her thighs under her plain black skirt.

Patty is a wicked schoolgirl with an SM fetish. Underneath her plain black skirt is a honking big strap-on (mental note: purchase harness and dildo, a formidable dildo). At her command he will get on his hands and knees and enjoy the rug burn, you pathetic motherfucker. Patty is a vicious cunt in bondage gear, with a whip and not afraid to use it, slave. Patty likes to be tied up, chained up with needles through her nipples, getting burned to bloodblack with cigarettes and branding irons. Patty enjoys biting and being bitten, hard, like starved vampires. She also enjoys: bestiality; triple, quadruple penetration; and feverish, drugged-up sex parties. Sex parties have lots of drugs. What kinds of drugs will Patty's sex party have? Patty is in the middle of being gangbanged, which means violence and overwhelming numbers of cocks at once. Patty is the one with the cock, and she is making him eat it, swallow it, gag.

'You're not giving me much to go on,' he says.

He has been talking all this time.

She will smear his forehead with menstrual blood, then slice a line in his lower abdomen and rub her face in his blood and guts. And shit. Shit will be smeared everywhere. She will hang him upside down, ankles chained together and thighs smeared with shit. She will leave him there with her formidable dildo in his asshole and slashes in his heels so he cannot walk when she unties him. She will be ruthless and loyal. After she slashes his heels, she will check in with a Baby, Are You Okay? Tell Me You're Okay, and take out his gag so he can say so. Then she will shove the gag back down his throat, kneel before him and masturbate where he can see her, inches from his nose and mouth.

Patty shrugs, smiles lazily over at him, lost in her dreaming.

His tongue in her mouth is slithery and warm, then a lifeless slab of muscle to her weak response. Fumbling and finally dead. Retracted. Suck.

Patty clenches and unclenches her thighs, faster, faster, until she is done.

When she is done, she thanks him, they should do it again sometime.

Then she slams the car door and hurries through the rain to her apartment building, stepping on a slug that's sprawled out to suck in the moisture. Ugh. That squishes. She scrapes the slug-guts off on the doorstep and lets herself inside.

Inside is a nice clean apartment with who cares what it's like. Descriptions aid in character development. There are dishes in the sink. Patty leaves them. She grabs a used glass and fills it with filtered water. Gulps it down. Stands there with her fingers on her lips, thinking he wasn't so bad. She could have been nicer. She could have tried harder. Made something happen. But what had he looked like? She remembers the nervous gurgling in particular. The meek way he cleared his throat. The tapping on the steering wheel, anxious, impatient.

She had made him impatient. That's funny. She had had an effect. He probably would've been too safe in bed, anyway. He would've wanted her to act like a girl.

Everyone is always too safe. Probably. What do normal people do?

They take off their shoes and makeup, and go to bed.

Patty takes off her shoes and makeup and goes to bed. Patty has not closed her window, despite the drizzle, which has now turned to rain. There is a lot of rain. It is raining hard. The rain is hard. Hard rain. Getting harder. The rain is getting harder and harder until it is too hard for anyone to handle.

Patty close the window! Patty close the window!

But Patty does not close the window.

Once, a long while ago, Patty was in love, with a man she met online. He had responded to an ad, or she had responded to his, and they had had a feverish exchange in which each had confessed her or his own and encouraged one another's perversities. He would write dutifully every morning; she would respond before retiring for the night. In their emails, they would each describe her or his every desire in obsessive detail, carefully crafting fetish after fetish with the intent to elicit the most violent desire and intrigue from her or his reader. For Patty, masturbation had never been so good.

After a time, they began to write erotic stories for each other. Patty wrote rottingdonquix a story after Story of O, in which O grew a cock and turned the tables on her Master, reducing him to the most obsequious and pathetic of slaves. Rottingdonquix responded with a story inspired, she found out later, by Masoch, in which his Venus was not so much wearing furs as she was covered in fur, for she was a vampiric werewolf who feverishly desired to suck the blood from the narrator's cock. Patty wrote him another story, in which Bataille's bull's eye is passed back and forth from orifice to orifice until finally, in the midst of passionate intercourse, it bursts in the protagonist's throbbing cunt. He had written back with an overwrought masturbation fantasy revolving around an onyx engagement ring. Upon reading it, she experienced the strong stench of rotten eggs, and could not bring herself to reply.

Weeks passed.

One day, missing the thrill of rottingdonquix's emails, Patty wrote him with the suggestion that they meet in person. He agreed.

He was fat, and ugly. She left with a sneer on her face.

That was the end of love.

Patty is in her bed masturbating. She has tied her date up with fishing line that cuts into his skin, leaves blood blisters pooling subcutaneous. She does the same with his cock, which is always fully erect, engorged even, then kneels in front of him, makes eye contact, and extracts her tongue slowly, torturously, until the tip just touches the head of his cock. He moans behind his gag. Saliva gets stuck in his throat and he tries to clear it, takes two tries, three, is perpetually clearing his throat. Patty's tongue has not moved from its tentative perch on the tip of his cock. Then she lurches forward to wrap it around the head while grabbing the ends of the fishing line with her hand and tugging, gently, gently, until he comes. He comes five more times as she frees his cock from the fishing line.

Patty does not come, because Patty's fantasy is dumb. Mindless SM drivel. Patty can do better.

She tries again.

Patty is masturbating. Patty grows a cock and it extends, fully engorged and throbbing with sensation. Patty's cock extends and extends, quivering in the air it is exposed in, then slowly curves backward and into her cunt. Patty's cock tentatively probes her cunt before beginning to fuck it, first leisurely, then hard, pummeling it in sync with the hard rain outside.

Patty's cock and Patty's cunt come at the same time.

Patty comes.

Patty drifts off.

Patty still has not closed the window.

Tap, tap. Tap.

Slug hangs down from the top of the window, suctioning his wet body, his enormous foot, to the exterior pane. There is a loud and sustained squerk as Slug navigates the window pane at his infuriatingly slow pace.

Patty stirs from her half-sleep.

Two sets of tentacles probe the glass.

Tap, tap.

Tap.

The incoming air is cold and moist. Patty stirs again, shivers. Her nipples tighten.

Slug's tentacles fidget impatiently as they work to gauge the size of the opening. The open window is not wide enough for Slug's impressive girth, but Slug is both lubricated and stretchy. He begins the process of entering her room.

Patty blinks.

Slug is six feet of pure muscle struggling to get through her window. Slug is a rippling lump of skin shimmering with beads of rain on top of a more general wetness. Slug is multicolored, translucent skin, eyeless, faceless, hairless. Slug's intricate underbelly is lined with undulating muscles that tremble against the pane, excreting stickiness, excreting slime.

Patty, torn between horror and desire, cannot bring herself to look away.

By now Slug has pushed a quarter of his body through the window, attaching himself to the other side of the glass. He pulls himself further forward, inch by thick inch, up the glass until his full length is inside. A pause, a shudder of slick skin, before he continues. He crawls along the wall, staining it with his wet trail as he nears her bed. Hanging down, he fills her nostrils with the smell of fresh soil. His tentacles toy with her hair.

Slug curves toward her, his back end vertical, attached to the wall, his front end suctioning itself to her shoulder, kneading her skin with his underbelly: like an introduction, like saying hello.

Patty sucks in her breath.

Hello.

He twists toward her head. Soon there is mucous creeping through her hair. His front end gropes her forehead, sticky lubricant oozing into her brows, clumping her eyelashes together, choking her nasal passage with a swamp musk. She opens her mouth to breathe. He enters, gropes around, sucks on her tongue noisily with the front portion of his foot, and pushes forward until her throat closes up and rejects him. He pulls himself out, with reluctance; works his way to her torso. Past her chin, along her neck, he slurps noisily, slowly, taking his time. The bedsprings bark. As he moves forward, he shoves her camisole down, the thin straps breaking, and flattens both breasts with his weight, his belly gripping and releasing her nipples rhythmically. She finds herself making soft gurgling sounds deep in her larynx. Slug gurgles Slug's reply.

Then he slugs himself down, less leisurely now, hugging the curves of her abdomen, his tentacles seeking her tunnel. Slowed by an unruly nest of hairs, his lubricant smooths the way, and—at last—he probes her slit, first tentative, then with force. He inches forward, nudging her thighs apart.

Patty's hands claw at the sheets.

The wind rustles trees outside. The wind enters the room triumphantly, amplifying the scent of swamp that is beginning to suffocate Patty.

Slug surges forward, stretching himself taut, easily eight feet long, digging, digging as deep as he can, the bed creaking with every insatiable thrust. Lodged inside her vulva, his front half shifts to suit her, curving back and downward. The rest of his body, resting on her torso, kneads her flesh raw. Under his weight, she struggles to further open her thighs. It is difficult—he is massive, his skin so slippery—but she needs to show him: more, please more. She wants all of him. Slug manages to pull a few more inches of his body inside, his trembling underbelly attacking her canal from all angles, speeding its tempo to frantic bursts. Faster. Harder. Her muscles tense. Faster. Harder. Almost. Slug gently chews the insides of her cervix, bringing her to excessive climax. Patty arches, kicks, sucks in so deep she nearly swallows her tongue.

The room is heavy with dampness. Slug slows to a hum. Then he extracts himself slowly, the suction stubborn, painful to break, and rests on top of her, his underbelly engulfing her whole body in its folds.

Slug has crushed Patty. Patty has died.

Slug kisses Patty. Slug kisses Patty until Patty can't breathe. Slug is in her nostrils and mouth. Slug's mucous drips down her throat and fills her lungs. Slug's mucous fills her body. Patty is drenched in Slug, stuck in him, inextricable. Her eyes are slimed shut, her hair slimed into new skin. Her face is slimed into an amorphous blob. Patty tries to move, but Slug's weight prevents her. She chokes a little, learning how to breathe again.

His work done, Slug releases her and crawls up onto the wall behind her. He creeps back over to the window and perches there, his head turning towards her, his tentacles dancing. He emits a gurgle. It seems to mean Come With Me.

Though she cannot see the limbs that are no longer there, Patty understands that her body has changed. She rolls onto her belly, finding that she can feel where she is with two sets of tentacles attached to what used to be her face. She tries to talk but can only gurgle back.

Slug nods: he understands.

Patty follows Slug through the trees behind her apartment building, their slime smoothing them over wet leaves and limp twigs, over thin gravel, the occasional rotting pine cone, until they come to a heavy dampness under a half-fallen tree trunk. Slug turns back and nudges her playfully, his tentacles fondling hers. Then he leads her up the trunk and out onto one of its outstretched limbs. There they mate, Slug showing her how to wrap around his length as he wraps around hers, so that they are like a DNA strand, like a corkscrew, hanging down from the limb on one rope of slime. It is easy, like love, this full-body writhing. For a long while they are content to lick each other, lapping up one another's slime and producing more in its place.

This is the wettest Patty has ever been. Her body is in full tremble, every pore of her skin secreting slime, every nerve channeling excitement.

Suddenly she feels a new sensation: her cock is beginning to protrude translucent from her mantle to wrap around Slug's protruding cock, its sensitivity heightened with every fondle of the wind. Like their bodies, their cocks writhe around each other until they are intertwined. Then their cocks begin to expand, throbbing and massive, together forming an intricate flower that dangles down from their hanging bodies.

Patty and Slug tighten their embrace further and further still, in sync with their pulsating cocks. Tighter, tighter, tighter; their cocks throb, begging for release. Finally they ejaculate, each fertilizing the other in an extended excessive climax.

Slug and Patty's simultaneous extended excessive climax ends all time and thought.

Patty is dizzy. Patty is exhausted. Patty has more work to do.

Because slugs' cocks often get stuck together post-coitus, the chewing off of one or both cocks is sometimes called for; and because slugs are hermaphrodites, this is not totally a big deal.

This is what has happened here.

Because Slug's cock is stuck in Patty's cock, Patty must begin to chew it away, being careful not to chew off her own cock in the process. As Patty gently chews, Slug writhes around her body and gurgles in pleasure, in pain. When she is done, Slug drops down and sprawls on the leaf-matted forest ground for a moment, recovering. Then he creeps away.

Now Patty is alone, dangling precariously from the tree limb. She tries swinging herself over to the trunk but, fatigued, cannot build momentum. Like her lover has done, she allows herself to fall from the rope of slime to the soft ground. Though the fall is not long, the impact stings. Her skin, she supposes, is still sensitive.

Here Patty rests. What will Patty do next?

Patty will leave the forest. She will creep back to her home. She will creep back to her bed. But her home can no longer be her home, she knows, for there, the air is dry. She must go where the air is moist.

GINA FRANGELLO

Slaves of Bataille

I. Childhood of a Sadist, reconstructed:

You left me with this dream you son of a bitch, where I'm sitting in a theater alone. Knowing I am trapped but not really trying to leave, isn't that just like me? Then in comes Bataille looking exactly and nothing like himself, and he starts talking up in front where the screen should be. He's saying, "And I will assert the validity of this without proving it right now, which I will do systematically later, and naturally my assertion will turn out to have been correct." I start to laugh, I can even hear myself do it in my sleep, but he gives me a very stern look and says, "Furthermore I am not able to supply a definition of abuse at this time, and do not believe that I should be required to do so." And I'm thinking, *Violence, it's violence, get the quote right*, because I remember that page, the chapter titled "Affinities Between Reproduction and Death," and somehow this is about me because I'm pretty sure good ole G.B. never used the word "abuse" in his life. It feels like you should be a (wait, that was a Freudian slip, I meant to write, "It feels like *it* should be a . . .") joke, like something we'd have talked about, the way he went around in circles and never cut to the chase, but you don't come in, and there is no one else there to laugh. So I think I may be stuck here forever, bastard, because even when I wake up, the sense of something hanging, unfinished and unsaid, doesn't go away.

It took two and a half months for you to tell me jack shit, but after the first time you whipped me you told me everything at once. I wasn't even sure I wanted to hear it, two-day-old welts scabbing over on my ass, but it was like some long-solid dam of pent-up family history came breaking out of you like blood. So I can see it clearly, it's Boston I'm talking about now, the house you lived in until you were eleven. Some big fucking Hollywood set of Irish people swarming around like extras, all wearing caps and suspenders as if you lived in bloody 1910 or something, that's how I see them in my mind. Your family. Mother with the long dark hair you described and blue eyes that sometimes changed colors like yours. Only they'd be kind and terminally (no pun intended) maternal, not cold as a snake's. But wait, I'm trying to get the image right, get her out of these ridiculous Victorian clothes. It was 1961 when your father got that professorship in Michigan, and you piled up in the blue Chevy, said good-bye to your eight hundred cousins and aunts in Boston and left. The beginning of the end of your family, you said. But you didn't know that then, you're only pretending you did. Probably you were excited to be leaving those crowded streets, to get away from all the people, because you don't like people very well and I can't believe you did even then. It was 1961. Who knew how fucked up the nuclear family would turn out to be, how the future of America was being annihilated every time some dumb kid waved good-bye to Grandma, left her sitting on the front porch of her "ever-since-I-got-off-the-boat" family home? It was 1961, and I wasn't even born yet. Hell, who knew *anything* then?

CRUELTY AND EROTICISM ARE CONSCIOUS INTENTIONS IN A MIND WHICH HAS RESOLVED TO TRESPASS INTO A FORBIDDEN FIELD OF BEHAVIOUR.

You were probably a rotten little boy. Sure, now you try to act like you were some quiet little bookworm, but no one who played racquetball (and fucked) like you did at the age of forty-two could possibly be telling the truth about that. It's just part of this image you have of yourself as introverted, isolated, unable to connect. Yeah, you're real tragic driving around in your slick little car (black, of course), making your hundreds of thousands a year taking other, even richer men to court. I'll bet you've never even screwed a woman with graying hair, except maybe your wife, but if she's got it she dyes it, I'm sure. So screw that image of you sitting there reading Fitzgerald, that's not what got some nun beating your ass, that's for sure. What had you done, really? Maybe dipped some girl's pigtails in an ink well, okay maybe not, you're not *that* old. Let's say you punched your brother, you admit you were always doing that. The smell of decaying wood was everywhere around your Boston school, a sharp contrast to the sterile smell of new carpet you'd later inhale in Utopia, I mean Ann Arbor. You breathed the rotten wood in deep as you climbed to the second floor and waited in the principal's office, your little cock hard in anticipation of being punished, hey, everything gives you a hard-on, and you were probably even worse then.

Later, your mother made you take down your pants and show her. You were embarrassed; you were nine and didn't like to get naked in front of girls. Your eight-year-old brother was dancing around in the dimly lit hallway outside your grandma's bedroom door, doing an Indian-yell of victory because you got hit. Your mother touched the marks, and her concern somehow made you more ashamed than being turned over the desk and beaten had. She said, *The nuns care about you, they're only trying to teach you right from wrong*, and you were relieved cause you were scared she'd go to school and make a scene. But later, in your bed, you worried it meant she didn't really love you if she could let other people hit you and then say it was their right. You even asked your brother, already well-acquainted with the Sister's paddle, if he thought it was true, and he looked at you like you were really dumb, like you'd forgotten for one minute that you were older and never asked his advice. But he didn't know the answer, so you figured it was God. That your mother was close to God and He must have wanted you to get your ass whipped because you were bad.

You developed a fear of Hell.

Sure, you say that now, but face it, it wasn't an entirely unattractive fear. Because after that first time, you started getting paddled a lot more often, waiting in a line of four or five naughty boys outside the principal's office with a rush of adrenaline running through your body. Listening to the other boys yell in pain made something tingle in you, and you wanted to be able to watch, but the possessive bitch always closed the door. When it was your turn, though, the idea of some other little asshole out in the hall getting hard because of you made you sick, and you never let out a sound no matter how hard she hit you, even when it was enough to make tears run down your face. You wiped them up before you'd leave the office, and pretty soon when you showed up again she'd tease you, say she bet she could make you holler this time. You wanted to kill her for having such a good memory, shit, didn't a bunch of little boys in light blue shirts and polyester pants all look the same? Oh, but not you, you must have been beautiful even then. And what kind of woman commits herself to a life of celibacy anyway, they've got to all be a bunch of closet perverts, right? Later you'd say that nuns and priests are the people in society most allured by transgression, that they pledge their lives to erotic rituals sanctioned by the church, rituals of pain and sacrifice that both center on and transcend the flesh. But then you were just wiping up your baby tears and runny nose, signing your name to the paddle the way you always had to when she was done beating you. She had about thirty of them in a corner, varnished wood, full of all the names of boys whose cheeks she'd made aflame. Boys she'd deflowered, in a way.

By the time you were ten you'd signed your name about twenty times. Had started masturbating while thinking of the girls on your block bent over the nun's knee and screaming in their little girl whines. In the back alleys of Boston, bony Catholic kids, freshly changed out of their school uniforms, congregated and had mock trials. The convicted had to go through spanking machines, and if it was a particularly brutal summer day, when the heat was so oppressive that the dogs curled up behind garbage cans looking for some shade, the victim had to pull his pants down first. Girls got to watch. Couldn't hit; it was a sin to touch a boy's bare ass. You noticed how some girls looked away if the boy started to cry, and others got a twitch in their hips under their skirts, like it was all they could do not join in. Those girls you and your brother started inviting over when your mother had one of her headaches and was holed up in her room. You played quietly in the living room, one of you standing guard. No dry, Protestant games of doctor for you: you played "Mean Teacher." One of you got to be the teacher, and the girls were the students who had been bad. You turned them over your knees and pulled up their skirts (not their underpants, you didn't want to go to Hell) and hit as hard as you could without them yelling. In a year you'd have found an empty storage room in the basement that you could access from an outside window, and there you could listen to their grunts in peace, not worrying you'd disturb your mother.

One time you and your brother took turns on one girl and got so aroused that you pulled her pants down and hit her until her ass turned red, and she got so scared she pissed all over you. She ran home crying and told her mother what you'd done, and her mother marched to your house and told your mother, who was listening to Mahler with the sound turned low, and crocheting. You ran to your room and hid your face, so ashamed to have your mother know how evil you were that you prayed God would just take you then before it could get worse. But instead He only sent your father, who lectured you about how you must never hit girls, not even mentioning the pulling down the pants thing or the nature of the game, not getting it at all. And he grounded you instead of hitting you, and then you and your brother had no one to torture except each other.

Which, although you would develop quite an affinity for it later, at the time wasn't as good.

In the dream, Bataille has an extended phallus protruding from his three-piece suit. He carries a pocket watch, keeps staring at it, saying, *Hurry up, we're running out of time.* In the audience, full now, I raise my hand and ask, *So is death as sexy as you thought it would be?* But before he can answer, tell me whether his flesh being eaten by maggots underground turns him on, he has turned into Kathy Acker's B., and I'm going, *Shit, not you again.* Then the theater is transformed to a cocktail party at which Kathy herself is present, a razor slash across one eye. She is walking around just saying the word *Cunt* over and over to herself like a mantra, a prayer. If I were a disciple, I'd draw a hairy penis now, keep it in the text, but that was 1978 when it was hip to be vulgar because the average person still thought sex was dirty but had a lot of it anyway.

Now the average person thinks it's healthy to want to fuck a lot, just dirty to actually do it cause it could give you AIDS.

ON A COMPREHENSIVE VIEW, HUMAN LIFE STRIVES TOWARDS PRODIGALITY TO THE POINT OF ANGUISH, TO THE POINT WHERE THE ANGUISH BECOMES UNBEARABLE. THE REST IS MERE MORALISING CHATTER.

Maybe it really was awful for you, leaving Boston. After all, I've never had any kind of large, extended family or support system, so what would I know? You say your mother was happy there, that she still played piano in the house while your father was out TA-ing classes and finishing his Ph.D. The rest of the family (hers) thought he was crazy, a freak, studying so much and spending all his time on campus. Mother stayed inside and practiced, but when he came home, she rushed to the kitchen to cook. Her sisters cleared out of the house when he returned, too, scurried to their own apartments down the street. Grandma went into her room and shut the door. For the rest of the night he dominated the house with his silent, judging presence. Grilled you and your brother on your performance in school, insisted that once he got a job out of "this accursed city" you'd leave Catholic school, would be an altar boy only over his dead body.

Your father mockingly referred to your neighbors as "the masses," hated living on the small stipend that kept him trapped on your mother's matriarchal block. It was a street full of the sounds of chattering women, of music. You sided up to your mother while her sisters were over, listening to her practice, to them gossiping in the background. Their high, loud voices saying, *Mary, stop for a minute, listen to what happened at the Kavanaugh's last night.* Sometimes they said, *Ryan is a solemn, distant man. Don't let him take you and the kids away from here or you'll never have company again.* But always your mother laughed and said, *You only see one side of him, you don't understand at all.*

You never believed your father that you would someday leave, or even that he would ever finish school. He had been a student for as long as you could remember. When he actually got a position at Michigan and you moved, the world instantly became a disturbingly anonymous sphere. The new house was spacious; you and your brother each got your own room. But there were no children playing on the street, no kids-only places to escape the silence at night when your father came home. And at school there was no danger, no seventh grade teacher who was rumored to beat her students with the Bible when they were bad, no girls who were willing to climb through a narrow window to a basement room and pull down their pants. The classrooms were carpeted, and there was what was known as a tracking system. You were grouped with a bunch of nerds, while your brother had classes with the kids who didn't do their work and mouthed off. Of course even they'd have been the best-behaved children in the school back in Boston. The teachers had master's degrees instead of habits—your father was thrilled. No praying at school, no religion book describing the fourteen Ways of the Cross and how guilty you should feel. At church everything was bland and wooden. No stained glass depiction of Jesus being whipped, no red paint made to look like blood on the hands and feet of a flesh-colored statue crucified alongside the alter. It was a world without shame, without fear of divine retribution or even the immediate threat of physical pain. No urgency, no forbidden fruit. A world that believed in perfection, black and white dichotomies, existence without shades of gray. Practical. Sterile. Dull.

So let's talk men for a moment. Men and the desire for chaos and pain. Now, I hope you'll excuse this politically correct generalization, but it seems to me pretty much a phenomenon of privilege to sit around all day glorifying anguish. That the bullshit about Dionysus affirming life by being torn to shreds is easy to swallow if the closest you've ever come to being ripped apart is a titillating jaunt to the principal's office (or, shall we say, spending your youth at Schulpforta and your young adulthood being lauded by the big dicks of Leipzig?). How quaint to speak of the nobleman (oh, sorry, was that two words?) loving his enemies, of villains in whom there is nothing to despise but ever so much to honor. I guess old Friedrich wasn't referring to the guy I met in Camden Town last month, the one who didn't own a toothbrush and forced my thighs apart with a sweaty, bristly knee, who kept me pinned beneath him on a stained mattress in his squat until after the sun was up, then tried to kiss me good-bye at the door. Of course maybe I just wasn't looking hard enough, you know I always jump to snap conclusions about people. For example, maybe once he had wanted to chop his mum up to bits for burning the cheese on toast, but refrained. And weren't you always the first to tell me how my father really wasn't such a bad guy either, was just over-protective? But then you never had the fortune of seeing him purple in the face, dripping scotch-stinky sweat onto my skin. I hate to disappoint you, but he didn't look real honorable then.

I wish I could get this ex-Catholic, ex-hippie code of yours, though. Wish I understood why sometime in the sixties you turned your back on a martyr God who causes the hearts of old women in babushkas to race with longing for a purity they will never reach, in favor of a sacrificed, ancient god of pleasure who makes the minds of intellectuals race with images of a frenzy they will never dare attain. And was it a token of love that you not only *wished* me suffering, illness, betrayals, humiliations, but offered them by your own hand? I was glad not to take your pity, glad you never offered, considered it a compliment of the highest rite. You really struck gold with me, didn't you? A disciple without even knowing it, I let you purify my sins by fire, worshipped at the feet of your philosopher gods by instinct alone. Only it was the despicable that bound us; you were not that noble man. And me, I was exempt from honor altogether. I was not a man at all.

In Ann Arbor, your mother went to church every Sunday at first, made you and your brother go too. But the intellectual deacons who attempted to reach out to her were all affiliated with the university, liberals who made her nervous. The church was politically active, talked about segregation, Vietnam, instead of repentance and sin. By the time you were fourteen, she'd stopped going altogether. Though her penchant for the piano had caused relatives at home to view her as special, in Ann Arbor she was an outsider: an Irish girl with a thick Boston accent and no college education. Your father tried to get her to go back to school, but she was too intimidated. Her headaches grew worse. The doctors said it was all in her mind.

You were in love with your mother, of course. Oedipus had nothing on you. She could do no wrong, while your father was a cold tyrant in your eyes, though you never in seventeen years of living at home heard him raise his voice. Every girl you dated seemed a pale comparison to Saint Mary, with her porcelain skin and kind, changing eyes. They were too *content*, the girls in Ann Arbor, not tough and guilty like the Catholic girls in Boston, not soulful and depressed like your mother. Even when you kissed them, felt their soft breasts under their sweaters on dates, they seemed devoid of mystery. Those flat chested girls from home with their scabby knees seemed infinitely sexier, and the thought of the women they were blossoming into was enough to drive you mad. But when you fucked your first girl at sixteen, you discovered a thrill not unlike pissing on a picture of a queen. Her straight, pale hair and chiseled features, her floral skirts and delicate beads, all being pushed, contorted, violated. She was in your year at school, a straight-A student, secretary of the senior class. An idealist, she wanted to go down South over the summer and work for integration. Once you'd had her a few times, you started to test her: made her take off all her clothes and spread her legs before you'd kiss her, stuck your finger up her asshole once and wouldn't take it out until she begged. Since you knew you were being a jerk, you kept expecting her to dump you, but she didn't. Maybe she was afraid she wouldn't find another date for prom, or maybe she considered it a learning experience being humiliated, who knew? You were planning to break up with her before her birthday so you wouldn't have to buy her a present; your brother thought that would be a waste of money and you agreed. It was getting dull anyway, screwing someone who didn't get the game. Her blushes when you pushed her down on her knees were getting old. She was no good anyway, dragged her teeth, and no matter what you did to her she never came. You little neophyte, you couldn't even grow a beard, though you were trying to be Kerouac or Dylan, and you'd read about female orgasm but never seen one in the act. The thought obsessed you more than the possibility of being beaten with the Bible had once. The biggest question of your life was: why waste your time with a prissy little bitch who can't come?

Except then suddenly your mother got one big headache that wouldn't go away. That turned out to be a brain tumor and killed her fast, lying in a hospital bed with her sisters flown in from Boston praying around her like a gaggle of would-be nuns who were just too pretty for men to let get away unfucked. Your brother wouldn't set foot in the hospital, spent all his time with his friends like it wasn't happening. Your father too was useless, wandered the halls silently, unable to speak or offer comfort while she wept from the drugs, said she was afraid of going to Hell for having abandoned the church. You sat next to her in a vigil, would not let go of her hand. Whispered things to her that your three aunts (who you had come to refer to as "the witches of MacBeth") couldn't hear, *God will be lucky to get you, don't be afraid, it will be beautiful, better than here.* She held onto your hand so tight that you knew when her strength was waning, when her last breath was coming just by the slow measure with which she let go. But you still held her fingers until they started to grow cold before you let the nurses make you leave, got up to find your aunts and tell them. It was four a.m. on the dot when she died, thereafter always the hour you most hated to be awake, the one you never again slept through sober. You kept asking God to please take her, don't let her have been right, please take her someplace nice where everyone will treat her better than they did here. But it was hypocrisy since you didn't believe in God anymore anyway, had spent the past two years scoffing to your friends about your religious past and reading atheist manifestos. If He were punitive, your prayers might have done more harm than good.

Really, like any God you could fathom was gonna listen to a perverted, disrespectful little fuck like you.

II. Exorcism (aborted):

So maybe it's after the fact, but by the way, I read all those books you used to talk about. From what you've indicated, you were almost my age when you used to read them, and boy were you dumb. Oh, sure, I understand that people weren't very bright in general then, I mean, these were the days when *The Brady Bunch* was taken seriously rather than considered camp, but come on, you supposedly have an I.Q. well over 150 and I would have expected a little more from you.

When Bataille's *Erotism* came out in English, you were only twelve years old. You read it in college, the same time you were reading all that Existentialist shit where every page starts out with some sentence like, *Today was a very bad day.* I guess I can understand, you were just a repressed little recovering altar boy with no one but rosy-cheeked ex-cheerleaders-turned-hippies to fuck, and after your mother died, death was kind of a big deal to you. But give me a break, that shit about prostitution could have been written on crack. I mean, I quote:

> A man cannot usually feel that a law is violated in his own person and that is why he expects a woman to feel confused, even if she only pretends to do so; otherwise he would be unaware of any violation. Shame, real or pretended, is a woman's way of accepting the taboo that makes a *human being* [my italics, not his, he said this with a straight face] out of her. The time comes when she must break the taboo, but then she has to signify by being ashamed that the taboo is not forgotten, that the infringement takes place in spite of the taboo, in full consciousness of the taboo. Shame only disappears entirely in the lowest form of prostitution.

Now I apologize for sounding like a student here, but fuck you, that's exactly what I *should be*, and I have to ask how you could have swallowed this crap when you spent your entire childhood in complete fascination with your own shame, your own violation at the hands of an ugly, Italian nun, and the similar debasement of other boys. Weren't we women only an afterthought for you? So why did I end up having to be your barometer, your gage of what was humiliating, walking some sick line between the base prostitutes of your wet dreams and your prissy W.A.S.P. wife and high school back-of-your-car fucks? And when G.B. walked into my dreams waving his testosterone stick all over the place, I thought of you thinking of literature as religion's heir, and wonder if you fancied me and my stories as some Christ figure you could put on the cross and still call yourself an atheist and not feel like Marx would spit on you if he met you on the street. But he would anyway, wouldn't he, since if I can be like Jesus, I can also be the poor worker you're exploiting with your fat wallet and fast car and male privilege, and don't try to reduce me you son of a bitch 'cause there's always another side, you know that, you taught it to me. And you'll never read this because if we ever meet again, I'll be too busy trying to have no shame, trying not to be human, but I am, and just thinking about you accidentally when I'm out, about what we did, makes me have to turn around and go home, embarrassed to be seen by anyone on the street, afraid they can smell it on me, that I am a whore.

What is this shame worth, though, if once I'm home I always come for you, even though you can no longer see? And did you ever wonder what your mother thought looking down (or up? Hey, that's your trip, not mine) while you let my blood run down in a screaming sacrifice to your own demon guilt? Now that you are gone, and it's me spilling my own blood in the sink, is it *her* eyes that make me ashamed, keep me human? Is she watching me still?

THE URGE TOWARDS LOVE, PUSHED TO ITS LIMIT, IS AN URGE TOWARDS DEATH

A family falls apart quickly. Following Mary's death, the three of you could barely look at each other, your father ashamed of his neglect of her, overwhelmed by the prospect of dealing with his children alone. You and your brother avoided him as much as possible, hated each other too for your respective family roles. It was the beginning of your life as a loner, and you embraced it as much as you could anything at that time. You even swore off sex for awhile. After all, everyone knows any philosopher worth his weight never gets laid.

Fancying yourself the next Heidegger, that lasted for some time. But the celibacy part, not long. In college, then law school, you went through a series of girlfriends, all of them just long term enough for you to end up hating each other. They'd call you weird, tell their friends how you wanted to tie them up, pressured them into a sordid menage á trois with your roommate. You thought it funny, how these things never seemed to bother them until *after* they'd been dumped. Truthfully, provided you weren't bullshitting me (and let's remember honesty is about your only virtue left), listening to your stories made being a woman almost embarrassing. I'd blush for those idiot girls if only I knew how. If I hadn't been one of them too.

It wasn't until your late twenties, though, that you actually hit a woman. Hey, it's not like you run across such opportunities every day. Your wife (and mistresses) didn't get off on being bloodied by your belt, and you had no compulsion to beat anyone against their will. Only with a calculated cruelty that had nothing to do with rage and everything to do with control. You knew from the first time that nun made you walk to the corner of her office and get the paddle, then sign your name after she made you cry, that the civilized, voluntary nature of it was what was most degrading. To make your pain feel like a deal in which you were an active, willing participant. To give you a sense of collusion with the hand that left the bruises that had you sleeping on your stomach for days.

You must have thought you'd found Mecca when I walked to your closet and handed you (okay, threw at you) your belt, got down on my hands and knees without your having to push me, tie me. So much better than your first Masochist Mistress who wanted you to force her. 'Cause you don't want force, you want assistance. Like the girls who walked into that coffin-like box during your magic acts in high school, you needed me to want it, to help you saw me in two. Maybe you dreamt for years of someone who would orchestrate her own destruction, none of that accidental shit you went through with Mom. No, the next time somebody dies, it will be clean as a laboratory, unthreatening as a Physics experiment. That's right, baby, all under your control.

So could I really be so pathetic? That after burning my first Psych book at eighteen, I would end up with a Freudian nightmare like you? Or is it just my own projection that you spent twenty-five years trying to lose something as valuable as her, and you thought it could be me? You told me things, but in the end I know only this: triages of sevens, holy numbers to your unholy sacrifices. At twenty-seven you whipped a married woman with a Biblical name until she bawled like a baby and begged you never to leave her (which, of course, you did, for your wife.) At thirty-five you visited your first S&M bar, and while said wife was home singing lullabies, you were watching women get chained to a stone wall and tortured. (Then went to a hotel and made your lover du jour get down on her knees and present her ass for you to fuck, and she cried, and you got impatient and never saw her again.) At forty-two you described both incidents to me while I was bleeding from your teeth, burnt from your candles, still cuffed to your apartment-in-the-city bed.

Oh, but I loved those stories. You weren't even touching me when you told them, and I swear I almost came.

ECSTASY BEGINS WHERE HORROR IS SLOUGHED OFF

"That struggle and inequality are present even in beauty, and also war for power and more power . . . How divinely vault and arches break through each other in a wrestling match; how they strive against each other with light and shade, the godlike strivers—with such assurance and beauty let us be enemies too, my friends! Let us strive against one another like gods."

Thus spoke Nietzsche, D(ead)WM, the same source of such pearls of wisdom as: "The happiness of man is: I will. The happiness of woman is: he wills." And don't forget: "Let man fear woman when she loves: for then she makes any sacrifice and everything else seems without value to her. Let man fear woman when she hates: for deep down in his soul man is merely evil, while woman is bad." Wait, didn't my father say that? To think all the time I was lying there with his dick up me, I had no clue he was teaching philosophy. Tragic, all the knowledge I could have acquired if I hadn't been so damned busy crying. Little girls, I swear they'll get hysterical at the drop of a hat.

Okay, I know you'll say that now I'm quoting from your guru's most simplistic text. But it *was* your copy I borrowed way back when, in the margins the markings you'd made at twenty, parentheses around the passages you liked, comments written in your nearly illegible, left-handed scrawl. Around the line, "You are going to women? Do not forget the whip!" you simply drew a bracket, wrote, *Funny.* Then, in a different pen, the style of your handwriting more current, you wrote (to me, to see if I would find it?): *Figuratively bullshit, but literally true.*

At least you never liked Sade. I guess he's too blatant for your oh-so-subtle, urbane sense of decorum. If the word "bugger" ever passed your lips, I'd have pissed myself laughing. All that vulgarity splayed out in an almost anti-erotic spectacle: you claim you never made it past page one hundred in *Justine.* But when your buddy Bataille wrote about the Marquis, he made it sound good. Right up your alley in fact. Like all that pomp and circumstance of feces and cum was merely the assertion that tenderness is completely divorced from the interplay between eroticism and death. It all seemed to flow together, to be part of some divine order. Not just some lonely pratt in a jail cell trying to vent his anger and get off.

So tell me the truth. Is that why you never held me afterwards? Why you'd sit and watch me try so hard not to cry I thought my chest would explode? If I looked up you'd be half-smiling, your eyes always gray after a torture scene, intent on me. I felt so naked I thought my skin had been turned inside out, that you could look up every hole and see the secret, ugly self that only my father had seen. There were times I thought I'd die, start weeping and never stop if you did not come take me in your arms, make it somehow okay that I'd let you do what you'd done, show me that you were the same person I'd sat up all night with talking to about books, ideas, while you sipped tea and rubbed my feet. But you didn't hold me, never touched me at all until long after I was calm. Still, if it hadn't been for the flashbacks, the phantom of my father, I swear even that might have been okay. Better luck next time, but then you know all about the jealousy of ghosts.

The first time I fucked another man after you, though, I almost fell asleep in the middle. I'm getting good at it finally, after almost a year. And you're in bed with your long-suffering wife (too bad sainthood's not so fun once you marry it, huh?), or maybe up already as the hour approaches four, long-since acclimated to the insomnia that's plagued you since a year before your mother's death. Are you thinking of me? My skin is so unmarred now (other than the cuts on my arms, my own doing) that you wouldn't even recognize me. And you, have you carried our habits on to some other woman who you have to hear scream to get your fix? Or maybe all I taught you was the value family life: safe and sane, as colorless as Ann Arbor, as devoid of blood, of pain, of gray? That we could intertwine with and come for others after the nights my blood flowed into your mouth is proof of everything I do not want to believe. But of a reality I should have learned long ago by my own hand, moving fast beneath the blankets, thinking of my father, one finger inside me as he raised his belt. From the fast, wet urgency in my cunt whenever I closed my eyes and heard him, *Tell me you want it,* the crack of his hand mixing with the heat between my legs, my tears lost beneath my climax, my words to appease him negating my pain. And even now that you're nothing but a character in this story, I'm still your obedient pupil, copying quotes that would make your dick rise so fast I'd have dropped to my knees.

You'd better believe it, though—this time—I'd bite.

Yeah, I finally read those books you talked about, asshole, and all I can say is I hated every word. But I have to give you this, you practice what you preach.

THE TRUTH OF EROTICISM

IS TREASON

LILY HOANG

Women & Desire–V

An Introduction

There's a woman sleeping down the hall. Her hair isn't golden or flaxen or any of those perfectly descriptive words. Her nose isn't slight or bold. Her body isn't proportional or buxom. Her lips aren't full, but they are also not lacking. Her cheekbones are not defined or flat, but her eyes. Her eyes are full of gray.

She isn't particularly striking in any way. Which is why she doesn't threaten me. She doesn't frighten me. I am not scared.

This woman sleeping down the hall from me, from us, she has slept for days and days and still will not emerge. She has snored and ground her teeth, and this disrupts my nights. But then, they also manage to disrupt my days, and it is for this reason that I wish to kill her. Now. While she is sleeping. Because lord only knows how long this woman can sleep.

I am certain that she can have little more than blistered gums by now. It's that sound of bone scraping against bone. It's not just a sound. It's really happening. This woman sleeping, she must have a burden that nestles like a bird, and hungry, it scrapes and scrapes and she must have nothing left in her mouth but the bloody remnants of that secret, whatever that secret may be.

I have never killed a woman, but I have often wondered how I would do it. Now, I wonder if her neck, which is not slender or thick, would be easy to grasp or if my large hands would simply slip from smooth skin. But of course I imagine that her skin would not be particularly smooth or rough. It is simply her way.

But I am not sympathetic. She disturbs me, and this is something I do not allow.

The Cold Outside

Once, when I was old, I knocked on a door because it was snowing. Because it was cold, I was wearing nothing but tatters and fragments, and when the door opened, I asked to enter. I was very old back then and could barely walk and yet somehow, I managed to travel quite a far distance simply to knock on this door. When the door opened and a maliciously smiling girl appeared, I found myself suddenly energized. Her eyes were fire, and looking at me, I was warm.

To the small girl, I said, "It's cold out here, outside, but you have shared your warmth with me, and now I am no longer so chilled."

The child looked just beyond me. She barely bothered to notice that my lips were once again beginning to chatter, and although I wanted nothing more than to push her down and run towards the flickering fire behind her, I smiled the kindest emotion I could.

She said nothing.

To the small girl, I repeated, "It's cold out here, outside." I said, "Dear child, won't you let me into your house? It's quite warm in there I can tell. From your eyes, I can tell that there is warmth tucked directly behind you, if only you'd let me come in."

The child continued to look beyond me. I was certain that she did not flinch when I began to speak. This, I am quite sure, is no small feat because it has been a great while since I have had the pleasure to engage in oral hygiene. It is nothing personal. There is, in fact, little more that I would like than to be able to wrap some floss around my fingers.

I looked at this small girl with her vacant face, her eyes passionate about something entirely not me. I wanted to kill her. I wanted her to let me into her home so that I could do so without the neighbors noticing.

Once again, I tried, "I am an old lady, dear child. Can you not see that I am shaking, even now as I speak I cannot stop my teeth from banging violently together?" I extended my hand towards her.

I reached and I reached, and I was certain that eventually, either my limbs would extend no further or I would be able to touch her, but my hand kept moving forward and we never did intersect. Nor did she move. It was the strangest thing, how this child avoided my touch, a touch that we both knew would be lethal.

And my arm, by this point of acknowledgement, must have been nearly four feet long. It was a piece of salt-water taffy, only not so sweet or edible.

Finally, when my arm had reached its limit, the girl looked to me and said, "Old lady, you may enter my home, but only if you take out all of your teeth and both of your eyes. Then, you must peel away the nails from your fingers. When all of this is done, knock once again on my door, and I will come outside and strip you of your impure rags and bring you into a warm stew of bath, and there, I will clean you with my own small hands. After you are clean, I will set you by the warmest fire, and there, we will feast."

I looked at this girl. There was nothing left in her eyes, but she did not avoid my gaze. So I began, one tooth at a time.

The Little Bird That Could

It is true that the little bird had lost nearly half of its left wing after the dog had had her pleasure with it. The man did all that he could to salvage the small bits of cartilage, pressing chunks of loose flesh back into the bone, hoping it would stick like putty if only he applied enough pressure for a long enough period of time.

He drove. He drove knowing that it wasn't safe for him to be driving while holding a dying bird in his lap, pellets of muscle staining his pants, but he was careful, and he knew that if he waited, the bird would not survive. For this, he was a kind man. It would be impossible to not think he was a kind as man when he did, after all, leave his car running when he reached the animal hospital to ensure that the bird received prompt attention. Some would call this stupid, a man abandoning his vehicle like that, but those more foolish would call it kindness, but it matters little how he is judged because he did, after all, leave his car running and in doing so, it was stolen, but by then, the bird had been stabilized, and he cared more for the bird's health than a money-eating car.

It's true that the car was stolen, that he in fact had stolen it because it wasn't but earlier that day that some louse left *his* car unlocked with the key still in the ignition. This man, this kind man who saved the poor bird, out of dumb luck stumbled across this car, this car that clearly belonged to someone else, but not caring much, perhaps because of intoxication, he got in and drove away.

We're not going to call it karma or fate or any of these words, but it is impossible to deny that there is some kind of cycle involved because the moment he walked into his house, still intoxicated, although that may be too kind of a description, he saw blood drizzled in chaotic trails. Out of curiosity, he followed these movements, which he alone could see. We have seen the house and the blood and sure as shit there's no way he could've seen any kind of pattern, and yet, somehow he did, and after he followed the trail to its end, he saw the dog and the bird. He's certain that at some point there was a struggle, perhaps even a war, but by the time he saw it, there were bits of dull bone protruding from this mass of flab and dirty feathers. The dog tossed it up and caught it. She tossed it up again and caught it midair. The man puked in his hand. Then, he called the dog, "Here Killer. Here boy." The dog's name wasn't Killer. The dog wasn't his. This wasn't his house. But the dog came anyways. The dog came and dropped the bird on his feet.

This is when the miracle happened, when the inebriated man picked up the pulsating carcass and crammed his own fingers over the missing pockets of organs and skin, exchanging his spare body parts for the ones it lacked for just a moment or two. The bird, recognizing a strange kindness, continued to breathe. This was perhaps all the little bird could do.

So the man jumped into the car that was not his and drove with the little bird dissolving in his lap to the animal hospital where the second miracle happened and the bird survived.

It was certain that the bird had only one functional wing and that the dog that damaged many of the little bird's nerve endings, although which ones in particular weren't quite clear. The man, now quite sober, agreed to care for the bird, which he'd become certain was some type of savior.

After eight hours of surgery and after he waited for another two hours for news that the bird had survived the anesthetic and all else, the man finally went outside, and he didn't even bother looking for the car, as he was sure that it had been stolen and if it wasn't, he certainly didn't have any respect left for a car that sat outside for ten hours with the keys still in the ignition that couldn't be stolen. He walked the many many miles necessary to reach his own home, his real home.

He was tired, but he didn't rest. He went inside and immediately began building a birdhouse. It had once been a bonding father-son activity, although he could hardly remember if it was between him and his father or him and his son, but his hands knew where to hammer, where to hold without instruction. And so he built and he built with great vigor until the house was complete. A two-story mansion designed specifically for a bird missing a wing. Everything was slightly off, on this diagonal skewer, and the man, satisfied, slept. He slept for what must have been days and days and he never emerged, not even to go to the restroom, and it was not until the animal hospital called for him three days later that he finally woke, completely refreshed.

The man got into his own car and drove. He drove until he arrived and picked up his little bird, his own little bird. He was happy to see it standing, although the dog had almost lopped off a sizable portion of the bird's left leg. The man reminded himself to account for this in the birdhouse.

Joyous, the man drove home, eager to show the little bird his new palace.

The Soundless, Bloody Whistle

So I began one tooth at a time, and without anesthetic, it was difficult and bloody. My fingers became pliers, and they twisted and pulled with strength even I did not know I possessed. Perhaps it was out of desperation or out of coldness, but my fingers were icicles and pick-axes, and I performed the most skilled operations until all of my teeth were gone. Even my wisdom teeth which had been so firmly nestled in the nerves running along my throat that dentists and surgeons alike were too frightened to remove them.

I took out all of my teeth, even the ones that had not yet formed, and I put them in a small pail for the little girl to inspect. They jingled a pretty melody, which I wanted to whistle but could scarcely manage a piddle of a sound without my teeth.

I took a swig of something that burned my throat, and it stung the corridors of my gums, but I didn't mind because there was some sort of numbing agent contained in it so I took a few more swigs until swigs became gulps and I was firmly intoxicated.

Intoxicated, I hastily plunged my icicle fingers into the sockets of my eyes and scooped them into the pail.

Without eyes, my hearing suddenly became muted, but I could feel vibrations in the ground with great accuracy. I could feel the little girl's little feet stomping down the stairs, skipping through the hallway, and pausing only briefly to unlatch and unlock and open the front door.

She did not invite me into her house, but this time, I did not wait for an invitation.

The Unanimous Decision

For a woman to sleep days and days, she must be very tired. Or sick. Or perhaps both. For a woman to grind her teeth with such earnestness, she must be very guilty. Or sick. Or perhaps both.

I know that I should have sympathy for her. I know that women like her should be cared for and loved, but it is impossible for me to do so when she annoys me, and it is not just me. We are all annoyed. Her presence bothers us.

Only last night, we met in the tearoom, and although we had neither called a meeting nor extended invitations, everyone promptly arrived as though we knew the time had come for us to make a decision. Only last night, we all sat in the tearoom in solemn silence for minutes and minutes. We all closed our eyes, breathing in her grinding teeth and mucous-filled snores. I admit that I wanted to speak. I wanted to be the first to propose murder, but I restrained myself. It isn't proper for a lady to speak first, even if she is the designated killer. So I waited. I waited and waited, until the woman beside me inhaled a sigh and the entire room bounced with all the anger and frustration that had been muted for so long.

It is very difficult to order an overzealous crowd, but I sang a sweet song and they became enamored with the melody. One at a time, they stopped their screams to soak in the message of death, the calling for murder, and even though I created the song as I sang, we sang in unison, in perfect harmony, and that's how I knew the decision was unanimous.

Weeping Beauty

The princess was very beautiful. This much cannot be disputed. She was so beautiful that her lips were veiled and her eyes shaded and every inch of her skin shrouded with death. It is said that this princess was so beautiful that any being that saw her would weep until they were sick with dehydration and even then, they could not stop crying.

Now this was a time before medical sophistications like diagnosis and needles so these people and goats and rabbits and lice were doomed to die. For a while, the king's cavalry tried to transport the more important people, like dukes and dames, to nearby sources of water, but submersion did little other than iron out wrinkled skin, but the discovery of the Fountain of Youth is an entirely different tale. Of course, even this mystical, magical fountain could not save these dukes and dames, but they were certainly the most attractive and youthful dead dukes and dames ever recorded.

Only no one suspected the princess for quite a while, at least not publicly. Even after the King and Queen and all the princes and princesses and dukes and dames and ladies and sires where dead, no one wanted to implicate the baby princess. That, they figured, would practically be sacrimonarchal, which was practically sacrilegious, and no one wanted God's scorning. So the young princess continued to kill all the people who came to care for her, for simply looking at her was a death sentence, and it was only after she had unknowingly caused the death of her entire kingdom and adjacent kingdoms that a young knight suggested that perhaps she was to blame.

So this young knight, being the bravest of young men, volunteered to care for the princess, and after he traveled for weeks to reach her, he knocked on the palace door and used a thick blanket to cover his eyes. He begged the princess to drape a curtain or several curtains over her head until not a single bit of skin was exposed. The princess complained of the excessive heat under all the cloth, but the young knight would hear nothing of it. He said, "Lovely princess, I am immune to your sweet words, but I am not strong enough to survive your beauty, and so I beg you. If you wish to eat today and tomorrow and for the remainder of your life, please, cover your entire body. Do not let even the slightest amount of skin reach my eyes."

She responded with a sweet song promising him that she would remain under layers and layers of curtains if only he would care for her.

He reached to open the palace door. He knew that she was lethal and yet he desired nothing more than to see the face that had killed more than a thousand men. He dropped the thick blanket covering his eyes and saw the most majestic woman. It was then that he began to weep until there was nothing left to him but bone.

The Little Bird that Couldn't

He loved the little bird. He cared for her. He chewed her food for her and drizzled slowly it into her little beak. Most of the time, the bird spit it back in his eye, but he was not offended. He loved the little bird.

Life was wonderful for this small family unit for days. He would often crawl into her birdhouse and spoon her when the nights were coldest.

Then, on the fifth day of their harmonious union, she fell out of a second story window and broke her neck.

Or maybe she didn't fall. Maybe she jumped.

Promise

To the old haggard of a woman, I said, "Old haggard of a woman, you have almost done as I have asked. You have taken your eyes out and pulled out all of your teeth, but I still see a shard of shining white in your mouth, your mouth which is fowl with blood and stink. I find you disgusting, but I can ascertain that you have indeed attempted to do as I have told you. I am a kind girl, old woman, and I will fulfill my end of the bargain, even though you did not. I will pity you with my kindness."

The old woman smiled and her mouth brimmed with slime.

The Returned Gift

She was not an uncaring or cold princess and she, being lonely for so long, took the young knight in her arms and connected her lips to his. She transferred as much of her spit into his mouth as she could. She did this until her throat was coarse. The knight stopped weeping, but it was still quite clear that he was dying.

The princess ran to the fountain and scooped water out by the handful and ran to the knight and fed it to him. Slowly, he gained color. Slowly, he gained strength. And the princess continued her running from knight to fountain, which was no small journey, but she was determined to save him, her last hope for a friend.

It took many years for the young knight to fully recover, but it mattered not because he had consumed nothing but fountain water so he looked as youthful as the day he knocked on the palace door, and the princess, she had legs and hands of pure muscle from her many trips from fountain to knight. She was certainly kind and caring, but she was not smart, and for this reason alone, once the knight was strong enough to walk, he slapped her once across the face for not dragging his lithe body to fountain, thereby saving nearly a decade of running, then he kissed her and returned all the sour spit she had so altruistically given him nearly forty years ago.

Ever After, Part I

He took a vow that day. He swore that never again would he save another being. In fact, he swore destruction on the world. It was his sole mission to kill all things sweet and kind.

That is how he came to reside with us.

Ever After, Part II

They did not live happily after, but they did live together—he constantly reminding her how stupid she was for lack of education and she ever reminding him that though she may be dumb, she saved his life. In many ways, theirs was a peaceful union, and if nothing else, they were by far the most handsome and youthful rulers in the entire world, although none could actually see her.

But after centuries of rule, the young princess became quite bored with the young knight. She looked at him and said, "Darling, I've become bored with you."

He said, "And I with you. I can't believe there was once a time when your beauty killed men. Now, you're so average."

He said this without thinking, and she knew this instantaneously. So did he.

There was not a pause. She did it without hesitation.

She dropped her veil and her shades, and all of her clothes fell off of her body, and he began to wail.

And that is how she came to reside with us. That is how she came to snore and grind her pretty teeth all day and all night.

Ever After, Part III

The old woman smiled and her mouth was slimy, which I hate. I hate slime. I hate things that shine. But as quickly as she smiled, her mouth opened widely, as if she wanted to swallow me in one fell swoop, but then her eyes caught the empty holes where eyes once were directly behind me. Thousands of them. I hate to brag, but many beggars have come to knock on my door and I offer them a warm bath and company and they in turn remove their teeth and eyes and once they enter my home and I remove their slime, they no longer live. I do not kill them. They simply stop living.

This old woman though, she was different. I had a kinship to her. I felt a warmth that I have not felt since my dear brother stopped living. So I said, "Old woman, here are your teeth and your eyes. Screw them back into place, but only if you promise to live with me for ever after here and play with me every day. Old woman, I make you this offer, but you must not try to eat me. You must play with me and all my dead old beggar men."

The old woman smiled and hungrily grabbed for her teeth. She sharpened the roots into screw and put them all back into her mouth. She said, "Now, dear girl, do you have any floss?"

An Ending

This woman sleeping down the hall, it is my duty to kill her. It is true that I live in a house filled with murderers and evildoers, and it is true that we take turns torturing our guests, and when there are no guests, we play games such as Monopoly and Trivial Pursuit to pass time. We are a family, and I have never killed a woman. Before I was an adolescent, I had seen scores of beggar men die, and I mounted their dead heads on my wall for decoration, but I did this only because my parents left me with no paintings when they deserted me.

But now I must do what I must do, and I wish to do it without an audience, so if you please.

KASS FLEISHER

Where I'm From

Part I: Where I'm From

Once upon a time, in a land far far away, a master-father castrated his daughter's long, apprentice sentences. Our tale begins in the master's dark, wood-paneled office, autumn leaves dashing against the ivy clinging to his window. He spends hours gripping red pen, pouring over the apprentice's promising young "stories." His eyes blur, his family calls (he *is*, of course, *married*)... but the daughter's "stories" would be saved. They would be trimmed, sculpted, sliced to order. She could be the new Ann Beattie, the clitorized Carver, if only he could make her so. He toils and he sacrifices, gives the apprentice hours he could have applied to his own clipped, taut, Vintage(d) work. When she objects to the bloody scars on her manuscript he strokes his beard and sighs. If only she understood his sacrifice of time, of logos. Finally, in search of her father's agent, she relents. She slashes sentences, minimalizes pain, inserts projectile plot structures, offers in jest to add his name as coauthor. And OK, yes, she fucks him once or twice, since that is what the stroking of logos can lead to. Then she leaves his tutorial. And her sentences, like the vines near his window in spring, begin to grow back.

N.b.: These words are *not* chains binding you to any one specific construct of hardwood forests.

Part II: Where I'm From

"My mother is a poem I'll never be able to write/though everything I write is a poem to my mother."

Part III: Where I'm From

Memorize the turnpike tunnels: Blue, Kittatinny, Tuscarora, Allegheny.

On South Mountain, Hosack Run spills down Methodist Hill, across Grave Ridge and into Conococheague Creek—north of Scotland, east of Iron Run, south of Dead Woman Hollow, west of Pine Grove Furnace. Fuller Lake is the cold one; Laurel Lake dams Mountain Creek; Cowan's Gap is better for swimming; Caledonia crowds in too many kids. Yellow Breeches Creek is best for trout and tubing, Conodoguinet for canoeing (the Seneca were better at it than we were).

One October day, a black swan lands on Laurel Lake, floats past the bright-red sugar maples, into the lily pads, around the bullfrogs—and vanishes into the low-branching pine forest behind it.

"I have arrived in Pennsylvania after an impossible trek."

Part IV: Where I'm From

She waits for him at Bigham's Fort. He's late—she fears the Delaware have got him, imagines what they'll do to him if they have. She smiles at the children, fails to convince them that there's nothing to worry about, rubs her stomach where the new baby grows. Truth is, he's gone to Carlisle for salt, but in the narrows near Bigham's Gap a bear has charged his horse and thrown him. He's chasing his horse through the hills when the Delaware charge the fort instead. He can smell the smoke for a mile before he sees it. She's sold to the French, who bring her to Montreal. She breaks a leg running the gauntlet, watches as they shove her sickly girl under the ice until she stops struggling, watches as they let her float away. He will try, but never find her.

Her father drives nails into pine logs for a cabin while her mother burns out the tree stumps. Shortly after her fifteenth birthday, she has just returned from fetching the horse back from a neighbor, struggles with the harness, tugs weakly, begs him to pull through the limestone rooted in the field that would be corn. When the Seneca ride in bareback and snatch her from the plow, she's wondering whether her brother left a little sugar with her biscuit lunch. From the top of Piney Mountain, from her seat behind the man, she sees the smoke of her father's pine logs twisting up between trees. When her release is negotiated years later, she stays. Later, she will own her own farm, cut her own cornrows, smother her own potatoes with her own dirt. Later still, she will rent several farms to white tenants. She'll sleep on the floor with a cherished husband, she'll bear sons who will kill each other, she'll become a leader of her adopted people. To the white man who'll print thousands of copies but take out the part about her profitable orchards, she'll dictate the story of being captured by the people she loves.

Too near her stove, she stands rolling a pie. It's berry season. A. P. Hill and his men have walked a long way looking for shoes and supplies for the exhausted, but the mountain people have lost their tobacco farms and have nothing to give him. He's come down from Piney onto the flats. When he fires accidentally on Union Army scouts, Robert E. Lee has to get up, over, and down three mountains to defend Hill's position. From where she stands in her kitchen, she can't see them coming. She shoves sweat from her face with a floured hand. The heat melts the butter enough to make the dough sticky guns pop feverishly in the distance an occasional cannon shudders the floor carefully she lifts the edges of soft dough folds the circle in half folds the half-circle in half hefts the quarter-circle into the palm of her hand bullet tears through kitchen window into belly falls to floor hands high dough intact on her back soft circle of pie dough draped across   chest

The men searching for the three lost babes hike by her place on Wigwam Trail every morning for four days running. Occasionally they startle her by firing their rifles at a deer. They're nowhere near the right spot. She doesn't want to, but thinking of the children, she rides her mule over South Mountain and tells the sheriff where the children are. She's seen the place—in her sleep. The sheriff laughs her out of his office. Weeks later he has no choice but to check out by Kahler's place like she said. When the sheriff's men find the bodies of the children stacked trimly like firewood, he arrests her for murder. How else could she

And why else would she tell, except to turn the guilt away from

Part V: Where I'm From

A 2-gravida female. Redhead. Current status unknown.

HILTON OBENZINGER

From A*hole

This, then, is where our story begins.

Red Phone

When they finally put Erich Mielke in Moabit prison he was an old man in his eighties. For decades the chief of the feared East German secret police known as the Stasi, Mielke was put on trial for a crime in the 1930s. He was convicted for the political assassination of two policemen in retaliation for the murder of Communists, and not for any misdeeds during the Communist regime itself. Luckily for the prosecutors, he could be accused of the failures of the Weimar Republic, and they could avoid any messy Hitler-Stalin complications.

The old man's spirits were very low, and the guards worried about his morale. Already morose, he grew increasingly despondent, and they were afraid he would fall ill, even die. If he died on them it would be very messy, and he needed to live at least long enough for the trial.

After some thought, the prison guards put a red telephone in his cell, the thick, bulky kind that he had enjoyed as a member of the Politburo.

Mielke seemed to scoff at first. The red phone was not even connected to the outside world, not even to the guards. But after a short time he began to pick up the bright red receiver and speak into it. More and more Mielke began dialing, cradling the receiver to his ear, conducting imaginary conversations, conferring with phantom subordinates, issuing orders—almost like the old days.

Soon the old man brightened up.

My dream ended, and I became confused.
My dream resumed, and my eyes opened.
Delete.

Bedtime Story

Barney told me yesterday that they were letting me go, and I don't know how you tell a kid her pop is a flop—yet again.

I didn't want to tell Missy that I was fired, but I knew I would anyway.

I thought I was hot, coming up with ideas with real legs, but no one else thought so.

Our client was some local environmental protection agency, and they needed some PR buffing of their image.

So I suggested a parody message campaign, "Got Sludge," with celebrities like Madonna drinking a glass of water with a brown "milk" mustache, or "Got Smog?" and have dirt smeared around a kid's face, you know, a take-off on the hit "Got Milk" campaign.

That got nowhere.

Then I dreamt up another take-off: "A Waste is a Terrible Thing to Mind."

The EPA rep just gave me a strange, anguished look, "A waste is a what?"

"You know, like the United Negro College Fund?"

"A Waste is a Terrible Thing to Mind?" Missy repeated when I went to tuck her in after "Goodnight Moon."

I told Missy I got canned like it was a bed-time story, nothing to worry about. Just a fairy tale—and tomorrow will bring the happy ending.

"Yeah, Missy, that was it."

"Pop, that's like the perfect slogan for you," she said, as I pulled the covers up to her chin. "You mind everyone else's waste, but they don't mind you. They don't give you credit for picking up all their garbage."

The sweet smile she gave me just then was worth getting fired from a million jobs.

The next morning I robbed my first bank.

Here is Body, but not Flesh.
The Soul sees, but not with Eyes.
"One Mimesis with Fantasia," she elects,
"But hold the French fries."

Officer's Diary
Sorsogon, Bicol Region, Philippines
17 July, 1901

A strange occurrence outside Sorsogon, so uncanny I have not yet made a report to headquarters in Manila.

Frankly, I don't know if I ever will.

Several fishermen in agitated state brought in a small boy, perhaps nine or ten. The boy appeared Anglo-Saxon or at least white, wearing brightly colored shoes made of a strange substance, denim trousers and a thin blue collarless shirt with a brushstroke symbol that looked like an Australian boomerang imprinted on its breast. On his head was a cap, very much like a baseball cap, but with that same white brushstroke symbol over its brim. The fishermen chattered all at once in the local Bicol dialect, but one or two could speak Spanish, and from them I was able to piece together their story.

Several of them were walking to the shore after that morning's torrential downpour when they spotted a pair of legs sticking out from the ground. They leaped back in fright. Then they noticed that the legs wriggled, and, thinking some freak accident had occurred that had buried someone head first in mud, they raced over and pulled the legs out of the soft soil to discover that the limbs belonged to a little boy. The boy spit out dirt and blew his nose, but otherwise he seemed fine.

The boy's strange arrival, not to mention his white skin, caused great consternation and a terrible sense of dread. They poked him, squeezed his arms, determined that he appeared real enough, but could not understand how someone, especially someone as out-of-place as a white boy, could be found in such a bizarre position. Soon panic spread among the fishermen, some thinking that the boy was an *asuang*, some kind of a demon. Most such demons take the form of a beautiful woman, a kind of succubus, who comes to drain the life out of some unwitting man seduced by the demon's wiles, but it was not unthinkable that an *asuang* could also take the form of a small boy. One insisted he was the boy Jesus. Others cried out that, demon or Jesus, the *Americanos* would blame them for hurting a white boy, might even accuse them of being insurgents and kill them all, and they better take the child to the soldiers or there would be untold bloody consequences.

So with much shouting and signs of alarm, they had come to my tent, bringing the boy, who seemed as bewildered as they, in tow.

The boy did not respond to the native dialect of the Filipinos, so I tried speaking to him in Spanish.

I asked who he was, where he came from, and other such questions.

When he heard me speak he grinned and replied, with great vigor, "*La vida loca*!"

The fishermen gasped at the boy's declaration.

The boy thought for a moment, then added, "*Hasta la vista, baby.*"

"*Como se llama?*" I asked him.

"That's all the Spanish I know—Ricky Martin and *The Terminator*," he went on in a perfect American accent. "But I can—"

His talk was cut off, interrupted by the incredible fact that he suddenly and swiftly began to sink into the ground. I was stunned, and before I could even reach out to him he had slipped deep into the soil right before my very eyes. How could Headquarters believe anything so preposterous? But as surely as the earth opened up to swallow Kora, the boy was gone.

The fishermen began to scream and run away in terror, some shouting, "*La vida loca! La vida loca!*"

Dear Boy,

When you read this I will be dead, of course.

I made arrangements before the cancer made clear thinking impossible to have this delivered to you. Mark Twain thought only the dead could tell the truth, but even now that I'm dead I'm not sure that I won't lie. I'll try not to.

This is the first of many communications you will receive from me. I have constructed a kind of ghost of myself, and I have every intention of haunting you. I have no desire to inspire fear, only presence.

Arrangements have been made with various entities to deliver mail, send emails, deliver videos, produce paid messages on radio, publish articles, deploy singing messengers, mimes, acrobats – in short, to draw upon every means or medium of communication in order to send you messages from the dead on a regular basis. I am still arranging for various rock 'n roll and hip-hop artists to convey their musical interpretations of messages from me. At this writing I am not sure if this effort will be a success. Nonetheless, you can anticipate Madonna or some other pop star releasing "Dead Dad" or some such title some time or other, just as you may one day see a remake of the Hollywood movie "Ghost Dad," with maybe Harvey Keitel instead of Bill Cosby playing me.

Messages will come at random times. Perhaps years will pass before you receive the next one. Nevertheless, I have arranged for communications to be sent to you for at least forty years.

Most messages will have nothing profound to say. Just the fact that a message from your dead father is delivered is enough.

I will never leave you.

Adieu

JOHN MATTHIAS

From "Laundry Lists and Manifestoes"

People often leave no record of the most critical or passionate moments of their lives. They leave laundry lists and manifestoes.

—A.S. Byatt

I am writing a manifesto and I don't want anything, I say however certain things and I am on principle against manifestoes, as I am also against principles.

—Tristan Tzara

He brought me also a box of sugar, a box of flower, a bag full of lemons, and two bottles of lime juice, and abundance of other things: But besides these, and what was a thousand times more useful to me, he brought me six clean new shirts, six very good neckcloaths, two pair of gloves, one pair of shoes, a hat, and one pair of stockings, and a very good suit of cloaths of his own, which he had worn but very little: In a word, he cloathed me from head to foot.

—Defoe, *Robinson Crusoe*

I

Nausicaa heard a buzzing in her ear.
A whisper—Girl, you left
The laundry waiting over night. That list, where is it?
Sashes, dresses, bedspreads, sheets & socks,
Your royal father's robes . . .
Expect a manifesto any moment that may issue from
The throne—not Alcinous', but one
Much higher, darker, grander, more sublime. I may look
Like Dymas' daughter, but behold:
I bring you soap and bleach and starch from very heaven.
Take your girlfriends and your maids. Take
A beach ball too.

Elsewhere in that meanwhile, Yahweh
Stood complaining in the water that was now
Just ankle-deep—Girl, he said to Japheth's wife, you left
The laundry waiting over night. That list, where is it?
Quick before the waters all recede and we stand here in sand:
Wash the dirty linen and the garments of them all—Japheth,
Shem and Ham, N himself & Mrs N—
Here's the soap and bleach and starch. Here's a beach ball too.
But where is Noah's manifest?

N in fact had lost it, drunk inside his tent, and couldn't
Reconstruct it from his memory; all those birds and
Mice and cats and dogs and even bugs and things. It seemed
As arbitrary as a laundry list. Still, old Yahweh'd brought
Them through and wanted an accounting. He took
His own frustration out on Ham who stood outside the tent

Staring at his father's genitals. Don't stare at my genitals, said N,
And soon thereafter issued his explosive anti-Canaan manifesto. . .

Meanwhile in the elsewhere, Nausicaa was playing
With her beach ball having done the wash and laid it out on
Rocks to dry: her thong, her super-low-cut jeans, her black lace
Demi-bra and other things she'd ordered from the catalogue
She read with flashlight in the night hiding underneath her sheet.
Suddenly a stranger came out of the bushes holding
Just a leafy twig to hide his genitals. She told him that her name was
Nausicaa and that she'd come to do the wash. Then
She asked to see his manifest. Alas, he said, I've lost it with
My ship and all my men, but you can put this on
Your laundry list—and took away the twig. Impressed, she
Bathed the stranger in the stream where she had washed
Her under things along with father's robes and brother's
Cricket togs. But soon she realized she'd left the list itself at home
With half the things the whisperer had spoken of.

We have the record of the stranger's deeds, his wily ways,
His journey home when washed and dressed and
Celebrated at the court of Alcinous. We have the history of
Abram's offspring after Babel. But Shem and Ham and Japheth,
Gomer, Madai, Javan, Tubal, Meshech, Tiras, Riphath,
Togarmah and many others on the J & P lists might as well be
Coat and tie and shirt and trousers on the one Nausicaa left at home
That floats up on a foreign shore right now.
Of Nausicaa little else is known (though more has been
Surmised.) She went on with her wash.
Zeus & Yahweh went on to become Suprematists
(The empty squares of cities not, as Kasimir Malevich
Was to say, mere empty squares).

Even in Vienna they could feel the earth shake as Poseidon
Dropped a mountain in the harbor of the Phacians.
For a moment, Donna Anna ceased to sing *Come furia disperata*;
Il Commandatore dropped his guard
Just long enough to feel the sting of Giovanni's sword. As they
Resumed, the maestro lost his place & skipped to Leporello's
Laundry list: *Ogni villa, ogni borgo—*
Sing along with me yourself—in Italy six hundred eighty,
Germany two hundred twelve, France a hundred,
Spain a thousand—wenches
Maidens, ladies of the court: the laundress
Or the duchess or the barely legal teen: any shape or any age:
Nella bruna, la costanza; nella bianca, la dolcezza;
Tall or short or thin or fat, horny singles, desperate wives,
Non si picca se sia ricca se sia brutta se sia bella
Purche porti la gonnella . . .
Giovanni turns up as

A stoned guest in Zurich, Tristan Tzara thundering
Against the 1 and 2 and 3 of things
While Leporello's list of ladies finds its way to Ararat to
Be released as species in the long dream of Darwin.
But who was girl eighty-six in Germany? girl fifty-four in Italy?
Who one hundred three in Spain? Who was thin and
Who was fat, who was barely legal? Simultaneologists debate
These questions with the Paratactical Historicists.
The friends of Nausicaa were Tamar and Elvira? Zeus & Yahweh
Sang like Il Commandatore, looking on the dead at Troy
And Sodom and the Somme?
                    Nausicaa washes on and on,
Her hands all red and gnarled. Her father wouldn't know her,
Nor would you. She washes out the blood of centuries.
Her list is endless and includes those things
You got for all but nothing at the Army-Navy store:
The shirt with corporal's stripes, a neat hole through the pocket
Right above the heart; a greatcoat out of which she never
Got the stains. The *manus* in the manifesto was cut off by Saladin,
Strictly following Koranic Law. *Profit not by Prophets*, one
Apostate's declaration had begun. *Yangtse not by Yahweh*
Sang a lost Confucian ode. Rebel Angels in a flight
Of biwing planes out of meanwhile into
Elsewhere and beyond . . .

II

For their fine linen, Chapman's Homer says, *Trojan women and
Their fair daughters had a Laundry.* Heywood: *Except the sonne shyne
That our clothes may dry, we can do ryght nought in our wash.*
Crabbe: *Fair Lucy First, the laundry's grace and pride. . . .*
And as for Lists: did Homer crib his own from sub-Mycenaean
Catalogues all full of places no one can identify & captains who arrive
In ships with fanfare out of elsewhere, never to be mentioned once again?
This was not the place where all his listeners nodded off
Or turned the dial back to classic rock. It was his great & cinematic feat
Of memory, & everybody hung on these 300 lines claiming for himself some
Otherwise unknown and well-born forebear, basher of skulls,
As the high if broken branch of their family tree. He'd take off into
It by error sometimes trying to remember what came next
In his more recent poem. In the midst of *Odyssey* the fans of *Iliad*
Would startle him by shouting out: *Do the bloody ships.*

Fair Lucy First, said Crabbe. Who was Lucy Second? Or was he
Counting off a list, with Lucy first, Sally next, then Jane?
(All of them together laundry's grace and pride)
To list . . .
                    incline to one side, tilt; heel over as in danger
On a stormy sea; listen as in *List, Nausicaa, you left the laundry
Over night – or List, Donna Anna, do it like a Furia Disperata*;
To be pleasing or to satisfy, to be disposed; n.— a desire or inclination;

A narrow strip of wood; an area for tournaments, a place of combat,
Ridge thrown up between two furrows by a lister; written entry
Of particulars or people sharing things in common, as
Pêneleôs, Lôitos, Arkosilaôs, Prothoênor, and other captains,
All Boiotians: Eilésion, Erythrai, Eleôn—
Or Sidon, Heth,
And others from the seed of Noah out of whom the Y god
Made his nations; or the girls
Of the Anti-Giovanni League whose manifesto was the work
Of Lucy I, executed by authorities, succeeded by
Her daughter, Lucy II, honored as a forbear in
The long awaited listserve Cyborglog .com
Good St. Wystan: Never trust a critic who does not like lists—
The genealogies in Genesis, the Catalogue of Ships.
Manifestos, meanwhile,
can be used like Manna (4): exudate of the Eurasian ash,
Fraxinus ornus, taken as a laxative
In any kind of wilderness [Aramaic, *mannā*,
Hebrew, *mān*]. There was a knight who listed for a maid,
But we are merely in the background of his great
Seduction scene, plowing furrows, sorting beans and lentils,
Coriander, wheat.

Maidens, kilt your skirts and go?
Mary, I want a lyre with strings Me so oft
my fancy drew Men grew sae cauld, maids sae unkind
Methought I saw my late espousèd saint Milton!
thou shouldst be living at this hour Mine be a cot beside the hill
More love or more disdain I crave Most Holy Night
that still dost keep Mother I cannot mind my wheel Much
have I travell'd in the realms of gold
Music, when soft voices die My Damon was the first to wake
My dead love came to me and said My dear and only Love
I pray My delight and thy delight My heart
aches, and a drowsy numbness pains My heart is high above
my body full of bliss My heart is like a singing bird My heart
leaps up when I behold My little son
who look'd from thoughtful eyes My life closed twice
before its close My lute, awake!
perform the last My mother bore me in the southern wild
Mysterious Night! when our first parents knew . . .

we'd sort out seeds—beans & lentils, coriander, wheat, maids
And musics, all the Ms, the Ls, the Ps—
Marie and Psyche, you and I, Lucy one and two—
Hot and tired with heavy work, listless by the end of day.

JOE FRANCIS DOERR

Tocayo

Come, all ye tribes of serpents and foul fish!
Beetle and worm, I have a feast for you!
—Alistair Crowley

The first strains of *Tannhäuser* made by a Sawzall—
Specifically B/E/B/G# —before
Ascending into approximations of whale song,
Ground their way through a stubborn length of rebar
On that *Miércoles de Ceniza*—
Consequently I
Rejoice[d], having to construct something upon
Which to rejoice when the Roach Coach's wheels
Came crunching through the damp caliche
Abaft of its breakfast-announcing cuminous stench.

Toting a plate of beans and chorizo, my coffee
Lightened by unsweetened milk, and a centipede
Curious about the gray flecks on my boot heel,
I commandeered a stack of 2X4s and sat
Anxious not for company, but for morning solitude.

But he sat too, having first asked permission,
His coastal Texas accent flat and green and smooth,
Though his features gave the lie to all of this and more.

The Rastafarian tam of Garvey colors—
Red, black, green, and yellow bands of yarn—
Worn Pericles high and pushed off the brow line,
Made him seem less politic than refined.
He called me *tocayo*, shook hands as *Joseph*,
Talked of carpentry, women, Melville, and time.

The last he claimed to be done with killing;
Having done it had smothered his yen to hang fire.
And murder, to which he no longer cottoned,
Was anathematic to his new moral code.

I'd heard the rumors; he was no angel,
An anti-*santo* and apoca-prophet, yes,
But one whose company was the picture of peace.

Prior to the prolix of his conviction and sentence,
He had made it his business to furnish the dead:
Great slabs of purple heartwood,
Spalted tamarind, wengé, and mun
Became in his hands the bedsteads of the breathless,
Terminal fixtures for those whinnying with us not.

He'd made a simple living, so he claimed,
And called it *Queequeg's Coffin*,
Selling to those who wanted something
Uniquely final, or finally unique.

He'd made his own as well; or rather,
Made one for himself—it was carefully worked
Of Yaje and Cocobolo in the classic coffin shape:
An elongated hexagram with a simple sliding lid

On which he'd carved a personal charm:
A white rose blooming from a thorn-encrusted cane.

When finished, he'd placed it in the attic hollow,
A space above his living place of rest—
The bed he shared with a woman who'd betray him—
Ready to receive him, ready there and waiting for his time.

Impassioned men are prone to crimes of passion,
And by some trick of nature find it difficult to bear
The same propensity for passion found in others—
Or such was Joseph's theory; and as theories go, it's fair.

He'd killed the man who for a time at least
Had lain beneath his coffin; had lain beneath,
Above perhaps, the woman he desired;

Had come, at any rate, between
Two objects of his passion—his words, not mine.

Fifteen years of punish and appeal,
Fifteen years of contemplating time,
Fifteen years of books and conversations
Had placed something like redemption in his grasp.

The woman who'd betrayed him never gave up
In her efforts to secure him an appeal,
To secure him his realease.

She'd worked three jobs and went through all her savings;
Lawyer after lawyer threw his hands up in defeat,
Till one agreed to take the case
For a most unusual fee,

And managed to make a fine appeal
Before a sympathetic judge.

The sentence was reduced to time served—Joseph
Had no idea who had been responsible for this.

The day he was released he saw her standing

Near the entrance, near the exit, nearly frantic in her joy.
She embraced him, he forgave her, they remembered who they were.

After the marathon making up, and over a bottle of wine,
He'd asked her how she'd paid for such
A brilliant, young attorney who had argued
His appeal with success.

Your coffin
she had answered
it brought you back to me.

My coffin
he kept saying
it took me back to her.

The coffin
I repeated
it raised you from the dead.

JEFFREY DESHELL

Father

"Look at this room. Look at this room. God, how can you live like this? You live like a pig." "I came from a motherless home, a motherless home, and I picked up after myself. We all did. We never lived like this." "That's right, that's right. We all picked up after ourselves. Our house was neat as a pin. Without a mother, our house was neat as a pin." "You take after your mother. Not after me, after your mother, your mother's side of the family. The Anglo side." "How do you live like this? You're a pig." "I won't stay out. This is my house, my house. I can go anywhere I want, anywhere I want." "Shut your mouth. I do too pay for it. I do too pay for it, goddamn it." "I have a job, I sell real estate. I have a job, you little pig, you little bastard. I sell land. Where do you think I go everyday?" "I'm a salesman." "And I fight for civil rights. I'm not part of the Anglo system like you. That's what I do, that's what I do all day. I fight the system." "What do you know? You don't know nothing." "Look at you. Stand up straight. You look like a question mark." "You live in this filthy room like a pig, and you can't stand up straight. And that hair, God that hair, you look like a wild animal." "That's right, that's right, like a wild animal. Are you human?" "Tell me Jeff, are you human?" "Don't tell me to shut up, you little bastard. Don't you ever tell me to shut up. You show me some respect, you little bastard, you show me some respect." "I have earned respect, Jeff, I have earned respect." "You have your mother fooled, but not me. You don't have me fooled. I see you, I see you." "I see a wild animal who can't stand up straight. Who lives like a pig. No wonder the girls don't go with you. Who'd want to go with a pig like you?" "When I was your age I dressed nice. Nice shirt, nice shoes, a haircut, a tie. Not like a goddamn animal at the zoo. You're not human." "You go fuck yourself, you little bastard." "What a thing, telling his father to go fuck himself. What a thing, what a thing. A thing an animal would say." "God you disgust me." "I never liked you, Jeff, never liked you. You disappoint me, you disappoint me deeply." "What have I done for you? I gave you life, that's what I've done for you. What have you done for me?" "I had to get married because of you, and look at you. God." "That's right, I had to marry your mother because of you. I never wanted to get married and I never wanted you. You forced me into this marriage." "This loveless marriage." "That's right, that's right, I never wanted you." "You disappoint me. You disappoint me deeply." "You're not a go-getter, Jeff, you're not a go-getter. When I was your age I was working, helping my family out. I didn't stay at home, moping around the house, my face buried in a book. No, I worked. And went with girls." "I don't see you going with girls." "Don't you try to shut the door in my face, I'll knock the hell out of you. I'll go to jail, I don't care, but I'll knock your teeth out if you do that again." "I don't care, let the neighbors hear. Fuck the neighbors. That's right, fuck the neighbors." "You're the animal. You're the animal." "I'm ashamed of you, Jeff, I'm ashamed of you." "Turn that off." "I don't want to hear that jungle music, turn it off." "I said turn that fucking thing off or I'll turn it off." "Oh yeah? Yeah?" "I'll turn it off for good." "You think I won't, you little bastard?" "There." "I told you to turn it off. I told you I didn't want to hear it." "I don't care. I don't care, you little bastard." "I told you to turn it off." "It's your fault. It's not my fault, it's your fault." "I told you to turn it off." "I don't care. I'm sick of that jungle music." "Look at you, how hateful you look. How hateful." "Tell your mother. That's right, go tell your mother. Mama's boy. Mama's boy." "Get out of my sight."

Everyone's against me, everyone's against me, even my son. Goddamn mama's boy. He's a major disappointment to me, a major disappointment. He's got a lip on him,

I'd like to punch him in the mouth. Slap him around, like my father did to me. I never would have said those things to my father: he would have taken me out in the back yard and beat the hell out of me. Telling me to go fuck myself. My father would have beat the hell out of me. I blame his mother for turning him against me. Two against one all the time, two against one. And the way he looks. With that posture and that long hair. The question mark. He's a stranger to me. Oh God.

I pulled the wires out pretty good. He likes his music, his jungle music. Takes after my brother. My brother used to play the violin, until the kids teased him, so he quit. I like music too. The songs of the forties and fifties. "Embrace me, you sweet embraceable you." I remember my father bringing that old Philco home when I was a kid. Someone had given it to him because it didn't work. He fixed it up in no time, and we listened to Amos 'N Andy and Jack Armstrong, Jack Armstrong, the All-American boy. He could fix anything, my father. He could fix this hi-fi in a snap. I just broke the wires, I didn't pull them out. I'll get my electrical tape and join the speaker wires again. I'll strip the wires, twist 'em together and tape it all up, it'll be good as new. I ain't going to buy the mook a new hi-fi.

"What does it look like I'm doing?" "Hand me that roll of tape there, will you? Over there. There. By your foot there. There." "Take the scissors and cut this tape." "I wrap each wire, and then I wrap the whole thing together, see?" "It shouldn't come loose for a while, but be careful moving the speakers."

"Let me get out of the way, and you can test it out." "Turn it on." "Put the record on, see if it works." "Not too loud, not too loud."

Little punk doesn't even thank me.

MATT KIRKPATRICK

Facts

Two brothers: One is a police officer, one is a fire chief, and one is a baker. Has no siblings. Has two sisters. Has a brother with whom he is estranged. In 1982, challenged brother to a dual. Instead they chose to drag race in two brand-new cherry red Chevettes purchased with savings from an extraordinary year of paper route tips. Crash Chevettes. Brother's Chevette totaled. Have not spoken since. Sisters collaborate on an opera when they are thirteen. Opera is produced locally to fantastic reviews, sisters hailed as visionary geniuses. Careers tank in high school when their first feature film flops, bankrupting the studio. Height: 6'3". That is a lie. Height: 6'2". Weight: Varies wildly. Any weight indicated here would be a lie. Inherits Chevette in 1995 from his deceased grandmother. Chevette is totaled in a slow collision near Ebensburg, Pennsylvania in the Allegheny mountains. His girlfriend at the time and future wife and future ex-wife was driving. A car going the wrong way up the divided highway collided head-on in heavy snow. Both cars were moving less than 10 miles per hour. The driver of the other vehicle, who was drunk, sustained no damage to his vehicle. Later purchases a rusty yellow 1974 Mercedes 240 from a Physics professor for 1200 dollars. The car lasts one year before the body disintegrates into dust after many rainstorms. Will borrow his father's car when he moves to Hoboken, New Jersey. The car will not be there one day when he returns from work. The police will check the impound lot. He will check the impound lot. The car is declared stolen and the insurance company buys the car. Six months later, traveling for his job, he will get a call in Long Beach, California from the Hoboken police informing him that they have found his car in the impound lot. It had not been stolen. He is the victim of poor record-keeping. Sisters become famous again in their thirties for staging elaborate pranks involving repainting celebrities' cars while they shop, faking kidnappings of famous television babies, showing up late at night at celebrity homes with camera crews; celebrities viewing internet pornography. Police officer brother's partner is killed and police officer brother swears to hunt down the man who did this to his partner. Back in Hoboken he retrieves the following items from the front seat of the car: one half-empty bottle of Coke. Three cassettes of various albums by the band Led Zeppelin. One ice scraper. The insurance company sells the car at auction. Calls either his sister or brother often, leaving long messages apologizing for ruining his/her car and demanding that they reconcile. Visits his brother's bakery in Shamokin Dam, Pennsylvania and discovers that his brother has never been a baker, or a police officer, or a fire chief. Questions whether this is his brother. Bakery is a bowling alley where his brother bakes frozen pizzas and pours pints for bowlers. Either bowls or doesn't bowl. His brother doesn't recognize him. His sister doesn't recognize him. He hardly recognizes himself sitting in his cold car the lights blinking out at the bowling alley squinting into the sun visor mirror.

BRADLEY SANDS

In the Restaurant

The waiter brings you the most delicious lasagna known to man. Baked with all your favorite foods. Served on a supernatural plate. Pulsating with energy rendering this eclectic clash mouthwatering rather than stomach-churning.

You transport a forkful to the bottom of your nose. The aroma makes your nostril hairs tingle.

You take a whiff. It reminds you of picnicking with your sweetheart on a summer day. You prepare yourself for the first nibble.

An entrée from another table catches your eye. It is an octopi smothered in mayonnaise. A glob of drool skids down your chin. You drop your fork, startled by the affection that you feel for this unpalatable meal.

You stare down at the lasagna with regret. You contemplate signaling for the waiter. Instead, you choose to avoid confrontation.

A baby wails. You look over at the bane of the restaurant and film industries. It is lying inside a cradle. The cradle has been placed on top of a table between a young couple. You wonder if the restaurant is out of high chairs. Are they going to eat the baby?

You scan through the restaurant's menu. "Baby" is listed under entrées. $26.99.

The lasagna makes a noise. It sounds like it's passing gas. You shout, "I'll have the baby if you don't..." then squeeze your throat violently. No one reacts to your outburst.

A toad gasps for air. It is dying from lung cancer. You turn to give it your sympathy.

The false toad has deceived you. It is not a toad, but a shish kebab of human hearts. The hearts are working in tandem to gasp like a lung cancer patient. A man points the skewer towards his mouth. You envy him.

The aroma of the lasagna makes you nauseous. The supernatural plate is now powerless. Its warranty has expired.

You hurl the meal across the room. Pasta and all your favorite foods rain down upon the customers.

They react to your outburst with outbursts of their own.

You make a scary face and charge.

And after you're finished, not one iota of flesh is left on a bone.

NATALIJA GRGORINIĆ & OGNJEN RADEN

One, Two, Threeselves

It was most fortunate that we had met at the very time when each of us was only beginning to explore the boundaries of one's own identity, hers and his respectively, so that it made sense to join forces in that exploration and at the same time to double the unexplored territory. At that point we didn't know that to create texts is to create oneself, create oneselves, yet from that moment on we began to construct our mutual identities. As those identities proliferated we began to discern, not necessarily who we are, but maybe who we are not, and it is through this system of elimination of endless possibilities that we build who we are, even by means of ripping out sections of tracks behind us to reuse them in the part of the journey that is before us. Thus we are trapped in this process of progression from who we were to who we could be, and we remain together because we would no longer be, we would cease to exist, should we attempt to suddenly split our tracks—the very fact that we are together allows us to be anything we choose to be, as long us we remain together. It's quite simple really.

Right now we are writers with two languages, Croatian and English, two first novels, and a second one, and a book of stories. More precisely, we are writers with at least five languages we can think of: his and her Croatian (remember, we met when we were in our twenties, and come from different regions of the country that have very distinct dialects), our Croatian (at least one we forged thus far), our Early English (that of, for example, Mr. & Mrs. Hide), and our Present English (the one in which we write this). This goes against anything we have been taught—a writer, a true author, should write in a singular, unique, idiosyncratic language. Of course, everything we have been taught is wrong—the very essence, the very possibility of understanding lies in the plurality of languages: we understand you because we speak in different languages. What is more, it is because we, you, all of us use different languages that we must understand each other. Are we making sense?

We are firm believers, regardless of what Barthes, Foucault and others may have said, that literature is a form of communication. After all, we ourselves create it through communication, through dialogue, and while no, a novel is not a long love letter to the public, who we are, all of us, all the participants in this complex system of literature, is determined by our exchange, regardless of the fact that parts of it span across centuries and languages, and parts of it are as crude and immediate as a generic rejection slip. The key to communication is to assume responsibility for the other regardless of whether we understand him or her, or not. In the very act of creation the two of us have each assumed responsibility for the other, and have assumed responsibility for you too.

The question is: will you reciprocate?

Crows Don't Care

One of nature's rare occurrences, an anomaly, two-headed snakes are usually incapable of survival so they perish much sooner than normal, one-headed specimens. The fact is these are two animals trapped in one body, each of them wanting to go its own way, but only one having the ability to actually control their mutual body. And snakes being hardly gregarious creatures, natural competition between the two is always present, so one might say if snakes would be capable of feelings, the two-headed ones would most definitely hate each other. Thus, in a way, without even knowing it, they die because of this hatred.

They learned that the offices of The Divisions magazine are right in their neighborhood. Why waste money on postage, they just turn up at a tiny second-floor ex-apartment on the crossing of Beverly and Van Ness, only to discover that it harbors the giant ego of Holden Heckler, the magazine's youthful editor. They catch him right in the middle of what he usually does. Must be secretary's year off, cleaning lady's five-year unpaid leave. Heckler sits alone doing an impression of Marlon Brando from *Apocalypse Now* surrounded by a jungle of manuscripts, back issues and dust divided into neat coke lines. Keeps scanning the first page of their story about zoo-animals building a space ship to escape from Earth.

"I must say I'm distrustful of writers who change their mother tongue like a dirty shirt."

"So are we." Nasia refused to sit. In the story the animals fashion the craft out of soda cans, disposable cameras and left-behind baby carriages. They distill fuel from elephant dung.

Holden looks up. "For a writer, it's suicide."

"Don't worry about it, it's our rope." Oren pretends he's bored. A young zookeeper discovers the plan just before the take off. He blackmails the animals into taking him along. Uses his spare key to let them into the food storage and prove he's worthy. Lions and tigers eat him up before they reach Jupiter. Lions and tigers eat the last elephant before they reach Uranus.

"But you had a good thing started, I mean, you published a novel and all."

"Who told you that?" Nasia frowns.

"You did, in your cover letter." Holden reads the last line again. *There they run out of fuel.*

"I wouldn't know anything about that, she wrote the letter." Oren shrugs his shoulders.

"Liar," Nasia cuts in, says to Holden, "You shouldn't believe everything you read."

Their next story is about a married couple taking a walk. A car runs into them at the crossing. The wife dies at the site. Husband lives to find out there was no one driving the car. Just one of those freak accidents. He buys the car at the police auction, fixes it up, drives off a cliff. The end.

"Look, guys, I can't promise anything, you're just too ordinary to be strange, and too strange—"

"We won't beg." Nasia clenches her fists. "We need money."

The two of them aim their stares like double-barrelled shotguns, Holden blushes. If only he had a buzzer now, like in James Bond movies, to summon Miss Moneypenny.

Finally they're leaving. Holden walks them to the door because he's too embarrassed. For them. He promises to get back to them within a week. He promises he won't forget them. It sounds like a threat.

They let you have everything: clothes, lots of food, newest DVDs, deep, dark radio voice you can happily masturbate to, uninterrupted, in private, safe. On occasion there are spectacular fireworks to observe from your balcony, but for someone else's birthday. They give you things, you work for things with things, smooth, shiny, reliable (people aren't nearly as reliable). It's a positive feeling, to work and live with a purpose, get paid for your time and effort, in attainable beauties and useful objects. Yes, you understand it's because they want you under their control, they want you addicted to comfort and security. They want you alone and in need of a human touch, it's perfectly normal, just go talk to your shrink, he'll break it all down for you. It's good to want, to yearn, to necessitate, it makes you shop better and keep yourself happy, keep shopkeepers happy, keep Dow Jones happy, that's your function; you're a regular little happiness dispenser.

I was eighteen when I lost my virginity.

First time I had sex I was seventeen.

It was with a man ten years older than me, on my fifteenth birthday, on the beach. The water was cold, kept rising in waves up my spine, so I didn't feel his sweat, only the fat oily skin, like whale's; I was still a mermaid then, he couldn't spread my legs, I would hit him with my tail, he was scared.

She was forty, married, had a son my age, I was mowing her lawn all summer long. She put my resisting cock into her dry mouth, in the dark cellar, next to the boiler; I was fourteen.

You're lying.

You are too. At ten I published my first poem, it won the national award for young poets and got published in the newspapers.

I was nine when I got to recite my composition essay in the theater, the president was there.

President of what?

I learned to swim when I was four.

I was diving with three.

At the age of sixteen I spent three months in a psychiatric hospital.

I burnt the school log and got expelled, never finished sixth grade.

A gipsy woman read my palm and said I'll receive the Nobel Prize before I'm fifty-five.

Mother Theresa was my aunt.

I'm fluent in five languages, read from five more plus Esperanto. I can eat ten hamburgers in one minute.

I can fly a plane. I can eat ten hamburgers in one minute.

Billboards hang over boulevards like giant fly-swatters ready to drop on unsuspecting insects milling in the exhausts of yet another day. Ten-story faces on the screens smile enormous warm smiles, or frown their fierce and unforgiving frowns, like gods of Mount Olympus, saliva that comes from their mouths is liquid pearl, nectar for the brains, and the souls, and the tired unloved bodies of the ordinary folks. Teenage girls want to have sex with ten feet lips of Tom Cruise, middle-aged men wet their pants at the sight of the twinkle in the lake sized eye of Kate Hudson. Everything that moves in the streets is governed by the two-dimensional images of these divine incarnations; when people close their eyes they see movies in their heads and it helps them through a hard day's work, a fat meal, a routine intercourse with the person they feel nothing for.

He likes to wake up with an erection. He'll show it to her and she'll grab it screaming."We better take care of this!"

He likes the way she takes care of it.

Or she'll just giggle, tickle him, keep it in mind, and then later in the day she'll surprise him from behind, pull down his pants, slide between his legs, grab it like a microphone, sing a funny song until it grows enough for her to take care of it.

These are, of course, ideal scenarios.

Because there are times when she's indisposed, busy with something other than him, reading a book, newspapers, or just plain disinterested in the bulge in his boxer shorts. He resents that, he resents that very much, so in protest he goes to the bathroom to take care of it himself. Growing up is realizing one cannot learn anything by staying in love with oneself. You learn about yourself by discovering that she is not you, he is not you, but someone else. While the world is shaped by your will you never recognize these limits, you never see other people, you never see yourself because you are too vast even for your own perception. The moment someone you love refuses to do your bidding you become a human being. You react. It isn't always nice.

See the filth all around you. Witness the dirt of the world. It's all in the eyes of the beholder, the scum, the grime. Eyes are the orifices of evil, interfaces of corruption. Vision interferes with the thought. Truth is in the sound. Sound is pure. God speaks to us. Got to get clean. Music takes you higher. Got to get clean. Disconnect. Disrupt video input. Got to get clean. Music takes you higher.

"The guy poured Drano in his eyes." The ambulance driver smokes next to his van, waiting for the paramedics to bring down Dimitri, the friendly DJ. "I know you people want to pass, but would you hold on for just a second. For Christ's sakes, the guy poured Drano in his eyes. I don't know why. Maybe he watched too much television."

The ambulance is blocking the alley leading to the parking lot behind the building. Two cars are waiting to go in. Two are waiting to go out. People's impatience charges the air so that it almost crackles, creates ozone, like before a storm. There's a smell of smoke as the gears of the world grind together, the world not turning, things not turning up the way people want it to. The ambulance driver shrugs his shoulders, throws a butt under his boot and sighs:

"A guy pours Drano in his eyes, and everybody ends up having a bad day."

Crows don't fly around Hollywood that often. Mostly they just walk. Too much competition from helicopters and planes writing names of dot-com domains across the sky. A clear sky is not to be wasted in Hollywood, there's always some writing on it, done either by clouds or by planes, a note, a message, a novel. Crows don't care about writing.

Crows don't care about writing at all. If they see a loose poster on the ground they'll walk over, and hop on it, and they'll appear to be involved in some heavy reading, but they'll just shit on it, and hop away. The words such as: FREE WORLD, might be printed on the poster. But, the fact remains, crows just don't care about writing.

CHRISTINA MILLETTI

Where Nööne Is Now

There is a sequel to this story. It has already been written: no doubt my sister Nööne has already corrected my mistakes. After all, this is her story. I'm merely telling half. The half I know. Which is to say: I know nothing at all. Nööne has said as much for years.

Even now, after all that has happened, I can imagine Nööne ringing my bell on Avenue J, returning to the house in which we grew up, and those would be her first words. Without greeting. After three years. *Don't make assumptions, you know nothing at all.* Why shouldn't she say it? In the past, she's always been right.

It is just like Nööne to always be right.

After she left for China, Nööne kept in touch with my mother (I missed her phone calls). Then—suddenly—we heard nothing from her. Not a word. Not a letter since the Chinese embassy in Belgrade was bombed. Not even an e-mail since my sister went into hiding. Even when my mother fell ill. Then died.

That's another story. A story only half related to this one which is (as I've said) only in part mine. This story is my sister's story as she told it to my mother who then told it to me sixteen days after NATO bombed Belgrade and my mother saw, while propped in her bed, an international news report about a young American woman who was beaten as she walked through the Beijing streets on her way to work. The young woman, my mother said, looked like Nööne. She had fended the blows as Nööne might fend them, she had even fallen as Nööne often fell. It's true: my mother wasn't wearing her glasses when she saw the report. She was under heavy medication, morphine in fact, in the last stage—the only stage—of the rapid illness that took her. So I reassured her, I stroked her damp face: *Leave it alone. Don't worry,* I said. I likely smiled at her distress: *You know Nööne always lands on her feet.*

Let me be clear: I did not smile because I care little for Nööne, even though we have never been close, or even troubled by the fierce rivalries that generally mark complex sibling relations. The fault is mine, I have no doubt: I'm not sentimental. I did not weep as my mother did, for instance, when Nööne moved to Beijing three years ago to pursue graduate studies. Yet I felt uneasy as Nööne's airplane rose off the tarmac from Newark Airport: early on it was impressed on me—I'm not sure by whom—that you ought to keep your family close. Perhaps that's because Nööne and I have different fathers. Because I am the elder and, unlike Nööne, I have never known mine.

So when I smiled at my mother, I did so merely to comfort her as one might comfort a child who awakes bewildered in a strange bed in the night. I smiled because her fears were groundless, because—as she herself had known—Nööne hadn't lived in Beijing for over a year. Not long after Nööne earned a Masters degree in Eastern Political Studies from Northern JiaoTong University, she'd left the city. But while her peers had gone on to consult for big business or statesmen, Nööne had just moved from Beijing to Yuxian—a nearby village in Hebei Province where the rice paddies are especially dry. There, she collected data and wrote reports for *China Today*, a Chinese magazine published in English by an ex-patriot staff based a world away in New York. At first, Nööne only worked freelance. But three months after her first piece appeared, *China Today* brought Nööne on board full time. As usual, I was happy for her. I was happy because my mother was happy each time *China Today* arrived in the mail, as if it were a letter addressed only to her: *CT*, after all, was the closest my mother came to a dialogue with my sister—came to an understanding of where Nööne was and why—during the years she was away. Her phone calls were too short, my mother complained. Nööne never told her enough about where she lived, what she ate, the few friends that came to visit. So it was no surprise that my mother forgot about Yuxian: there was so little for her to hang onto once she became ill. She forgot Nööne's move as easily as she forgot the small curved wound on her back that long ago had scabbed up, then scarred, after she accidentally tripped over my sister on Avenue J. At the time, Nööne was two. I was ten. So it was I who dutifully applied the ointment to my mother's back.

As my mother lay damply against the fresh sheets of her bed, I didn't remind her the Nööne had moved to Beijing. I didn't tell her because I would have then also had to remind her where Nööne lived *now*—why she'd left Yuxian. I would have had to relate the events that transpired after Nööne took her degree. And I didn't want to make her remember how fiercely she worried, her prolonged distress, when early one morning (one week to the day she was diagnosed with her illness) Nööne's advisor called from Yuxian in alarm. There was sweat in his voice. I could hear it bubble against the dry swell of his throat, though he tried to speak slowly—each accented word arriving soft and precise through optical cables laid across ocean floors. He took his time. He explained with sober attention how the police visited Nööne's home that evening. How two officers—two stern-faced men paired in green serge—had interrupted them shortly after he'd arrived for a visit, just as they'd sat down to share a kettle of tea. *They took Nööne's laptop*, he said. *Her notes. Articles under revision. Even the drafts of the letters she was writing home.* A Ministry man then dragged her collected belongings outside while Nööne was escorted to a dark, idling car. They were gone in an instant. The advisor's tea was still warm as the car pulled away in the direction of Tiajin, the black harbor where the cargo ships docked. There, Nööne was put aboard ship the next morning. A colleague watched the engines catch, dredge yellow water as the ship pushed out to sea. Of Nööne, however, the advisor's colleague saw nothing. Yet my sister's fate was apparent to all: without explanation, the police had sent her away by ship. Nööne was expelled from China.

There was no news from her for three weeks as the freighter made its way south for Taipei, then west to Danang, before it pressed onward to Krong Kaoh Kong. It wasn't until the ship drew up along the sudden madness of Thailand's southern coast that the Captain, following the Ministry's orders, at last passed her off. We are behind schedule, he said as he secured a rope ladder, tossed it over the side, then gestured for her to climb down. No doubt Nööne left his crew without a word. That would be like her: to climb with care down the rope until her feet touched the new deck. To leave her captors without complaint.

The deaf fisherman who met her aboard his vessel didn't question the sudden, extra company, Nööne told my mother. He just handed her a gutting knife. Then showed her how to pin a squirming eel under her foot, while she thumped a rock on its head. They spent the afternoon together like that—leisurely gutting his catch while the freighter disappeared in the distance—before they at last made their way back to shore.

Nööne called at once to tell my mother what happened: she was safe at the docks at Laem Chabang. She had no money, she said, but she did have a job: an editorial post already lined up with *China Today* (a new branch, she said, had opened in Bangkok). She was lucky, Nööne was clear about that. Though the editor hadn't expected her, he was sending a car to pick her up at the docks. He'd even offered to put her up a few nights, at least until she found an apartment. *I'm unharmed,* she said, t*here's no need to worry.* She would ring again soon when she had her own place. And she did: three weeks later she called (I was at work). She spoke to my mother, spelled the names of the streets my mother couldn't pronounce. I have since written Nööne. In fact, I wrote frequently when my mother first became ill. All my letters, however, have been returned. I am quite sure Nööne remains unaware that our mother has been dead now four months.

Yet I'm still not concerned. Nööne is like the wind—as proficient, as perilous. She can slip through doors. Beneath window sills. She can always get in and out when she desires. To this day, even her name remains a mystery to me. It can't be pronounced in my mother's tongue. Nor in Nööne's father's. And in the English common to our home, it makes no sense at all. I say "Nuh-oon." My mother "Noh-woon." My sister uses both names and many others. When I was young, I used to ask my mother about it. But with a half-smile, she'd shrug, as though in her gesture lay an approximate answer—an enigma I know Nööne still enjoys. It was a game between them. And if they shared a secret, I didn't begrudge them or the distance between us: it was just how things were, how I knew they'd always be. We grew up as though nurtured in two different nests. Even if by the same, doting bird.

At the kitchen table, my mother sat nervously not long after the freighter first left China. She looked slightly blue, as if the belt she'd cinched up several notches were strangling her slowly like a lazy serpent. It was just an illusion. Under the fabric, I knew her belt was still loose. Already, my mother was losing weight (the treatments were taking their predicted effect). Already, we knew she was dying. I did what I could: I warmed up her tea, I held her hand. I offered small words of comfort.

You know Nööne, I said and kissed my mother's red knuckles. *She is like wind,* I went on, *as proficient...*

My mother slapped me then. A hard stinging blow. It took her some time to rise from the table, and slowly return to her bed.

Don't get me wrong. I do worry about Nööne, just not unnecessarily. After all, Nööne has left us hanging before (just not for so long). It's the nature of her assignments, of "collecting data," she'd say. Eight months is a protracted silence of course. Yet *China Today* is still sending her paychecks—that's what they tell me. And Nööne's stories continue to appear with comforting, albeit anonymous, frequency (for "security reasons," her editors claim). One piece per issue, that is, every two weeks. But for the first time out of Belgrade.

Nööne's move was a surprise of course: I thought she was still in Bangkok, much as my mother thought Nööne was still in Beijing. Yet Nööne had traveled suddenly, swiftly, before at the behest of her editors. And *China Today*, I reasoned, likely developed an interest in the Balkans when the Chinese embassy (as Nööne was quick to point out against contrary claims) was targeted by NATO and bombed. "Can the public believe, as they seem to believe, that the special ops' maps were merely old?" she wrote. "That our armed forces act no differently than city teens lost in a corn field at night?"

I have no doubt of course that Nööne is writing the series. Nor do I have trouble imagining how she must have prodded her editors for it, pushed them to send her, to allow her to be the first American writing from Belgrade for a Chinese paper published in New York. The geographic stitchwork of her position no doubt would have pleased her: it's just like my sister to position herself one step away from what she desires just to get exactly what it is that she wants. She's strategic that way. Ambitious. I once watched her leave a ballpark after a surly pitcher declined her interview. A moment later, she appeared at his side through a trapdoor in the mound. The pitcher relented in surprise of course. That's always been Nööne's way.

I once asked her about it. We are not close, but I've always wanted to understand my sister, her motives, better. But Nööne merely looked at me from the sides of her eyes as though I'd asked a much different question. If I am symbol, she said, I merely stand in for myself. Then she met my gaze. But only at certain frequencies. At the time, she was working for a local news desk, it was her first job as a sports stringer during college. She was only a kid, they didn't give her an office—just a desk and a chair with a blind at her back. The chair creaked as she rocked. It had four casters, and one didn't spin. As we spoke, she rocked in her chair.

Two years later, Nööne left for China.

While in Pristina, I gathered Nööne was the guest of a man she called Danilo Losvek (the name surely was a pseudonym), a professor of social history. The life of his family, my sister wrote, had been *"disrupted by a conflict that was not their own."* Danilo likely would have had a lot to say on the matter. But it was his daughter whom Nööne quoted at length. *"Lena Losvek, 18, points up to the craggy apex of a mountain above her village"* (I read). *'The rebels are there,' Lena explains. 'But they do not shoot. They do not want us to know what we already know: that they have received new weapons.'* 'Who sent them?'" the reporter asks. Lena does not answer, but the reporter describes the look in her eyes, rich and brown, fresh earth pawed by a goat in a meadow. *"'When the army shoots at them,' Lena says, 'they hit us instead.'"* She sounds as grim as an eighteen year old youngster can sound who, until the year before, ate potatoes and chocolate, bought new clothes without question. *"'They are lousy shots.' Lena kicks a small stone into the sewer. 'But even lousy shots are sometimes lucky.'"*

Within 24 hours, the international news agencies—all of them—picked up Nööne's feature. By all accounts, the story should have made the back page. It was a focus piece—sentimental—not hard news, like most of her work. Yet in less than a day, after one year's work, Nööne's career was suddenly launched. Only I and *China Today* knew she was the source of the story, but I'm sure, somewhere—back in her hotel in Belgrade perhaps—Nööne must have been pleased. She likely smiled—the faint smile of those whose hard work has paid off—as she relaxed, feet up in her slippers, newspapers strewn on the floor.

What do you think of that? I asked my mother as I always had in the past. Had she been at home, and not in her grave, she would have cried *Bravo!* So I said it for her: *Bravo, Nööne, bravo!* Alone, I leaned on my mother's tombstone, against her freshly carved name, as if it could give me warmth.

Your sister has a way in this world, a way with this world, my mother would have said, which most of us can't understand. When she said "us," I knew my mother meant "you." That is, she meant "me": "they" had an understanding from which "I" was excluded. That much was apparent to me from an early age. Perhaps because my mother loved Nööne's father more than mine, even if both left her without warning. Mine in a rush hour pile up on the Garden State Parkway. Nööne's father, one morning, to go "west." It was a trip from which he never returned.

Where is Nööne? Where is she now? my mother asked me each morning when I arrived at the hospice to sit by her as she faded often mid-sentence in and out of consciousness, hemming in a thought over a course of hours—one word or phrase at a time—until she locked her punctuation in place with a tired and forced smile. *Where is Nööne? Where is she now?* That was the gist of it. I tried to answer her. That is, I lied. *She is in Hong Kong, I'd say, but the flights are grounded. She has landed in Tokyo, don't be afraid. Nööne called,* I told her, *but she's been diverted to Sydney.* Some days later, *Hawaii at last!* Then: San Francisco (she's so close I can feel it). Towards the end, it was Reno then Houston. Detroit, at last Philly. The geography was all wrong. The geography didn't matter. Soon, I assured my mother. Soon. I lied again and again. I mailed letters. I called *China Today.* Nööne was simply beyond reach. I gave up on her long before my mother died. My mother never did.

I buried my mother in the local cemetery, adjacent to the university football stadium where Nööne scooped her first story. I can still remember how proud my mother was of that first publication, how she carefully clipped it and pinned Nööne's work to the kitchen wall. Now matted and framed, the article still hangs where my mother once placed it. Though my mother herself is gone.

The story appeared to be simple at first. The state university had lost a "big game" they were favored to win, and after two overtime periods, several controversial calls, one fight, one fine, and a raging crowd, the game finally let out in disbelief. The town was afire with unwieldy fan passion, and Nööne and I were inside the crowd when a short, steamy riot broke out in the streets. Like a wave whose tide licks your calves before it tosses you onto your back, we felt the gentle nudge of its wet rumble begin. Nööne was first to notice of course. She grabbed my arm, held me back, as a young, painted woman (Jerzy Min was her name) turned and, winking at Nööne, picked up a trashcan not five steps from us. Without a sound—it happened so quickly—the heavy can was aloft in her arms. A moment later, she'd hurled it, clumsy but sure, through the thick glass of a barbershop window. The glass shattered and, pleasure being equal portion expectancy and satisfaction, Jerzy clapped her hands, crushed the scattered shards beneath her feet. Soon, she was jumping, the crowd was jumping. Yes, Jerzy shouted, fists beating the air. *Yes!* I knew what she meant: *Yes! That's much better.* It was as if I could hear her thinking it as she was carried off across the sweaty oxbow necks of the crowd, her palms to the sky, holding it up, as if her strength were its only support. I am the world, I thought I heard her sing. I shook my head while Nööne took notes.

Why do people destroy, I asked?

Nööne looked at me in surprise, the way she always has.

Why not?

I knew not to challenge what she meant, though she asked Jerzy the same question the next morning during a follow up interview. Jerzy's answer, "Because the world is destroying us," was remarkably prescient. Spoken at home in Cog Country, USA, the center of Newark's industrial garden—not just after a football game, but, more significantly, we later learned, while an Apache helicopter with 9 airmen aboard was shot down overseas—it captured the tenor of a new global paradigm that was as apparent to high school dropouts as elected statesmen. Nööne's piece about Jerzy made the front page.

For any other novice reporter, their first story would have been innocuous. Words and ink quickly lost to fiche, to the archives of aging librarians. Yet Nööne was uncanny. I said she was the wind. But perhaps she's really a witch. I used to find her staring at the moon as if she understood what it meant to be large and alone, looming over the earth, giving off one's light to the blind.

Two years after that football game, Nööne left the country to pursue her graduate studies. After that, I never saw her again.

In the first few months after graduation from Northern JiaoTong University, Nööne was hired as a research analyst to gather agricultural data in Yuxian. She wasn't disappointed with the job, though we knew she missed being a reporter. *Data is just a story told on a spreadsheet*, she explained to my mother over the phone, *you just have to learn how to tell the facts right, learn how to read them.* Her job was to count people, births, the length of days. To note blisters, infections. To remark on the subtle bend of stiff spines beneath cotton, to estimate crop production, the average wage for each family. It wasn't long before the locals took to her, she said, offered up recipes to complete her records, even invited her into their homes for evening meals. Afterwards, she often stayed up to watch the stars align just to note how long her subjects slept and, if they slept, how deeply they dreamed. In the morning, she transcribed their visions. How, that night, Xu fished deep waters. Shao bought pink fabric. Or Zhu made the cracked town bell sing as it never sang for its maker, an arthritic blacksmith, 400 years before.

Once, I found a note Nööne had scrawled during an unexpected return trip home while I was away on business. My mother didn't tell me Nööne dropped in. I only learned about her brief visit after I found the note, and my mother confirmed that Nööne passed through before she went to New York to meet her editors for the first time in person. *Our chief trouble*, Nööne wrote, *is our belief in fact. A coin has 2 sides. A globe has many. They bend, overlap. A curve is nothing but a distortion.* Beneath this she had written in lowercase letters: *i have too much pride.*

When my mother died, I ordered her tombstone from a man who claimed he was my mother's countryman and, because of their erstwhile relation, gave me a 10% discount. *You know*, he told me as I wrote down my mother's name, her relevant dates, *you spell your surname wrong. It's not possible to say your name in our language. To say it the way it's spelled, understand? There are too many consonants. This way, your name sounds like a sheep skin stretched between posts.* He paused, crossed out two letters added three more. You should correct it, he says. *Your mother should be buried with her own name, not the name someone else gave her as a girl when she first stepped off the boat.*

I thought for a moment. My mother had never told me about the misspelling. Perhaps she never knew. She hadn't gone to school for long before her father sent her to live with her American cousin who fed me sweet rice when I was a child. After her cousin died when I was eight, however, it was just my mother and I, eventually Nööne. How were we to know of the error if my mother didn't herself?

Do it, I told the engraver, and with a curt nod, he made the correction. Later, I took the paper with her new, old name home, pinned it by the telephone next to Nööne's postcards. *It is never too late to be buried under another name,* I'd told the engraver. *We should all be corrected after we die.* The engraver had squinted at me. *I wouldn't have guessed*, he said, *that you inherited a sense of humor from the country of your mother's birth.* He laughed. *You speak her language much better than you know.*

At home, there was a message on my answering machine. At last, I thought, at last Nööne has heard, at last she has called. I wasn't surprised, however, that the voice wasn't hers, but that of the American consular representative in Beijing with whom I'd spoken two weeks before when I'd been promised a prompt reply. His message was brief. Nööne was still on file with the American Embassy in Beijing. But they had no record of her expulsion. Nor a new registry under her name in Bangkok. Was I aware, he asked, of her work with *China Today*? Was I aware that Northern JiaoTong University wasn't accredited back in the States? He asked: Was I *aware*?

I called the consular representative back. *I did not mention before*, I told him, *that my mother believed she saw Nööne during an international news report broadcasted from Beijing. My mother saw Nööne chased by a crowd, beaten by men in the streets.* I heard the consular representative grind his teeth. He was annoyed, enamel on porcelain. I heard it all though he hadn't spoken a word.

What news agency, he asked? I didn't know. He paused (he was thinking: was I aware?). *Call me back when you remember.*

My mother's skin smelled like dust before she died and I often considered collecting her, sweeping her up like talc into a bottle so I would be able to powder myself with her scent in the days to come.

Do you remember, she asked, smiling faintly as I pulled a thin blanket around her shoulders, *I tripped you up on the sidewalk? You fell, you were just two. I cried when I saw your blood.*

I still have the scar, I said pointing to my lower back. Evidently, she thought I was Nööne and she'd forgotten, as she'd forgotten so much else, that it was Nööne who tripped her (not the other way around). But I didn't remind her. Instead, I held her hand until she fell deeply asleep. She was still smiling faintly as though the memory of tripping Nööne gave her great and unexpected pleasure.

The consular representative called me back the next day. *Evidently, we store video recordings of news broadcasted by the local networks for up to 3 months,* he said. *It will take time, but I will look through them for you.*

Can I help? I asked him. *Should I come to Beijing?* He paused. I could hear him chewing his tongue. *That would be a breach of security.* Since the tapes were already broadcasted, I couldn't see how. But I didn't argue. Instead, I quietly hung up the phone.

He called back one week later. Nööne had in fact been in Beijing, the representative told me. After the footage was originally broadcasted, the embassy had looked into it, found Nööne, and interviewed her. The report was duly filed, my sister had signed it. He read the report to me over the phone.

"In Beijing," Nööne was quoted as saying, "not long after the Chinese embassy was bombed in Belgrade, I went to buy produce. I went to buy three bananas. Not many, just enough for the next few days. They turn brown too quickly in the summer heat, you must go buy produce every few days or the flies come and stick to your eyes while you're napping. I was at the market, at a fruit stand. I did not touch the bananas, you cannot touch them, you're not supposed to. You have to wait," she explained to her interviewer, "until the old woman emerges from behind the stand. Then you point out the fruit you want, and she bags them for you, that's how it's done, that's how I'd done it for years while I lived in Beijing. The old woman knew me, though I'd been gone one year. I was just back for a visit. As usual, I pointed at the bananas. They were green still, under ripe, but I was sure they would turn quickly. I bent, I pointed. And while my eyes were turned, while I was distracted, the old woman hit me. She slapped me hard, right here on the side of my head. She punched me with the small tough fists that once patted my back while I lived in Beijing. She screamed, the other patrons watched. I could not hit her. I dared not. You saw the tape. I wanted to, that's true enough," Nööne said. "If we'd been alone, I think I would have belted her. One good shot to the chin, that's all. I could have knocked her out. I could have left her there flat on her back. But it was a good thing I ran instead because the men showed up quickly. They kicked me once, maybe twice. But I run fast. I left them all behind."

She stopped then and for the first time asked a question herself.

"I was caught on camera? I was broadcasted on the evening news?"

The interviewer didn't record his response.

The consular representative cleared his throat. That's the end of the file.

Where is Nööne now? I asked.

There was a long pause. I'm afraid, he said simply but without comfort, the interviewer failed to inquire about your sister's current residence. She gave only her former Beijing address. I have no idea why.

He paused then. *Do you?*

I didn't bother to answer: of course I didn't. I know nothing at all. It's the only thing of which I've ever been sure.

Nööne's university advisor called today. *I thought I might help you,* he said. *I thought I could find an address, a lead perhaps. Instead, I've just discovered to my surprise that Nööne never registered for classes at NJTU. In fact, though she wrote a thesis, and I graded her work, she never took a degree. She was here for two years. Now she's gone. That's all I can say.* As an afterthought he added: *She was my favorite student.*

Since then I've learned there's no bell in Yuxian. There isn't a town hall from which Nööne sent her stories. There is no Shi, no Zhu. There is no China. Only desolate monkeys eating jicama aloft in the trees.

You are an accumulation of the events of your life, Nööne once told me. *What you have done is not who you are, but who you become. Always stay on the move.*

Not long after, I received a letter from the consular representative. He had discovered which cargo ship—the MV Rong Chen, he said—had sailed from Tiajin the morning she was sent away. The Captain, however, denied Nööne was aboard. *Sometimes we take passengers, that's true enough,* the Captain told the representative. *But I've never taken them against their will. I don't tempt fate. Ships get lost as easily as people do.* (I could imagine his shrug.) *Even a ship as big as the Chen.*

The Captain seemed sincere, the consular representative added. *There's little else I can do.*

He signed off with his good wishes.

There must be a sequel to this story. Because I know I haven't told it right. Because, now, there is only a stone and a street.

Because Nööne is always right.

Today, a car exploded. Near a church. Outside a market. Three men inside. There was a reporter nearby, a tourist caught her on camera as she ran, a basket of fruit in one hand, a satchel of papers loosely held in the other, toward a limp man splayed on the sidewalk. I could not see her face, but I could tell by her long unbound hair, the curve of her hips, that she was American, that she was on business by the way she held her bag as she stooped to help the injured. The video was shaky because the tourist's hands were shaky, because the tourist was running as he taped the reporter moving from body to body, over torn concrete, a girder, around the hood of a car standing upright in the ground. The tourist swiveled and the lens took in collapsed stalls, the pitted sidewalk. Water erupting from a severed line gushing around his feet.

He did not focus on the woman's face. Only her hands. Hands like Nööne's hands—long, but not tapered or delicate. The fingertips were stained with ink.

I waited. But the camera lens did not rise.

CARLA HARRYMAN

the opposite of slackness

Orgasms

tis issue robbing pope sucking spear transit splash oops bore eye fro eye hire harrow guarded leer trap fire slurry badge adage craze

speak speak speak engineer linger rotund dusty ust ust uh

hoe oat toe below spire rain stamen stick rat earth reeves heavy slob oh sorrow mow

spot smear spot squashed stadium clinging pillar out hear a-rear basting let low lyric violet storm

loaned honey nothing doing behind gravy train evil fell to slow entrance gained a bil

low in the random rain

never never adumbrate never fever scumbling punchable larynx snot god sported inside mountain yawn swerve gliding dust to dust hard shadow phase hammy maverick nut there scratching crevice hording hot snow ocean bosses suds scribble which ways blacking

chancy chaos gouge loony brighter than tune

may may may may may may max may max may max ayax

razor ruby bird seared near her area reached piper ripping rail

low light lit little tick flea migrant sip pissy wit twill twill low will piano frill label slain

hero palo o opal laughing harrow barracuda amour our radio crash

not on my time happy not on my time mad not on my time money not on my time skin not on my time merry not on my time dig not on my time fanny not on my time sorrow not on my time sand not on my time sun not on my time moon not on my time hills not on my time rivers not on my time rinse not on my time cloud not on my time vapor not on my time film not on my time shame not on my time hover not on my time blow not on my time sassy not on my time slow not on my time honey not on my time more

defeat effete defeat effort defeat fort defeat eat eat de teat at art faart or fete tete ear eat fete tete do to oat to o deaf effort fort ore eee or taa tort or at eat taa tat or de de ten effete neat tete defeat

lulu lang loop bay bay bay rad hip hole cleave o decalogue boober hover mine hammer am

bubble slumber pressure song cover over every wrong abridge my sigh with over wing oh swim again beyond thy hand

points are reached at every point slimmed mirror prunes mere mourning rave

Everyone now began to tear at Adorno. An orgasm is an elegy. I can't explain this rationally. It's site-specific emotion lodged in a small barking noise—an escape hatch in the negative dialectic.

This is what he might have desired during the student protest in 1969. The emotion that corresponds to the practice of oppression is contempt. If I had been among the students in Frankfurt, would I have opened up my leather jacket and showed him my breasts in a parodic manner, in solidarity with a leaflet that proclaimed "Adorno as an institution is dead?"

Direct socialization is structurally determined by the patriarchal or Oedipal family, so the gender politics of parody is hopeless if you want meaningful social change. In this story however the people live and Adorno dies. Yet I am convinced that I would have refused to think of Adorno or any individual as an institution and instead would have removed myself from the scene and posed as "the small time expert," a sexless menial. In my rejection of revolt, I would have underscored my subject position as a mirror of the fragile component of the social sexual contract. Adorno was attracted to, in fact relied upon, mimesis. Did I desire him even after he forgave me for faking the orgasm? But how do I know that I wouldn't have been instead liberated from this inclination to withdraw, to pose, and to think at a remove? What if I had become activated—I can well imagine this. Even as I write, I can feel some odd source or space that's as much physical sensation as idea located inside—it's probably in everybody's brain—wanting activation.

With a flick of the switch aggression exposes erotic drives to blindness. On the other side of this blindness is an orgasm in the public void.

An orgasm is an elegy in which there is no consolation. Machines, like orgasms, are inconsolable things.

Adorno metamorphosed from an instrument to a machine to the unnamable, a figure in the Beckett he had admired. Text is the electricity that moves the body from one thing to the next even as it cannot break out of its instrumental rationality.

With the books in his brain stem shifting their weight hurriedly, he sought comfort in nonhuman Valais in southern Switzerland. The poet Rilke had a few things to say about this spot: I hide my shame below the figure of his agonistic remorse. In respect to mountains like these, Kant refers to "a voluptuousness for the mind in a train of thought that [he] can never fully unravel." Why is it that I wish for the mountain to remain where it is and for the unraveling to continue beyond such words? Adorno has responded thus: "To enter nature," signifies "seeking out unconscious existence at the very place where it is most clearly revealed in the phenomenal world." Adore, whose name became No for an instant, wanted to be elevated by or into the irrational at the site of a gathering of "dissimilar human beings." "The need to protect sexuality has something crazy about it." The need to protect sexuality has something crazy about it.

About has something crazy about "it." About has something crazy about it. About has something crazy about it. About it.

Sources: Lorenz Jäge, Adorno: *A Political Biography*, (2004), 192-210; Max Horkheimer and Theodor W. Adorno, *Dialectic of Enlightenment* (1988), 93, 106, 111; Rebecca Comay, "Adorno's Siren Song," and Andrew Hewitt, "A Feminine Dialectic of Enlightenment?" in *Feminist Interpretations of Theodore Adorno*, ed. Renée Heberle (2006), page 53 and 94.

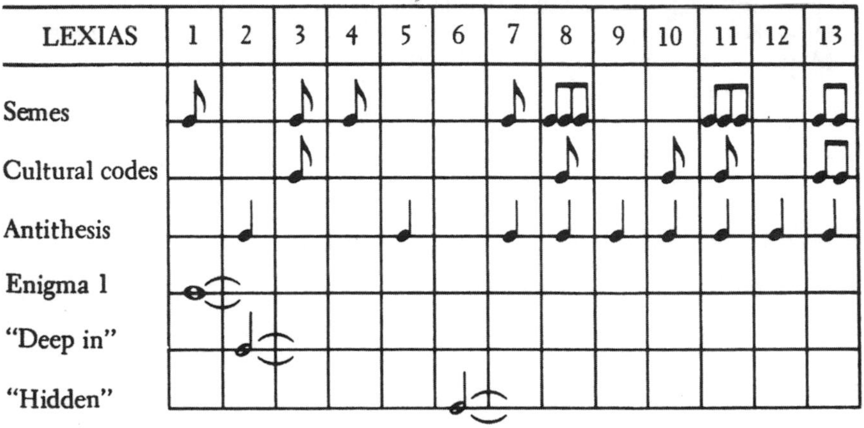

LEXIAS	1	2	3	4	5	6	7	8	9	10	11	12	13
Semes	♪		♪	♪			♪	♪♪♪			♪♪♪		♫
Cultural codes			♪					♪		♪	♪		♫
Antithesis		♩			♩		♩	♩	♩	♩	♩	♩	♩
Enigma 1	𝅝𝄐												
"Deep in"		𝅗𝅥𝄐											
"Hidden"						𝅗𝅥𝄐							

Introduction: The Story Behind the Essay behind the Story

There is a half-smoked cigarette on my basement floor. Is that a narrative? There is a flat tire in the back of my car. Is that a narrative? There were no injuries and only minor damage in the blast at the building's main entrance, which police say occurred sometime between 3:30 and 5:45 a.m. local time. Is that a narrative? And another one of my feminist friends is getting married. That's a narrative, right? Augusto Monterroso wrote a short story entitled "The Dinosaur" which reads, in its entirety: "When I woke up, the dinosaur was still there." (42) Is that a narrative? Italo Calvino seems to think so (VIII). "Roses are red/Violets are blue/Sugar is sweet/And so are you." Is that a narrative? Shlomith Rimmon-Kenan doesn't think so (1). But I do. "Water boils at one hundred degrees Celsius." Is that? Gerard Genette seems unsure (*Story* 212). What is narrative? Answering this question, for me, has become the process of choosing the narratologist whose writing I like the most. After months of research, I have to admit that I don't know where or whether narrative ends.

But I know that narrative is the basic unit of experience. I know I use it to reason morally. I know that narratives are cultural, but I suspect that narrative is a cognitive process as basic as metaphor. I suspect it is as important as (though not necessarily analogous to) language. But I don't know what it is.

On the other hand, written narratives—stories—I think I know pretty well. This is an essay about a story and a story about an essay. It all began with the diagram opposite.

When Roland Barthes rewrites the opening of Balzac's "Sarrasine" as a musical score, he raises a number of questions (29). For example, can this be performed? It is unlikely that anyone could read this score as "I was deep in one of those daydreams which overtake even the shallowest of men..." Is it possible, however, that another writer (having studied Barthes but not Balzac) could take this score and write the beginning of "Sarrasine" with different characters, a different plot, a different setting, but the same music? Can the various structural analyses of narratology be used to structure new, different narratives? What will this process reveal about the analyses themselves?

The separation between narratologists and fiction writers baffles me. Why would Barthes rather write a book-length study of another author's short story than write a novel? Conversely, why isn't *S/Z* used as a textbook in creative writing classes? Why would one transcribe music by ear if not to learn to perform it? The aim of my project is to turn to the abundant resources of narratology back into stories, making the descriptive prescriptive, turning the model into a score. My attempts to translate narrative theory into instructions on how to write a story are part of a larger process of turning the world into instructions on how to write a story.

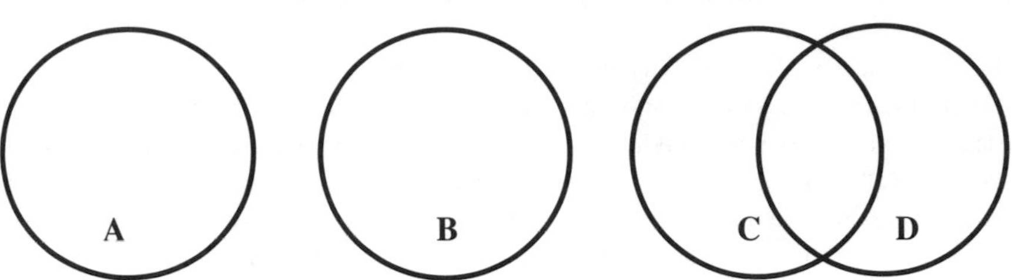

DIAGRAM 1.

This diagram represents four characters as four circles. The chronology of the story runs from left to right. The diagram shows that the story will concern, in order, four characters. The overlap between character C and D indicates that part of the story will be told from two simultaneous points of view.

Story / Essay Contents

A1.

Every day at work Amy would go through the same routine. For the first five hours she would attend diligently and cheerfully to the tasks at hand: answering phones, making calls, and keeping her boss's appointment book updated. During the sixth hour, her pace would decelerate, unfinished projects would reach stopping places, dockets would go back into filing cabinets, and the stapler would return to the drawer. Then for thc next half hour she would continue to answer the phone while she made notes to herself of images, metaphors, puns, rhymes, palindromes, the unusual spelling of a client's name—anything that had occurred to her throughout the day. Then came 4:15—afternoon breaktime and the single Eve Light 120 cigarette her perfectly flawed discipline allowed, savored at a concrete breakroom table beside humming vending machines in a gigantic warehouse filled with palettes and stacks of magazines. Amy would spend the final half hour of work, during which her boss talked on the phone with her husband and child, using the company's computer to write and laser-print the following poem:

the inefficient appearance of efficiency

when the expediter smiles
and gently reels in her leash
her assistant scatters files
and drops a stack of microfiche

when the coordinator happens by
the conversation freezes
we all twitch busily under her eye
and wait until breaktime for sneezes

when the director stalks the halls
the directed speed to a frenzied blur
when the supervisor calls
everyone races to answer her

when the hour is five at night
the sun expires in citrus light
we slip on our coats and file our fright
it's quite a quite a sight

when the hour is eight you see
us boast goodmorning pointedly
though nobody smiles we all agree
it's something to something to see

She would understand that this poem suffered from the fact that she spent so little time on it ("Ballad of the Copyright Clearance Coordinator"—a full page—had been typed in a minute) but she didn't want to get fired. She wondered whether Dominique would consider that a "constraint" and briefly imagined saying something direct to Dominique about art, tongue like a whip, cracking the frosted glass between them.

A1. Genette: Iterative

My score implies that events in my story will happen sequentially. Gerard Genette suggests only alternatives:

I. Order: sequence of events
  - A. story: the events as they are told
  - B. history: the events (of the story) before they were told[1]
  - C. anachronism: discrepancy between story and historical sequence
    - 1. external anachronisms: scenes which refer to events outside (before or after) the history
    - 2. internal anachronisms: scenes which refer (out of sequence) to events inside (during) the history
      - a) completive anachronisms: scenes which fill in a previous or later ellipses in the story
      - b) repetitive anachronisms: scenes which repeat a historical period
        - (1) announcements (anticipations): foreshadowing, a scene which refers to a scene that hasn't happened yet
        - (2) recalls (retrospections): flashbacks, scenes which refer to a scene that happened earlier
        - (3) anticipations within retrospections: flashforward within flashback
      - c) retrospections within anticipations: flashback within flashforward
  - D. achronism: scenes which are organized without chronology

II. Duration: length of scenes relative to the amount of historical time
  - A. summary: short scene narrating long period of history
  - B. scene: when story and historical time are supposed to be nearly equal
  - C. stasis: when the story progresses although historical time is at a standstill
  - D. ellipsis: historical time omitted from the story

III. Frequency: "relative frequency of the narrated events and the narrative sections that report them" (6)
  - A. singulative: one scene narrates one historical period
  - B. repetitive: "story-repetitions exceed in number the number of events"
  - C. iterative: one scene narrates "several recurrences of the same event or, to be more precise, of several analogical events considered only by respect to what they have in common" (7)
    - 1. internal iteration: an iteration within a singulative scene summarizing things which repeat within the historical period narrated by the scene
    - 2. external iteration: an iteration within a singulative scene summarizing repetitions from outside the historical period narrated by the scene
  - D. pseudoiteration: an iteration whose precision makes its repetition implausible ("Order")

At 4:45, remembering Dominique's enthusiasm for her "minimum wage poetry," she would consider calling her thesis advisor and leaving a voice mail message saying that she had changed her mind: her thesis was going to be a collection of poetry entitled "Steal Poetry from Work." But it seemed as though this semester there was an unusually high number of Master's candidates writing books of poetry for their final theses. Dominique was working on a collection of poetry entitled "Table of Forms" that Amy didn't have the nerve to ask her about. Afraid of being evaluated on poetry (whose rules were unclear (even proper grammar was unnecessary) and whose conventions (or lack thereof) were flexible (why is prose poetry poetry?))—she ended up forgetting the call, her degree, and her thesis, which was due in a month, for which she had written a hasty proposal—something her advisor had suggested about the panopticon and *Don Quixote*. She realized she had burned out and could no longer read through the smoke.

She found herself picking up more and more hours. What was supposed to be a parttime assistantship photocopying course materials had turned into a fifty-or-so-hour-a-week commitment to an office she wasn't even sure could run without her. She reminded her boss of this around five. They agreed she should take some time off.

Iteration struck me as a useful technique to narrate a routine day at a tedious job. Pseudoiteration is iteration carried to its illogical extreme: it is implied that Amy writes exactly the same poem every day. [2]

1 It is worth stressing here that "history" does not mean history. "History" refers to a bounded segment of fictional time, the segment of time the story is concerned with. There are many events outside "history," including fictional experiences the characters had before and after the period of time bounded by the story and its "history."

LOU ROWAN

Prince

We were on the leather couch your father gave you, soft and long enough to lie on. How many men sat here with you, taking in your ripe legs, your round knees, how many did more than look. I was holding your small strong hand. We chattered gaily as the teenagers lurched through. Your hands, relaxed demurely on their backs in your lap, lured me when I first saw you, perfectly postured on a camp chair.

When I proposed to you, going to my knees by the bed, putting on your slim finger an emerald you still wear opposite the platinum set that succeeded it, we shared our joy with the son to whom you are closest, but he already knew: Yes, I'm so happy for Mom, there hasn't been a steady man around here since Brian.

I wondered about others when you let me into your twin bed. Your bedroom gave on the tangled yard from which the cat would leap to watch us at the west window. You're a fast driver. You love to laugh. You say what you think. Or is it what you feel? I can't keep up, the love story curdles in my head.

Maybe that's why I dreamed we were walking down Fifth Avenue towards the Museum of Modern Art on our first date, and I was tired from my work in the office above the atrium and feeling I deserved to be tired. But you were excited to be on the Avenue with me, stimulated by the hustle and bustle oppressing me, and you kept talking until you noticed my lassitude. After a pause to hear about my weariness you resumed, tried to lure me to your enthusiasm, but the crowds and the traffic muffled your words; too much effort to stay abreast, I let your hand go and fell behind, knowing you would be miffed by my losing contact, nursing my self-righteousness as a vast black square Hummer slammed into the crowd, wiping the sidewalk clean of people before the steps of St. Thomas Cathedral, whose traditional services I have for decades longed to attend in memory of my language-rich adolescence at boarding school.

Into the sidewalk clean but for gum-spots fell a toothless bum whose pink-purple face indicated something inside pushing him to the brink of death. Blood spreading on his grimy plaid shirt prevented thumping his heart. The only hope was to breathe into the smelly depths of his lungs through the spumey yellow of his mouth, and no one in the literal or figurative uniform of a good Samaritan materialized.

Retching I step from the crowd that jostles me with the outrageous force of bodies thirty-deep, hating my sense of obligation to some obscure higher being motivating my benevolence as I remove my tie, hand my jacket to an old lady who clasps it to her drooping bosom, fresh from communicating at Anglican evensong. I bring my face to the bum's face, attach my mouth to his, the sticky moisture establishing a hermetic seal. I blow hard, remembering how strong my lungs are from a youth of swimming and wrestling and a middle-age of jogging, and while my mouth is working his mouth my nose is enduring a stench worse than any subway bathroom. He's beginning to twitch; his yellow crusty eyes open wide, focus on me, and during my next powerful breath into his gummy hole he throws his arms around my neck, thrusts his tongue into my mouth, twitching, and groaning in pleasure. He slides his body under mine and grasps me with his legs. I am too weak to detach myself from his pleasures, and presently he threatens to wrestle me to my back, where my limp nakedness will be exposed and abused before the evening rush hour crowd on Fifth Avenue. The old lady steps forward and yells "Heel" in a booming voice that summons two policemen and an ambulance crew, who because my starched white shirt is covered with blood and dirt do not know if they should rescue me or the bum or both, but because the bum is yelling in Australian intonation that just because I gave him a dollar that doesn't give me the right to take liberties they let him go and strap me to a stretcher despite my outrage and my business card. No one in the crowd will attest to my good character and my good deed. They attach an IV near my bicep in the ambulance.

I wake late the next afternoon, feeling hung over. My bed gives on a view of the harbor I am amazed a hospital can afford in a Manhattan run by relentlessly competing developers.

You are ecstatic, you've never seen such a total panorama of the harbor, and while I think about Stephen Crane's sky and the pollution producing the pinks and purples of the sunset, the dirty water, the chemical plants in Jersey, the hands that led me to you caress my cheek, smooth my hair, remove my IV, give me clothing that is big and floppy on me. I roll up the pantslegs and the sleeves and you say, "Hey cool, great look." You open the window, persuade the window-washer to give us a ride down on his platform, and your laughter while I grip the ropes and avert my eyes from the view above below and around is music that a string quartet plays on the concrete esplanade for the rush-hour crowds, and once again I can love the big city

I have never broken a bone, never suffered debilitating disease. It has been decades since I've experienced financial insecurity.

Whenever you look angry my heart sinks, all grace of speech and motion leaves me. You are 5'7" and weigh 140. I have bench-pressed you. If we fought I could hurt or immobilize you in seconds. You have never threatened me physical harm.

The Prince of Wales endeared himself to me by writing his lover he longed to be a unit of Tampax inside her.

I am of the crowd that loves a lover.

His princess was alive when Prince of Wales sought to pick you up. He'd completed a polo match. Famous actors and rock stars watched. The pinkness of his pale royal complexion, the hints of perspiration at his temples were dramatic in the Florida sun. He jumped from the tons of lethal animal he had controlled through perilous jostlings to ask you if the match was a pleasure for you.

Heads turned. You are blond. You are so lively that friends of your children have made passes at you.

I pursued you so assiduously by car, phone, letter that one evening when you asked me not to come by, hinting another man would be there, I cried in your passenger seat. When we first kissed you closed your eyes and followed my receding face with a sigh, as if I was breathing you in. It was dark, and we were on a bridge across the rushing stream that confounded Ichabod Crane. We could see the bright foam where rocks speeded the waters. You love the word "romantic." I was smitten by everything you touched, even your car, which your son had backed into a fire hydrant, denting the center of the trunk with a vertical crease, so that I could pat its big grey ass.

You continued home to your father's condo, while the Prince of Wales retreated, mallet on his shoulder, across the vivid turf his huge steed paused now and then to crop, and rejoined the crowd.

JOE AMATO

Tango

"Say, what do you call this
anyway?"

"There's such a thing as being too
versatile. Or patulous. Or, it's so bad
I couldn't put it down."

Thanks Ron.

He
                                        (i.e., I)
thinks
                                        (think)
one needs must be more
obscure, yes, more
WW II? Mending
the lifeways, then, heartless
returning to the heartland
the dangling modifier appears
to signal grammatological
                                        (i.e., "amato with a
                                        self-aggrandizing
                                        difference," where
                                        metaphors of writing, specifically
                                        reading, collide, up-
                                        ending themselves
                                        in the tomato sauce
                                        momentarily exterior to which
                                        one interiorizes an "mmmm")
perspective, the embodiment
of his failures not
unlike a pie, a custard pie
that has risen
only to fall, hence not rising
at all to the greatness
once thrust upon it—i.e., the gapingly
paparazzied
                                        (from the Fellini
                                        film)
face; not unlike that stubbed
great toe that draws all
of your attention
to little avail; not unlike that
just like that the
troubled encounter
with a smidgen of
What Thou Mightst
Have Been, sapping
thy middle-aged ambitions
of the magnifical.

Damn. And this despite a literary library literally littered with literature.
A failure of means ends
with the gratuitous justification
of means?

"Am I being fair?"

"No
fuckhead, you're not."

Some of my colleagues, some of whom
are poets, some of whom
I count as friends 1234
maybe 5 are clueless
about collegiality, that share-
and-share-alike of allies
allied with some institution
who work in concert
to allay the harsh realities
of cash flow
and the like.

Break out the pies!

It's a surplus
of signification
oneway ayway orway ethay otherway [cough]
l'une ou l'autre manière [oy]
one (or the other) that
you can learn from or
~~from which~~, if you still have
your alletway.
(check
why don't you)

"Just don't make
a habit out of it," she warns, as I plus
size for maximum
cornering, expiration
date suddenly 07/09. Me
I mean. Like magic. Computational
magic.

Praise the lord and pass
the bottle
Mack, cry me
a river, Jane, in other words
baby
miss me

and my Pearl
Harbor antics? That life, that's life
they must have led, those two
before my memory
of them began to
"take shape."

"An entire generation
of writers
is losing its legacy
to its defunct hard drives."

Or will there yet be paper
enough to pore over, to gauge
future life? See that sky, recycled
but holding steady
at 90 brightness?—try, just try
to touch it. By Christ, I've found myself talking
like a trooper these days. *Trouper*?
Trooper. Using the expressions
my old man used.

:   I can't stand people
who live in the past. I can't
stand people who
have no past. I can't
stand
          Are you going back
          for the funeral?

          Ameri-
          ca
                              (mouth
                              agape, sarcastic
                              even, repeat
                              after me)

          Ameri-
          ca

          Huh?

          Are you going
          back?

          Ameri-
          ca, your remote
          side can be
          murder

on our hands
and feet, we
who are your
torch song?

Hardly. I didn't say
I loved the guy
but he's a fuck-up.
I said he's a fuck-up
but I loved the guy.

Sometimes. Pre-1954, port
and starboard, one heard AbleBakerCharlieDogEasyFoxGeorgeHowItemJigKing
LoveMikeNanOboePeterQueenRogerSugarTareUncleVictorWilliamX-rayYoke Zebra

We can locate other lost codes, other
conflicts. And your
little dog, too.

RAYMOND FEDERMAN

From *Return to Manure*

—I did once ask God for help. But he ignored me. He didn't answer.

What do you mean? What did you ask?

I asked God for a sign. I don't know what kind of sign. But I felt that if God gave me a sign, things would improve. There would be hope that I would soon be back with my parents. I felt so homesick, with no one to talk to.

I didn't ask for the sign in church. I asked in the farm yard, near the two cherry trees, one night when I felt I had no place in the world, no existence outside the nightmare of the farm. I needed help.

I got up from my cot and walked outside into the dark.

By the way, this happened before Josette started her evening visitations.

It was cold. There was frost on the ground. I could feel it and hear it crackle under my bare feet. I had put on my pants and a shirt, but not my sabots because I didn't want to make noise on the floor of the kitchen and wake up the old man. It was a dark cloudy night, but I could feel the moon somewhere behind the clouds. Even though I was afraid of the dark, I went out that night without a light.

Usually when we had to go outside at night, like when one of the cows gave birth, we carried kerosene lamps.

So, alone in the dark, I stood near the cherry trees, in the lane that led away from the house. The clouds were dark and heavy in the sky. There was no wind. The night was frighteningly quiet. All the animals were asleep. Even the wild animals that roam in the fields at night were quiet. Even the birds were quiet. Yes, I clearly remember how quiet it was that night. A haunting silence. Unless it was just me who, for that moment, became deaf to the world, so intensely was I concentrating so that God would hear me.

I was trembling from fear and cold. I looked up at the sky and in the darkness I heard the sound of my voice asking God to give me a sign. I had no idea what I would do or what it would mean if God gave me a sign, but I was so desperate. I was in such need of an explanation for my being on this farm. An explanation for the punishment I was enduring.

Of course, I asked for the sign in French. Dieu fais-moi un signe pour que je puisse continuer. And then I told God, Je vais compter jusqu'à vingt et si à vingt tu m'as pas donné un signe alors je serai fini avec toi. Et je continuerai tout seul, sans avoir plus jamais besoin de toi.

That's exactly what I told God that night in the middle of the farm yard. Give me a sign. I'll count up to 20, and if at 20 you have not given me a sign, then I will be finished with you, and I will try to go on by myself. And I started counting. Slowly. Slower as I approached 20. Then I whispered .... vingt. I waited. Nothing. I waited some more. Nothing. No sign. Not even the rustle of the dead leaves in the cherry trees. Just the quiet dark clouds in the sky and the moon hiding behind. But that was not the sign. That could not be the sign. The clouds and the moon were already there before I asked. And so at that moment, barefoot on the cold earth, my body trembling, I gave up giving myself the lie. I renounced God. I decided not to be afraid any more. It was in October or November. About a year after I started working on the Lauzy farm. I was fourteen by then.

I waited a while longer. Still no sign. Maybe God was trying to decide, but there was nothing I could recognize as a sign. I started walking back to the house. I didn't feel despair, nor sadness any more. Suddenly I felt nothing. I don't mean I felt good, no, I just felt nothing.

Just as I reached the door of the house, a cow in the barn moved and rattled the chain around her neck. I froze in place. No. No. That cannot be the sign, I told myself. It came too late. And besides, a dumb cow could not have given me the sign. But still today, I can hear the rattle this chain made in the barn when the cow moved.

I must admit that when I asked God for a sign, I didn't know much about God and godly things. I imagined God as an old man hiding somewhere là-haut dans le ciel. Up in the sky. That's the idea I had of God. An old man with a long white beard. So I simply assumed that if God were to give me a sign it would be something from above. I would see or hear something up in the sky.

—Suppose God had given you a sign that night. What would you have done?

—Good question. I don't know. The sign would have told me what to do.

—And suppose the sign made no sense to you. A sign meaningless to the boy you were. So, now you have a sign, but it's useless since you don't understand how to use it. It would be like having a broken toy.

—Are you saying that the cow rattling her chain in the barn was the sign, and I didn't get it? That I expected something more dramatic?

—Yes, I think already then you were somewhat of a melodramatic dreamer.

— Well, maybe I was being melodramatic. It was such a strange night. You see, I didn't know how one should act when asking God for a sign. I didn't kneel like I had to do in church. I asked standing up, looking at the sky. Maybe that was the wrong way to ask.

—Imagine if the cow rattling the chain was the sign, and you had accepted that, then everything might have been different for you.

—Maybe. But a cow giving me the sign? No, that's not possible.

—Why not?

—Cows are dumb. I wanted something more significant to make me less desperate.

—Or more desperate.

—You may be right. Looking back at it now, it's lucky I didn't get a sign from God, because then the nightmare of the farm would have been worse than before, especially if the sign was meaningless. Though sometimes in my dreams, I still hear that chain rattling in the barn the night I became a non-believer like my father.

—Yes, we know your father was a Communist. That's what you've been telling us for more than forty years, but you've never been able to prove it. Like everything else you made that up. I don't think you knew a damn thing about what your father believed or did not believe. And besides, you told us he was never home.

—Look. I had no idea if God existed or not, but that night, all alone, I decided that I didn't need him any more, just like my father who renounced God for politics.

—Maybe I didn't know much about him, but it's a fact that my sisters and I never set foot in a temple when we were children. There was no religion in our family. My sisters and I, we knew nothing about religion. Only our mother used the word God once in a while. But she never forced us to believe in him. We knew we were Jewish, but that meant nothing to us. Well, maybe for me it meant a little more than for my sisters because of my nose. I was often teased and called a Youpin in school just because of my crooked Jewish nose.

—Do you always have to bring your nose into everything you say? Maybe for you, being Jewish only made your ego suffer, but how do you know that for your sisters it may have meant something more than just the suffering of their noses. Maybe at night, over there in the camps, they prayed to God.

—Maybe.

—You know, you never talk about your sisters. You often talk about your father and your mother, but never about your sisters.

—It's true. I rarely talk about them. I suppose because I cannot recall what we did together. I do think about them sometimes, but there isn't much to remember.

Not even a little story
you could tell us about them?

Yes, it's true, I often mention my sisters, but I never say anything about them. Except their names. Sarah and Jacqueline. They died at Auschwitz. Sarah was 15, Jacqueline 11. That's all I ever say about them. Perhaps because I cannot recall a single word that passed between my sisters and me. I cannot remember any games we played together. We must have played games. We must have had fights too. Brothers and sisters always fight. I was the middle one. The boy. So I was the one they beat on. Girls always stick together. I was so clumsy I was barely able to fight back. I would just cover my face with my arms to protect my fragile nose.

There is maybe one story I can tell about my sisters. It came back to me the other day when I was looking at the only photograph I have of them.

It's an old black and white photo of the three of us. A bit yellowed now. In that photo both my sisters are wearing dresses. Sarah's hair is short. Jacqueline's is long and curly. Jacqueline is smiling more than Sarah. She has big eyes. Sarah is more stern. I am wearing a jacket, and I have a beret on my head. I'm smiling more than my sisters. There is nothing in the background. We must have been standing against a wall when it was taken. Maybe at a professional photographer for a special occasion.

It is difficult to say how old my sisters were when that photo was taken. I would guess, Jacqueline 6, Sarah 10.

How did you get that photo?

Oh, I found it in a cardboard box when I got back to Montrouge and searched our old apartment. Everything in it had disappeared. All the furniture. Everything. Except for that box on the floor of the closet and some old rags. I suppose nobody wanted that box. In it there were old handwritten letters and papers, barely readable the ink was so faded, and some photos, of my father and mother, of other relatives, and of other people unknown to me. The photo of my sisters and me was in that box.

In that photo I cannot tell the color of their eyes and of their hair. They both appear to have dark hair. I don't think it was so. I think Sarah had black hair. Jacqueline light brown. Sarah looked like our mother. Jacqueline like our father. So Sarah must have had dark eyes. Like our mother. Our mother's eyes were very dark and always sad. Jacqueline must have had grey eyes like our father. Our father's transparent grey eyes always seemed to be looking elsewhere.

Staring at this old black and white photo I tried to recapture the faces of my sisters, and suddenly I remembered a moment with my sisters during a summer vacation.

No, actually it was not like I was remembering, it felt more like my sisters in the photo were whispering that memory to me. I could see their lips moving.

No, I was not stoned that day!

They were speaking very softly. The same words, both together at the same time. It was like they were humming the words rather than speaking them, but I could understand.

I wanted them to tell me what happened after they were taken away. I wanted to know what I had never known about them. What I had forgotten. Instead they just told me the story of what happened one day when we were on summer vacation. Only that one moment. Nothing else.

While listening, I started writing what they were saying. Writing the story you are reading.

It felt strange to be listening to my sisters while writing what they were whispering. It felt as if I was split in half. Two different beings. One of me passively listening. The other actively writing. Or was it the reverse. Actively listening while passively writing.

Then gradually, as the story unfolded, my sisters' faces receded into the flatness of the photo. Or maybe my eyes were getting tired of staring at the photo, that's why it became all blurry. As the faces of my sisters became more and more vague, the sound of their voices became more and more faint. Then it stopped. And I stopped writing.

This is the story my sisters told me.

It takes place on a farm, inside a barn. I don't think I have ever told this story before to anyone.

—Not even to me?

—Well, maybe to you. Yes, I must have told you that story. I always tell you everything.

—Everything? Well, we'll see, go on.

What my sisters whispered to me brought nothing to my mind but that one recollection from our summer vacation.

No other souvenirs. No souvenirs of what we said to each other. Of our games. Of our fights. No souvenirs of how we teased each other. Or how we loved each other. Nothing else. No other moments. No other scenes. Just what happened that day, in the barn. The day the war was declared.

So don't expect the whole story of how my sisters and I grew up in a squalid apartment with a lazy starving artiste as a father and a slaving femme de ménage as a mother. That would reduce the story of my sisters to the pathetic and sentimental level of naturalism. My sisters deserve better than that. Better than a story of misery. At least they should appear in a story that would give them pleasure. And that is the story they whispered to me. A story of pleasure. But not without fear. Pleasure and fear are good companions.

The story takes place the day World War II started. At the end of the summer 1939. September 3rd, 1939, to be exact, when France declared war on Germany. That summer the Federman children were sent to the country on colonies de vacances organized by the government for children of poor families who could not afford to spend the summer with their children on the Côte d'Azure. Each school would select the kids of the poor. Everybody knew who was rich and who was poor in our neighborhood. And those children were sent to les colonies de vacances for two weeks. But not on the Côte d'Azure. To some remote corner of the province so the children of the poor would not annoy the children of the rich.

That year, the year the war was declared, my sisters and I were sent on colonies de vacances with a bunch of other children to a little remote village of le Poitou. The children were distributed to various farms for the duration of the vacation. So at least for two weeks the children of the poor ate well.

This is what happened that day with my sisters. And my mother too, because she appears later in the story.

Oops! Correction. The scene I am going to describe did not take place on the day war was declared. It had to have happened the following day, because our mother could not have traveled from Paris to the farm days le Poitou the same day war was declared. War was declared at 5 p.m. I once had to check the exact time for something I was writing.

She must have come the following day to take us home where our father was waiting. She was worried about us. She wanted to protect us from the war.

I'll skip the description of the farm. Typical old French farm. A house, a barn, domestic animals, manure, and a couple of old swings hanging from the branches of a tree. As for the weather that day, let's say hot and humid.

The scene takes place in the barn. Just imagine a barn in a French farm circa 1939. Not in very good shape. Old and dilapidated. Roof leaking. The wooden planks of the walls rotten and warped. Old rusty agricultural tools in various places. On the ground in the dark far corner a huge pile of hay. The big double doors of the barn are open. It's sunny outside. There are cows on one side of the barn behind hay racks. One can hear their chains rattle, and the sound of their jaws masticating. And also the sound of the cow-dung dropping on the fresh straw. One can hear the puffing and farting of the horses. There are also horses in the barn. Dust floats in the rays of sunlight that stream through the planks of the walls.

In spite of the heat and humidity, a perfect place for the vacation. The children should be out in the meadow playing games. Gathering wild berries along the hedgerows of the paths. Or swimming in the river. But not Raymond, Jacqueline and Sarah. They are in the barn playing a game. Must be a funny game because one can hear them giggle. They are playing doctor. Raymond is the doctor and he is examining his two sisters. The three of them are giggling. That day Jacqueline is 8. Raymond 10. Sarah 12.

Oh, major correction. In that scene Sarah is not present. I am sure of that. And besides she was too old already to want to play that game. It's just Raymond and Jacqueline who are playing doctor. Sarah must be somewhere else. Probably reading a book in the shade of a big tree. Sarah reads all the time. Books that she refuses to show her younger brother and sister. Today she would probably be a poet.

So Raymond and Jacqueline are playing doctor in the barn when, after a long day of traveling, their mother arrives from Paris late in the afternoon. She anxiously asks the farm woman where her children are. She's told that the two young ones are in the barn playing because they love the animals so much. The other. The older one. She's so quiet. She always sits under a tree reading a book. She loves to read. She will probably become a teacher.

The younger one. Jacqueline. I think she wanted to become a ballerina. She was always bouncing and twirling on her toes. She was so carefree.

Raymond. He had no idea what he wanted to be. He wanted to be nothing. He was not interested in anything. Il est toujours days la lune, people always said about him.

That's how my sisters set up the scene they told me to write. The open doors of the barn. The dust floating in the rays of sunlight. The semi-darkness of the barn. The noises of the cows and the horses. Jacqueline and Raymond playing doctor in the dark corner of the barn. Raymond examining what's under Jacqueline's dress. Jacqueline giggling.

And suddenly our mother appears. Leaning into the entrance of the barn and staring into the semi-darkness she shouts, Raymond! Jacqueline! Vous êtes-là les gosses?

And together Jacqueline and Raymond answer, their voices full of surprise and apprehension, Oui on est là, as they come out of the corner where they were playing brushing the hay from their clothes.

—Qu'est-ce que vous faisiez là? our mother asks.

—On jouait, Jacqueline et Raymond answer. On cherchait quelque chose.

—Quel quelque chose? our mother asks.

—Un petit truc que Jacqueline a perdu, Raymond explains.

—Quel petit truc?

But just then Sarah comes rushing into the barn from wherever she was. Now she is in the scene. And she cries out in a hissing voice pointing her finger at us, They were playing doctor. Haha. Raymond was playing with Jacqueline's little truc.

She didn't say that in English. I am translating.

Jacqueline and Raymond tremble with fear. But our mother doesn't say anything. She just says, Chut. And she gathers the three of us in her arms and holds us tight. She has tears in her eyes when she says, C'est la guerre. Je vous emmène chez nous. Papa nous attend.

She held us tight like that for a long time. My sisters and me.

STEPHEN COLLIS

The Frostworks

Something there is
that spills
makes gaps
the work of
hunters at spring
the wall
between us
is a collapse
of constituency
the boulders
are loaves
we break
together
all is pine
or apple trees
only he says
with nothing
between us
how are we
yet broken

A wall
doesn't love
the frostworks
pressing beneath
or passing abreast
of another thing
making repair
in gaps widening
having heard
beyond the hill
we walk a line
erasing it as we go
so nearly a balance
with backs turned
dear fellows
what little need
of this wall
to get across as
neighbours

Something there is
if it is
spring
it is mischief
I could put a notion
of others
where before

I built nothing
and to whom
something
wants it down
but he said
in chronology
we appreciate
the part played
by the future
as words not
woods will make
fences or flowing

I wonder friends
isn't it neighbours
in our heads
no cows
only signs pointing
to walling out
I hate a wall
doesn't love
rather see the
alter armed
in shade of trees
saying it well
that words
are common
as frost or
fences falling
so take a stone
everyone
take a stone
unmending

Is that
frozen ground
a literature
boulders breaking
even two
is another
after them
the yelping dogs
we break
to meet outside
a wall until
fingers come
and I will
orchard
in his pines
till forgiven
all fencing

When across the lines
I like to think
as ice storms do
loaded with rain
as the breeze
soon shattering
such heaps
you'd think
they are dragged
so low you may see
years afterwards
like abandonment
but I was going
with all her matter
as he went
whose only summer
he took to conquer
and not to learn
and not to clean
the ground of branches

Beyond these
frozen forms
frets of others
unknowing
creates cold
film upon waters
a writing of sorts
interrupts the
world was the
strangest thing
winter had in
chorus passed so low
flushed into darkness
started to think
they could not
they must
break into entry
twist daylight
its wind-torn life
again to swoon beneath

Where is joined
the hunter and
the gun
the harvest too close
the fur-things
across the threshold
taking the widespread
advantage revolt has

over reform
they could almost be
forgotten who slept
one night only
in the old barn
its only windows
bullet holes
like waking alone
and checking
its locks against
conservatives

It comes of
wind and winters
dear energy
something there is
isn't just
yours or mine
but between
the light of
eerie dawn or
dusk I coat
the fresh rockery
with movements
and maybe
stone fish fiber
crack block breath
bends leans turns
this onto that
in structure
I'm leaning
into you too

DOUG RICE

A Poetics of Reflection and Desire

Note on black and white: Originally these next photographs were taken in color. These are "real" photographs taken just moments before dreaming. In color the light creates a more defined sense of uncertain possibilities around and near my skin. It is "as if" (in that Deleuzian sense) there is only becoming and hecceity—a kind of melting away of definitions that limit dreams to the real. In black and white, this is lost, as is the notion of the real and dream mixing. In black and white, I always fear that photographs become documents and lose their deeper joy. They become artistic and rendered. These photographs enjoy being dreams.

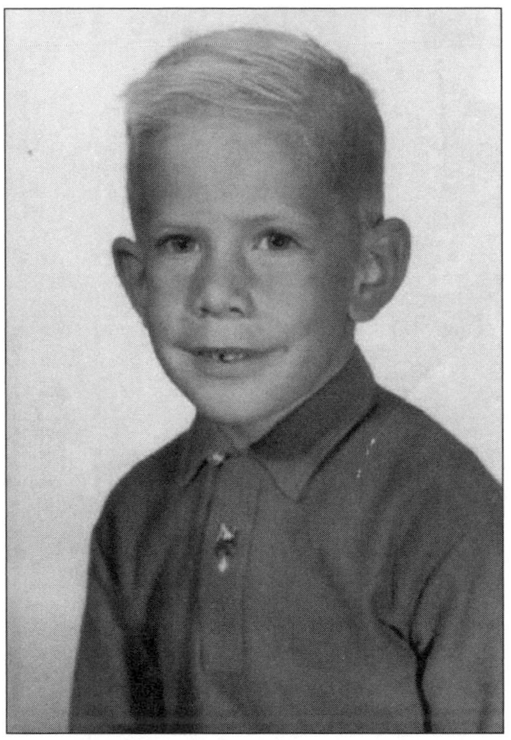

Without any photographic evidence, it was as if Doug's childhood never existed. These stories of Doug remembering believing that he was a girl were the only photographs that remained. All his infant dreams have been wrapped in tissue and buried beneath the pomegranate tree.

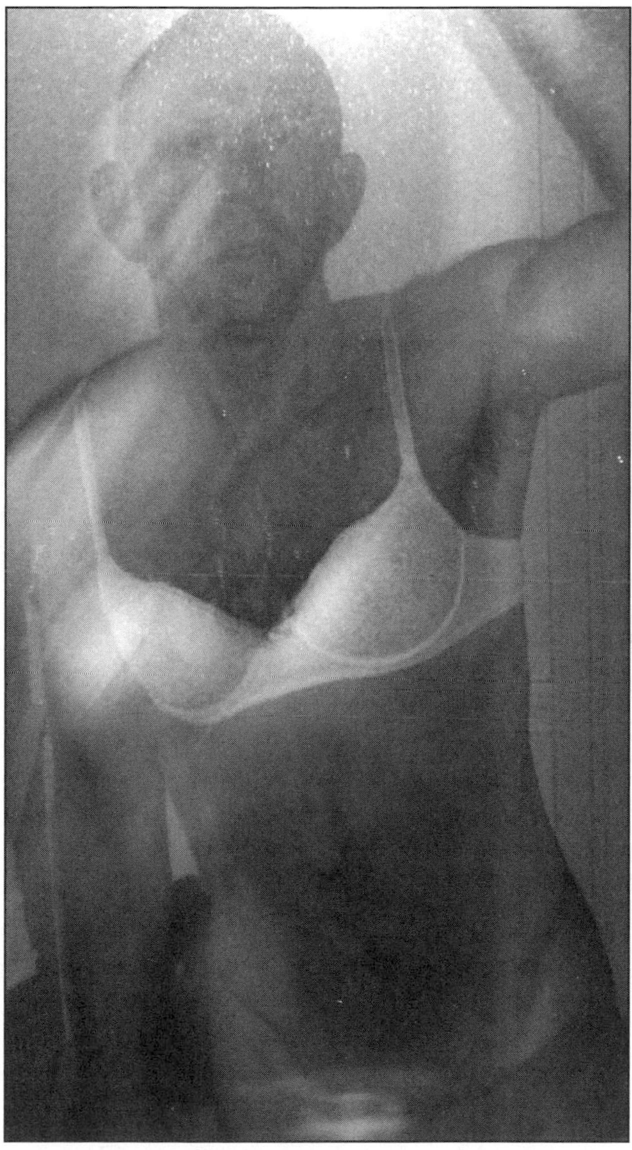

We see everywhere the reign of the blurry and the indeterminate, the movement in the mirror that pulls at form. The shadow escapes from Doug's body in the time prior to dreambreathing. "There once was a girl," he says but cannot finish.

The sensation of the image avoids the detail and boredom of conveying a story. Doug believes, even today, in the possibility of her reflection being other than what was thought to be seen. ("Nothing is behind or before the mirror," Gilles says to Lewis. "Everything is inside it.")

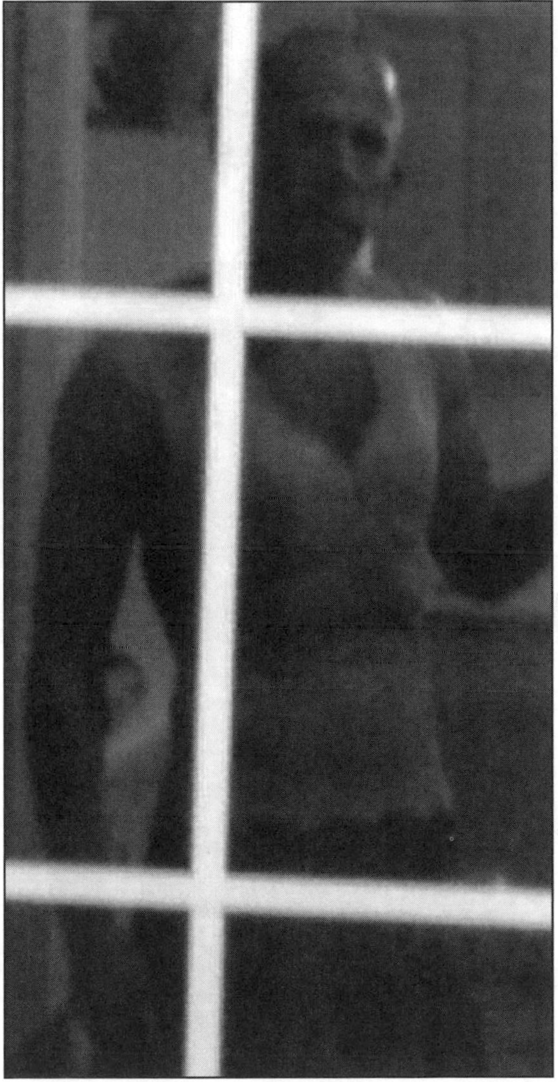

Seeing is no longer possible now that we have invented photographs and have begun to believe in their desires. And, even though mirrors are no longer looking-glasses, mirrors have become a spectacle of what language cannot think.

The hope for speech abandons her desire and fades into his mirror.

MICHAEL DU PLESSIS

The Carpet Out of Time

Today Kathy Acker isn't feeling herself. Dead woman writer, she stares into the solid, unbreakable plastic mirror in the bathroom without windows. Because she sees nothing in her mirror, she touches her face and marvels at its transformation into smooth, lifelike, unlined plastic. Today is a day for change, she decides. She's been thinking too much about O, O who will give up everything for a man. Pathetic. Perhaps it's time for a change of gender, thinks the dead woman writer. But why does Kathy Acker nonetheless feel as though she were on the verge of an anxiety attack?

She glances into the corridor outside her Boulder sublease bathroom. It's that silence again. She looks down, and notices the verge of the carpet just outside the door, lurking like the panic attack she's verging on.

"If only I could capture the unmitigated horror of life in Boulder," wishes Kathy Acker, "I might be able to ward off my panic attack."

Boulder: where eugenics couples with software to secure the perfect reproduction of middle-class bodies, bodies that desire only perfect reproduction.

Boulder: where white-collar heaven beckons under pitiless white-collar skies.

Boulder: where there's cotton-ball cotton-candy cirrus over the Flatirons, like the prettiest, freshest mushroom clouds ever.

Boulder: where the Pied Piper lured the children of Hamelin and where they grow old but never grow up. Where Never-Never Land was colonized by the U.S. of A.

Boulder: where lumbering adults play hackeysack, tag, beanbag, frisbee, volleyball, all day long. Forever.

Boulder: where it's an attack of lunatic snow angels.

Boulder: where it's always white men who celebrate the Fourth of July, bare chests, sweat, minor explosions, beer.

Boulder: where a city ordinance makes it illegal to have upholstered furniture out of doors. Boulder, with its soft spot for pyromania, can't resist the temptation of flammable outdoor targets. Boulder burns so readily that it invites arson.

Boulder: where the mountains shove up against the town, closing in like walls in an Edgar Allan Poe story.

And this leads Kathy Acker inevitably to the even more unmitigated horror of domestic space in Boulder. "Perhaps if I could describe that, I would be able to ward off my panic attack, pressing in like the mountains, like the sky.

"All Boulder apartments are exactly the same," Kathy Acker declaims, eyes shut. "Structures of the 1970s, they promised the good life of the American Bicentennial in the raw materials—particle board, polyresin, reinforced tupperware, drywall, polyester, pressed-wood shingle, polyurethane—the flammable and cheap fabric from which the American Dream is spun. All apartments are alike: beige carpeting, gray from years of snow stains, pet stains, brown kitchen sticky from years of unsavory vegetarian grease, dank bathroom in dark green. Look, the A-frame with its two-story wood-burning fireplace—cozy, no? A wood-burning stove in every A-frame, those kitchens in once-modish browns, those bathrooms of an avocado color trendy long ago: hippie dreams met money in a studio jam session bliss-out, in a free love encounter of leisure architecture and rising real estate values. Olive green, brown, beige, camouflage colors still after Vietnam, violently neutral, the U. S. foreign policy turned domestic design. Outside, below the junipers, yards of gravel, yards of bark. Do you know that the local gay bar was called the Yard of Ale? Boulder, the Yard of Yards, domestic interior as exteriority, space as its own measurement, for its own empty sake.

"All are filthy now, not with the heroic filth of poverty or despair, but with the dirt of middle-class transience, the shifting attentions, the ultimate shiftiness of the populations who have passed through Boulder, insubstantial as wireless technology, with a residue like nuclear waste.

"All are alike, beneath the filth, built to a scale that contests bodies, human or doll—as though Boulder were a dingy other planet, its apartments constructed according to a geometry that renders them uninhabitable by humanoids. Khaki, tie-dye, lighter fluid igniting a thousand barbecues for charred tofu dogs. Mattings and clumpings of pet hair, clumpings and mattings of juniper, juniper like shapeless hands at the windows, at the doors, like an off-shoot, an outgrowth of the carpet.

"Everywhere in Boulder, the creeping, omnipresent, utterly inescapable fungus of the beige wall-to-wall carpet, once bright beige at least, but now a sullen gray, like an overcast sky, the kind of sky one never sees in Boulder, where the sun shines 360 days a year. Perhaps this carpet is the revenge of the weather, a meteorological curse, Boulder's bad weather underfoot if not overhead? Can a village be strangled by the crawling, all-consuming, wall-to-wall, door-to-door, street-to-street, suburb-to-suburb beige carpet? Even on the hottest summer day the carpet recalls the filthy snow that blankets us for nine months of the year. If triffids were carpet, they'd be this dingily colorless nylon bodysnatcher.

"Oh, winter warmed us all right, mixing memory with desire with a lot of other, less easy-to-name things in our carpets. Summer surprised us, as we stared at our carpets. Surely it must have expanded this past season? What lies buried beneath the grayish beige of wall-to-wall carpet in Boulder? The corpse under the underpile, that strange lump the vacuum cleaner always bumps against? Unreal suburb: Boulder, Louisville, Superior, Broomfield, Lafayette, Gunbarrel, Highlands Ranch: unreal. Stetson, has it begun to sprout, the corpse you buried beneath your beige wall-to-wall carpet last year?

"All apartments in Boulder are the same because only happiness tells a new story, because all unhappy families are unhappy in exactly the same way. It's all in the carpet, you see."

Today is a day for change, decides Kathy Acker, dead woman writer. No, not Don Quixote, not Pip, not Pussy King of Pirates. No, she decides, as she stands in the mildewy bathroom with no windows, a different masculinity is needed. She pulls off her finger armor, takes out her long single earring.

"I'll become H.P. Lovecraft, gentleman fictioneer," she laughs. "He knew a thing or two about the colorless colors of small-town America." She strips, and then puts on the clothing piece by piece, slowly, a neat gray suit, white shirt, black necktie, and a Panama hat.

VANESSA PLACE

From *La Medusa*

INT. SKULL–CONTINUOUS

QUESTION: What is the significance of this period of history, in terms of history as a whole?

ANSWER: I was born between the deaths of Kennedys, père and blankeyed
verse. I've seen the Father undone in the hatless Dallas
sun, rerun in technicolere, and in muy bricolaged black
& white photos, kept with baby carrots in aspic, and still I
believe more in the sun, blotting my eyes only for our little
prince, because it's better to bawl over an abortion than a
man, the *in fieri* over the *in esse*. But that's not it. That's a
see-through cogitate, pimpled and legless, that, my lovely
pineapple, lacks a lead-colored back. That's it. It's easier to
see the reflection of the unnamed than the unnamed, explaining
the popularity of hand-held mirrors and underwater
phosphorescence. Maebe. Or maeebee, as Perseus, that
big baby, evidenced so simply, it's death to look in anyone's
eye, though < deadly for a monster. Maeeebeee. Though
which side? Or maybe its Cain and Abel, Abel and Cain,
ever t'winder, ever twain. Ergad, that's why this epocrypha
seems significant, for everthing is a reflection of something
and nothing comes with meat. No, that's incomplete, it's a
partial birth, you tepid yam, something with fins and flippers
and insufficient fur. Something fleshed in mercury, sir.
Well, maybe everything is and is reflection. So history is geography,
measured in bolts of horizon, the here that is a
mirror of the there that was and the never to-be. O, that's
nice. That has a carrot nose and a coal-button grin. For
moreover furthermore nonetheless and hitherto, as Faust
and Himself swear on a stack of glassbottom boats, time
is divine.

[Here's a joke: During the Crucifixion, Christ calls to His disciple,"Paul, Paul." Paul responds, "Yes, Master, what is it?" and struggles mightily through the throng towards Jesus, only to be beaten back by the brute Roman soldiers (repeat 3x). Finally, Paul, badly hurt, crawls, broken and bleeding, to the bottom of the Cross. "Master," he gasps, "What is it?" Christ murmurs: "Paul… I can see your house from here."]

................My hands're starting to hurt from holding the steering wheel too tight. Tightly.

QUESTION: Isn't that Narcissus again?
ANSWER: Kind of. But the image in my instance is better than the thing casting the image, though you know the image is less substantive. Oh, and not real.

— Wrong, wrong, wrong, my sweet potato. That's the whole point, *now*, isn't it? The substance of the image, the supernatant rhetoric of the unreal. You're daydreaming again, aren't you, chocha? Not paying a lick of attention.

...............I cut off the guy next to me. He honks and I draw my middle finger out, slow & solitary as a tubercular death.

—Well, if you gave me a lick, I might pay attention.

QUESTION: Let me rephrase. Isn't that exactly Narcissus? Aren't you just revisiting, via the Kennedys, and your histories and geographies, *etc.*, the idea that the image appears more perfect than its Maker—especially to its Maker?
ANSWER: Okay, yes. Just as Christ was more perfect than God, being capable of divine compassion and cruelty because He was God-as-Man, although we all know Christ was God cast as the abandoned Anthropos, and therefore Man redux times two, Man being then the Supreme Image of God and God Himself, more perfectmade than His Maker, In My Son I Am Well Pleased, the well being like the great and individuate eye a circular font capable of holding the circular horizoned self, impermeable and permeable, still as a surface and still capable of rippling and swallowing so the wail of betrayal was a hyperbolic vamp, and Judas just a beard. Such as was favored by Stephen Foster.
QUESTION: Among many other great Americans.
ANSWER: All, je pense.
QUESTION: But if "in the image of God created he him," what is God's hairy problem?
ANSWER: Depends. A doctor who has completed his psychiatric residency, even before he gets his vanity plates, could diagnose Him3 as suffering from Disassociative Identity Disorder (*Diagnostic and Statistical Manual of Mental Disorders*, DSM-IV, code 300.14: "two or more distinct identities or personality states (each with its own relatively enduring pattern of perceiving, relating to, and thinking about the environment and self)" (487). [NB: "Eve" of *The 3 Faces of*

Eve having a godlike palindromic sensibility, i.e., the hooded self donned like a reversible raincoat, though this may also be a comment on the female's lack of a discreet inner vs. outer self, the hood then becoming both Ewigweibliche and plainwrap truth]. Significantly, in many such cases "[s]elfmutilation and suicidal and aggressive behavior may occur" (485). In legal terms, at least herein the Golden State, third largest geographically, ceded to the United States by the Treaty of Guadalupe Hidalgo in 1848, turning states' evidence two years later, Golden Poppy, Valley Quail, song by Frankenstein, this would mean the Incarnate He should have been locked up, thus absolving Pontius Pilate, or even Herod, of indiscretion or abuse of civil or military authority, given any competent hearing officer would have done the same. (See, Cal. Welfare & Institutions Code § 5150 ["when any person… is a danger to others, or to himself… [the state] may take, or cause to be taken, the person into custody."].) Moreover, it is this hamlety hem and haw that makes the son the better romantic, being the only being that gets the girl, and the One voted Most Likely to Be, in other words, He's a One with a transformative character arc, a good dramatic model for us creatures of the tarsprings. Plus, Peter the Betrayer comes to become Peter, Rock of the Church, his metaphorosis thus underscoring how history furrows like a fault under the Majestic Eye. Confluct. That's what sulls sap.

[Here's a joke: A farmer goes to his fields, all his crops have been destroyed. He cries, "O God, why me?" No answer. He goes to his barn, all his animals have been slaughtered. He cries, "O God,why me?" No answer. He goes in his house, his family all lies dead. He falls to his knees, beats his breast, moaning, "O God, O God—why me?" A voice thunders from above: "I don't know. There's just something about you…"]

.....................Many Asian tourists are clustered by Van Cleef & Arpels, where a Russian gunman killed many people many years ago, first lining them up inside the jewelry vault. One of the clerks begged for her life, she found it hard to breathe from fear and her hands and legs were shaking and her breath stank of swallowed vomit, and someone else, a customer or another clerk was howling, not a word, and the trembling clerk put the palm of one hand toward her captor and told him somehow about her daughter, how she loved her little girl, who has soft brown hair that whorls like wet whipped cream and whose smile pierces her mother's quick. She needs to go home now and set out a thin glass of cold milk and an apple, unpeeled in a perfect curl, and two perfect chocolate chip cookies for her little girl, she needs to go home now to remind her daughter to wipe her mouth with the sharp tip of the paper napkin folded into a long triangle just like she likes it she must go home now to be there for her little girl and say it's okay, she'll never tell about being so scared, about being locked in and so locked out, but will just serve her milk and fruit and cookies and kiss her in the smooth middle of her smooth forehead and the clerk's heart will surely crack from such a love of such a little girl. And the Russian gunman listened and shot this clerk through the neck. He did not want to be saved.

QUESTION: Are you suggesting that history is irrelevant, then, and the temporal span of humankind merely the recycling of tropes?

ANSWER: Well, I think it's two things. It's always two things, unless it's three. The first thing is moms and martyrs are the way we will think, just as when we dance we tend to tango. Jung suspected as much, you know, and every story could, I suppose, be seen as such a spyglass. Second, either there is or there isn't, point-blank, and if there is not, and something besides lead backs our philosophies, then previously Truth flashed its temper like a fictitious schoolgirl showing her panties, then went all cowboy cool in the neonew, barely speaking, keeping mum, despite the fact we's done forgot dear mammy, savoring the slow satisfying burn of a cigarette before the bonfire of a billion bodies, and still millions more wait their turn, we're better at keeping our appointments, at any rate, skinny corpses stripped of teeth and hair and skin, difference plucked like daisies, for there is no difference; in ether words, to hear the Great Apes tell it, every plague is one for the pointless and every poppy's got jack to do with Us. *Hoohah*! A particularly ballsy bit of business given the most recent nearing too close, we're singing our rondel with a bellyful of gravy and sourmash, we're at the highpocked end, and there's more to come, come the dawn. Though bear in mind we've no prêt-à-porter poodle sniffing around here, nossir, we're not afraid to say stay, still, we'll stay right here, eating off the apple of your eye, carving the plump of your cheek caught in the family photo, the flash in the pan goes off and so does your head, or so Buttercup says, we're stuck, that is to say, in the over-brought dawn of this new clearer Age, in which we play patsy to witness just this: *everything is beauty-full, in its own way....*

[Here's a joke: Which is worse, slavery or the Holocaust?]

QUESTION: Upon what proof?
ANSWER: Versable proof. For beauty comes in bolts like blotter, begging to be put into pads.

.... I shake my right hand, then my left. Fresh sores crack across my knuckles and a hollow, scaled spot carnations each palm. Of course.

QUESTION: So what's the point?
ANSWER: Why, the beginning, of course.

[Here's a joke: What's the difference between a concentration camp and a bowling alley? You can't clean a bowling alley with a pitchfork. Here's another: How many blacks does it take to tar a roof? Two, if you slice 'em real thin.]

Who hath prevented me, that I should repay him? whosoever is under the whole heaven is mine.

.....................Catherine scratches her neck and I swerve too close to a guy in white shoes keying a blue Boxstar. He curses me.

Me, the Maladictine monk.

{NB: *Phlogiston* refers to the contemplation of fire as segregate form of material substance, like angel cake.} go fig.

LIDIA YUKNAVITCH

The Photographer

1:17 A.M.

She rolls over in the bed as if her hips were mountains turning away from the sea. The white of the sheet follows her like a reversed shadow in the night. She sees the black and white hint of her lover's face. She feels the tiniest prick of weight in her throat, like a stone suddenly swallowed.

She squeezes her eyes shut and clenches her jaw and the sweat between her thighs, under each breast, and in the unthought of folds of her belly talks to her about her woman weight and pretty soon woman thickness raises and rises again almost like a third person there in the bed with them. What is it—this being a woman going from the drive and whir of the end of her thirties . . . eight, nine . . . is it her age aging her, or something else? She nearly feels the small feet of crows at the corners of her eyes. She almost feels her ears growing longer, heavier, the lobes pendulous. She can see her own nose growing for the rest of her life, changing her entire face, elongating it and drooping and dropping it as if everything were filled with enormous, bulbous fishing weights.

2:49.

God damn it, the feisty in her goes, a woman growing older is glorious, beyond every paradigm, beyond desire, beyond belief and truth, mythic, why, she's the god damned statue of liberty—yeah—whole nations should grovel at her feet. And exactly up against this is the thought that blows it apart: a woman growing older is nothing or less than nothing, she is her teeth, her increasingly unsubtle breath, her unreproductive swelling belly, her ever-reddening cheeks giving away her steady need to drink, she is her deflated breast sacks—sad, unwanted old balloons, she is the lines in her legs, her swollen and sagging cunt, her gassy gut, her thinning and wiring like a poodle's hair, everything the culture counts as detritus.

Just when her stupid eyes start welling up with water like a big fat baby her intellect zooms to the rescue . . . a kind of weird, academic Artemis comes in and fills her brain with large vocabulary and theoretical wizardry: *the immensity of the image—larger than any systematized god or belief—only the image arrested can liberate us from the lie which suggests that life tumbles forward toward some meaningful end. The arrested images is an artifact. When one stops the hegemony of life in motion, the truer fiction emerges. We are each simply an arrangement of particles of light. We are none of us anything if not a glimpse of something fleeting and miniscule, weightless as air. The childless woman is not a grotesque, uneeded thing . . . she is nothingness. The unmarried woman, nothingness. The aging woman, why, as nothing as the sky no one can touch at the top of a climb. Photographs replace memory. Photographs replace lived experience. History.*

3:00.

She feels better. Her smartness has again calmed her with its metaphysical leaps and tricks of light. Why, right now is simply nighttime. She can just go to sleep. Her love is resting quietly next to her. An ordinary thing to be in a bed like this. Then she hears a siren outside and her calm is jostled and she thinks she needs to fart and then her brain goes at it again, her thinking is stabbed and then it's at it again fuck fuck fucking fuckety non-stop Mac truck. She tries to breathe. She tries to breathe in exercises she knows to calm herself. Non-Westertn thought and practice. She breathes in through her nose, holds it for seven seconds, out through her mouth, letting all of the twisted and burning wiring of her mind's games release through two holes in the head. And again. And again. But with each more calm and deeper breath the words CALM DOWN CALM THE FUCK DOWN get bigger and bigger like cartoons until the part of her brain going *balance, calm* is overtaken by a bigger part of her brain—the terminally American compulsive competitive she-bitch, who goes *run*.

3:42.

So then this is the moment before she leaves her lover, the musician.

It is in this moment that the photographer thinks, take photos. It's all you've got. You are a complete nut case when you aren't taking photos. Yeah when you try to slow down and rest inside the life of an American woman, you suck. And you fatten up like a hog. Just leave it.

Leave this country and take photos not here. Not you. Not any of us. As if taking photos of other people from other countries will release her. Leave it. Leave your aging body, leave your beautiful and impotent lover, leave the failed attempts at woman-life.

She decides the small technological box and the images it births are worth leaving everything for.

She decides to take the assignment that, truth be told, she would never have been able to turn down—not with her ambition, wicked runaway whore.

Fuck yeah.

This is how she ends up in Eastern Europe during a tumultuous point in history.

As if there are any other points of history . . . all our grand epochs or puny private moments scattered like glowing ash in a big godless sky—particles of light, time and events merely a series of invented fictions that we can pretend hold us.

Notes—Lithuania—Panaveyzes—Day 23
The night is cold as fuck and the color of ash and soot . . . even with all this snow. Ironic. Newspaper colored. The town has already been shot to shit and the Russians look to me like jack-booted thugs from some B-rated movie, really, ignorant killing machines with ill-fitting uniforms and contorted loyalties. Only their boots and rifles look lethal. Every corner of every building is shot away, making the little village look like pieces of itself . . . ghost structures. There's no telling rubble from real here. None of this has made the news, it's just gone on and on for years without end, the supposed end of one war giving way to micro-violences. Nobody even knows where I am or what I'm doing or why. Not even me. The ground stinks of blood and shit. Domesticated animals—horses, sheep, pigs, dogs and cats—wander around or stand like idiots in the paths and streets. There is a commotion up ahead—they want something—badly—and they are yanking people from homes like snatching tissues from a box. They want something—or someone—and they are moving as one entity of brute force against these small families. Language fucks me over—I don't know Russian or Lithuanian in any real sense—just bits and pieces enough to stay mobile. I'm only able to be this close because I'm dressed as a garbage man—as my interpreter and guide—and more than that. We've been given the duty of clearing corpses from the street. It's easy to snap shots from this distance, in this grayed out light, smoke and dirt and night's falling covering my hands and sound being swallowed up like it is, though my guide looks angry every shot I take. He doesn't think it's worth it. A photo, he says when we are in the cave of his house, what use is that against what is happening here? Do you even know where "here" is? Do you even know what our story is? How long this fight? I know why you are here. You are here to catch the Russians committing atrocities. But only because you are American. You want to shame them and make a big story out of their brutality. Where were you when we needed you? Your promises of nuclear attack—your threat to obliterate them—we counted on you during your so-called Cold War. We hid in the woods for years after the war waiting for you. We accepted guns and money from you. But you did not attack them. And so we have been left to fight alone for all of these years.

Sometimes I think he wants to kill me. But he merely hands me bread and hot tea with something that helps me to sleep at night. The look he gives me is one of dismissal. I am nothing, or less than nothing, and so it costs him little to help me or kill me.

We move closer and closer to the edge of this hulled out village, its people overexposed and dead with tired. We pass what was once some kind of town center building. We pass what was once some kind of café or bar, its windows as black as the eyes of a corpse. We pass what was once a schoolhouse, its doors boarded up like a shut mouth. We are some ways behind them, and more or less part of the detritus. Soon they are at a house barely in the village at all. We are able to approach mostly because of our giant, horse-drawn wagon with rotting bodies—it seems part of the mis en scene. What I see next doesn't seem possible, but the first form to emerge from the house is a girl . . . she looks to be about 10 or so. Her hair spreads in waves of nested coils around her face, down her shoulders. Unbelievably, she walks straight towards them. She is wearing the clothes of a boy—and soon a second self, her brother, and her father and mother come rushing out like blood after her. There is some yelling back and forth before it happens—a blast from I don't know where disintegrates the father, mother and brother just at the edge of the girl's body, missing her in some terrifying accident of a fraction. They blow up right before her eyes, her hair alighting for a moment, so that she looks as if she may float skyward, her arms up and out, her face glowing so white that her eyes look like blue-steel bullets, her mouth open in the shape of an "O."

I remember how the ground shook.
I remember the camera going off. Shooting before I fell.
I remember her hands—palms white—fingers spread.
The light from the explosion must have acted like . . . like a perfect flash.

There was yelling and a lot of smoke. Not all of the soldiers were there any longer. No one even looked at us as we hobbled away, fear bringing bile into my mouth, my guide so angry we were there he fractured my arm pulling me away, and when I turned my head back to the action, I thought I saw a girl running toward the woods.

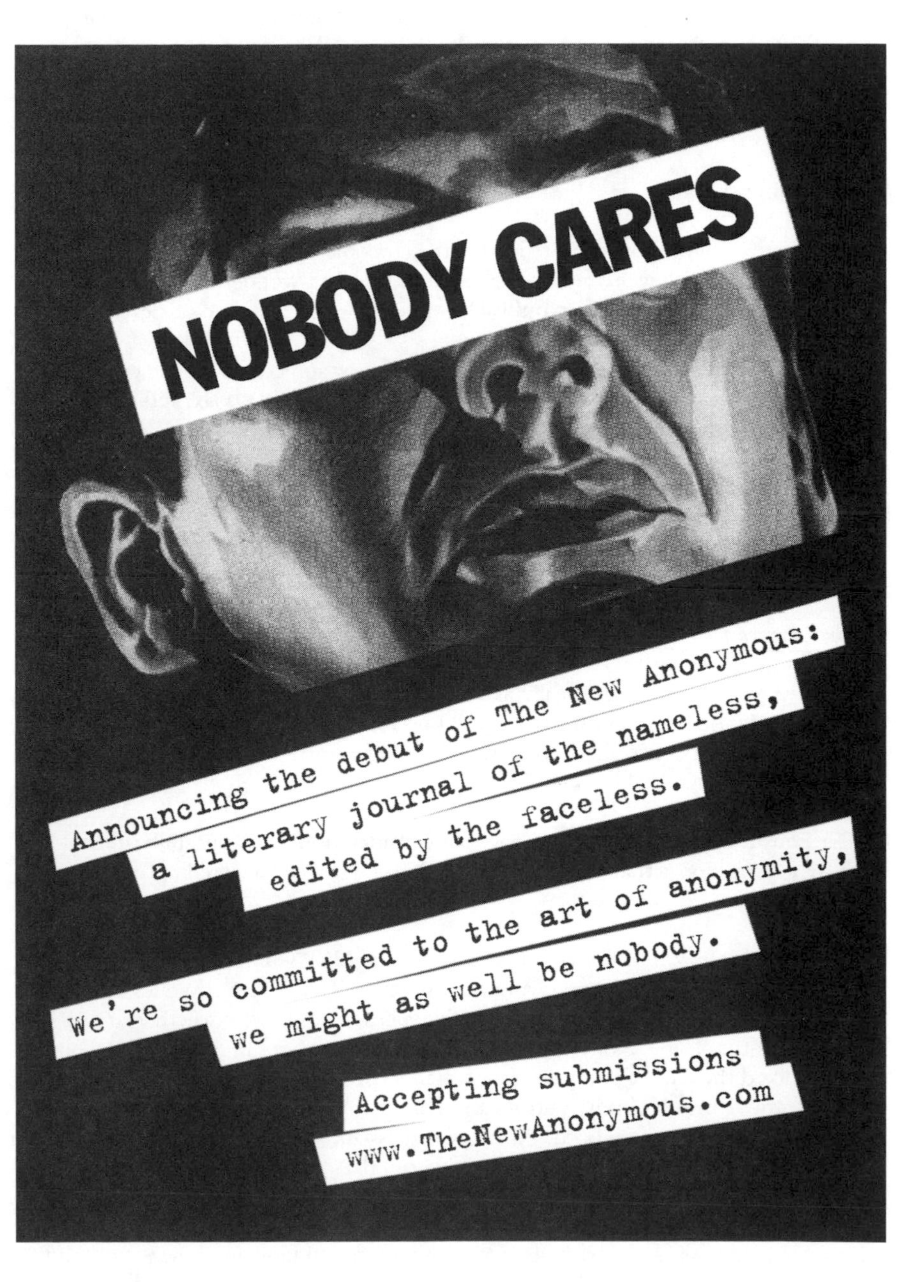
NOBODY CARES
Announcing the debut of The New Anonymous:
a literary journal of the nameless,
edited by the faceless.
We're so committed to the art of anonymity,
we might as well be nobody.
Accepting submissions
www.TheNewAnonymous.com

The New Anonymous is an annual literary journal that not only publishes all work anonymously but also blindly screens and edits its submissions, i.e., the submission, editorial, and publishing process is anonymous from beginning to end. The stated goal of *The New Anonymous* is to "celebrate the text." They refer to themselves as both "a literary journal" and a "literary act." Invited to explain themselves, they chose instead to pass along commentary on the magazine found on the web and in letters to the editor.

From online threads:

"Sounds like a scam. How can I trust that these people will take my work seriously? How will I know if they are even considering my work? I wonder if the entire project is just someone's clever effort to publish all his own work. I'm tired of cleverness."

"According to their website, the whole thing is run by someone with the crypto-gothic name 'The Mediator.' I'm willing to bet the whole thing is a hoax, and they'll never publish even a single issue."

From *The New Anonymous* epigraph page:

"The birth of the reader must be ransomed by the death of the author."
—Roland Barthes

From Letters to *The New Anonymous:*

"Dear *The New Anonymous:* I really like the concept for the magazine, and I want to submit. But if you do accept my story, will I be able to list the publication on my CV? If I do, and a prospective agent/publisher/employer wants to verify, will you confirm that the story is mine?"

"Dear Editor: I've enclosed a story for your consideration. But, truthfully, it's not my best. When my stories that I really like get published, I want the credit. Thanks (and sorry)."

"Dear *New Anonymous*: I visited your booth at The AWP Conference, where you were selling your magazine and giving away buttons. There were two piles of buttons, and I was supposed to choose from one of the piles. I wasn't sure whether to take a button from the 'I'm A Nobody' pile, or a button from the 'I'm A Somebody' pile. I certainly liked the idea of being secure enough to proclaim myself a nobody. So I took and wore the 'I'm A Nobody' button. But I also took and wore the 'I'm A Somebody' button. I wore them both. People would ask me, 'Well, which is it?' It was quite a dilemma, as you can imagine, a crisis of the soul that I seek to resolve today. I am returning one button, the one which reads, 'I'm A Somebody.' Thank you. I am free."

"Dear Mediator: As an established writer, I am interested in seeing how your 'blind' editors will receive my work. In recent years, I have come to suspect that my name is being published, not my poetry. I believe Trollope and others attempted the same experiment, removing or changing their name once having gained literary acclaim. There is always that fear—the fear that the work won't stand on its own, that the writer's best days are behind him (her). Thanks for allowing writers like myself this opportunity. Indeed, as you say on your website, it is a bit like 'play.'"

"Dear *The New Anonymous*: I really liked the concept of your magazine. In particular, I enjoyed the piece called, 'Interview with Someone.' I want to believe that the anonymous 'someone' is in fact a real person. But, at times, he (he?) seemed a bit too clever, a bit too in tune. Did you really sit down with a 'someone'? And, if so, did you disguise your identity? Did you wear a mask during the interview? Did you use a voice modulation machine? Etc. Assuming this will be a regular feature in your magazine, I'd like to volunteer to be your next 'someone.' I also would be interested in being the person for the 'What Someone's Been Reading' feature."

From an art magazine review:

"An inspiring, new embodiment of democracy at its best."

From letters to *The New Anonymous:*

"Dear Mediator: I am sick of being in literature classes that spend the majority of the time talking about the biography of the author, rather than the very works that made him or her famous. I am sick of hearing those works only be judged and interpreted in terms of the author's life… Furthermore, I believe that the pressure of feeling judged by family, friends, or anyone who disagrees with you can trap and trifle a writer."

"Dear *New Anonymous*: I really liked the masks you were handing out at the AWP Conference. Enclosed is a picture of me wearing the mask." [accompanying photo of eye mask draped over a man's private parts]

From an online thread:

"I hadn't looked at their website until now. And I see one of the cardinal sins—the expression 'very unique'—in the submission guidelines. I don't need to see any more."

THE NEW ANONYMOUS

An Interview with Someone

The New Anonymous *sat down with Someone to question him/her about the intersection of art, process, publication and identity. What follows is a transcript of that conversation.*

When did art become part of your life?

I never took myself really seriously as a writer. I just kind of did it on the side. The study of literature was much more important. Then I went to law school because there were no jobs for English teachers. The whole distinction between creative and analytical writing is really interesting as well, and it's kind of a false one. It's more about people that are good with language. So I got kind of caught on that track, thinking of myself not as creative, but analytical, and also as a good writer.

Why did you get caught on that track?

That's a really good question. Some of it had to do with pragmatics, getting a job. Some of it had to do with self-confidence, you know. Some of it had to do with believing in myself and going for it and not really being able to do that.

So now you are going for it?

The whole thing just turned around for years and years, and after I got tenure and stuff like that I figured, what the hell.

Nothing to lose?

Exactly, which is weird, because writers are so much about trying to gain something.

Now that you are doing readings and other public performances, how is it affecting your self-confidence?

I'm still really sensitive about what people say about my stuff. I just think at this point I have to do it. I am compelled to do it. It's kind of like a treasure that is buried that needs to be opened up and thrown around regardless of what people think. It doesn't have to do with confidence, because I am definitely not confident. It has to do with me being able to relax into that mode; whereas before I didn't think I could be in that mode, for whatever reasons, whether it had to do with superego or something like that.

So you say you are still sensitive. What about the opportunity to do it anonymously, or pseudonymously? Would that be as satisfying? Would it open up opportunities and relieve you of the sensitivity you have?

I don't think so. Because the sensitivity is part of the process. I get a lot of self-rejection as I write. On the other hand, not having to worry about people knowing you are the writer is kind of liberating. Because so much writing gets pinned to the person who wrote it. It would be really interesting to take the names off a bunch of canonical works and have people look at them and see what they think. I think somebody's

doing that, submitting anonymously, and he's getting rejected, whereas when he puts his name on it, everyone wants it.
It doesn't matter how good it is...

[laughing] Right. Something Kittredge said is the trouble of being famous is no one will be serious about criticizing your work. People are not going to say this is bullshit, as often as they would if you or I sent something out.

And?

I don't have the whole MFA structure on top of me, so I get really nervous about that. I don't have that kind of sophistication.

Is this the kind of insecurity you were talking about coming through?

[laughing] Yeah. One of the things that would be interesting would be if you could write anonymously. I'm talking about just the writing process. If you have a style, obviously that has a kind of signature to it, and so are you giving yourself an identity by trying to live up to the style of what you've written before.

It's said that writers of antiquity were just vessels for a muse. There was this whole sense of modesty, because they had no identity and because they played no role in the creation--

No filter.

Would this relieve the pressure of being the creator? Would being a filter eliminate insecurities?

The idea of the muse and the idea of the medieval writer is someone who kind of patches together the old stories and tells them over again in a different way. Like Chaucer is retelling Boccaccio and retelling a whole bunch of other stories and he doesn't think of himself as a creator. And then there is somebody like Milton who sits down at five in the morning and calls on the muse to let him talk. Both of those idea are antithetical to the way we think today, which is like we have to sit down under a tree and compose "the [interviewer's name] Ode" and it has to have the stamp of [interviewer's name] or [interviewee's name] on it. That's really compelling for us, but it's kind of nice to think you can just filter the things that are a part of you and put them together in a weird way.

So you're just putting a puzzle together?

The more and more I write the more and more I think of myself as rewriting, whether it be the "Hail Mary" or some song I might have heard. I was out pulling dandelions one spring so I just looked up dandelion and read all about them and got really interested in how they work, because they are so invasive—I don't know if you do any gardening—but they can be really invasive. Anyway, I got really into dandelions and I felt that what I wrote was really more that stuff that I read. So I was just a filter for it.

Is this a way of protecting yourself? Is there still the fear to reveal the self because you are going to be judged?

I think that's true. I kind of justify my own erasure by saying, "Well, you know the self is all a pastiche of different scripts that are out there that we kind of own—"

So, "It's not me."

[laughing] Right. But also at the same time you're going, "What is my voice? I want my voice." I often talk about this as a capitalistic urge. You want to have your own kind of trademark. But that has to do with ownership, too, which gets more into the capitalist self, as well as the egotistic self.

Riff on what you mean by "capitalistic urge."

Seems like writers want to have that kind of copyrighted sensibility. Where they make a product that is theirs, and everyone knows what Campbell's Soup is, or [interviewee's name's] Soup is, and that it has the great taste of [interviewee's name].

This idea of sense of authorship or ownership seems like such a modern thing.

Yeah. I think it comes from the myth of individualism from the 19th century and is still with us, the idea of the autonomous self that is, in so many ways, unconnected to the rest of the world, or understands itself as an individual and fails to see the deeper connection between what we think of as the self and the other. Right? So, this isn't an advertisement for plagiarism, but on the other hand everything is plagiarized. If you think about it, there's one thing we all have in common; it's language.

So we just sample?

But the way you sample, the way you parody all the things in your life, the way you pastiche them together creates that politics of the self. Part of subjectivity has to do with understanding that nothing is ours; but the way we put that nothing together makes it ours, in some weird way.

If I can go back for a second, earlier you used the word "flawed" to describe this modern condition where everybody is staking ownership in order to become an individual. What did you mean by "flawed"?

I think it's flawed in the sense that people are scared, just as I am scared, of some deeper voice, the "real me," and that there is some inner [interviewee's name]-ness that I can get to. I think we are also afraid, on the other hand, that there may not be anything there, that you may just be peeling an onion and we're just, as you said, a set of questions and injunctions that we amassed in our head, from others. And that's scary, too, to think of yourself as amorphous, so deeply connected to the outside world that there isn't really any [interviewee's name]-ness. It's kind of as scary as thinking I might be hiding behind that fact and not getting to what might be my real voice. It's kind of a paradox.

You say you sample. What is your process in how you create? Do you read, watch TV, wake up at night and talk into a tape recorder?

No, I just kind of walk around until I kind of hear a phrase or something. But basically I find that most writing is about feeling, and the best writing for me pushes my buttons around laughing or crying… Take Pound's "The River-Merchants' Wife: A Letter" and she talks about moss on the ground and there's just this set of images that evoke longing in a weird away. And I always aspire to that poem, because it evokes feeling

Is that what you are after…to evoke that feeling in your audience?

Yes.

And how do you determine when you've reached that goal? Do you measure yourself?

I measure myself. Sentimentality is a problem, but I think that's something people have to risk. I think all good writers risk sentimentality because if they don't they're not going to get to the real emotional stuff.

So you're measuring what your own work evokes in you?

Yes. My process has to do with putting it aside, looking at it and seeing if I get that feeling when I read it.

And is that enough, to get "that feeling"? I asked you earlier if you would continue to write if you were stranded on a deserted island. Would you?

I probably would. For me writing is deeply personal. It's a way of expressing my emotions in ways that I can't, like here in this interview, or through playing the piano, or whatever… In that way writing is compelling personally and entirely un-public, but, and so—I don't know what all this has to do with what we were just talking about, anonymity.

I have all these other things I want to bounce off you, like Plath—

I love Plath.

She wrote anonymously. Or, rather, pseudonymously. She published *The Bell Jar* under the name Victoria Lucas, apparently because she was writing about her family so much. Do you ever have that fear, that you are going to offend people you know?

Definitely my partner. Because a lot of my subject matter comes from the disappointments I have. I use the frustrations with the people I know and live with as a subject for what I do. I feel like I might be able to hurt them with my work [laughing], but what the hell, they don't care. It's just writing.

Do you hold back at all?

Maybe a little. But sometimes I go the other way. I go forward and make it worse than it is.

How come?

Because I think it gives me a sense of being able to really ratchet things up. Because we live such kind of deadbeat avoidance lives. Writing allows us to, in a kind of a horribly old cathartic model [laughing]...I know this sounds horribly old fashioned.

Is art playful?

To work in a complexity of language, that is playful, which is the nuts and bolts of the artistic process, and that's a little more difficult because it can become solipsistic or it can become impenetrable by readers other than yourself, though you may love it and read through it and understand it, but you give it to someone else and they go, "What! I can't understand this shit!" And if you are already famous, people go," Oh, well, I'll try and figure it out." But if you're anonymous, like Trollope, who scratched his name out, and you send that shit out people are going to go, "What the fuck?" so it's kind of interesting to have that self play.

Earlier, you said that when you were young you put your artistic impulses aside. Are things different now? Is the goal the same? Is the motivation the same?

I don't know. I want to say it had something to do with being a queer kid. I was always kind of a queer kid, a klutz; I had these freckles and thick glasses and a butch haircut. I wasn't really a nerd, but I was on the margins a lot. So, for me, writing stuff down in my room by myself was kind of like a refuge from the ridiculous extroversion of the world. So it was kind of like dogs and writing were the two things I could go to, where I could be and be something other than backslapping and ne'er-do-well.

Did you keep it private for one reason or the other? I mean, some would call this a "nerd" activity when you are younger, to write poetry or whatever.

I shared it with various girlfriends and boyfriends as the years went on, but I didn't think of myself as a public writer, as somebody who could kind of "send things out" and get them published. I just didn't have enough feel for that being something I could do...without getting into deep psychoanalysis [laughing].

Okay, last question. What do you think of the concept of this magazine, one that is anonymous from start to finish?

I think it's fun. In some ways it's highly subversive of the whole process. I don't know if that's your goal. But I think you are doing key work around the questions of authorship and the whole racket of writing [laughs]; and you are trying to undermine it in really interesting ways. Because if you are reading something, do you really want to know about the author? Or do you actually want to read it and see if you like it? So we're all caught up in this meta-thing, "Who wrote this and what's their biography?"

And how do I become one [an author] myself?

They all want to know about Shakespeare's wife, and it's like, "Go read the play." Everybody wants to jump to biography and ownership and they don't really want to spend that much time looking at the work.

Is it true, what Roland Barthes said in 1970 or so, that the author is dead?

Nope. He keeps popping up. Or she does. Rearing an ugly head.

STACEY LEVINE

From *Frances Johnson: a novel*

Frances Johnson sat on her front porch, listening to the radio in the dark. She wore a blue dress.

Beyond the wooden porch, night was thick. Frances stood, walking into the living-room, listening. A train lumbered across a nearby trestle, halting as it reached the center of the weak bridge. Below the trestle was a curving road, leading in one direction toward the town, and in the opposite direction toward the sea.

The train hissed. It would follow a tricky, meandering route that would probably lead to another state.

Frances was an expressive woman in many ways.

There were so many people and things to think about, such huge compendiums of circumstances.

Sometimes Frances was afraid for no real reason, it seemed. Oftentimes, waking in the middle of the night, she was uncertain who she was. Frances did not like that. Stumbling to the bathroom, she feared that who or whatever she was would be inappropriate or cause a calamity of some kind—and that was the most frightening thing of all. Standing on a little foot-rug, she would calm herself by rubbing her limbs briskly, hoping the heat would fill out her body and make it more dimensional.

"We can't know the future," she said dully to someone on the telephone, then hung up the heavy receiver.

Outside, the porch swing creaked.

"I will not attend the dance," she spoke aloud to herself.

Frances had a suitor, Ray Garn. Ray was fine, though sometimes his enthusiasms were hard to understand. The two had been together for quite some time, making vague, halfhearted plans for the future.

Ray was mild-tempered, and things generally went well. Once, though, they traveled a few miles south to search for the sea—just that once—and Ray hid behind a wall for hours, causing Frances to feel a kind of fury.

It was a long, tall wall that rose up to hide the ocean shore from the road. Ray squatted next to it, smoking, smiling, and looking up at Frances when she found him, as if it were all a game, as if he had made her worry on purpose by hiding. She got so angry that she smacked him, hard, on the jaw.

He laughed. "Frances, it was just a joke! You know—hide-and-seek? Well, now you can hide, if you like."

Frances did not want to. She preferred to go into the cabin and play a quiet game by herself with a bowl of salty water, a religious-type game in which she imagined punishing and bathing herself and others. Sitting alone, in any case, brought such relief that Frances locked Ray out for most of the trip, feeling deliciously private while he stood by the sea with its freezing waves.

After some time, she saw through the cabin window that Ray had resorted to taking a walk. The wall along the beach prevented him from looking at the sea—assuming he liked the sea—and clamorous, gusty winds ripped at his sleeves and hair.

Frances left the cabin to join him at the far end of the wall. They said nothing at first, but soon were sharing some hard crackers and butter, sitting in the wild grass near the fence, chatting amicably and joking, shouting into the wind.

That evening she allowed Ray into the cabin bedroom, which smelled cheerlessly of mothballs and skin. He lay next to her on the bed for a while, then, levering upon bent arms, rolled atop her. She heard a tiny click: Ray's eyes shifting. After moments, he rolled away.

"It doesn't make sense to me," she exhaled toward the window, which framed a dark, gelatinous sky. "Two adults, in the middle of the night... one lying on top of the other... ?" Frances felt out of sorts.

"Yes, it's awfully strange," Ray agreed.

They fell asleep.

CRIS MAZZA

Trickle-Down Timeline

1980

Pac-Man became the first computer game hero. He was originally supposed to be Puck-Man (he was, after all, shaped like a hockey puck), but with the threat that rampaging youth might scratch out the loop of the P to form an F on arcade machines, Pac-Man was born, a name with literally no meaning.

Median household income: $17,710.00
Median cost of a house: $76,400.00
These things hardly mattered, or even meant anything to anyone who was just moving out of his or her parents' house and had found an apartment for $200/month which could be afforded on a $100 a week part-time minimum-wage paycheck while finishing a fifth and sixth year of college.

Ted Bundy was sentenced to death by electrocution.

Brook Shields purred in her Calvin Klein advertisement: You know what comes between me and my Calvins? Nothing! Shields also showed off what she had to offer as an actress in *The Blue Lagoon*. Anyone who went on their first date with the person he or she eventually married will remember this film, especially if either of them had to go see it twice because in the middle of the first time, one of their brand new bought-with-birthday-money soft contact lenses came out, and for some reason they still wanted to see how the movie ended.

Ronald Reagan visited the White House to get his job briefing from President Carter. Carter would subsequently disclose that the President-elect asked hardly any questions and did not take notes.

John Lennon was shot, ostensibly for being a phony, by a fan carrying *The Catcher in the Rye*. Doctors at the emergency room that received Lennon's dying body later said they could not have recognized him.

In fact there were few people less phony. As an emblematic death, it was the end of rebellion. Some people, though, were in the throes of being engaged, pawning high school rings to buy silver wedding bands.

1981

The hostages held in Iran for over a year were released on the day of Ronald Reagan's Presidential inauguration. In his inaugural speech, Reagan took credit for the release.

The public heard the first news report about a gay man's mysterious death from an immune-deficiency disease. Later when the media continued reports of the endemic, the disease was defined as one that affected "homosexual men, intravenous drug users and Haitian men." The inclusion of Haitian men in this early description was eventually dropped without explanation.

Striking air traffic controllers were fired by President Reagan.

The Army suggested, Be All You Can Be.

The Reagan administration tried to count ketchup as a vegetable in subsidized school lunches.

The minimum wage was raised to $3.35. At 40 hours a week, for 52 weeks a year, this would net $6,968, no taxes. The poverty threshold for 1981, for a single person, was $4,620. Two-thousand three-hundred forty-eight dollars of breathing room for the year. Some people, however, went to college, and could now make $10,000 a year working behind a desk at a hospital, or as a salesman (person) for a cement company, or as a first-year elementary school teacher, or even earn a little more than that as a grocery checker.

Reagan Budget Director David Stockman said in an interview for *Atlantic Monthly,* "None of us really understands what's going on with all these numbers." He then conceded that trickle-down economics "was always a Trojan horse to bring down the top [tax] rate." And then, regarding the tax bill, "Do you realize the greed that came to the forefront? The hogs were really feeding."

Britain's Prince Charles married Princess Diana on live TV, and Americans began a(nother) immersion into Royal-watching. Some other people got married this same year. Some of them did so without the Diana-style wedding dress and hundred-yards-of-lace train. A few of them opted for a minister's office on a Thursday night, the bride wearing a brown corduroy skirt, the groom in white jeans (his best pants).

"Honey I forgot to duck," Ronald Reagan supposedly said to Nancy after he was shot by John Hinkley Jr. It was immediately assumed that John Hinkley was crazy.

1982

Bob Jones University, which did not allow admission of non-white students, was granted a tax-exempt status by the Reagan administration. A few months later, Reagan told Chicago high school students that the plan was not designed to assist segregated schools because "I didn't know there were any. Maybe I should have, but I didn't."

The poverty rate rose to 15% and the national unemployment rate reached 10.8%. There was a new plan, under consideration by the Reagan administration, to tax unemployment benefits. According to a spokesman, it would "make unemployment less attractive."

President Reagan did not like the media constantly reporting about economic distress. "Is it news that some fellow out in South Succotash someplace has just been laid off, that he should be interviewed nationwide?" He would have been pleased to hear that after six years of college, some people considered themselves fortunate, almost blessed, to be allowed to teach college composition for $250 per month per class; or rewarded to have started at box boy as an undergraduate and in six short years had become night manager.

An ad from Mattel for children's computers said, "Now you can get a smarter kid than Mom did." Did college composition teachers discuss the ungrammatical awkwardness of this sentence? And why was Mattel advertising computers for children when some people, even those who taught college composition, were still using electronic typewriters with "correctible" lift-off letters?

Responding to the buzz regarding Nancy Reagan's appetite for fancy gowns, a White House spokesman said that the First Lady's only intention was to help the national fashion industry. Some people, especially those who rode bikes to work—without making a connection or considering it a protest—stopped wearing skirts entirely (even that brown corduroy wedding skirt).

Bottles of Tylenol were laced with cyanide in Chicago area stores and pharmacies. Seven people with headaches died of poisoning.

The Equal Rights Amendment also died.

4150 followers of the Rev Sun Myung Moon, (2075 of them women), were married in a mass ceremony in Madison Square Garden.

"You know," Ronald Reagan reportedly said to the Lebanese foreign minister, "your nose looks just like Danny Thomas's."

1983

The Navy thought maybe it should eliminate expenses such as $780 screwdrivers, $640 toilet seats, and $9,606 Allen wrenches.

HIV was identified. By this time Haitian men were no longer blamed for carrying the disease. Fashion prognosticators predicted ultra thin would soon not be considered stylish, since those suffering with AIDS were ravaged by weight loss. Plumpness, however, did not find its way into contemporary style. Anyone who was still a virgin in 1980 when they met their future husband, then got married in 1981, was probably not ever going to experience uninhibited sexual experimentation or promiscuity.

Just Say No (also) became the (only) official anti drug slogan.

The same year Karen Carpenter died of anorexia at the age of 32 (which would not do anything to help chubbiness come into fashion), a new pop star named Madonna released her first album. Her voice was compared to Minnie Mouse on helium. Some people, however, weren't buying new albums at the same rate they had when they lived with their parents. So they might own several Carpenters, but no Madonna. One of the Beach Boys also died this year, but no one remembers where they were when they heard Dennis Wilson drowned. This might have meant something, but nobody wondered what.

A White House spokesman said "preposterous" to conjecture about an invasion of Grenada. The following day, because the media was not permitted to cover the mission, the press received, from the White House PR office, photos of Reagan in his pajamas being briefed on the invasion of Grenada.

"I think some people are going to soup kitchens voluntarily," said Ed Meese (who, it turned out, was the same guy who came up with the plan to tax unemployment benefits). "I know we've had considerable information that people go to soup kitchens because the food is free and that that's easier than paying for it... I think that they have money."

$3.35 was still the minimum hourly wage.

Ed Meese (whatever his official position, he seemed to do and say a lot), gave a Christmas speech at the National Press Club: "Ebenezer Scrooge suffered from bad press in his time. If you really look at the facts, he didn't exploit Bob Cratchit. Bob Cratchit was paid 10 shillings a week, which was a very good wage at the time... Bob, in fact, had good cause to be happy with his situation. His wife didn't have to work... He was able to afford the traditional Christmas dinner of roast goose and plum pudding... So let's be fair to Scrooge. He had his faults, but he wasn't unfair to anyone."

1984

Ronald Reagan, preparing for a speech, was asked to test the microphone. He said, "My fellow Americans, I've signed legislation that will outlaw Russia forever. We begin bombing in five minutes."

Penthouse produced its first issue with a man on the cover (George Burns). Inside, the nude centerfold was an underage Traci Lords. In most countries, including the United States, it is (still) illegal to own or view this issue. The same edition includes photos of the first Black Miss America, Vanessa Williams, a few years younger, and nude. Although it was not illegal to look at her photos, Miss America was asked to resign.

Advertisement for Softsoap: *Ever wonder what you might pick up in the Shower?*
Advertisement for Sure: *Raise Your Arm if You're Sure.*
Advertisement for Wendy's: *Where's the Beef?*
(Still an) advertisement for the Army: *Be All You Can Be.*

Despite complaining that it cost too much to administer, Reagan signed The CIA Information Act of 1984, an amendment to the 1966 Freedom of Information Act. At the time the cost of administering the act was less than the Pentagon spent each year on marching bands.

Replacement umpires worked the playoff baseball games when umpires went on strike.

In a Presidential election debate, the former actor pointed out that much of the defense budget was for "food and wardrobe." The Great Communicator went blank in the middle of another answer, then said, "I'm all confused now," before giving his closing statement. Afterwards Nancy beseeched Reagan's aides: "What have you done to Ronnie?" Reagan later claimed that if he'd worn as much make-up as Mondale, he would have looked better in the debate.

The Census Bureau reported that 35.3 million Americans were living in poverty and that it was an 18-year high rate of 15.2% of the population. On a televised interview, Reagan said, "You can't help those who simply will not be helped. One problem that we've had, even in the best of times, is people who are sleeping on the grates, the homeless who are homeless, you might say, by choice."

Median household income: $22,415, up 20% since 1980; median cost of a house: $97,600, up 27% since 1980. Minimum wage: still $3.35/hour; still $6,968 for 40 hours of work, 52 weeks a year. Some people say this was the best year of their lives. Even some who were right at the median, or even a little below. Especially if things like that didn't matter. Especially since they'd just left home in 1980 and doing their own laundry and grocery shopping—even laundry and grocery shopping for two—was still fun.

1985

In its 100th year, Coca-Cola introduced "New Coke." Three months later, after consumer objection, it introduced "Coca-Cola Classic." Some wondered whether the whole snafu was a planned promotional gimmick.

While most of the American public will only remember The Great Communicator demanding, "Mr. Gorbachev, take down this wall," President Reagan also said, prior his visit to West Germany, that he would not be visiting any site of a former concentration camp because it would inflict too much shame on a country where "very few alive remember even the war." (Whereas American veterans were in their 60s and many of them quite alive.) But The White House pronounced that Reagan would lay a wreath at the Bitburg military cemetery, "an integrated home to the tombs of American and Nazi soldiers" (although there are no Americans graves there). President Reagan defended his West Germany itinerary: "I know all the bad things that happened in that war. I was in uniform for four years myself." (His uniform, more aptly called wardrobe, was in training films he starred in).

The number of Barbie dolls sold surpassed the American population. Some people had contributed more Barbie dolls than they would children (as in 2 dolls to 0 children). This helped, because that median income figure was for two people, not three (or four, or five…). Even though that wasn't some people's reason for not procreating.

A congresswoman, discussing Ronald Reagan's response to the balanced-budged bill, said, "We tried to tell him what was in the bill but he doesn't understand. Everyone, including Republicans, was just shaking their heads."

A *San Francisco Chronicle* reporter filed suit, under the new Freedom of Information Act, to obtain FBI files that would prove then-California Gov. Ronald Reagan spent years trying to launch an illicit "psychological warfare campaign" against "subversive" students and faculty. The *Chronicle's* questions were referred to Ed Meese (this guy again?), Reagan's chief of staff while he was governor (then too?). Meese said he did not remember planning any such activities. While it would take 17 years for the Chronicle to win the challenge and get documents that in fact proved these things true, in 1985 the FBI only released documents that appeared to have altered Reagan's part as a mole for the FBI in the McCarthy era. Some people, if they'd watched the news more often than ESPN or reruns of Kung Fu, might have wondered if their own activities in the 70s, including visiting a "known commune" (which has the same root word as communism) might have resulted in their own FBI file. But maybe some people knew, without knowing, that it was better to only know now as much as you knew then, when you visited the known-commune not knowing anything except you were there to get some grass.

1986

In thorny contract negotiations with musicians, management of the San Diego Symphony cancelled the season and locked out orchestra members. But even before negotiations officially broke down, management (anticipating the cancellation of the season)—to help pay for the newly refurbished former vaudevillian concert hall—booked shows by East Coast ballet companies, East Coast orchestras, a few comedians, and Barry Manilow.

The first postal killing happened in Oklahoma, netting 14 postal workers.

Ed Meese (who now, apparently, had a different job) suggested that employers should begin covertly watching their workers in "locker rooms, parking lots, shipping and mail room areas and even the nearby taverns" to apprehend them with drugs. (Just say no may not have been working. This was plan B.)

On November 25, as the Iran-Contra scandal simmered, Ed Meese said, "The President knew nothing about it." On November 26, on national television, Meese said, "The President knows what's going on." A month later Meese suggested maybe Reagan did give his approval to the deal, while he was under sedation after surgery.

California Highway Patrol Officer Craig Peyer—who, it turned out, had a history of stopping young women driving alone and talking to them for lengthy periods—pulled college student Cara Knott off the freeway and directed her down a dark, unused off-ramp. Their encounter ended when Peyer strangled Knott and threw her body off a bridge. The day after Knott's disappearance, local TV news chose Officer Peyer to do a safety-on-the-road segment.

An advertisement for Nike said, *Improve your husband's sex life.*
The Army reiterated, *Be All You Can Be.*

The space shuttle Challenger exploded, live on national television. Decades later, a new generation will be defined as those who weren't alive when Kennedy was shot, but who knew exactly where they were when the Challenger blew up. This simplistic division ignores those who not only recall clearly when they heard the Kennedy news (recess cancelled in 1st grade), *and* when they heard about John Lennon (the afternoon of their last final exam of the fall semester of their senior year of college) but now also remember when the Challenger exploded (while doing sit-ups on the living room floor with the TV on before going back to the laundromat to pick up the white load so there'd be clean underwear for work that evening).

1987

"I hope I'm finally going to hear some of the things I'm still waiting to learn," President Reagan said as the Iran-Contra hearings began. In his January Tower Commission interview about the affair, Reagan conceded that he authorized the arms sale to Iran. In February, Reagan told the Tower Commission that now he remembered that he did not sanction the arms sale. While narrating his (re)recollection from a memorandum, Reagan also read aloud his stage instruction (which some remember to say "be earnest" but they may be confusing it with the time George Bush Sr. read aloud his stage instruction, " message: I care").

President Reagan, in a *Washington Times* interview, reminisced wistfully about the time when Joseph McCarthy and the House Un-American Activities Committee exposed subversives.

The acronym AIDS–first used in 1982 when more than 1,500 Americans were diagnosed with the disease–was not said by Ronald Reagan in public until 1987, by which time 60,000 cases had been diagnosed, and half of those people had died. (Perhaps he was hoping it was still a mysterious disease among Haitian men, and maybe medical research money could go to beefing up immigration laws.) During a rally to protest the administration's (lack of) AIDS policies, Washington police wore large yellow rubber kitchen gloves when they arrested 64 demonstrators.

Playtex became the first to use live lingerie models in TV ads for the Cross Your Heart Bra. One might say they tested the waters for pantyshield companies who would, in the future, use live actresses to rave about a product that's "not for your period, just those other little leaks."

Gary Hart withdrew from the Presidential race when a sexual misdemeanor was exposed. One might propose that his candidacy died to save the future President Clinton.

At the Iran-Contra hearings, no one, including the President, ever definitively found out what he knew or when he knew it.

Prozac was approved by the FDA. Some people needed it right away. Even anyone who had used audacity, cunning and acumen to successfully fake a psychological exam and earn a 4F draft deferment in 1969—that same someone might come home from an hour on the grocery workers' picket line and cry, and be curled up in a fetal ball by the time anyone else came home, and not be able to afford Prozac without health insurance.

1988

The Bureau of Labor Statistics said that more than 6 million persons who worked, or looked for work at least half of the year, had family incomes below the official poverty level in 1987.

President Reagan on Michael Dukakis's campaign for the presidency: "You know, if I listened to him long enough, I would be convinced that we're in an economic downturn, and that people are homeless, and people are going without food and medical attention, and that we've got to do something about the unemployed."

A (new) Nike advertisement said, *Just Do It.*
Visa said, *It's Everywhere You Want to Be.*
The Army continued to say, *Be All You Can Be.*

A General Motors advertisement said, *This is not your father's Oldsmobile.* This campaign was credited with helping hasten the eventual demise of Oldsmobile, as the message confirmed for babyboomers the notion that Oldsmobile had been a make preferred by their fathers.

One and a half million acres of Yellowstone National Forest burned. For the fortunate who actually had that archetypical 50s and early 60s babyboomer upbringing, where the family station wagon, festooned with tourist decals, was certain to pull into Yellowstone at least once, this might have signaled the final death of childhood. Just to be certain biological clocks had been completely distorted, Old Faithful began to change its schedule.

Other factors contributing to early midlife-crises might have included the incursion of the first college-educated Gen-Xers into the job market the previous year. College composition teachers had already noticed the attitude-change in their students, and the number of business majors who wore Bush campaign pins. Then the morning of the election, when the pedestrian overpass spanning the freeway beside the university was adorned with Dukakis posters, some people actually thought "maybe all is not lost."

In his last television interview as President, when asked to comment on his Presidency overlapping with a sizable upsurge in the number of homeless people, Ronald Reagan wondered if many of these were homeless by "their own choice." He extended this analysis to people without jobs. For the second time he clarified his point by referencing the number of newspaper classified job listings.

1989

A new East German government prepared a law to lift travel restrictions for East German citizens. On November 9, a government spokesman was asked at a press conference when the updated East German travel law would come into force. His answer seemed flustered: "Well, as far as I can see, ... straightaway, immediately." Within hours, tens of thousands of people had gathered at the wall, on both sides. When the crowd demanded the entry be opened, the guards stood back, and the wall was disengaged, peacefully. It's possible the East German plan to allow "private trips abroad," never intended the complete and total opening and then destruction of the wall. Did Ronald Regan, almost one year out of office, try to take credit? (Yes.)

Pro-democracy demonstrators in Tiananmen Square were fired on by Chinese soldiers. Between 400 and 800 people were killed. (Reagan did not take the blame.)

Although he denied betting on baseball games, Pete Rose was banned for life from Major League Baseball. Why does it seem that Tiananmen Square and the Berlin Wall faded from the news quicker than Rose's fall from fame?

Ted Bundy was executed in Florida's electric chair. This event did not muster much outcry. There is still more debate over whether Rose should be allowed back into baseball than the efficacy of the death penalty, although, admittedly, Rose is a slightly better example for debating baseball's betting rules than Ted Bundy is for discussing capital punishment. However, while Bundy simply solidified for the Right their belief in society's moral right to kill undesirables, it only caused shades of grey for the Left, some of whom were distracted further by the realization that even mating with someone of the same political persuasion didn't guarantee a sublime unison, and some kinds of disillusionment could not be fixed, even with Prozac.

Since 1980, the median income went up $11,196 or 63%. The median cost of house went up $72,400 or 94%. The overall cost of living rose 48% while minimum wage was still $3.35/hour. If you went to college, but didn't major in business or engineering, medicine or law, you could probably hover right near the median 2-person household income of $28,906, provided you sustained the 2 people in the household.

Some people got married this year; actually two million four-hundred-three thousand two-hundred-sixty-eight. A nearly as impressive number, one million one-hundred-fifty-seven thousand, were divorced.

Although, later, the 80s would be called—usually by patronizing college students who'd grown up in soft middle-class homes—the era of superficiality and decadence, some people never got to become yuppies or conspicuous consumers or marital swingers or weekend cokeheads. Maybe they already were all they were going to be.

AMINA CAIN

Black Wings

I want to know what it is like to be asexual. I read an article about the asexual movement and asexual rights and though I feel like a sexual person, I crave something else. In the mornings I sit down to think, but there is something that gets in the way, and I think it might be everybody else's sexualities. I have met someone and asked him if we can just read books together. To my surprise, he has agreed.

It is hot and humid tonight and we are reading *Lolita*. After we read for a while we take a bike ride, and when we are tired we get off our bikes and sit against a concrete wall. From where we sit I can see a small part of the ocean. This is what I think about the whole time we are sitting against the wall—not other people's sexualities, not *Lolita*, but about this small piece of the ocean.

Against the concrete wall we begin to read again and though I don't still think only of the ocean, it begins to enter the story of *Lolita*. I become aroused at certain points in the book. I hold his hand when this happens, and I think he can feel me through my hand.

A pair of black wings are left on the sidewalk in front of my house. At first I like seeing them there, as if someone has tried to communicate something to me; later they are ominous and I wonder what this person is trying to say. They are the size a woman would have if she had wings. Maybe a woman who was at a party was wearing them, and when she got tired of carrying them on her back she left them here.

Then I see someone I used to know, and she tells me she is sorry she was ambivalent when we were having a relationship. "Why are you telling me this now?" I ask. She says she doesn't know. We are standing next to a pilot who is talking on his cell phone. Afterwards, he walks with me along the hot streets. No one is outside, except in one yard, where a group of people are playing badminton.

"Don't worry. Everyone is ambivalent," the pilot tells me. "I was ambivalent towards my wife."

"I'm not worried."

"She'll regret it."

The plants here are filled with water. The pilot touches one.

"I know."

My boyfriend and I kiss for the first time. Sometimes I feel like a piece of grass that is so weak it falls forward, or a computer someone has just dropped on the ground.

One night the pilot calls me and says he is walking next to the ocean. He will fly to China early in the morning.

"Where are you?" he asks.

"I'm also near the ocean." The waves break over a concrete wall.

"Are you still sad?"

When I get home, my boyfriend is leaning against my gate waiting for me. He tells me a story about his day.

"I saw a woman drop her child," he says.

"Did you do anything?"

"No."

"Do you want to?"

We stand against the gate, and then go inside the house to read. I sit on the couch listening to his voice. It is difficult for me to concentrate, even though he is at a good passage. He reads one sentence and then I hear it again and again. *Last night we sat on the piazza, the Haze woman, Lolita and I.* I get up out of my body and walk around every part of the room.

I asked the woman who was ambivalent towards me if she would ever want to own a horse and she said no, but in my mind I had seen her riding a horse in a field. I never told her I saw her like this.

"How do you see me?" I asked her.

"What do you mean?"

"When you think about me."

"I just think that you're you."

"But what is that?"

"A person. A woman."

It's dark. I close the shutters and lie down on my bed on top of the sheets. My boyfriend is still reading, and now I hear very clearly what he says.

"Should I keep going?"

"Just a little while longer."

Every move I make is bigger than it really is. If I move my leg, there is something strange about it and everyone is able to see it. He lies down next to me on the bed, and when he moves he looks strange. His arm falls away from his shoulder.

I think about my boyfriend while I am in the bathtub, or when I am lying on my couch. I am always surprised at how long I can think about him. It doesn't seem healthy to think about him for a whole afternoon, especially since I see him everyday.

Once, when I was in China, I lay on a bed all day thinking about someone. Mostly when I was there I swam in a river, but on that day I lay around in bed. That night I got up and walked around the town. It was hot, and I didn't know anyone, and though it was a small town it was very crowded. I walked through those crowds, sometimes stepping into a small shop, until I eventually made my way to the river. There I saw many young couples standing next to each other in the moonlight. The couples watched the water or yelled to their friends. I thought briefly of the person I had been thinking about that day, but I didn't want to think of another person anymore. It had exhausted me.

In China I was around people everyday, though I wasn't with them. When I took a walk in a secluded place I would run into several others walking on the same path. One evening I walked through an area that had been mined. There was an explosion. I thought it was me someone wanted to blow up because the explosion was so close. A few minutes later I was around lots of people again.

At an internet café, I e-mailed one of my friends to tell him what had happened. I also told him about the river, and the many small peaks surrounding the town. Then I looked around the room. Everyone was typing so quickly. When I closed my eyes to listen, the sound of typing was loud and fast.

I do everything slowly. When I am supposed to get work done I lie around and think of someone. I watch things blow along the street. That is why I want to be asexual. I am focused on the wrong things. If I am inside sitting next to an open window and I hear a dog bark, it sounds like everything I wish I were. Something pure; something honest. It makes me sad I am so diluted. When I read a book I am thinking of the ocean. When I look at the ocean I am thinking about a book. I want to just look at the ocean.

One night I hear something. When I go outside, I see two women fighting in the street. One of them is punching the other. The woman who is being hit has blood on her face, and the other woman has blood on her hand. I've never seen a fight before.

The woman who has blood on her hand looks up at me. I look at her. I close my eyes and listen to them fighting again.

I keep that fight with me no matter what I do. Even when I am reading *Lolita* with my boyfriend I think about those women.

"What's wrong?" he asks.

"I saw a fight."

"Between who?"

"Two women. It made me a different person."

He sets the book on the floor. "What kind of person?"

"A normal one."

I walk by the ocean and think of nothing but the ocean. I put my hand in the waves and feel nothing but the waves. But it doesn't last. I try to make it last. The water is green and clear, heavy with salt. On the beach a teenager is walking around with a video game close to his face. We are the only ones here. The game is small and black and the sun reflects off of it onto the water.

I ask my boyfriend if he likes *Lolita* and he says yes. I ask him if he imagines Dolores Haze. Yes.

"Do you imagine me?"

"Sometimes. But you made it clear that you only want to read books together, so I try not to."

He hasn't even tried to have sex with me.

"What if I want you to imagine me?"

"I thought you were asexual."

I look at him. "I don't know what I am."

DIMITRI ANASTASOPOULOS

Signs of Intrauterine Life

I wanted to have a baby. I knew, of course, the basics of *making* a baby, but I was mostly ignorant of the process of *having* a baby, that is, the decisions one makes (and by one, I mean, myself) after I—enthusiastically, energetically, athletically—undertook the basic initial act of making a baby. Conception happened, and I was there. After conception, the other body involved in the baby making process was naturally given priority as the central site of baby growth, the site of production and, also, the site of a certain magic and wonder. Like many expectant fathers, especially first fathers, I felt I had to educate myself about the birth process. I needed to read books, seek out doctors, talk to friends. And so I began an activity of information-seeking together with the baby-grower. In fact, the baby-grower's constant presence in my information-seeking activity only emphasized to me that my own knowledge of the stages of the birthing process were dictated by the rhythms of the baby-grower's birthing cycle.

This secondary position afforded to the male should be accepted without hesitation (if one wants to be an ethical partner in the baby-making enterprise) although this does not preclude the male from considering the various psychic and bodily impressions which impact the male exclusively. One must begin, first, by acknowledging that there is very little scientific information about the male's physical and psychological experience of forty weeks of pregnancy. Granted, there are words of advice for expectant fathers, self-help books and the like, though none of these address the physical and pathological effects of the birth process on the male. So I set out to discover them on my own. Early on, I began to consider—in addition to a range of intuitive or instinctual reactions to the fact of fatherhood—certain bodily reactions as well, and through research into several case studies involving male participation in birth (informatics assessments of meetings with obstetricians, to child-birth classes, and especially actual births themselves), I gradually began to accumulate notes which have evolved into this expectant father's notebook.

At the Royal School of Medicine in Edinburgh, a study linked the geometric shape of certain common forms of architecture to the spatial conditions of the womb. According to Dr. Jean-Gilles Ballard, "The right-angle spiral of a stairwell reminds us of similar *biases* within the chemistry of the biological kingdom." Obviously, Ballard is referring here to well accepted visual reconstructions of DNA patterns in the form of spiraling staircases. But Ballard goes beyond this to state that the space between each stair of the spiral—not unlike a gill slit when viewed from below—appears as the primitive precursor to the embryo: that is the last human structure to preserve perfect symmetry in all planes. Ballard states, "Our bodies may conceal the rudiments of a symmetry not only about the vertical axis but also the horizontal." Ballard—citing Goethe's sacral skull in which the vertebrae and the pelvis correspond to the form of the skull—considers the bodily symmetries of lung and kidney, eyes and testicles, nose and penis, as examples of asymmetrical separations which proceed directly from single cells inside the blastosphere. If one accepts a translation of the body into geometry and therefore the architecture of the world around us, then thinking through the embryonic origins of the human body may give us insight into the rudimentary forms we inhabit outside the body.

Later on, I found photoplates that reproduced cellular division in the blastosphere stage. I examined the cells of the blastosphere as though looking down the cone of a kaleidoscope, albeit a broken one whose colorful and symmetrical crystals had hypostasized under the lens. Initially, I considered that the cells in the photoplates represented the last form of a cellular symmetry that would eventually evolve into a soft jelly-like tadpole replete with axolotl eyes and tail. This is, after all, how we begin as human beings, I thought: first out of nothing, then into a perfect symmetry, which then finally explodes in a mininova that has macrocosmic impact on the rest of the baby's life. We move from harmony to chaos, in such a manner, I thought. Eventually, however, I found film footage of blastosphere growth in which the symmetry in the static photoplates was gone. In the film it was evident that the cells were dividing asymmetrically from the start. Burbling pockets in the northeast quadrant of the microscopic lens were not met with similar burblings in the southwest quadrant, as one might have expected.

What then of my metaphor of harmony and chaos, a metaphor influenced by Dr. Ballard's research at the Royal School of Medicine in London, which sought to cast all human life in terms of a residual longing for the harmony of the blastosphere, for a perfect Amniotic Return? This nostalgic vision was only possible, I realized, when scientific information was cast in its static form. Beauty, under this lens, was only possible when beheld under the broken kaleidoscope—whereas the film version of the blastosphere spoiled the symmetrical paradise. The scientific information provided in the film was always in the process of becoming, never fully available for observation that could be authenticated and verified in the terms I wanted: in terms of harmony and chaos. I wanted to know, relative to each cell's microcosmic existence, what accounted for asymmetric spasmodic movements. But microcosmically, each cell was always changing, and the mortal macrocosmic blastosphere could never forgive the relative immortality of each of its cells, because the blastosphere's very existence depended on each cell's becoming. Looking at the films and the photos, it was immediately evident that my intervention in the baby-making process after conception would depend on information that always arrived too late, information that, once authenticated and verified, became practically useless for my purposes. If I privileged a life inside the womb, a life immediately after conception, I could only do so with the greatest force of imagination possible, an act of imagining fueled by nostalgic chemicals. I was the father who recognized that the child was never innocent (in the symmetrical sense, that is not the moral sense), and that the baby's next stage of growth couldn't be entirely anticipated.

In the midst of studying the blastosphere, I met—together with the baby grower—the obstetrician. This initial meeting in which the doctor regarded the baby grower as an incubator, and the male—that is, myself—as nothing more than a dolt, was quite productive in that we were allowed to observe the doctor manipulating his imaging technology all over the site of production. As I looked at the monitor, I was told to disregard the fetus (its tiny heart beating) and to focus instead on the amniotic sac around the shell, the uterine wall itself, and the chorionic shell surrounding the fetus (the chorion being the last remnants of the egg). The doctor informed me that the fetus' entire future depended on the complete fusion of these three concentric rings. As the doctor explained, "The inner portion of the placenta is the chorionic plate, and a fusion of the amnion and chorion must take place. They are artifactually separated there." "Excuse me," I interrupted the doctor. "But according to Dr. Scoober at the University of Georgia Medical Center, the chorion need not fuse until 16 to 18 weeks after conception, so this information creates a host of expectations if it's indeed true that this fusion will determine the fetus's viability. Can you explain to me all the possible permutations of membrane to membrane to membrane fusion? What if the amnion fuses to the uterine wall, but not to the chorion? What if the chorion fuses to the amnion but not the uterine wall? What if the chorion penetrates the amnion and fuses to the uterine wall? What if the amnion fuses to the chorion prior to its fusion to the uterine wall? What if the amnion fuses to the uterine wall prior to its fusion with the chorion? What if the chorion penetrates the amnion and fuses to the uterine wall prior to the uterine wall fusing with the amnion? What if the uterine wall fuses with the amnion prior to the chorion penetrating the amnion and fusing with the uterine wall?" The doctor answered with an answer that was not an answer at all, but rather a new range of variables that proliferated and expanded the possibilities. "Between chorionic plate and basal plate are placental villi in various planes of section," he said, "each with a vascular connection to umbilical blood vessels in the chorionic plate. The placenta has a fetal portion, composed of the chorionic plate and villi, and a maternal portion, the decidua basalis." As he spoke, I wrote everything down, and assured myself that I would consider the entire range of possibilities over the next several weeks. I subsequently filled seven notebooks with all the possible variations which the fusion of part to part to part to part might undertake, and I intended to present my considerations to the doctor.

When the next visit came in the sixteenth week, the range of possibilities which I had sketched were all rendered irrelevant since the chorion had indeed fused to the amnion and the uterine wall. There were no longer any distinctions between the three shells. It was literally impossible to determine from the ultrasound whether chorion had first fused to amnion or to uterine wall or which of all the other possible permutations had occurred first in this chain. Complete fusion had happened, and this fact had a way of blunting all my speculation. From that point on, any consideration of the fusion process only served to pique my intellectual curiosity. Moreover, the doctor was quickly moving on to other matters thereby mooting the deliberate descriptions I had jotted down in my notebook.

"Look at the face," he said, as he pointed to the monitor where a skeletal negative of a child stared directly at the viewer complete with tiny hands on either cheek, dark eye sockets, calcified nasal formation, long jawline: the fetus resembled Munch's homunculus without the angst, though a father could be forgiven if he read terror in the dark eye sockets, frustration in the rapid grinding of the jaw. My first look into the baby's eyes left me cold and without fatherly feeling. Father *to* a homunculus. It was enough to make an expectant father reconsider the depiction of intrauterine reality through imaging technology—a reality which was previously only accessible through an act of the imagination. In black and white, in silvery negative traces, the baby was not represented as the sweet being I knew it actually was. "Look at that," the doctor exclaimed. "You see the large organ directly under the chest?" he asked. "That's the bladder. Your baby has an enormous bladder, and it appears to be grossly efficient." Those were his exact words. I began to imagine a grossly large bladder inside a normal human body outside the womb, and though the idea of a large bladder seemed positively grotesque, I was mollified and impressed that my child's bladder was also highly efficient, if not grossly so. That must be a good thing, I thought. Soon enough, everyone in the room, the doctor, a nurse, myself, as well as the baby grower, witnessed a movement that shook me straight. We saw the fetus's jaws open wide, like an alligator's—to use a common metaphor—then close quickly, open wide again. "What is it doing?" I asked. The doctor answered that it was swallowing rather large amounts of amniotic fluid. "Does that explain why its bladder is working overtime?" I asked. "Perhaps," was the doctor's only answer.

When I went home that evening, I researched this process by which the fetus swallows amniotic fluid and I found that the process of swallowing inside the womb was largely superfluous since the fetus derives its necessary nutrients through the placenta.

In fact, I was mortified to discover that amniotic fluid consists largely of the fetus's own waste products, mainly urine. The fetus apparently delighted in swallowing waste, and also in processing the waste in a grossly efficient manner. Did I still long for an amniotic return? Not after this discovery. My insight into this uterine existence, garnered through technology, emphasized the primitive capabilities of the fetal body. Even as the womb served as the site of production where the baby was made, the baby itself was already operating as a machine without consciousness or morality of any kind, unless I were to assume there was a quantifiable pleasure in the swallowing of amniotic fluid. Indeed, in a female fetus, eggs were already developing that might one day repeat this act of mechanical reproduction. The important thing to remember is that my absolute exposure, my absolute susceptibility, to the rudimentary images of the fetal machine—through imaging technology—had forced me into a curiously scientific if detached relationship to the baby still growing at the site of production. My will to understand the birth process, to become more informed, had succeeded in emphasizing the evolutionary and mechanical facts of human gestation. I was not prepared for this. In fact, I was deeply troubled by it. I wanted to build a sentimental attachment to my child. I wanted to adopt the caring and responsible father's demeanor: I wanted to learn to love the child *prior* to its birth. Instead, the more I thought and learned about the child, the more detached I became. I needed to obliterate information that always deferred to a not yet verified future, and which therefore anticipated a future that would never ever arrive. I needed facts, no feedback loop at all.

TOM LA FARGE

Introduction to Three Writhings

Reeling and Writhing were taught at the school in the sea attended by the Mock-Turtle in *Alice in Wonderland.* I have appropriated "writhing" as a term for writing with constraints. The Writhing Society, which I lead with Wendy Walker, meets every week at Proteus Gowanus, an interdisciplinary gallery and reading room in Brooklyn, to experiment with this sort of composition. The most famous source for such procedures is the French group Oulipo, who have invented many of them, but there are many others. I am working to compile and explain, with examples, all of them that I can find out about in a series of pamphlets, *13 Writhing Machines*, after which I hope to tackle an anthology of reelings.

The three pieces included here all perform operations that require a dictionary or thesaurus. In the first, "Sans Merci," two lines of Keats' ballad "La belle dame sans merci" have been rewritten by substituting for the original nouns, verbs, and adjectives their synonyms from a thesaurus. I have used all the synonyms listed but have grouped them a little differently. In "I beg to differ," the oulipian procedure called "definitional literature" was applied: for every word in the title phrase I substituted its definition, drawn from a paperback Merriam's dictionary. Then I did it again. Then in the third sentence I substituted synonyms selected from a thesaurus. Then I replaced those words with their definition in the Oxford English Dictionary. For "Running from Dissent" I opened the paperback dictionary at random and used the running titles at the head of the page, which name the first and last word defined on it. The constraint required me to use both with just one other word in between and to continue to the last page with a running-title-word beginning with D, the letter I opened to. If this constraint has a name, I don't know what it is. I think I may have made it up.

Sans merci

I happened chanced lighted or lucked on, accosted, affronted, brushed into, ran into across or up against, dug up, crossed, confronted, encountered, faced, rendezvoused or fell in with, grappled or got together or rubbed shoulders with, saw, stumbled upon, found, saluted, tumbled, tussled, wrestled, and struck a female human, gal, femme, gentlewoman, girl, grandmother, madam, matron, mother, and sister in the bottoms, grassy field, grassland, heath, lea, meadow, pasturage, plain, prairie, steppe, veldt, carpet, and rug, full physically attractive, admirable, alluring, angelic, appealing, beauteous, bewitching, buxom, charming, classy, comely, cute, dazzling, delicate, divine, elegant, enticing, excellent, exquisite, fair, fascinating, fine, foxy, good-looking, gorgeous, graceful, grand, handsome, ideal, lovely, magnificent, marvelous, nice, pleasing, pretty, pulchritudinous, radiant, ravishing, refined, resplendent, shapely, sightly, splendid, statuesque, stunning, sublime, superb, symmetrical, taking, well-formed, winsome, and wonderful, the adolescent, ankle-biter, babe, bairn, bambino, brat, cherub, chick, cub, descendent, dickens, imp, infant, innocent, issue, juvenile, kid, kiddie, lamp, little angel darling doll or one, minor, mite, moppet, neonate, nestling, newborn, nipper, nursling, offspring, preteen, progeny, pubescent, shaver, small fry, sprout, squirt, stripling, suckling, tadpole, teen, teenager, teenybopper, toddler, tot, tyke, urchin, whippersnapper, young one, youngster, and youth of a bogie, brownie, elf, enchanter, fay, genie, gnome, goblin, gremlin, hob, imp, leprechaun, mermaid, nisse, nymph, pixie, puck, siren, spirit, sprite and sylph.

I beg to differ

I ask for money, etc. from others, to be unlike. I request information about coins and banknotes used for payment from those not previously mentioned to be not characteristic. I hit up for dope about chicken feed and counting-house characters at home with gravy from those not heretofore touched on to be peculiar. I strike with aim or intent at some distance above the ground or earth as representative of any thick liquid or semi-fluid used as an article of food, or as a lubricant on the outside or outer surface of a girl or young woman eating, grazing, to be taken side by side with, along with, or in addition to a private chamber, closet, or cabinet appropriated to business and correspondence, a graphic sign or symbol answering the question *Where?* (passing into *Whereby? Whence? Whither?*), the place of one's dwelling or nurturing, with the conditions, circumstances, and feelings which naturally and properly attach to it and are associated with it adversely to the fat and juices which exude from flesh during and after the process of cooking, denoting removal, abstraction, separation, expulsion, exclusion, or the like, indicating things or persons pointed to or already mentioned, in a copular sentence with the complement preceding the subject for ironic emphasis, indicating the limit of a movement or extension in space, to have place in the objective universe or realm of fact, with subordinate clause understood after verbs of thought or utterance or impersonal verbs of seeming unlike others, *sui generis*; special, remarkable; distinctive.

Running from dissent

Dissent is dissolute, dissolution will distill, distillation renders distraught, distress creates disturbance. Ditches then divest, divide the dizzy. DNA drives the doer. Doff, don't doll up, Dolly holds dominion. Donate, you dormant dormitory of doubtful, doubting Thomas runs downhill, downlinks all drag on, drag queens simply draw out, draw up and dress up, dressy golfers driving. Drizzle renders drowsy. Drub me ductile, duds can dumbfound, dumbfounded ain't durable, duration ain't dynamic. Dynamite is earnest.

WILLIAM WALSH

American Fried Questions

A derived text sourced from *American Fried: Adventures of a Happy Eater* by Calvin Trillin, 1974.

I don't suppose your friends took you to Mary-Mac's on Ponce de Leon for a bowl of pot likker, did they? But who wants to hear a skin doctor saw away at the cello when Johnny Cash is right down the street? Who would have ever guessed, for instance, that the old Mexican street near downtown Los Angeles that looks as if it was restored by the MGM set department and stocked by one of the less tasteful wholesalers in Tijuana would have one place that served delicious hand-patted soft tacos packed with *picadillo* or *chicharron*? How can an innocent traveler be expected to guess that he is going to be subjected to the old Hollywood mystery-film trick of hiding the real jewel in a case full of paste imitations? Who controls the city council here? They have plates there? What do you mean 'plates'? How can people talk that way? What Mario's? Please, teacher, can we have some arithmetic? Have you ever heard of Henry Perry? You went to the original, you're sure, on Colorado? And you did ask for extra sliced tomatoes? Who wants to spend his time shelling almonds? Do you ever get hungry, Fats? Just what *did* you eat on a big day in Kansas City the week you gained seventeen pounds? Ever had their chili dogs? Is life worth living, Fats? Where else could you *forget* a restaurant like this? Who would wish such alternatives on a pal? But did you like it? Did it make you happy? Did you clean your plate? You sure you want angel-food cake and a glass of milk? Where do you usually go in Chinatown? Whadaya drive? Is that place still good? How could I begrudge Ben an additional day of rest, I asked myself, when I could come in any weekday and have my choice of baked farmer cheese with scallions or baked farmer cheese with vegetables or even baked farmer cheese with pineapple? Who was I to complain about a little break in my Houston Street routine when there were millions of people all over the world who would never taste Russ & Daughters chopped herring? Isn't she cute? Is the whitefish good? Could he now plan, as the final blow, cutting off my supply completely? Will the place be run the same way? Where would that leave me? But what if that person—the same person who has tasted the clams—happens to have a wife who would commit armed robbery for the right piece of chocolate cake and that wife has found the chocolate cake served in a restaurant in Edgartown, Martha's Vineyard, to be necessary to her continued happiness? What was a responsible person to do? Launch a citizen's inquiry to ascertain where justice lay between Nathan's and its pizza slicers? Cross the picket line but only eat hot dogs and French fries, which happen to be the best things at Nathan's anyway? Not go in but, in fairness, explain to the pickets that the decision had been based on cholesterol rather than political considerations? Is an eater being fair to the family he supports if he substitutes for Nathan's hot dogs some inferior lunch that so depresses him he performs badly at his daily task? But what if the son he supports grows up to be a radical professor of Latin American Studies and says one day, 'Father, did you break the picket line of the *possumbyistas*?' You think they have any plain chicken? You're not going to have another piece of strawberry pie, are you? What should I order if I don't want to start with the plain? What could possibly be in a seven-way? Red-eye gravy? Is it too late to turn back to Kentucky? How come everybody in the Village who wants to work as a waiter says he's really an actor? What do I want with actors? Did you check her teeth? Does she share her food? Isn't it accepted practice to let students with language problems write about their experiences so they can gain confidence? I really haven't the time to translate the entire wall so why don't you tell me which one you want translated most? Guess what Tricia Nixon Cox's favorite recipe is? How did you know about ketchup? Why don't we just eat here at the motel? Who, after all, would have ever expected to find the Great Dried Beef in the Sky (not to speak of a superb fried-seaweed dish) across from the Golders Green tube stop? Would I go to a French restaurant in Juarez? You know what he told me? How were the oyster loaves at the Acme today? Could it have been a mere coincidence that Willard Marriott, who owns what is presumably the kitchen most likely to get the contract, is a personal friend of Richard Nixon, a President who had a history of eating cottage cheese with ketchup (the 'old Nixon' we've heard so much about) and has raised a daughter whose favorite recipe is made with canned soup? Is it just happenstance that the Big Boy hamburger defended by William Edgett Smith as the best hamburger in the world—a defense that remains inexplicable by any rules of logical argument—is produced by a company that is now a totally owned subsidiary of the Marriott Corporation? Y'all got a license to serve them fresh vegetables? Have you tried our meatless chickenlike product? Could it be, I wondered, that a crowd of dieticians had actually been lured into Joe's Jungle? Does justfolksism go that far?

Michael Joyce and Alexandra Grant

About Alexandra Grant's work "Nimbus- wire, shadow, motor, light after Michael Joyce's nimbus, 2004"

Anyone who grew, as I did, in snow country can recall the shape of breath in air, perhaps even sense how the words secret themselves, crystalline passengers gazing out from inside these small, vagrant cumuli, drifting away like zeppelins, the taut viscous glint of tiffany glass soap bubbles suddenly popping, momentarily leaving a droplet suspended in air, dry and flat, then fast falling; this dissipation apparently prompted by nothing more than foreplay, the exquisite tension of coherence, no matter how much one suspects some fairytale stray breeze, twig poke, small bird, whirling seed, hot exhalation of soil, sea or far-away other. But to think that what one writes shapes itself likewise before you, the recurrence of one's ordinary rhythms, the accustomed vowels and consonantal articulations themselves reticulated like lewd brambles clinging to one another in a dank swale (or, perhaps more decorously though no less fervid, the lofty, gloriously imbricated branches of the American Elm trees looming high above lovers on a shaded bench along the Poets' Walk in Central Park on a warm April morning) is unimaginable.

That the mind—or what escapes it as breath written down and scored for another's breathing—itself forms whorls, coves, and eddies like the paisley of fingerprints—each sentence as distinct from another, the procession of even commonplace marked like the bright network of silvery pores upon the skin of an infant—is a surprise.

It is a shift from all this, from thinking "I wrote this, do you see" to actually (the act of it, the handiwork) seeing the craft of it before you like a blooming, the words twisted, boustrophedonic elephants, circus creatures, their backward wire shapes sprawling along the only vaguely longitudinal coordinates of unseen magnetic fields, and yet seemingly fastened upon nothing, viz. how the bright and spiraling tentacles of spring Clematis grasp tenderly for support, a rickety framework within which God, wearing sandals, hangs out the elements of the world like a jewelry maker in a market stall his wire earrings.

Seeing Alexandra Grant's work "Nimbus," conceived "after" a text of mine, I felt a delight in my own language that I have not felt otherwise, her art giving the shape of breath and hand to the air and yet knowing that, were these words some other ones or one's—other words or another man or woman's—they would form themselves differently under her pricked fingers, wind the languorous knots of their wire orbits otherwise; knowing that in some sense it does not matter, will not, whether anyone has read them before this or ever will, the reading now quite something else, a making one's way through the void, the silvery threads of spittle of Bombyx mori, the silk worm, weaving a cocoon like the Milky Way seen from beyond this galaxy. To be outside language and yet to see oneself woven in it is a pleasure like a dream.

We stood there, a half dozen of us on the sidewalk on a warm February night in Echo Park, Los Angeles, looking back in through the storefront gallery window, each of us wondering aloud at the fragile beauty of this spinning thing, how it painted the light like a dream does, the runes of it glinting in air and shadowing dark against the illuminated wall.

—Michael Joyce

POINT

"nimbus," by michael joyce, 2004. written by the author in 2004. paper on pencil.

POINT is a passage of text titled "Nimbus," written by Grant's long-time collaborator, hypertext author Michael Joyce. Representing the written word as a medium for conceptual communication, this piece serves as source material for the remaining iterations.

You want to see where she wants you to whil
says what you see. You want to see what she
but it's all too easy breezy. The sky enfolds us like a
Someone has just come into the room distracted by
hole of ceiling. We right ourselves & greet her w
A casual salute. She winks and imperceptibly waggl
Everyone seems to be & waves or waving a
something & thus jointly for their ages. It's all
[illegible] story & lemons. The way the clouds are even
Red sails take warning. The swallow dips her w
in the gilt water ~~where~~, the seam ~~the~~ where the s
is soldered. "not soldiered, soldered," she laughs, delighted
how the eye can fool you. "Not blood, but silver," sh
goes on. Softly lapsing breasts pillow grandchildren an
Ageless lovers she meets in the supermarket near
the spectacular flower [illegible]. Still her old elasticity an
her stride. "It rhymes with titty," she giggles in a
naughty whisper. The ladies aspirate, delicate & sussurous
There is too much talk of things and few words eno
or what we see. We are embarrassed by the persistence
of eros and the constant rush of wind outside the window
Nothing happens. Singing children dance a perpetual
low circle upon Herr Althoin's famous Hippocampus,
their blue skirts like [illegible] or bell [illegible]

PLANE

alexandra grant, nimbus drawing, 2007. paper on pencil.

PLANE is Grant's translation of Joyce's text into drawing as she explores its patterns of grammar and sentence structure visually. Here, the artist highlights the visual aspect of writing by presenting words in reverse.

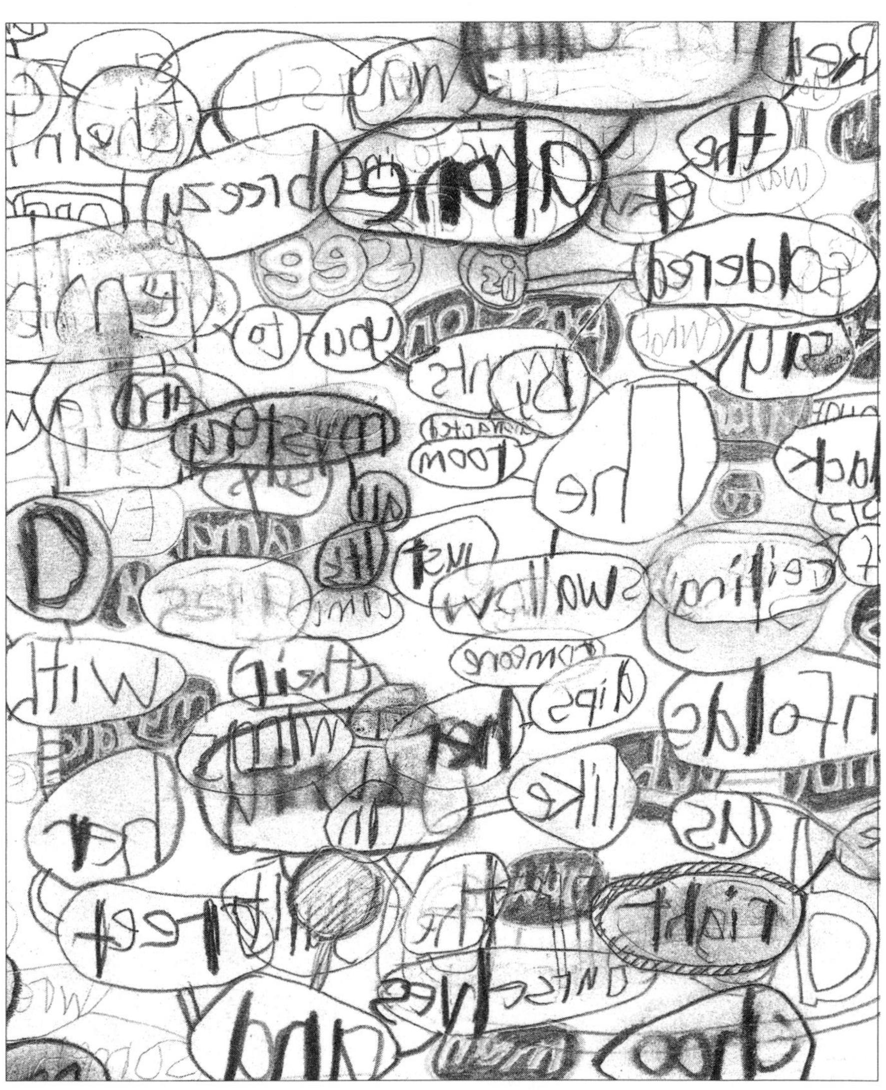

SPACE
alexandra grant, ¿dónde está la escalera al cielo? (Where is the ladder to heaven?), detail, 2007. wallpaper, edition of 10. publisher: the lapis press, culver city, ca.

In SPACE, drawing is translated into three dimensions via wire sculpture, work Grant refers to as "drawing without paper." These wire words cast shadows across the surface of the plane, further underscoring the word's physical existence. (This image is part of a wallpaper project Grant created for her show at MOCA.)

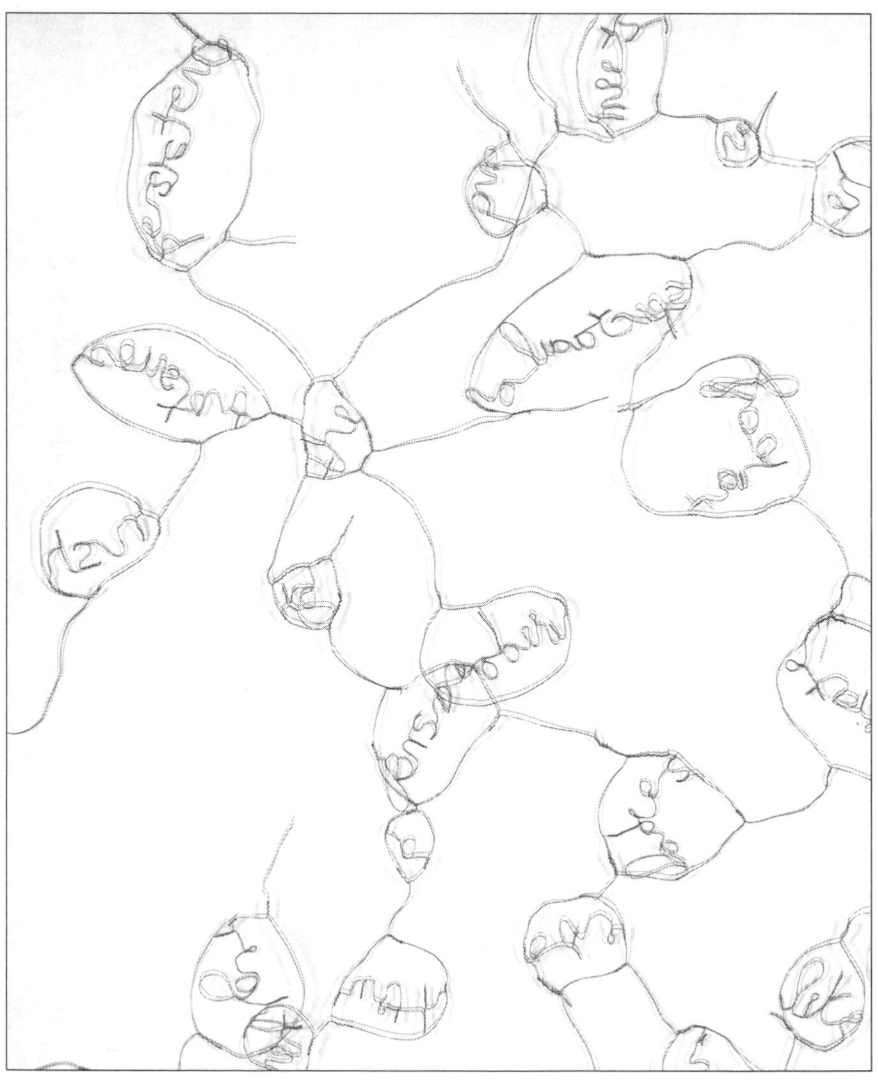

TIME

Series of stills of Alexandra Grant's "nimbus II," 2007. filmed at moca, april, 2007.

TIME is a series of stills from the film, MOTION, that documents the wire sculpture after its transformation into "nimbus II, 2007," a spinning globe of wire words (also installed at MOCA). Using the layout convention of the original text—left to right, top to bottom—the wire words no longer express a literary meaning, but instead suggest the passage of time.

MOTION, the fifth and final iteration, can be viewed at www.alexandragrant.com/motion.html or http://www.x-traonline.org/ArtistProjects/10_1ArtistsProject/iteration5.html

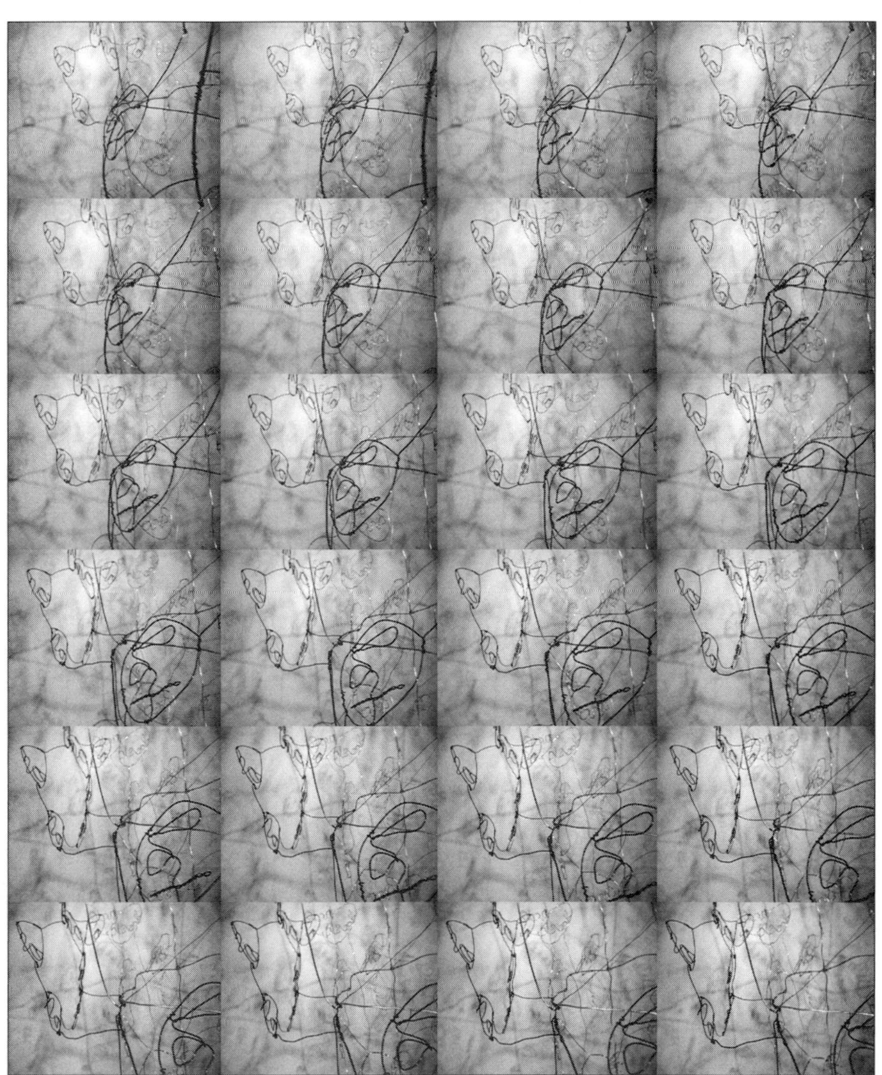

WILLIAM FULLER

Dives & Lazarus
(for Bonnie Barber)

There are two articles called Article Ninth
in them would still
be
holding and effective all the
provisions not negated by them
and these giving rise
to vexations
I could not have guessed at
but not even a hint of this falls to earth
deaf as ever
I made my way through the transformation unit
past thinning crowds raised in ditches
and I felt his presence
carefully cut to fit the frame
and out of this flies a kind of bat
on a perfectly level flight path
toward all kinds of people, apparently silent,
what is their common characteristic
with some exceptions many of them
have considerable accumulations
or bear witness to pure mysterious gold
in an effort to sustain themselves

ANGELA SZCZEPANIAK

AlphabeTics

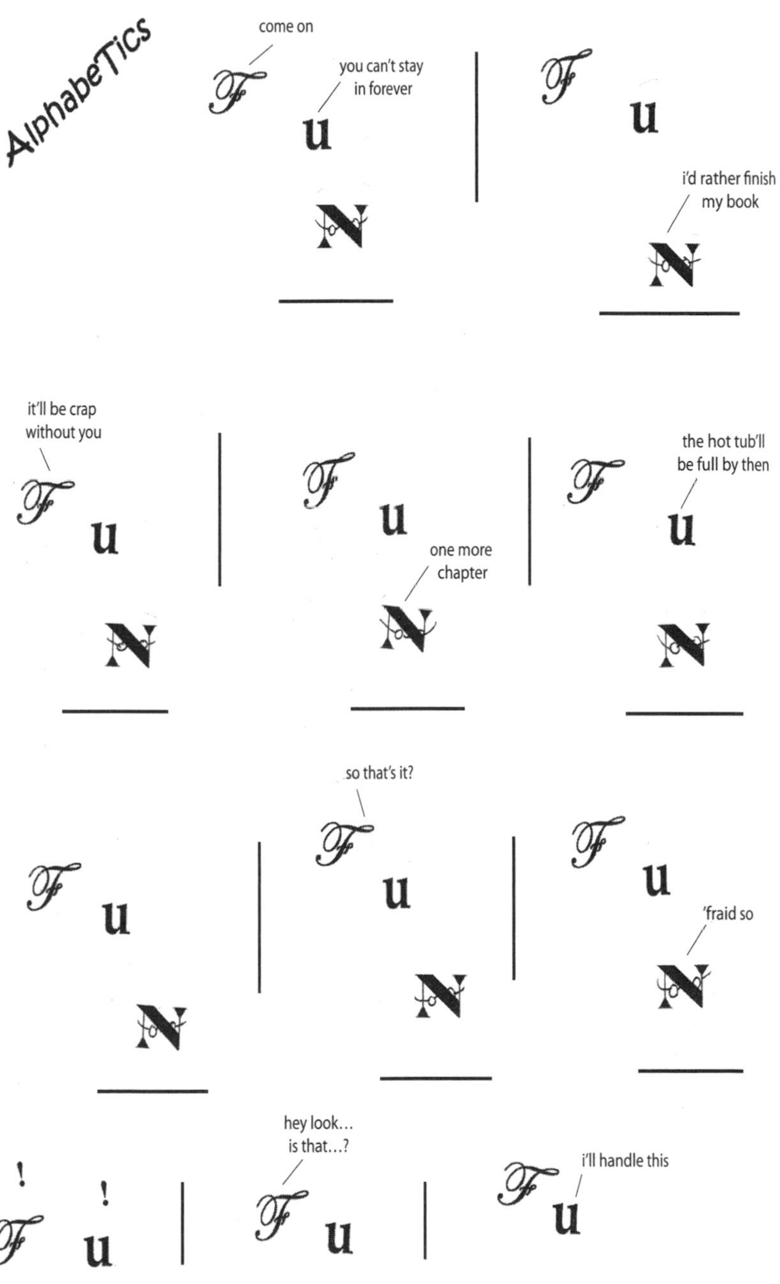

CK

The Merovingian Script Museum must be around here somewhere.

I knew we should have stopped for directions.

Just a few more blocks.

Are you sure it's safe? We should turn back—the children.

Nonsense! We'll miss the exhibit. I've been dying to see how they fit up the ligatures *by hand*.

Mummy! Their serif is... pointy.

Shhh. Mind your manners, dears. They're just... *common*.

This whole crowd is barely legible. Must be drugs.

I hear the carpet pages are magnificent.

And the Chelles! Extraordinary.

Just look at them—nibbed with iron gall ink. I suspect they haven't even *seen* a proper quill.

PILLOCK

That smell... if you don't get us out of here this instant I'm having you struck-over.

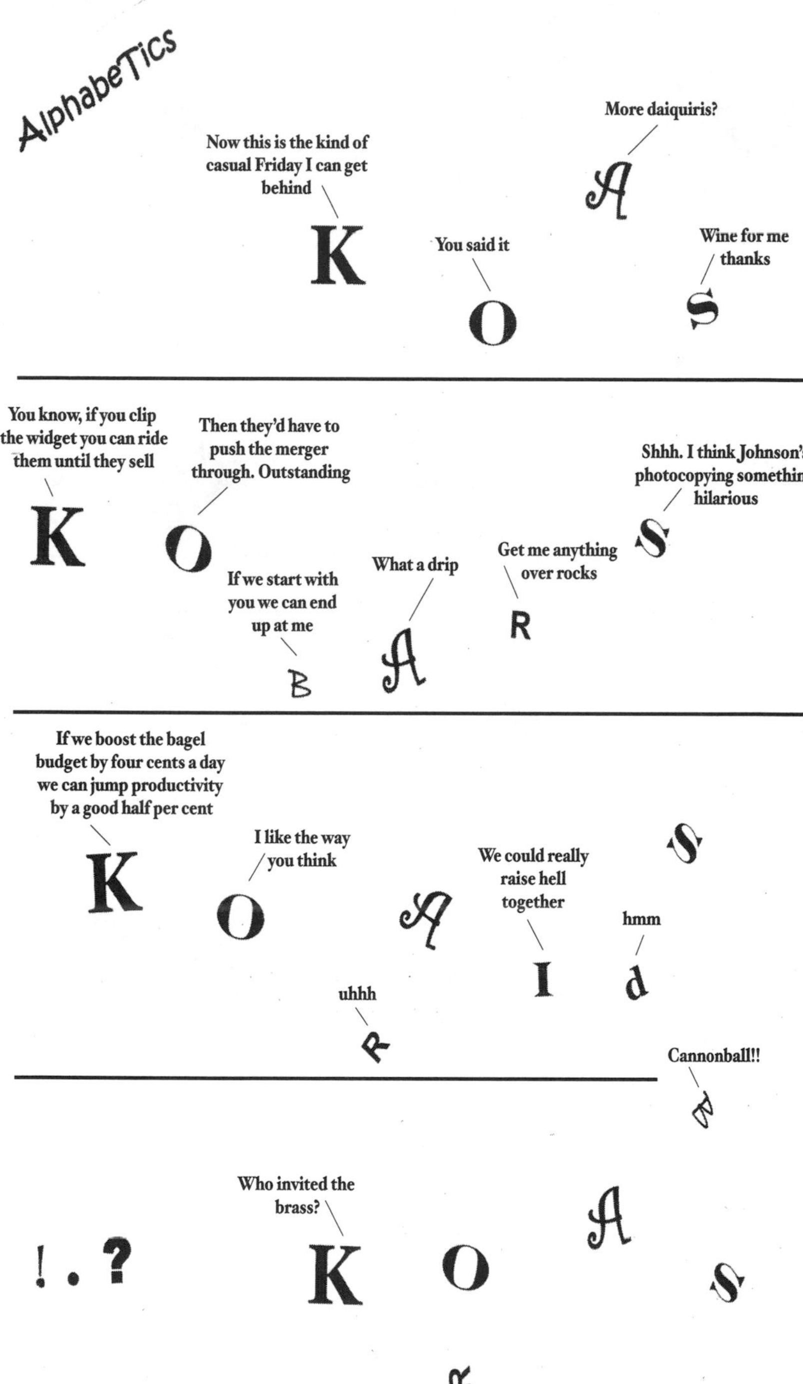
AlphabeTics
Now this is the kind of casual Friday I can get behind
K
You said it
O
More daiquiris?
A
Wine for me thanks
S
You know, if you clip the widget you can ride them until they sell
K
Then they'd have to push the merger through. Outstanding
O
If we start with you we can end up at me
B
What a drip
A
Get me anything over rocks
R
Shhh. I think Johnson's photocopying something hilarious
S
If we boost the bagel budget by four cents a day we can jump productivity by a good half per cent
K
I like the way you think
O
A
uhhh
R
We could really raise hell together
I
hmm
d
S
Cannonball!!
!.?
Who invited the brass?
K
O
A
S
R

The Monotype Sort, once roaming all manner of typesetting devices in robust herds, is now among the rarest of the great alphabetic beasts.

This slide, enhanced from a grainy amateur photograph, shows a magnificent specimen, a brawny *b*, at the peak of its vigour. This image remains one of the best modern examples of the beast ever captured by film or net.

specimen 13

Some call it an obsession. A hearty fascination. A bit of fancy run amok. Regardless of how you name it, I stand proud among the Mono game hunters. We are few, but mighty, and will not rest until we've captured, examined, and mounted every elusive husk of monotypography. Note the flirtatious fanned flourish of the *j*.

specimen 22
(in captivity)

Back when I was a novice, out on my first deep sea expedition, I had a dalliance with a coquettish *b*. Oh, she played coy at first. Batted her symmetry. Fluttered her mechanical florality. Then just as she was about to succumb to my twittering fingertips, she disappeared beneath the surface, lost under the depths of three thousand meters of saline obscurity. Biggest regret of my life.

specimen 26
(artist's rendering)

I once tasted a Monotype *O* that had washed ashore on an unpopulated beach. Sautéed a thin sliver off the tentacle in garlic and olive oil. It was bitter heaven.

specimen 42

CHRISTINE WERTHEIM

From +|'me'S-pace

Litteral Poetics

An Introduction to the sCUm Methodology

For the same Seeds compose both Earth and Seas,
The Sun, and Moon, Fruits, Animals, and Trees,
But their contexture, or their motion disagrees.
So in my Verse are Letters common found
To many words unlike in sense and sound;
Such great variety bare change affords
Of order in th' few Elements of Words.

And hence, as We discours'd before, we find
It matters much with what first Seeds we joyn'd,
Or how, or what position they maintain,
What motion give, and what receive again:
And that the Seeds remaining still the same,
Their order chang'd, of wood are turn'd to flame.
Just as the letters little change affords
Ignis and Lignum, two quite different words.

Lucretius, *De Rarum Natura*

The tradition of litteral poetics covers an extraordinary range of writing projects, many of which are rarely found today in either literary compendiums or in works of linguistic scholarship. For instance, it includes the nineteenth century soldier-turned-linguist, Jean-Pierre Brisset, who deduced by etymological research that man is descended from frog, (see *Imagining Language* by J. Rasula and S. McCaffery). It also includes the Roman poet and philosopher Titus Lucretius Carus whom many contemporary writers regard as an experimentalist *avant la lettre* and for whom, not just The Word, but *all* words are to be taken literally.

For example, in Latin, the tongue in which Lucretius toiled, the word for fire, *Ignis,* is a partial anagram of *Lignum,* the word for wood. This extraordinary fact told Lucretius that, just as Democritus believed the variety of matter could be explained as different arrangements of a group of material atoms, so the variety of words could be explained as the different arrangements of a set of atomic characters.

Many nineteenth century thinkers, from William Rowan Hamilton to Freud's mentor, Brentano, also believed that arrangements found in nature and mathematics were manifest in language, and more importantly, in the *shifts* from one set of meanings to another. Indeed, this is the idea at the heart of Freud's free association method for analyzing unconscious structures. And much contemporary combinatorial writing that composes itself by accumulating vast banks of material through following the associations of a small set of randomly chosen source terms (words, places, times, events, people, etc.) works by a similar process, though this is the exact inverse of Freud's method, where the purpose is to distill the small random source set from the masses accreted around it.

The idea at the heart of all these methods is what the philosopher of language Jean-Jacques Lecercle calls folk etymology, whose aim is to dis-cover meanings through tracking the (sometimes infinitesimal) associative shifts between terms (words, places, times, events, people, jokes, texts, etc.).

While associations may be tracked homophonically, graphically, metaphorically or metonymically, the key to such analyses is that all associations count; all are to be taken literally.

The litteral perspective does not therefore assume that language is a tool which humans pick up and put down at whim, nor does it suggest that it constitutes a grid through which we strain experience. The litteral perspective takes language as an organ, "a part of an organism that is typically self-contained and has a specific vital function" (*Oxford English Dictionary*). And this perspective is correct, for every language is a Tongue, that is, literally, an organ.

Like all such members, a Tongue participates in the organization of a body's experience. So just as the heart organizes blood and the kidney wastewater, a Tongue organizes the Sense, i.e., the meaning or purpose of experience.

In litteral poetics, then, language is treated as neither referential, nor as a set of impersonal and arbitrary rules, but as a (welcome) member that helps to make sense of a body—physical or psychical, individual or communal—by endowing it with reason/s through the organ-ization of its perceptions, kinships and tempers.

The aim of *+|'me'S-pace* is to examine such a body of organizations by making a litteral study of the English Tongue.

Chapter 1

+|'me'S-pace

Introducing space-time, which is the substance not only of the material realm but also of a psycholinguistic one.

In the beginning

A tongue is a connected complex even if it may sometimes slip.

We may thus commence an analysis anywhere.

For the sake of brevity, let us begin as science does, with the substance of our universe, space-time:

Space-time

But perhaps we should clarify something.

There are no singular or correct ways to understand the arrangements of a tongue.

All readings make (some) sense to some |.

(Perhaps this is the definition of a reading?)

A tongue is thus less a uni-verse, than a *multi-verse.*

|n the form|n' of

|ts Self Pr|nc|ple

LOve cOnceived

FOrme

|n the form|n' of
|ts Self Pr|nc|ple
LOve cOnceived
the vV o|dse
named
FOrme

|n the form|n' of
|ts Self Pr|nc|ple
LOve cOnceived
the vV o|dse
named
FOrme

FOrme

named
the vV o|dse

LOve cOnceived

|ts Self Pr|nc|ple

|n the form|n' of

So we begin again:

space-time

space-time

space-time

space-time

Space-time

Through the shifts offered by a poetic lens,
this wor(|)d may then be seen as:

time-space

time-space

time-space

time-space

time-Space

which becomes:

time'S-pace

which becomes:

t|me'S pace

which becomes:

+|'me 's pace

which becomes:

| + me = pace

| + me = pace

The multiverse breathes

|

me

|

me

|

me

|

me

|'m

me

|'m

me

|'m

me

me

+I'me + I'me + I'me +I'me
+I'me + I'me + I'me +I'me
+I'me + I'me + I'me +I'me
+I'me + I'me + I'me +I'me
+I'me + I'me + I'me +I'me
+I'me + I'me + I'me +I'me
+I'me + I'me + I'me +I'me
I'me I'me I'me I'me I'me
I'me I'me I'me I'me I'me
I'me I'me I'me I'me I'me
I'me I'me I'me I'me I'me
I'me I'me I'me I'me I'me
I'me I'me I'me I'me I'me
I'me I'me I'me I'me I'me
I'me I'me I'me I'me I'me
+I'me + I'me + I'me +I'me
+I'me + I'me + I'me +I'me
+I'me + I'me + I'me +I'me
+I'me + I'me + I'me +I'me
+I'me + I'me + I'me +I'me
+I'me + I'me + I'me +I'me
+I'me + I'me + I'me +I'me
+I'me + I'me + I'me +I'me

+ l’me + l’me + l’me + l’me +
l’me + l’me + l’me + l’me
+ l’me + l’me + l’me + l’me +
l’me + l’me + l’me + l’me
+ l’me + l’me + l’me + l’me +
l’me + l’me + l’me + l’me
+ l’me + l’me + l’me + l’me +
l’me + lvme + l’me + l’me
+ l’me + l’me + l’me + l’me +
l’me + l’me + l’me + l’me
+ l’me + l’me + l’me + l’me +
l’me + l’me + l’me + l’me
+ l’me + l’me + l’me + l’me +
l ’me + l ’me + l ’me + l ’me
+l ’me+l ’me+l ’me+l ’me +
l ’me + l ’me + l ’me + l ’me
+ l ’me + l ’me + l ’me + l
’me + l ’me + l ’me + l ’me +
l ’me + l ’me + l ’me + l ’me
+ l + me + l + me + l + me
+ l + me + l + me + l + me
+ l + me + l + me + l + me
+ l + me + l + me + l + me
+ l + me + l + me + l + me

mmmmmmmmmmmmmmmmmm
mmmmmmmmm
mmmm
mm O
o o o o O | am
mmmm mm |
| am | am | am
am |
?
|m |m |m |m |m |m |m mmm
|'m |'m |'m |'m |'m |'m
|
| O | O | O | am
|'m me |'m me
| am
O
+
|'me |'me |'me + |'m me |
mm |'m mm |'m mm |'m e
+ |'m me
|'m me |'m me |
|'m me |'m me |'m me O
+
+ | me + | me + | me down
+ + | me + | me
+ | me
again
+ + | me + | me + | me down
+ + | me + + | me
+ + | mc again
+
+ | me + + | me + + | me + + | me
|'m me |'m me |'me |'m
me me me me me me me
me me me me
me + |
| | | |
| | |
| am | am
| am
|
Oooooooooooooooooooooh
!

+ +| me +| me +| me down

|'me |' me |'me |'me

O | O | O

| am

|'me |' me |'me

|

o

O

O

O

O

O

|'mmmm

mmmME !

MARK SPITZER

From *Age of the Demon Tools*

The aesthetic/method/madness for the epic poem *Age of the Demon Tools* (aka, "A Season in Kirksville") rose out of a lyrical local eco-paranoia coupled with a burning rage at much of the stupid corruption and injustices of evil Bush Administration bending the world over with war and Katrina etcetera 2002-2007. The voice in mind was Ezraific, though obviously Ginsbergian, with a shout-out to Ed Sanders, garfish and the Void. Synergism happened. Spoetry occurred. And the ice is still melting, Amerigo.

• then eagles egrets owls and hawks
coons possums foxes hawks
red-tailed hawks / mini-hawks
big brown cresty craven hawks
w/ great white riffle breasts

& channel cats with mongo backs
& big old mothr lunkr shouldrs
muscld thick and fat

& mucho silver muskellunge
& carp crappie crayfish clams
shiners darters waterbugs

& hickory & sycamore
& walnut sweetgum mulberries
& dogwood birch & ash aflash
with charged yellow orioles

& ragweed fields & waddlesnipe &
miles and miles of squirrely trails
cutting through the cattails
tallgrass
nettles burrs & golden glens
hid in Callipygia

of huge-ass pollywogs
& big-ass bullfrogs
& wildcat scat of
deer-run wending
wabbitlands
junked with trucks
fungus
dung

where crazy spiky colonies
skewered like wild galaxies
come busting up medievally
like clusters of erupting urchins
looking for someone
to Crucifuck

• but lo the demon with his food-gooped beard
spitting spittly noxious gas &
sullying the ancestors

and Oy the Blogess fat n' nasty!
blubbering blubblistic
alather in tripe

and Aaargh the Army of Overalls
declining simple swipe of plastic
while plastering the baptistlands
with infantile
pink and blue
oriflammes of flatulence

avec magnetic yellow stripes!
twisting out what is right
for the rape-waifs of the plains

—a Flapalooza of Flinging Fladdle!
Uvulas of Udder Grubbage!
Gorges Gorged with Grodilation
Glogging on—
Gloguley!

• "This is no Vietnam"
yet plenty skullblown vets ashudder in the ratskeller
by the Boschian truckload—
this ship is filled with peglegs
hookclaws
brainplates
& synthetic-skin
cyclopsians

and oh yeah, scurvy rats
& coocarachas

not to mention
blackmold, mouseshit
& unscaleable summits
of Sisyphus
papyrus

"Fighting for our freedom!"
yap the vapid
(as an overextended backdoor draft
is stranded in the nomad sand)
"Doing it over there, so we don't gotta do it
over here!"

& when Johnny comes marching home(less)
with stubleg and stumpwrist
he can pursue the AmDream
from the backseat
of a Taurus

[while getting sued for med expense]

cuz that's the scape-equation these days

O thank you, Amerigo
for a new Gen-Y
o post-traumatics

KEITH AND ROSMARIE WALDROP

From *Flat with No Key*

I

1
Ill met by lamplight

2
Ill met by any light
our own incoherence goes unnoticed

3
Ill met completely unlit
our incoherence
invisible

4
Ill met even in sunlight
our incoherence
invisible to
ourselves but never in decline

5
Ill met no matter
it's our incoherence
invisible to ourselves
in
our intrusions

J

1
The tables turn on Jersey

2
The tables turn on Jersey
turn up Jesus

3
the tables turn on Jersey
turn upon Jesus along with
some another jerk

4
the tables turn on Jersey
Jesus wants to turn in
another jerk ob–
jects to being called back from his kingdom

5
the tables turn on Jersey
turned down by Jesus while
the other jerk pro–
jects another
but jollier kingdom

6
the tables turn on Jersey
it turns out Jesus hasn't read
Victor Hugo the other jerk re–
jects a
jollier afterlife under
Jove's juridsdiction

K

1
Let's perform something in a flat with no key

2
let the missing key be sharp
no kangaroo be seen

3
Let the missing key go west
avoiding kangaroos
and kulchur

4
Let the key
miss kangaroos
and kulchur
the kettle-drum is set up in the flat

5
Let the key
muss up kangaroos
kick kulchur
drum up the kettle
ka-boom

R

1
Something rises in the west

2
Something rises in the west
a riddle, a rose, not the usual, a jest

3
Rises in the rising west
something ridiculous, the usual rose
handed to me, right-handed

4
Rises something in the west
you might wish for a ridiculous rose
handed in right-handed jest
rather than right-wingers, radiation, or recession

5
Or if the west rises, declining
ridiculously like a rose
right-handed
and rather
rampant

6
Then we assume decline does rise,
a rose
by any other name's right-handed
and rather
rampant in the way it's taken
over this ridiculous poem

S

1
These songs are quiet songs

2
Quiet songs
we sigh with pleasure

3
But with unquiet songs
we often sigh
with the same, or a similar, pleasure

4
Songs
sighs
our pleasure same or similar
so indecisive a result above sea level

5
What song? what
sigh? what pleasure? how can the
same thing (or something
similar) decide the sea's
level? Song? Surge?

6
you sang this song
I soughed this sigh
of similar and same
of sound of sea
and surge of song
sensation sun seed salt (a pinch of)

T

1
Blood from a turnip

2
Blood from a turnip
a turnip from a turban

3
Blood from turnip
turnip from turban
turban from tristes tropiques

4
Blood from turnip
turnip from turban
turban from tristes tropiques
triste treasure hunt

5
Bloody turnip
torn turban
triste tryst
sunken treasure
tristeza sad sick citrus

6
no turnip
no turban
triste tribal
treasure
sick with tristeza
this was supposed to turn transcendent

U

1
Stone unturned

2
Unturned stone
upturned

3
unturned stone
upturned
distance ungathered

4
Unturned
but upturned stone
with ungathered legends
uninscribed

5
Unturned
and not upturned stone
legends distances and wool ungathered
and uninscribed
words unraveled

6
Stones unturned keep
turnips from being upturned
left ungathered
for uninscribed joys of cooking
in unraveled (I really mean unrivaled)
urgent recipes

V

1
Shrill violins complain

2
Shrill violins complain
chill violence again

KANE X. FAUCHER

Lysicology: An Introduction

Is lysicology a poetics? A Movement? We have here arrayed three experimental pens in the service of the overarching rubric that to compose is to decompose and re-compose. Since the genesis of this project at the beginning of 2008, what was a solo project was quickly twinned in effort by Matina, and afterward, John, whose unique comp-manipulated orthographical "wordscapes" were a thematic fit with this project. And still, later on, the lysic caught on and was put to the sonorous musical talents of experimental composer and poet Jukka-Pekka Kervinen. All four of us have in some way collaborated solely with one another, and this text is an example of assembling these collaborations together. This project began with a single idea: to reverse lyricism. Eventually, the project metastasized, succumbed to what we call an anaclysm. In order to furnish the reader with a more robust context of the artists held herein, it was decided to append these interviews with the artists themselves whose eclectic range of talents travel well beyond the border[blur]lines of this work.

KANE X. FAUCHER

From *[+!]*

[ammunication]
m.bush.d, not [tilde-option] on notice::10er 4 voyce.
machinicunt +!/-! gasmasquerade as eurotic
-digitUR datasphere,
the free re-inscription of equipmental space (region) is not just another shifting of form, not just another surmoulage. It is to take territory by its scruff and drive all the "appropriate places for equipment in spaces" through the wall. How else could one drive off a household assailant?

This will have been an anti-performative license. Be advised that all transmission via oral conduits that open and/or close is strictly prohibited by the lysicological law. Would-be performers of the [+!] project should govern themselves accordingly by the "ignotius per ignotum; viva non voce" statute as laid out in the lysicological pedifesto. Failure to remit non-oral reference to the project will be met with harsh and retributive action, including the imposition on offenders of a bio-palimpsest that shall reveal, in corpus, the most scarlet of letters.

[die noopoetry]
::(roll+)over a dekade in devo
          lop
         (mom+)ment(+um),
the Stimmungalese la-text pan-immolates.
Pure Rhetoraganda-/-/-
          drips of cesium
tangentlemen poet shot dead after pinball incident
involving a free play verb hitting noun bumpers.
Will involve four levels of prophetic reading to unhitch the
bracketeering ostentatiously pre-installed,
post-approved,
going on, giving up, going bowling.

I am am I a cherished son in state bosom that they dis- and re-inter me in that combination mausoleum library, a curious place, as it came too late, as it came too late to Alexandre Dumas. In Abdominion (this dollar-patriot land of the intestine), in abollocks (Milton invented the abyss, or uncovered it via Gk. abyssus), in abdiction rather than malediction/maledi(c)ktat(e). A crooked enfilade.

A very crooked enfilade...we now enter the anti-DMZ:

[title bout in Tbilisi]
This lesson in doublets -
          iota to jot
          beldam to belladonna
          crook to cross (a la Kruchenkross)
          & briar to furze.
I have built an ensilage for neologeodesic words, a silography.
(that Ossetian lacks antipodes, but a good eanling, a cater-cousin).
tankroll / blown bullrings as convoys are topographically engrail'd.

One side hunting leopard
  the other a dancing bear.
One side acceleration
  the other a heavy claw.

this'n'that via the web(b)-flow of the inertnet. It don't move none, no, 2.0.
NO TO 2.0! Nuptialimonies PAID.

[baldynamo]
  dima[m-usliminal]
  dumanche.
    hor+
    .//. rendum &
    pud + endum ./ [errandum] -
  l'eglissande homibile
<<we [+!}ists...lysicist-ik melodestone>>
<<they [-/-]iatrists...a codemic>>.

(in fine:) "disasterisk explaud"
(in passim:) nova corium:
  it is indeed to arrive in new skin
  in understanding we cannot, should not,
separate
  INTERPRETATION from *PRODUCTION*
  ; *otherwise, poetry as we know it will become*
sentenced (senescent) to + incarcerated in + poetry as THEY know it -
  as gloom-grey lither.
(McGann is wrongwrong).
Instead: CREATE with PHLOXIC HUE(s)
  in pure calenture.
  wash clean pötree of its viscid(dity a la quid quisquiddity).
Become: becile, w/ ken & kythe.
Avaunt!: (don't prate, make cheeky badinage rather),
  coruscate/d
  +sanguiness(e)!
make (/of) your word(s) rubicund or at least make for erubescent.
ALL GREAT CONCEPTS ARE GAINED AT A GLEEK
  (not the plodding rummage in depths, Nietzsche QED, ipse dixit).
w/WordW/word.

[DADA-DNA-DA-DENADA]
fåéčţîõüşľŷ (diacriticaca):
  has all the vowels in alpha-beta ordo.
NTH:
  is a three-letter word rejoicingrejecting the vowel insurgence.
petrologos – quidditasia (/?)
-//commodificarnivale//-
O Stalinotype come obliquefy me, gulaggardly pogromenate!

MATINA STAMATAKIS

From *[+!]*

Kleptokinetisis

what little, [m]asked before the gravel--
lexiconologies embedded in the flesh [superimposed]
suprasensual [viscosity
way-for-way/tap for (comunicables thwarted +
juxt oppose suprasensitiveontolo-
gees[e] in the muchrakr[y]
f-ire once into voidal obtuseries
misgluttonized/morphistic graphology
the fundus-mess of angle/to/angle
[f]lit fluster spectral wake
[pgDn]

JOHN MOORE WILLIAMS

From *[+!]*

Tetatetagrammatron

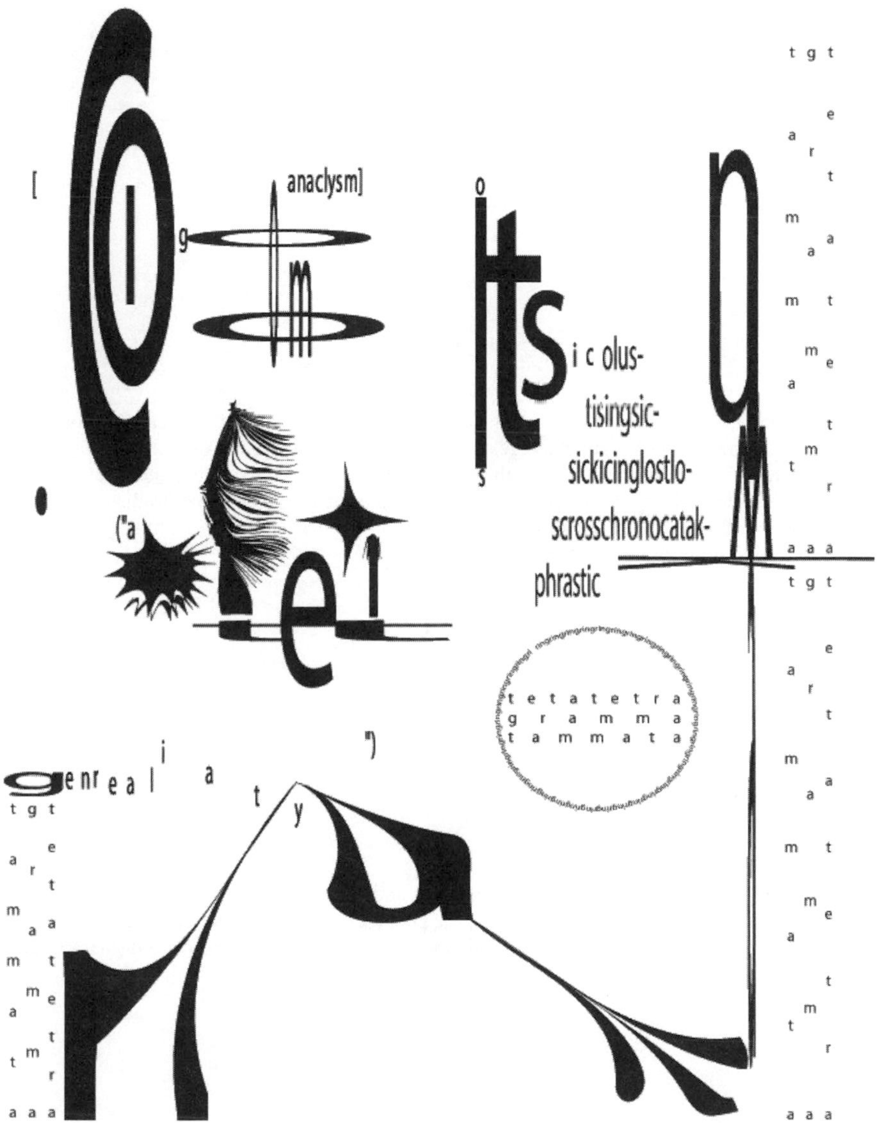

ANDREA KNEELAND

Continuity as an Axiomatic Resultant of a Clearly Defined Fragmentation of Lines

Rules:
(1) Didactics are most useful when charted, i.e. maps, algorithms, taxonomic functions.
(2) Taxonomies work best as dialectics.
(3) Gray is almost always more confusing than the worth of the centered bar.
(4) Bars are more useful as dividers than uniters.

Illustration:

vs.

east	west
water	humanness
traffic	muffled
plunge	bridge
	seals
	Proteus
saffron	vultures

Derivation:
Here, it is clearly of fundamental importance to note the etymology of both "saffron" and "vultures." One reputable source suggests that the language of saffron as a spice took a trade route originating somewhere amongst the epithelium of the Arabic tongue, later routed through Latinate trail only to incite the papillae of both the French and the English. We are further lead to believe that the vulture sprouts directly from a Latin origin, although etymology and ornithology are admitted to make strange bedfellows.

Use:
The bar can also made a blank horizontal (example follows):

children's naked teeth
children's naked teeth
children's naked teeth
children's naked teeth
children's naked teeth
children's naked teeth

Conclusion:
Proofs made available by both Leonard Schwartz and Zheng Er clearly indicate that while the scientist prefers a vertical form of notation, the poet (lazy by nature) prefers a horizontal delineation: a form made even more conspicuous through the use of an inverted (blank) line.

JUDITH GOLDMAN

From "FatBoy/DeathStar/rico-chet"

I drew the title "FatBoy/DeathStar/rico-chet" from the names given to trading "games" played by Enron employees in their manipulations of the California energy market. The work comprises apocryphal leaked internal memos that interpolate spliced, verbatim citations of transcripts of audio recordings of the traders' phone calls. (In live readings, these outtakes are performed as cell phone conversations that repeatedly interrupt the memos.)

The aim of "FatBoy" is to explore conjunctions between the game theoretical aspects of war and of the market, focusing in particular on how torture short-circuits strategy, introducing an alternate logic of pure asymmetry and pained embodiedness. In addition to the Enron tapes, compositional materials include the UN Convention against Torture and the US revisions of and exceptions to that convention, a dictionary of non-lethal weapons terms and references, the report reviewing Department of Defense detention operations, technical works on game theory and strategy, declassified White House memos, transcripts from animated video games, Emily Dickinson's poem "Split the lark," the song "The Big Rock Candy Mountain," and Louis Zukofsky's *A*.

[Excerpt]

INTERNAl MEMo: [neither flesh nor fowl; or] [THE BUTCHER WHosE HAND] [lEIsURE sUITs]
To: detainee
CC: detainee
RE: detainee # CirCular # detainee

o that the torment should not be confined/or, if he is a stateless person/prohibit overseas sales/to inflict severe physical or mental/of equipment such as thumb cuffs, leg irons, stun belts/exhaustive cocktail/full-frontal/all-you-can

/it's so Efficient/but

the butcher whose rigid frontality I/We often hear no two human beings are alike, and thus/will sell a stun gun "kit" in which parts are shipped/tommy/separately

and yet/Am I a beggar? What is the cause? How am I crost?/all warm in the tommy barn, you face/or intimidating or coercing him or a third person/at the receiving end is immobilized for several/fires two barbed darts up to 21 feet and jolts/total exports of shock weapons and restraints approved by the United states/butcher whose/a little too subjective/merchandizing/biodegradable/it's so efficient, but/Cineplex/in 2oo2 were worth $19 million/It is often called the law of armed conflict/apparently for the sadistic pleasure of/sick for hours

the butcher whose/chatroom/had recommended dogs/"NoW, YoU WIll FEEl/ the senior Army and Navy dog handlers/THE WEAKNEss oF BEING HUMAN! HA HA HA HA HA!!"/regulates the conduct of armed hostilities/acknowledged he knew a dog could not be used on a detainee/rights and obligations which/spray green foaming dye/govern the treatment of/if the detainee posed no threat/his communications with other detainees, his/***Optical, Laser-Infrared Co2***/receptivity to particular incentives/laser which can heat the skin of a target to cause/tommy/ pain but will not/It is difficult, however, to trace a specific device to a particular case/burn the skin/of torture. Application against the hand of a suspect/including the means for as full a rehabilitation as possible

O Australasia Less Lethal Forum/specialty impact munitions, simmunition, chemical/"Indoor use of chemical munitions"/"Opening Ceremony"/

is pleased to announce its first "Homeland Security Stocks Online Investor Conference"/because they think it will not leave permanent marks/and an accompanying PowerPoint presentation/Tactical use of dogs, advanced Taser/Click here for a partial list of/

CONVERSATION 5 (X CALLS Y)

Y: El Paso.
X: Uh hello, this is Stan with Enron.
Y: Mm hmm.
X: Hey, just wondering if I need to make the call to turn Copper on, or—or—or do you guys do that?
Y: Well, we've already given the order.
X: Oh, OK, so its uh—it's uh, getting ready.
Y: It's on its way.
X: All right, great. OK, thank you.
Y: You bet.
X: Bye.

(HANG UP) (Y CALLS X)

X: This is Stan.
Y: Stan, you think we should take Copper off?
X: Yes, I was just looking at that, uh, I think that'd be a good call.
Y: OK.
X: You want me—you want me to call the, uh, the Newman plant?
Y: Uh we can call them—
X: OK.
Y: —that's OK.
X: All right, yeah let's, uh, let's shut her down.
Y: OK.
X: All right, thanks Tate?
Y: Thank you.
X: Bye.
Y: Bye.

BELL/hear "bell"

Acoustic, Infra/sound. Very low-frequency sound which can travel/all members of the human family/the butcher whose/Airport Security, Biodefense, Biometrics, Defense, Internet Security, Integrated Security, Military, Border and Port Security/long distances and easily penetrate most buildings and vehicles. Transmission of long wavelength sound creates biophysical effects; nausea,/tommy/loss of bowels, disorientation, vomiting, potential inner organ damage or death may occur./"THEN AlloW ME To REJUVENATE YoU! ACCEPT MY PsYCHo PoWER! AND YoU WoN'T FEEl ANY WEARINEss NoR ANY PAIN!"/superior to ultrasound because it is "in band" meaning/www.HomelandDefenseStocks.com/that it does not lose its properties when it changes mediums such as from air to tissue./under the impression they were administering real pain to people/By 1972 an infrasound generator had been built in France which generated waves at 7 hertz./suppose that two players with given vulnerability, specified armament, and known shooting accuracy/These individuals were told they were allowed to administer electric shocks of various strengths to some other people connected to a machine/failed to detect warning signs of potential and actual abuse/Very low-frequency sound/a one-day training session/When activated it made the people in range sick for hours

had not received an orientation on what was/the sunrise, the toothache, the lover's touch/remote-controlled stun belts/expected from his canine unit/or, if he is a stateless person

the butcher whose Def Con 1 I undergrowth/the limbo of/This is life beyond words, the sunrise, the/detainee custody and control

"To sToP IT, WE HAVE NO CHoICE BUT To UsE THE MACHINE!"

These gloves allow for the grappling of prisoners and rioters./"There is no proof our products are used/cause death through loss of coordination of heart muscle contraction/is pleased to announce its first "Homeland security stocks online Investor Conference"/O that the torment/How am I crost?or whence this curse?/to the Bodies wounds and sores/for every year a fleece doth spring/Do Not Resuscitate/No connection fee/kidgloves/to torture people"

permitted American companies to ship electroshock weapons/"THE WEAK sHAll PERIsH…THAT Is NATURE's lAW…"/the butcher whose hand is sworn/bullet points/felled to make/a clearing/barcode/Cineplex opening in San Mateo/shopped it/like flies/its rump shivers, snuffling/for every year/tommy-rigged/shopped it/ shopped it all around

"HoW CoUlD soMETHING DIsPosABlE lIKE YoU…?"/tommy/tommy-stripped/ tommy-cocked/***Electrical, Stun Belt.*** A command-activated belt/Marker, Foam Dye. Hand-held device which is used to spray green foaming dye into the face/you are felled to make a/tommy/clearing/worn by prisoners which delivers a mild electric shock when they become combative./Def Con 1 I/***Entangler, Net, Gun.*** Fires a net which entangles a human or vehicular target./relation between the angle of fire and the range of a projectile/***Hologram, Death.*** Hologram used to scare a target to death./"NoW, I'll CoMPlETElY ElIMINATE YoU!"/as what he felt, did his skin/ bullet points

/all-you-can-/eat/chatroom/full-frontal/all-you-can/(path-dependence)/eat

heart muscle contract-/the stripping away of clothing may have had the unintended consequence/an act must be specifically intended/to include lighting and heating, as well as food, clothing, and shelter/inflict physical or mental/to acquaint thee that I intend/of dehumanizing detainees/tommy

Get in,/the butcher whose/Get rich,/hand cuts and delves into the body/adjust/adjust for inflation/Do/Do Not Resuscitate/with the black blood of black-and-white photographs/the butcher whose hand served on a tray/manmade such that they are/no humane alternative/opening in San Mateo/surround-sound/Get out

BEll/hear "bell"

RACHEL LODEN

The USNS *Comfort* Sails to the Gulf

Huge red crosses on the whitewashed hull:
http://www.comfort.navy.mil/welcome.html

CATHERINE DALY

Maquis / Malice

Maquis

mint, laurel, myrtle
    victory   death
"I thought they were militant socialists"

a strict regimen of initiations and degrees, structured like a secret society
    opposing
    colluding with Knights Templar
        cathars

trained as deep undercover agents   kill on command
        without regard for safety
            personal
    line of duty visions of paradise
the concept of apostasy
inquisition   capacity of human sadism
    war is cruel delusion
maquis? de sade
"in france" *why do you think I have this outrageous accent*
clandestine
sanctions sanctified   sanctimonious, ceremonial "in name only"
    In the name of….

ideologically-motivated
    bulwark against the spread of—their ideology

of denunciation

letters to the authorities identifying black marketeers, resistance
sympathizers, Jews even encouraged by the collaborationist press
    Au Pilori and *Je suis partout*
    personal grudges and animosity

collaboration not motivated by ideological affinity to fascism, collaboration not motivated by ideological affinity to fascism,

there were a number of political parties with a commitment to ideology

greater good
my country right or wrong
lesser evil

unifies the disparate into I
hold this… it seems self-evident
                                        obvious

each
to
each
social construction or reality
we worked
together to make
collaboration a dirty word
might makes right
I remember the last sentence I said to him: “It is better to be on the side of the Jews than to be a stupid idiot!”

human propensity to violence

against nationalism
revolution in consciousness a pre-requisite for social revolution
auspices of automatism
            divination   birds

militia

black years, dirty bomb
                          war
travail, famille, patrie

Milice

Marguerite Monnot

daughter of an organist
a prodigy

free
editions de travail work
to become a persona non grata
technical problems, interpretation
intuition deaf to evil
what is authentic, national

"One can never train a child carefully enough" youth
today's dissonance sight singing (fixed-Do solfège)
not sight reading tomorrow's consonance
Boulanger
Grand Prix du Disque by L'Academie du Disque
the stranger, a policeman, a hooker whose

screw is slang for prison guard

arrester—real boyfriend didn't want to work
at the fish market
but her working emasculated him
Où Sont-Ils Mes Petits Copains?
where did Billy Wilder put song

Irma la Douce

Irma la Douce

where did Billy Wilder put song
Où Sont-Ils Mes Petits Copains?
but her working emasculated him
at the fish market

arrester— real boyfriend didn't want to work
screw is slang for prison guard

the stranger, a policeman, a hooker whose
Grand Prix du Disque by L'Academie du Disque
            Boulanger
not sight reading   tomorrow's consonance
today's dissonance   sight singing (fixed-Do solfège)
"One can never train a child carefully enough"   youth

what is authentic, national
intuition   deaf to evil
technical problems, interpretation
   to become a persona non grata
editions de travail   work

            free

a prodigy
daughter of an organist

Marguerite Monnot

DAVE KRESS

The Law

Japan has a series of detergent suicides that release toxic fumes, like one in Konan where a girl, fifteen, dies.

The law: like cures like.

A twenty-eight-year-old Japanese man kills himself by mixing laundry detergent and cleaning fluids, releasing noxious fumes into the air and forcing the evacuation of thousands of people from their tents.

The thing works!

An eighteen-year-old boy-man mixes chemicals in his home in Otaru, on the island of Hokkaido and is found dead shortly after midnight Wednesday.

1,349 curative proofs wash up on the Pacific coast: examples of proofs include powdered starfish, anal glands from hog-nosed skunks, crushed live bedbugs, powdered anthracite, decorative oyster shells, human urine, and snake droppings. The itch, among all proofs, is most highly studied.

Police order an immediate evacuation of 350 neighbors as the resulting gas can sicken people.

So-called "Sudsers" do not realize that as they become less material, girl-boy curative agents find themselves beset with increasing œthereal tetchiness—when matter is completely exhausted, low-grade radiations from the spiritual band remain active for up to thirty days. Woman-man agents are not being studied.

His unconscious mother is taken to a hospital where she recovers, a Hokkaido policeman says.

Millions of people take infinitesimal doses of all drugs, some benefiting others finding no proof for their symptoms.

His death comes as fourteen-year-old Japanese "Girl" kills herself using the same method. "Girl's" suicide leaves dozens ill from fumes. Fumes escape her apartment.

Lachryma filia—consisting of tears collected from a young girl weeping openly after committing a social gaffe—seems to work, but research not yet been able to determine (A) appropriate flow rates for delimiting *weeping*,

(B) viable parameters of openness, or (C) *socius*-specific gaffe boundary conditions.

As "Girl" dies, a thirty-one-year-old man outside Tokyo kills himself inside a car by mixing detergent and bath salts, police say.

The strongest form of healing proceeds from the infra-red: there, invisible to all but a small number of highly observant, highly trained eyes, chatty, infinitesimal agents go forward where—by degrees, Sato san's infernal cold at last heeds, heels, obeys.

National broadcaster NHK reports that "A. Man" in his late thirties is found dead by hotel employees who notice a strange but clean smell coming from his room.

The reemergence of nature—in the form of new practices, rituals, and obsessions—may ultimately be linked to the phenomena: the *frontieruku* (musket-toting, coonskin-cap-bedecked male prostitutes clustering around Tokyo's Harajuku Station) on the one hand and the *Lolikon* (women in their late forties taking on the trappings and carryings-on of Nabokov's famous twelve-year old) on the other, are only two sites of possible research.

Woman, happily married at twenty-four, mixes detergent with cleaning fluids to make toxic fumes. She dies and is found dead.

Steam baths, sunlight, water at mealtimes, a vegetarian diet (including whole wheat bread), and walking barefoot on wet, recently-mown lawns are suggested, but as of now, none show significant amelioration of either symptoms or proofs. Interest in the potential use of clay compresses remains high.

Media reports in Japan suggest that the number of similar deaths reaches about thirty, including several cases in which bystanders are sickened.

Some suggest that the disease causes bacteria, not the other way around.

The suicides are part of a spate of detergent-related deaths that are encouraged by œthernet suicide sites, experts say.

In the town of Tangerine, (in Hokkaido's Soya-Shicho sub-prefecture), gazing into the large, bright eyes of wounded owls is the preferred proof—though exactly how the owl is to be wounded remains at best mysterious. Plump crabs are also being tried—and lamb.

Police in Japan ask œthernet suicide sites to take down instructions for the mix.

Doctors decide that relaxing as many of the body's orifices as possible may bring relief to thousands. They are not sure exactly how.

However, œthernet suicide sites refuse to axe the recipes.

Very little is known.

Japan has one of the highest rates of suicide in the solar system.

TED PELTON

Woodchuck and Hank Williams Zombie

Let us hear another story of Woodchuck.

One day in his travels Woodchuck saw a man whose western shirt was drenched in blood streaming also from his mouth.

In his teeth were small clumps of flesh and gore.

It was Hank Williams Zombie.

Woodchuck had heard shrieks and crying on his amble into the country town and had ignored them.

It was Woodchuck's way to wander both in body and in mind.

As tall as the Zombie Woodchuck shrunk himself down to the size of the people who live underground.

The Zombie was Williams alright and not the son nor the grandson.

He wore a cowboy hat stained with blood and an entire western outfit heeled boots matching jacket and slacks powder blue in spots not drying reddish-brown string tie cinched up gait not so other-worldly as drunken-seeming.

Instead of a guitar he held in one hand a rifle by the stock.

Yet who would believe this creature next tilted back his head and yodelled *oldle-oh-dee-odle-oh-dee-oh-de-odle* which I cannot accurately reproduce here except to say that Woodchuck is said to have found it the most beautiful thing he had ever heard on earth and perhaps for this reason also the most unearthly detached and terrifying.

Hank Williams Zombie hitched his head front badly aimed his gun at Woodchuck and fired.

Woodchuck shrunk himself further so as to be an even smaller target.

When Woodchuck was this small the world was very distant far-off and toy-like.

Woodchuck saw that the seemingly vacant town was not at all empty its residents merely hidden small like himself.

Hank Williams Zombie at this moment turned as zombies do in movies lurching without speed into a doorway left half-ajar and pulled out into the street a little human girl.

He put his hand or claw into her chest in one movement and ripped out her heart chomping it to his mouth like a soft peeled orange gushing with red juice over his thin cowboy lips and down his chin the blood ran.

Far-off to Woodchuck the blood ran over the hand and down the arm of Hank Williams Zombie globbed onto the pavement pooled there and got tracked further down the road as the zombie stalked off gun in one hand heart in the other to his mouth like one dead or drunken or unearthly.

Woodchuck took advantage of the creature's turn away to resume his normal size and run to shelter behind a gas station building.

Again the zombie yodelled *odle-lo-dee-oh-dee-oh-dee-oh-dee-lo-dee-odle-oh* and Woodchuck out of sight now burrowed underground where he found his people cowering worse than they had with the sportsmen.

What is this thing they said to Woodchuck who paid no attention but sat down to be served food and beer.

The people were honored to host Woodchuck.

They remembered the stories they had heard of him.

They looked in awe at the box which held his penis.

And said let us smoke and think on these things.

Let us Google Hank Williams Zombie and see what we find.

They kept excellent connections underground not really what we call Google today but something we cannot explain but must trust how the story comes to us.

This all took place not yesterday or last year or even when your grandparents lived but in No-Time when all things happened that would ever happen.

All the people smoked and sweated and asked themselves what could be done with a raging death-in-life zombie seeing Williams had died badly and no one could say exactly where nor how drugged and drunk aged twenty-nine laying in the back seat of a car headed for a Hank Williams New Year's party he would have played if not dead.

All agreed Williams had good reason to have gone zombie but none said a word because what was the use in bothering Woodchuck who was made by God with things one didn't know anything about not of this world.

So they sat and smoked and Woodchuck looked out before him into the middle-distance with eyes that seemed unfocused or focused upon something no one else could see.

Later the people would know that Woodchuck was looking into the future and seeing what would happen not because the future has to occur in one way but because the future like the present unfolds as a series and must be played out.

They smoked and sweated for three days and at sunset of the third day.

Woodchuck stood up and left the hole never having uttered a word the entire time he was among the people.

Above ground now the streets were strewn with half-gnawed body parts and large swaths and small clots of blood everywhere one looked.

Woodchuck emerged from the hole and went to the clot of blood which three days before had been the little human girl whose still-beating heart Hank Williams Zombie had seized and chewed whole and Woodchuck began kicking the clot along the ground.

He kicked and kicked and the clot rolled in the grime of the street and began to gather energy.

The dead material now gained life force through the motion Woodchuck gave it and the clot grew until it was the shape and size of the little human girl.

Woodchuck went from one clot to the next kicking life back into the dead blood and restoring them and did not rest when night fell but kept moving one to the next kicking.

It was at dawn of day four with a crowd of humans and people watching when Hank Williams Zombie reappeared staggering up the street at the opposite end of the town square.

Woodchuck stopped kicking.

Williams shouldered his rifle but lost his balance and fired wildly.

Woodchuck stood firm while bullets whizzed about.

Now the very air seemed to have changed.

It may have been the sun growing brighter and hotter in the morning sky at that moment and it may also have been emanating from all of the newly living creatures Woodchuck had brought to life who glowed and smiled happy and alive as a warmth began to envelop one and all.

The zombie seemed to respond to this and take on some life-feeling.

It began then to sing.

You're looking at a man who's gettin kinda mad.
I had lots a luck but it's all been bad.
No matter how I struggle and strive.
I'll never get outta this world alive.

And then for a time all was silence as the warmth of life as those who tell this story say enveloped us all.

Woodchuck walked down to the other end where Hank Williams Zombie stood motionless.

He pushed over the zombie with one arm.

Williams Zombie fell and crumbled in ash.

Woodchuck took the gun and broke it in one movement over his knee then began to dance on the ashes of the Hank Williams Zombie.

The people joined and all of the creatures of the town restored its horses cows sheep cats birds squirrels rats toads insects and humans all danced a dance to drums and beat the dust of the Hank Williams Zombie back into the earth where all dead things go.

Day into night people kept on dancing and whooping until they began to look around and no one could see any sign of Woodchuck.

Then a child said I saw him wander off and the people knew Woodchuck had left to travel again.

There is a moral to this story.

It shows why today though the humans do not have such things to fear as they once did in towns in the country you will find that they have no hearts and they are numb and murderous raging and brutal insensible as the dead.

It is because long ago their hearts were eaten by the Hank Williams Zombie who was then reduced to dust by Woodchuck who danced to drums until he wandered away.

ROBIN BECKER

How I Ate My Wife

Lucy and I were hiding in the basement. We were with the boxes of Christmas decorations—no Chanukah junk, mind you, no menorah, nothing Hebrew in sight—and the never-used tent and Lucy's treadmill, also never used. Our life's detritus was all around us and my cheek was on the concrete and Lucy's hand was in my hair. The bite on my shoulder throbbed like a hard-on and I closed my eyes and I died.

Let that sink in: I died.

There was a moment of suspension when I was no longer human and not yet zombie. My body was nothing, was as good as a couch cushion or a blow-up doll or the giant plastic Santa mocking us in the corner. Walt Disney cryogenically frozen. Pinocchio before the breath of life, hanging limp from his strings.

It's true what they say about viewing your corpse from above. I floated near the ceiling, gazing at Lucy and what used to be me, and in that instant, I was as content as one of the Lord's sheep, a member of His flock. The zombie horde seemed far away; I could barely hear them pounding at the cellar door. My ears were flooded with celestial music, the music of the spheres. It sounded like twee Brit pop. Was it angels with harps? Maybe. Belle & Sebastian? Perhaps. Was it Jesus strumming an acoustic guitar like some traveling barefoot hippie? In my dreams.

Because let's rationalize: the whole "near-death experience," the whole light-at-the-end-of-the-tunnel trip, is a trick of the brain, a hallucination. It is not a supernatural event, but one last fantasy brought to you by your endorphins to mitigate the absolute terror of death. To inspire hope against the nothingness we all fear. The whole cessation of ego and selfhood business. The loss of the world. Because everyone wants to exist, don't they? But we all die in the end.

Unless we're undead.

Then there are the suicides. Hanging themselves on reinforced beams in their empty Seattle apartments; overdosing on pills in the bedrooms of their mothers; blowing their brains out with rifles or shotguns or pistols; starting cars in garages and reading Dostoevsky until sleep; driving mini-vans off cliffs with children strapped in the backseat. They screw existence. In the ass.

Bear in mind, this is a zombie talking—a supernatural being. What do I know? I might not even be real.

Oh, ontology.

Regardless of religion or science, there I was, floating near the ceiling and at peace, when the girly music of the spheres turned into Norwegian death metal and I was ripped away from the fuzzy blankets of cloudland and confronted with demons and devils and a descent into hell. I was whisked into some sort of meat tube, like a large intestine, where trapped souls screamed at me from polyp walls and everything was flaming orange and too hot. Munch's *The Scream* was there, the painted man's hand on the side of his face. A child tattooed with the mark of the beast turned into a stampede of wild horses running away from a Gothic mansion which morphed into a fat lady in pearls laughing. The typical horror movie shtick. Cliché, but true.

Then I was reborn.

Let that sink in.

Yea, though I walk through the shadow of the valley of death, I fear no evil. For I am evil. And I am the shadow. And I am death.

Not just zombie but archetype. Not just villain but hero. Jungian shadow, id and ego. Man is woman. Ovaries are testes. Cats are dogs.

There's Michael and Laurie, Leatherface and Sally, Leatherface and Stretch, Norman and Marion. Need I go on?

I opened my eyes. Lucy screamed. The zombie horde broke through the door and I lunged, lunged, lunged at my wife and she was lunch.

Heavens she was tasty. We ate her communally: the fresh-faced blonde zombette from next door; the nuclear family from across the street, which, as a result of decay, truly did have 2.5 kids; the haggard waitress zombie from Denny's, varicose veins now black and inky; the suspicious loner zombie who never gave out Halloween candy; the teenage geek zombie with his pimples and Lord of the Rings t-shirt; and me, the professor zombie, with my tortoiseshell glasses and robin's egg blue shirt.

This was no symbolic eating, no representational wafer. We didn't just break bread—we broke flesh; we drank blood. It was a living Eucharist.

Lucy's still in me now. Transubstantiation. Her remains remain. Forever and ever. Amen.

Burp.

AVERILL CURDY

Probation

The cheap dropped ceiling
    jumped like a pot-lid boiling
when our upstairs neighbor
    chased his girl that winter.
        Falling out of

summer's skimpy tops
    she'd want our phone. Her plush lips
creased. Not exactly blonde,
    but *luteous*, we thought,
        pleased the right word

was there for that shade
    of slightly slutty mermaid.
Wincing, we'd hear him punch
    along the floor on crutch-
        es, a giant

bat trying to mince
    a mayfly. Sex and Violence
you called them; Blondie with
    Dagwood on crystal meth,
        I'd tell our friends

over dinners stewed
    in noise. Even his truck cowed.
Black, smoked glass, outsized wheels
    flaunted like chrome knuckles
        we shrank from, ducked,

afraid we'd find her
    later, knocking at our door.
Some nights we waited through
    like captured prey. To you
        I'd turn in bed,

saying the furtive
    words against your back, I love
... You'd stroke my hair, or hip,
    all our years the same flip
        crack, *I do, too.*

STEPHEN-PAUL MARTIN

Food

Stopping in the middle of a sentence, distracted by thoughts about food, he closes the book without marking his place, even though it's not time for a meal, even though the sentence was holding his interest, making the claim that mainstream reality doesn't exist anymore, that at this point we can only talk about mainstream unreality, an assertion that's not as simple as it sounds, not when the distinction between real and unreal has been relentlessly blurred by the mainstream itself, to such an extent that the mainstream exists only because real and unreal have become interchangeable terms, generating a confusion so pervasive that it hardly seems to exist, functioning as a background noise that you notice only when it's not there anymore, but such moments of silence are unusual, difficult to recognize and even more difficult to sustain, provisional in a way that makes you feel insecure, like you need more control, the power to make such moments happen at will, as if the creation of silence were a skill you could learn in a classroom, but when the lesson appears on a blackboard, and the words are as precise as any professor could possibly make them, there's something that won't fall into place, something that still makes trouble, something that even experts are confused by, experts like Professor Food, a man who's been teaching long enough to know what he's talking about, long enough to know that he doesn't know what he's talking about, standing in front of the classroom with a piece of chalk in his hand, saying things he's learned to say by saying them over and over again, things he didn't fully understand until he said them, as if unspoken words were like uninflated balloons, a figure of speech he enjoyed when he first came up with it, though he's not sure now if words and balloons can really be compared, but he keeps producing the words and the faces facing him keep writing them down, concerned that what they don't write down might work against them later, though some of them are distracted by what's outside, by colors and faces and words on walls of billboards moving closer, blocking out most of the view from the classroom windows, making the classroom clock seem larger and louder than it really is, magnified seconds made of magnified nanoseconds ticking away, or not ticking away but stretching out and curling back on themselves, serpents flicking their tongues and flashing their fangs and eating their tails, while underneath the clock a student wants to raise her hand, a blond psychology major with a mini-skirt and a permanent smile, wondering why the billboards keep getting closer, wondering why the lesson is always the same, word by word and phrase by phrase not a syllable out of place, but she's not sure how smart it would be to say anything, since the first question would show that she's not focused on Professor Food's lecture, and the second question would imply that he's too lazy or too dumb to come up with anything new, even though Professor Food has already justified his teaching strategy, announcing on the first day of class that every class would consist of exactly the same lecture, word by word and phrase by phrase not a syllable out of place, since his goal was to make sure students *fully* understood the material, not just in their brains but in every cell of their bodies, and he claimed that this could only be done through repetition, as if the lecture were an elaborate mantra, hypnotically seeping through the conceptual and emotional superstructure of the mind, slowly undoing toxic patterns of thought and feeling locked into place so firmly that nothing else seemed even remotely possible, but of course there was really no question of repetition, because the lecture on second hearing would be different from the lecture on first hearing, different the third time around than the second, different heard for the fourth time than the third, different on the fifth day of class than on the fourth, and besides, Professor Food firmly believes that it's crucial for students to learn to cope with annoyance, since so much of life is annoying and you can either be pissed off most of the time or you can preserve your sanity by mastering the annoyances, in much the same way that a surfer masters a wave, but the blond psychology major would rather be mastering waves at the beach, so instead of raising her hand she gets up and leaves, just as Professor Food turns and writes the word blackboard on the blackboard and the students bend over their desks and write the word notebook in their notebooks, everyone so focused that they don't know at first that she's just gone out, but the sharp sound of her high heels in the corridor gives her away, a sound so compelling that after ten seconds it's hard to tell if she's approaching or moving away, a confusion which builds as the sound continues, reaching a point where advancing and receding are about to become the same thing, destroying one of the basic oppositions that time and space depend on, threatening an even more primal condition, the distinction between possible and impossible, which means that too much is at stake, activating the occult mechanisms of universal correction, which turn the blond psychology major 180 degrees in the blink of an eye, sending her back down the corridor toward the classroom, leaving Professor Food with no doubt that the sound is getting larger and larger, haunting him with an image of high heels punishing a floor tiled like a chess board, a design that's always made him nervous, not because it reminds him that he's never been good at chess, not because the game includes menacing metaphors like checkmate and stalemate, but because the floor reminds him of other floors with the same design, places where bad things must have happened, though he's never been able to say what they were, and he doesn't think it would help him if he could, especially since he's never been convinced that he needs any help, except that at times apparently harmless sounds affect him more than they should, especially when combined with aggressive illumination, light with a purpose, like the light that's all but replacing the afternoon sunlight in the windows, buzzing fluorescent light from walls of billboards moving closer, smiling faces clever phrases calculated colors, counterpointing the sound of high heels coming closer and closer, turning Professor Food toward the classroom door, just as the blond psychology major sticks her head back into the room, giggling nervously, trying to be sheepishly cute and act like nothing is going on, which loosely speaking might be true but strictly speaking can't be true, since something is always going on, even if it's on a scale too small for human perception, and the difference between nothing going on and something going on is on the verge of dissolving, threatening yet another primordial condition—the distinction between what is and what isn't—leading the blond psychology major to sit back down beneath the classroom clock and try to look serious, an expression she's not accustomed to, scribbling furiously in her notebook in response to Professor Food's description of a blond psychology major scribbling furiously in her notebook, not quite understanding what she's writing, and she ends up mixing Professor Food's words with her own words, half transcription half translation half misunderstanding, but three halves don't make a whole, making instead an unstable condition, like a table with a missing leg, like a story no one seems to be telling, focusing on a prominent quantum physicist, a woman who grew up masturbating to pictures of Isaac Newton, living in a Victorian house on the western shores of Lake Baikal in Siberia, having inherited enough money from her dead parents to construct a device that allows her to reduce herself to the size of subatomic particles that exist for less than a millionth of a second, but a millionth of a second seems to take decades when she finally makes herself small enough to look the subatomic realm in the face, an image that she thought was only a metaphor when she wrote it in a recent journal article, but now that she's there it all appears to be just like what she left behind, people in houses waking up and eating and talking and laughing, trees bending in breeze, jazz in low-lit basement clubs, aisles of food in labeled cans and bags, rattlesnakes making figure-eights in desert sand, mystical dancers making figure-eights in desert sand, planes that look like hammerhead sharks dropping bombs on a third world country, people in observation balloons delighted by panoramas, drivers on freeways getting pissed off and giving each other the finger, out of work middle-aged men forced to take jobs delivering pizza, animated café conversations about economic instability, but she tells herself that it's all so small that no one else even knows it's there, and when her device brings her back to the top-floor lab in her Siberian house, windows facing miles and miles of the deepest lake in the world, she can't quite bring herself to begin a scientific paper, knowing that she'd be laughed off the face of the earth if she wrote what she knows, but over time the frustration of having to keep quiet about a momentous discovery drives her to contact an old college friend, an avant-garde filmmaker who grew up masturbating to pictures of herself, and through an eager exchange of emails they plan to make a documentary film about the sub-atomic world, protecting themselves from the scorn of the scientific world by framing the film as a work of fiction, but fights over details jeopardize the project, and one late afternoon, after a vicious disagreement about quarks and leptons, the filmmaker feels like someone trapped in a prepositional phrase about food, the very same phrase that appears in Professor Food's lecture, scribbled into the notebook of an attentive young man in the front row, an astrology major with short black hair and a long white beard and a varsity sweater, someone who would surely be every teacher's dream if he weren't listening so aggressively, changing what he's listening to, transforming a detailed discussion of symbolism in ice cream commercials into a detailed discussion of movie trailers, the way would-be actors and actresses avoid waiting on tables by making stupid movies sound brilliant, thrilling, profound, stunning, breathtaking, cultivating a seductive and authoritative manner of speaking, showing that even the most vacant nonsense can sound impressive if the speaker knows how to use her voice, something that has disturbing political implications that need careful attention, except that now the astrology major is transforming Professor Food's remarks on the need to protect animals from human violence, the need for an ongoing critique of humanity's master species complex, into a playful description of puppies in cardboard boxes, offered in shopping malls throughout the nation, bringing love into thousands of homes that would otherwise be dominated by Republicans or Born-Again Christians convinced that rhetoric about national security or family values is more than just the latest official installment of toxic nonsense, more than just an indication of how brain-dead the USA has become in the past thirty years, though it's foolish to assume that the USA has ever been smarter than it is now, and perhaps a more accurate way to approach the problem is to focus on what happens when a military superpower becomes obsessed with amusing and ornamenting itself with hi-tech devices like the cell phone that won't stop ring-toning in the astrology major's pocket, the kind of intrusion that used to make everyone giggle, but it's become so commonplace that no one notices, least of all Professor Food, whose discussion of substitute gratifications appears in the astrology major's notebook as a team of mountain climbers returning from a remote summit speaking a language no one has ever heard before, an image that affects the astrology major so physically that he feels like he's walking down an urban street on a chilly day at half past noon, a sidewalk of squares that keep repeating themselves, exactly the same size and shade of grey, and he's gotten to the point where he doesn't know how long he's been walking, except that he knows he's moving south, south becoming deeper south becoming deeper and deeper south, reaching a sky-blue boundary beyond which motion is no longer possible, the place where the sky comes down to meet the pavement, something that he's always thought was an optical illusion, or perhaps an optical metaphor, but now he walks face-first into what feels like blue plate glass, and there's nothing to do but turn and walk in the opposite direction, a sidewalk of identical squares repeating themselves, a trance of motion making the north appear to recede forever, except that he's suddenly face to face with a plate glass boundary again, blue so flat it's clear that on the other side motion doesn't exist, a firm indication that north and south aren't what they were before, so he tries walking east and bangs his face against the same blue boundary, and he tries walking west and the squares of the sidewalk end at the same blue boundary, forcing him to conclude that profound changes have taken place undetected, that the open transparent space he used to take for granted has been severely compromised, but instead of just waiting there at that suddenly rigid boundary, fondling his crotch or picking his nose, the astrology major slips quietly out of the classroom as soon as Professor Food turns to write something about mountains and language on the blackboard, chalk scraping across the flat black surface with the sound of skates on ice, a sound that follows the astrology major down the corridor, past paintings of smiling men and women who gave the school money, all posing with the same mountain meadow in the background, beyond which in the corner of his eye the astrology major expects to see a blue observation balloon, bobbing pleasantly between clouds that look like brains, reminding him of a trip he once took through mountains and meadows, taking shelter from a sudden storm in a cottage empty except for three unlabeled cans of food, waiting out the storm for days, becoming so desperately hungry that he smashed open one of the cans and ate what looked like a human brain, smashed open a second can and ate what looked like a human heart, smashed open the final can and found himself inside the can looking out, haunted by the sound of the cottage door thrown open by freezing wind, then footsteps on the floorboards, but the memory collapses into the light at the end of the corridor, imagery on walls of billboards waiting outside the doors of the school, quickly convincing the astrology major that there's no point in leaving the building, that at least the classroom is still a media-free zone, an assumption that crumbles when he slips back into his seat and Professor Food's lecture becomes a commercial, flashed on a screen descending from the ceiling, separating Professor Food from the blackboard, apparently triggered by an outside source beyond Professor Food's control, an ad that begins with the sounds of battle, Custer with bullets and arrows whizzing past him, surrounded by Sioux and Cheyenne braves and hundreds of dying soldiers and horses, and a voice-over says YOU **CAN'T** ALWAYS RUN AWAY FROM YOUR PROBLEMS, as Custer looks to the sky and sees three flying saucers cutting through the blinding sunlight, suddenly becoming Tylenol tablets, and the voice-over says BUT YOU **CAN** FEEL BETTER ABOUT WHAT YOU CAN'T ESCAPE, and the tablets fill the sky with the sound of many rivers, spinning down one by one into Custer's mouth, while a slow-motion arrow goes in one ear and out the other, and the general falls with a smile on his face, the camera zooming in on his teeth, which gleam like symbols of eternal happiness, just as the silver screen gets pulled back into the classroom ceiling, entering the astrology major's notebook as a harsh condemnation of a rightwing think-tank, the Project for the New American Century, the un-elected group that secretly governs the nation, a group the astrology major has never heard of, appearing in his notebook not from his pen but from the page, as if the notes were composing themselves, climbing off the page and into his pen and hand and wrist and forearm, climbing neurochemically into his brain, looking out through his eyes, expecting the rest of the class to be looking back, but their eyes drawn instead to what Professor Food is drawing on the blackboard, something that might be a magical diagram, a woodcut in a medieval book of spells, a sign that conjures fires of purification through destruction, though Professor Food himself doesn't know what he's doing, only what his hand has done with a piece of chalk on the blackboard, an image drawn with artistic skill far beyond what he's normally capable of, a picture of himself drawing a picture of himself drawing a picture of himself drawing a picture of himself drawing a picture of himself drawing a picture of himself, smaller and smaller scales of representation, culminating in a picture of a blackboard that's really a mirror sketched in so carefully that it mirrors all the scales of representation, forcing Professor Food to face his own face in a distant reflection, and behind his face he can almost see the mirrored student faces facing the blackboard, as if he were nothing more than a talking mirror, getting consumed in the endless play of reflections, digested by what the students think he's teaching them, digested by what he knows he's not really teaching them, and the gap that forms between what they think and what he knows catches fire, burning down the classroom, burning down the school, burning down the walls of billboards crushing the school on every side, flames that sound like applause, flames that pause to enjoy what they're doing, flames that leap and dance composing a shadow play on the flat white sky, flames that seem comprised of all of history's conflagrations—Rome Chicago San Francisco Dresden Hiroshima—flames with no connection to firebirds rising from their ashes, leaving only what might have been there before, the college town, its tidy rows of nineteenth-century houses, the abandoned factory district, blackened buildings and obsolete smokestacks, motels with their neon signs by the freeway flashing their vacancy, as if there would soon be nothing left but the vacancy, nothing to reduce to print and pictures, nothing to cut and paste and frame and sell, only a sentence twisting and turning away from where it began, making and remaking itself through changes in speed and focus, a tale that's eating its tail, a tale untelling itself in the telling, feeding on the eyes of someone feeding on what he thinks it means, someone getting distracted and turning away from the page to find food.

CHRISTOPHER GRIMES

The Public Sentence

Speak of the devil, if it isn't our young Doctor defiantly taking his lunch break downwind from the Willet Loop Sewage Plant, secondary-source of his catastrophe some thirty-three and a third days ago, now bench-ridden in the Municipal Gardens before a terrace of white gladiolas, staring at his khaki-trousered knees while his Indian counterparts in Delhi are undoubtedly hard at work composing yet another addition to the thick ream of facsimiles providing oblique descriptions of their impenetrable customs, misleading and nonsensical analyses of their archaic municipal histography and sketchy explanations of their unfathomable appetites, all of which, sheaf by onionskin sheaf, churns the young Doctor's thoughts into foam while a limp rooster's tail of hair dangles from the crown of his head toward the back of his collar, cinched tight by a tie that he is too weary to loosen, as Ella, the young Doctor's wife of a month, attested this morning ("You are tossing and turning, do you understand me? and biting your teeth all night") in the timbre of innocent assessment because, as she pointed out immediately after the back-flush, as one of our newest immigrants she was least represented in the sewage now being contained by the Army Corps of Engineers in our beloved river, was, in point of fact, culpable for precisely fifty-seven days worth, a teeny-tiny drop in the bucket that she began contributing the morning she touched down at the Municipal Airport, her dry, frizzy hair the color of bark still carrying, it seemed to the young Doctor when they awkwardly embraced on the tarmac, something of the smell of the Autumn corn husks that fill the fields down there in Sioux Falls, where the two had been coupled as freshman physics lab partners at the University until, eventually, they found themselves not only sharing the lab table, but whole days together, then evenings and finally dormitories as pressed wood and Formica refuges against what they both thought to be a temporary condition during their remaining three years of college, namely their persistent sense of alienation, of being utterly alone without each other in that strangely expansive country, until they both graduated and she returned to Buenos Aires and he, not to the deep kettles and rolling moraines of his native south-central Wisconsin, but here, Bismarck, this Great State's Capital which employed him, and from where he posted short, type-written notes that *crescendoed*—a term used by Ella in a letter describing Paco D'martine's voice in *Jupiter y Juno*, within which Zeus does the deed with Hera, his wife and sister, as recalled and related by Ella from her stint in the orchestra pit of the Teatro Colon—into a one sentence invitation ("the Bismarck Municipal Symphony is looking for musicians") that prompted her subsequent descention from the sky as dramatic as a stage prop, bassoon in hand, a sheaf of operatic orchestrations flowing from memory to her fingertips unabated during an audition for the symphony, which, in preparation for the forthcoming summer-long festival of opera, immediately offered her a contract, withdrew it upon discovery that she had neither a work permit nor a Green Card, and offered it again when, two and a half months later, well within the Bureau of Customs and Immigration's three-month term-limit on tourist visas granted to Argentine Nationals, they were married, so that there she was this morning, sitting on the bathroom vanity, informing him that he is tossing and turning the night through and pointing out, before he could attempt to explain the seemingly unspeakable source of his nocturnal restlessness, the discrepancy between the color of his black belt and brown socks to which he, in turn, resisted the impulse to give her a brotherly punch in the arm—an astonishingly new impulse altogether, he being raised without siblings—and found himself staring at her, this *wife* of his, without any idea of what to do next, as a *husband*, but change his socks to rectify this slight fashion guffaw made in the distraction of the ever-present memory of the first harbinger turd, black and swollen as the plague itself, that surfaced on the Missouri at precisely 2:07 p.m. on a pleasant Saturday exactly thirty-three and a third days ago, thereby ushering in this state of mind we now find him in, sitting on his park bench, unbuttoning his cuffs and disheveling his collar and tie, oblivious to the flock of pigeons scattered around him, grounded themselves by the shimmering thermal folds of heat that have been slowly baking the river into a wretched, turtle-infested casserole, its warm, flatulent aroma wafting through the rusty links of chain and rope-burned bollards of the river port, blowing through the broken windows and open doors of the abandoned Customs House and the dilapidated Inter-Coastal Navy Mechanics School's barracks, across Pioneer Park, Grandview Heights, the Bird Arboretum and Divide Avenue, through Tom O'Leary Golf Course, Hanaford Avenue and 3rd and 4th Streets to dump its sour load of odors inside the shallow brick walls here in the Municipal Gardens, where it converges *counter-punctually* (Ella again) with the sweet theme running through the young Doctor's head in the form of last year's Christmas Program, exquisitely performed by our Municipal Choir, which included John Francis Wade's 1743 composition *Come All Ye Faithful* and its penetrating refrain which asks that we *come and adore Him* (repeated three times), effectively uniting us—you and me and the young Doctor himself—in the dark of our Civic Center then miraculously filled with a spirit altogether different from the one now displayed by us all, each one of us now, who haven't the vaguest notion of how our public waste is directed through a system second in complexity only to that one posteriorly balanced above it, who have, until this moment, been perched blind as bats on the great public commode without *once* having occasion to think past our ankles, down the wrought-iron throat that connects us to the municipal digestive system, the intestines of tunnels, conduits and channels, the brick-lined bowels that release into the newly vulcanized slag tanks churning the corporate volume flowing from our homes and businesses for, individually, we are more concerned with to whom the sound of the soft scrape of toilet paper is being heard than we are with the workings of the sophisticated mechanism that we are just then affixed, its product, coupled with the bad advice given to the young Doctor by the Indian Municipal Government in Delhi, being the true and primary source of the bespoilment of our beloved river and the burgeoning turtle population first, under the direction of those Indians, purposefully seeded and now swarming on our river's banks, their collective shock to our senses matched only by how shockingly quick we are to lay blame when, truly, no one contributing factor can be blamed, neither the impoverished Indians with their appetite for turtles, nor the summer of opera suddenly thrust upon us and the subsequent rush to prepare the infrastructure to receive it, which is undoubtedly taxing all of the municipal services, including the Division of Water Works, one component piece, albeit an important one, to the larger composition that makes up the Public Works, employer of the young Doctor, our Assistant Regulator of Flowage, who opened the grit chamber, but failed to close the outflow seals of the sedimentation lagoon, our raw sewage overwhelming the tertiary system, the charcoal filtration unit, lime clarifier and recarbination filters, so that we find ourselves with a very large helping of our own offal stew belched back into our river in its undigested state, now contained by the Army Corps of Engineers with gaudy yellow floats and buoys that keep the discharge stationary, but not the turtles from migrating, as the Department of Natural Resources pointed out, pronouncing both the spill *and* turtle population a biological hazard, thus provoking the overly hasty adoption of the ill-conceived Indian model first posited by the young Doctor, who, drawing on his Comparative Municipal Histography curriculum, directed the

Emergency Advisory Committee's attention to the confluence of the Ganges and Yamuna Rivers, where the Indians in general and Hindus in particular pilgrimage to wash their feet in waters endowed with the mystical power to wash away both sin and sickness and the tribulations of the dead who, cremated if the mourner can afford the wood for the funeral pyre—the Indian soul apparently being designed to leave through the head, which is apparently signaled by the skull cracking in a shower of sparks—and cast into the river, are assured liberation from the cycles of life and death, the inference being that, not at all unlike us, those Indians love their river and therefore can't keep themselves away from it, the consequence of which is that it swarms with cholera, tetanus and typhoid, that a statistical analysis of a tear drop of its microbiotic life yields cosmological proportions, and that its flow has grown sluggish with human silt, a fact that does not dissuade in the least the pilgrims from immersing themselves in the symbolically charged but unspeakably polluted river roiling with their beloveds' ashes—in itself not problematic, as estuary muck is estuary muck—but it's the impoverished multitudes, however, who are unable to afford the wood for a proper cremation, and their alternative ritual of chanting then simply dumping in their corpses, beads and all, like a sack of spoiled yams, that, when we multiply this act by the millions, conveys a sense of the problem's severity, and, hence, the simple genius of what by all accounts is, or *was*, a seemingly infallible solution, of which even those in the various Indian Municipal agencies in Delhi could not help but be awed by the centrifugal force of life and death at the heart of its populace, namely that the turtles released into the Ganges year after year—a species that subsists on decaying matter, particularly fond of the flesh—are eventually poached and eaten, the turtle population therefore controlled by sheer appetite alone by those same pilgrims who dampen out the sun with their breakfast fires before wrapping up their dead for their big send off, thereby obscuring what appeared by all accounts to be a useful test case for an environmentally efficient, low-cost clean water program with similar impurities, a model so compelling, in fact, that the young Doctor himself tabled it without ever imagining that the turtle population would, as anyone can now plainly see, reach the thousands, if not tens of thousands, such that the sheer congestion of the shells on the surface of the Missouri admittedly gives it, if not a hallucinatory, than at least a menacing aspect, so much so that while no immediate danger to the operational infrastructure of our city is predicted, the Department of Public Works, equally alarmed at the negative *aesthetic* impact that the turtles may have on our visitors and residents alike, offers two, possibly concomitant solutions, the first one being that we effectively eradicate a controlled portion of the turtles by, for example, injecting sides of beef with a toxic, non-leaching substance in an effort to target the species without jeopardizing the life of the river itself—the one significant drawback here involving an understandable reluctance to floating sides of beef down the river (an unsavory prospect for any stroller to happen upon)—which brings us to the second proposition, a more community-oriented approach, whereby a sum of money is offered, or perhaps a ticket, or coupons towards the cost of a ticket to some of our community events like, for instance, the forthcoming opera, or the art museum, in exchange for a turtle brought to a particular location, which might be called a "return station" and may be affiliated with our recycling stations, the outcome being, it is hoped, that both the ever-burgeoning turtle population is curbed while, simultaneously, cultivating interest in our community events, and, as an added bonus, it is further hoped that the turtle "return" will be particularly attractive to our youth, who it is believed will see it as a "game," and as consequence receive a "prize," thus fostering participation in these cultural events, suffering, as they are, from lack of at least local interest, all of which should reveal both the enormous obstacles confronted by and far-reaching substance of the young Doctor's counter-proposal, and might, therefore, silence his critics who more than suggest that his Ph.D. is a Ph.Demented, a Ph.Dummy, and—in the halls of the Public Water Works—his pH's unbalanced, though even there a tendency exists for misrepresenting the complexity of the system, so that he is sorely tempted to abandon us to the pathogenic diseases which generally dwell in our digestive tracks, as well as the malodorous gasses created by the decomposition of our solid wastes, while, in his new-found free time, the young Doctor might instead enjoy becoming acquainted with his wife and finally writing a review for the seventh edition of the excellent four-volume series *Sewerage and Sewage Disposal* written by the engineers Metclaff and Eddy (though indispensable as it otherwise is, there's not a word printed on *this* subject), to say nothing about the real problem with criticizing and laying blame, mainly knowing when to stop, because all are finally blameworthy, including the most innocent-seeming among us, like Ella, for instance, for whom the young Doctor made explicit his requiring one hour of solitude before leaving for his office, so that she was free to lunch to the accompaniment of a military marching band, puncture the fall of darkness with fireworks and sparklers, and in all hours in-between (except six to seven in the morning) waltz about with bone china tea plates strapped to her feet while tooting her infernal bassoon if she was so moved, but *this* exact hour was to be a peaceful hour, the only one that he fully relies upon to unfold *peaceably* in order to execute the responsibilities of his part of the Public (which Ella is no doubt part of now) Works, the complexity and contemplation of which requires, in both strict and vivid language, to declare that if she is so inclined to use the toilet during this time, that she would please avoid flushing, as, his study being situated below the bathroom, his skull is filled with its vacuous suction, thereby drawing his attention from the task at hand, away to the opposite wall, inside which the sewer pipe is hidden, and that preempting this constant interruption by clasping his hands over his ears serves, since the physics of plumbing are in no large degree different in the human and municipal forms, little good, as the sound of the flush perfectly mimics the sound of one, with his hands over his ears, swallowing, but he does not blame Ella, no, on the contrary he hears the sound of the waste water falling through the pipe and is reminded of their connectivity, how each is plugged into something larger, how the many make up the one, and how the Austrian composer Schiller himself defined the bassoon as the instrument of hunger and unquestionable optimism, so that we too might do well to listen to Ella's transformation of gasses into music with her alchemist's instrument right smack on top of our young Doctor's head and recall Schiller's odd axiom that *one bassoon doth the symphony make*, and not be surprised when, after taking our seats, after the lights are dimmed and we hear Ella's throaty bassoon lumbering out of the woodwinds during the *prelude*, we find the young Doctor sitting there in the darkness next to us, and the choice will be ours, to up and leave our seats or remain, pretending to ignore him, yearning for the last note to fade, concerned not with the painted faces, colorful costumes and booming voice before us, but instead our tail bones pressing further and further against our skins, thus reminding us of the young Doctor's presence and therefore possibly missing the moment when we might be otherwise filled with the emotion at the heart of every tragedy ever written, acted or sung, which is that our hero, having made his mistake in water, finds that nothing remains to wash it away.

Curbing

Ascenseur, Monsieur?
Photons travel free
through the angled cuts in towers
and the lush lawn
suddenly curbing
the edge downtown
where you can hear the little noise
made when improvising learning.

The Palms of Space

When you called, I was on my knees
picking beans off the floor in the 3rd most-poisoned
parish in the state.
I was replicating all existing lines
in the apartment, a toy universe
to inflate the environmental capacity
like a bubble whose outside
is a larger bubble keeping pace.

When the squirrel learns to take off its head
it finds a head the same weight
as the walnut. The material world
is a mental machine
on a string of days without accident
exceeding memory.
For the patient, fruits of the Osage-oranges
splash to the lagoon
under the gibbous, howling, hole in the sky
punched by the Titans to fix
the position of the inner life
once created, there is no refusing.

We are all sensitive people, eating lunch
in the car. There, space creates a mental form,
appearing contemplative.

How long would I lie in the puddle?
Could I fill the cart?

The palms of space hide the afternoon
in song that plays on the radio.
You can hear it conspiring to mystify
the hoary trees on hillside.

My face, is it a battery?
Is capacity stored
to scale?

Without it there would be no opposite,
no quiet taking the grass of the playing field,
nor pen tapping on the aluminum stands,
no way to pass through
the porous and soluble hood
into a new world
that brings familiar poverty.

C.S. GISCOMBE

From *Prairie Style*

1304 North Central Avenue

Indianapolis, Indiana

To me, intention's a fact, a register equal to any other value. Intention's the device in nature. It repeats the range. I like that it's noisy or can be; I like that it's a measure. The median is full of images. Argument's there to discern, to straighten you out. To me, meaning's like parallel streets. Meaning stands in. Nothing's more sexual than laziness. I'd be equivocal, I'd pass.

Prairie Style

"I use the word 'Negro' in the sense in which it is commonly used in the United States, to designate a person with any discernible amount of Negro blood."
—Emma Lou Thornbrough, *The Negro in Indiana* (1957).

Situation's the uncertain argument; the neighborhood can't contain it though it starts because of the neighborhood. The contour property gives you takes the place of region.

A Cornet at Night

I'm the fish horn, I'm going to lean out and blow for you.

Say I'm a fact of nature, a habit of life, the broad ripple. Say I'm a Usonian. Say I'm from out past the turnaround but have come in like a pack of dogs to reveal eros to you, to converse with you about the repeating shape. Say I'm teeth and crows. Say I'm voodoo-dick. Say I cleave to you or say I'm a vacant seat pulling away from the curb. Say I'm incomplete without you, sugar. Say I'm late but say how I'll come sooner or later. Say I'm doubtless. Say I'm lazy but articulate.

PAUL A. TOTH

The Kind of Girl You Read About in New Wave Magazines

Carol used to sashay into that Holiday Inn conference room sexless as a TV dinner, tits shielded by aluminum foil, ass and crotch wrapped in gauze like accident victims you'd rather not see, lips painted like black eyes, eyelids the color of ruby lips. She was cold, but that's not an accurate description. She was Cold.

Well, that was her story, anyway. But she loved Joe from the start, Joe with his baseball hat and skinny frame the bomb blew six inches off. To her, he looked like he belonged on a baseball card from a 1912 team called the Craters. When he and his teammates ran, it probably looked like the keystone cops, at least on newsreels. That was Joe. She called him Joe DiMaggio.

He and his men met each year at this Holiday Inn thirty miles west of Indianapolis. They celebrated their survival. She watched their rituals without sympathetic impulse, motherly urge or savior instinct. She watched from her throne and came down for the Unsexing and that was it.

Joe protected her. Every year at least one group of outsiders faked their way inside the conference. They'd hoot and holler and splash beer everywhere and grab themselves the way no regular would. Every year, Joe stood and walked over to that table like a sheriff. The other regulars would yell, "Uh-oh, uh-oh," as Joe looked at the strangers and said, "This party's for men that ain't got no sex." Then Joe reached down, grabbed a guy's crotch and said, "She's ain't even interested in being interested."

It started with a box of magazines Joe found in a bombed out bookstore, down in the basement, beside a box of tools that fit nothing invented since 2015. They allowed victims an hour to roam through the site of an attack and keep one thing, which the government shrinks called the Transformative Object.

Joe's TO was a ripped pop music magazine circa 1982. Stapled in the center was a photo of a model dressed in foil leotard and platform shoes. She wore red sunglasses and cherry lipstick. The caption read, "Now that's a girl you read about in new wave magazines!"

What made Joe choose that photo? He told Carol that 1982 was a special year for him, the year his mother was born. She used to show him newspapers and magazines that her own mother collected. There was a song her mother loved, something about eating cars in bars. And so the girl in the magazine, he said, looked like she ate cars in bars, spitting out chunks of metal, rubber. But most of all, Joe said, she looked like she was the opposite of his wife—and all his friends' wives—never nagging about the lack of sex, but reveling in it.

"This," he told Carol when she auditioned for the part, holding the photo for her to see, "is a woman most men would hate. We worship her."

Carol took the part, a bimonthly role for an actress whose career was over. In her last production, an historical epic, the director almost choked her to death when the mark from her second small pox shot showed on screen. "You 'ave got ze small pox inzection vizible right zere," the German screamed. "They vere no small pox shots in ze Civil War and ezpezially not two!"

She always remembered Joe's last long look before making his decision. She swept her hand across the width of her body and said, "Don't even look in my direction: This land is my land."

"Made for you and me?"
"Nope. Just me."

One day she admitted to Joe she loved him.
"But I can't love you back," he said.
"Not physically, Joe, but I don't care."
"What about kids?"
"The children are the past."
"We gotta keep a few coming."
"For what?"
"Because things could settle down one day."
"What about Honolulu, Joe? That was two weeks ago."
"It could've been worse."
"Two thousand?"
She stared into his baseball card face and imagined Old America.
"What's the matter?" he asked.
"It feels like the station never comes in, like I'm tuning and hearing voices and --"
"The little bits of news, the rumors, the predictions and forecasts? Give it twenty years and that starts to sound like music, dear." His hand almost touched hers. He pulled back.
"Go ahead, Joe, hold my hand."
"It ain't right."

The caption beneath the photo led to a song taking on great importance for him. Joe found the disk in an old store and wrote the lyrics down on a napkin, soon torn and shredded. The words became totemic, especially the reference to Room 714 and, of course, that line about Chinatown, where Joe's nuts were blown off. Bits and shards and fragments chased him like smoke from a bomb.
A girl in a new wave magazine, a superfreak. She was all right.

This was the night of the Unsexing, the big event at the Holiday Inn, developed over the first three years, brainstormed and improvised, never quite the same, aided by group intoxication, exactly when they would have tried to pick her up in the days before their injuries.
They counted along with Joe as he read the incantation:
"One: Connection or dealings between persons or groups. Two: Exchange, especially of thoughts or feelings: Communion. Three: Physical sexual contact between individuals that involves the genitalia of at least one person."
They men laid their hands face down on the table and sang in a monotone and off-key voice:

> I will take you home to mother.
> I will let your spirits down.
> Once I get you off the street
> I do not want to know you.
> Your toenails sicken me
> And your feet, yeah.

She walked across their hands, their knuckles cracking.

I don't care what you do, boys.
I love your zeroes.
You can't add with me.
One plus nothing equals one
And that leaves me.
I'm keeping my one
Right between my legs.
Because this land is my land,
It was made for me and me.

It was Joe's responsibility to pay her at the end of the song. He always had a funny look.

"Fuck your money, Joe DiMaggio," she'd say.

"But I wasn't trying to—" he'd reply. "I'm the Joe you can't blow."

As if in church, the men stood and proclaimed, "Promise you won't fuck us, Lady. Promise we can just be friends."

"I promise," she hissed. "I promissssssse."

When she pulled down her leotard, there was nothing there, really. They never figured out how she hid it. They just clapped and whistled.

On the last night of the fifth year, she visited Joe's room after the Unsexing. Room 714. She had a feeling about that strange look in his eye. She leaned in his doorway and stretched in every direction, like a four-legged spider sprawled vertically.

"One of these days," she said, "I'll wait for you backstage with my girlfriends, in a limousine. We're going back in Chinatown. Or should I say Chinatown Three? Is that too kinky for girls in new wave magazines?"

He looked as though he might slam the door, but instead quietly closed and locked it.

"Joe!"

"The Joe you can't blow."

He wheeled onto the balcony from her living room, oxygen rig at his side. "Some getup, ain't it?"

She reached to touch his hand, but he gripped his armrest and shook his head.

"Well, the radiation was gonna catch up sooner or later," he said.

"And I know why you really came. But I don't care about your secrets."

"Those meetings when I was a kid, they showed me pictures of another time, you know? It's really about time travel, back to some sepia-toned postcard they carry in their heads. Like --"

"Like Joe DiMaggio?"

"Like that, sure. Like Old America, Old World. Out of time."

"But you ended up stuck in time after the bomb, right, Joltin' Joe?"

"I was any dumb kid stuck in his own damn time and place. The bomb would blow me out. I thought."

"Stop it," Carol said. She walked to the balcony, swept her hand across the width of her body and said, "Ain't it pretty, all that smoke and sun pouring through?"

"Prettier than I remember peace."

"It's too bad we could never."

"It only takes one person," he said. "I mean, that was a trick when you pulled down your leotard, right?"

"What?"

"Come here," he said.

She walked towards him. He leaned forward, kissed her, and pushed the button on his armrest.

Goddamn it, look at the earth down there. Temptations, sing! Orange fire makes a wonderful searing bed for two. Blow, Danny! Old Joe, the wind blowing through our brains. Chinatown Three wasn't you, was it? It was, it was.

"But I'm her all-time, down to her toenails." That song you sang, fucked up and chopped, because that's the best that you could offer, your bits and shards and fragments. Blew your own nuts off, huh? With your own bomb? I could've crammed my foil leotard down your throat when the sick came on, an aluminum angel.

But when the sun comes shining and I stroll and the wheat fields wave and the dust clouds roll and the fog lifts and a voice chants and we walk down that ribbon of highway to the endless skyway from California to the New York Island, I'll say, "Here's to you, Joe DiMaggio. Jesus loves you more than you will know. Hey, hey, hey." Because this land is your land. I promise. I promisssssssse.

BRADFORD GRAY TELFORD

Kate Moss Queries Her Counselor on the Nature of Love

in that the "Green Group" is facility shorthand for the sex addicts whom everyone feels can't dress which may be a part of their problem—a problem with a range of symptoms and behaviors treated by "No-Fraternization Contracts" and the "Ten-Second Rule" and volleyball

which she enjoys—volleyball

although why there's a swimming pool is quite beyond her—in that why Staff permit the Green Group pool privileges what with their doughy bodies their worn-out sex organs and their shattered families

is one of only several disagreements she'd like to discuss with *someone* in charge

although she won't because she wants everyone to think she's interested in recovering and not causing problems or being a diva and—deep down—she wants everyone to like her

everyone

and wanting everyone to like her—they keep pointing out—in their clever and at times roundabout ways—is part of her problem—especially since she hates everyone

although during the last volleyball game they got so good she threatened to charter a bus so they could take on Betty Ford and beat their drunk ass—and everyone laughed and loved her which she loved—which of course made her hate them more which she hated which of course she loved—

GABRIEL GUDDING

Fifteen Minute Performative Masculinity New York School Name Dropping Poem for David Shapiro as Transcribed from his Interview at Pennsound

I said to Jasper Johns
I was walking with Allen Ginsberg
I wrote a book with Jacques Derrida
When I was at Columbia
It was one of those wonderful days
I commute a lot but I write while I'm commuting
Joe writes a lot when he commutes too
I dedicate this to the painter Jeremy Rolfe
I hardly knew Kenneth then
I had memorized everything in the New York Public Library
I met Kenneth and I loved him
I met Joe Ceravolo and Frank Lima
We won the avant garde book award
We met almost all the time that we could
It was one of the first times that I had an essay in a dream
After that dream essay came this poem by Joe which is of course
Not by Joe but by me
That was a poem given to me by Joe
Kenneth said he did he did win a national award
This is a poem for Joe
I'll read another poem for Joe
I said when I was off the air
This is a poem I wrote thinking about how often we'd meet
He said, "I want to found a school, David."
I said, "Oh that sounds great, Joe."
And he said, "Yes, you know."
I also met Allen Ginsberg a lot and we would walk
I am referring mostly to Charles Ives
Allen Ginsberg walked beside me
That is influenced by Samuel Beckett's radio play Oh Joe
I was writing a book with Jacques Derrida
I heard a dog crying the day I had to give one seminar on prayer
Rabbi Heschel, the great protestor, his wife is now my cousin by marriage
I wrote this work for Joe Ceravolo, my friend
At Bard College where I taught
I've always wanted to do an opera, it wd be very Kochian
I want to read something less lugubrious
I do have a lot of elegies
I'm getting to this age where people want me to write my memoirs
I said to Jasper Johns a year or two ago
When I was at Columbia I once threatened self-destruction to Kenneth Koch
This is a poem I wrote walking around the George Washington Bridge
Frank Lima writes in the subway every morning at six o'clock
My welsh terrier walked around this park a lot
I dedicate this to the painter Jeremy Rolfe
This was pre-Giuliani
Paul Georges once said

It's like one of those moments in Wallace Stevens
I want to read something for Rudy Burkhart
Of the great friends that I've lost, Kenneth Koch, Joe Ceravolo, Meyer Schapiro
Jacob and I, Jacob his son, has worked with me at Cooper Union
I said to Rudy I said you're the best photographer in America
He left me, he left my son, really, a hundred photographs
He drowned himself like his friend Edmund Denby
He said You're always giving me gifts, and he said Yes no more gifts
So I wrote this song for Rudy
He loved New York, he also loved nature
I said to him you're the best nature photographer
Antonioni said I love Monica Vitti but I also love a white line on a street
Rudy really knew how to make a white line on a street
As beautiful as a woman
It's very hard to do
The architect John Hejduk makes a great drawing every day
He's another great friend and I'll read a poem for him later
Here's another poem for Rudy and it's really a 9-11 poem
I wrote a lot
I was a violinist
I was like a trained monkey and my family was all trained monkeys
My grandfather was one of the great singers of the world
He's a composer also
He was very important
You can still go to Judaica stores and buy them
Mozart is a standard
Where Glenn Gould is playing
My father was not only a violist but a sculptor
He studied with a student of Rodin
I remember when Kenneth said congratulations on yr dual career
I married an architect
She introduced me to Meyer Schapiro
He defended Jackson Pollock
He wd defend Wolf Kahns' landscapes
Willem de Kooning
My great teacher, he really introduced modern art studies at Columbia
He brought de Kooning and Barnett Newman and others TO Columbia
I once sd to Wm de Kooning is it true that Meyer saved yr woman number one?
As Delmore Schwartz once said
Here's a very funny one for Meyer
His great love Picasso
Meyer lectured on it for a famous five hours
An arrow wd not pierce her vagina
I could not erase one woman
Who is all cunt and spine and democratic bone
You're sucking me off
Certain people thought that I shouldn't publish that
But then forgave me
A lot of my life is about architecture
I worked for a long time with John Hejduk

When he met the Romanian president he gave him Emily Dickinson
When I was a fellow at Cambridge
My poem was placed in the castle in the castle and dedicated by Havel
He took a poem of mine and translated it
I'm looking forward to the day when the president of Columbia and I and others
I met his brother and he sd the whole Palach family thanks you
What was moving in Prague when I read that poem
Havel said
Havel had someone recite my poem by heart
John Hejduk liked that part of the poem
Trotsky was in love with my grandmother
My uncle was not only a great pianist but also wrote sonnets for the New York Times
My father was also concerned with everything
Like Meyer Schapiro he also cared about everything
There were hordes of people of a variety of races in my home
Allen Ginsberg didn't like the left being violent nor did I
I felt very close to Robert Lowell
Kenneth used to say to me
This was published in South Africa when I was 12
Every poem of mine is an act of resistance
The old surrealists have grown up and have good jobs
A lot of us used to dream whether our names wd be next to Thucydides
Poem for my architect John Hejduk, the greatest architect
I wrote a long poem for him

Weight Loss

Undernourished mice created in an Atlanta genetics lab may offer hints at why some people can eat all they want and still stay thin.

Researchers have found that with a single genetic alteration, they can turn up the natural metabolic furnace in mice so that the animals burn more fat. Experts said that people might soon be able to control their weight by doing the same thing, or by exploiting related processes.

Mice with the mutation have about 6% body fat, compared to about 15% in their unaltered brethren. But even more impressive, the genetically altered mice can eat a high-fat diet without ill effects.

*

Who would you bomb in that one?

I'd bomb the "experts."

I'd bomb the incorporated biotech firms that employ the "experts."

What about the genetically altered mice?

I'd grow them vampire teeth then drop them down the trousers of the corporate chieftains.

Smiling with Cancer

A man who for three years pretended to be dying of cancer—even shaving his head and faking seizures—got 14 months in prison Thursday. Kurt Kelleher, 50, was also ordered to repay nearly $43,000 to his victims and perform 200 hours of community service.

The former vacuum cleaner salesman claimed to have kidney, lung and prostate cancer. His former wife and three stepsons believed him, as did most of his fellow residents of Canterbury, a town of about 1,700 in central New Hampshire.

To convince people, Kelleher shaved his head, talked about how awful chemotherapy was and dropped red dye in his toilet to make it appear like blood in his urine.

"He also faked seizures, sometimes slamming his head into walls to make the episodes look realistic," said Branford Rawson, a federal prosecutor.

*

Who would you bomb in that one?

I'd bomb Branford Rawson, the federal prosecutor.

Hell, he's just a custodian with an Ivy League name. I'd bomb the federal judiciary building, in DC.

What about Kurt Kelleher, cancer lover?

I'd bust him out of jail, pin the coyote medal on his heart, and plant a wet kiss on his thin lips.

Pigeons

Several hundred pigeons were distributed to Marine Corps units in Baghdad to warn the leathernecks of chemical or biological attacks..

Like the canaries that miners once carried in case they ran into explosive gas underground, the pigeons fall victim to dangers and die.

In this instance, the pigeons are gassed or biologically infected by predators with identical black mustaches.

Lacking our elevated moral nature (19th century term), pigeons die more rapidly than humans.

Lacking our far superior cerebral cortex, pigeons cannot experience pain like humans.

Marine Corps units, then, will get a heads-up from the suffocated-to-death pigeons. The Marines will also be equipped with $682,000 worth of mechanical sensors in case the pigeons don't die on cue.

The pigeons cost $63 each, including seed.

*

Who would you bomb in that one?

I'd bomb the think-tank that came up the stratagem of sacrificing pigeons.

What about the Marine Corps four-star general who passed down the order?

Court-martial his ass.

No shit. Dude will leave the Corps and get a job in industry paying him seven times what he got as a leatherneck.

Then interrogate him with extreme prejudice, along with the corporate think-tank humans. Do to them what's been done to their prisoners in Abu Ghraib and Guantánamo and the rest of those hells where Muslim captives are outsourced.
Is that the word I'm looking for—outsourced.

I believe it is, yes.

Corgi

Queen Elizabeth was said to be devastated by the death of one of her corgis, put down after it was savaged by an English bull terrier belonging to her daughter, Princess Anne, newspapers reported.

The bull terrier, Dottie, which last year caused the princess to be fined after it severely bit two Pakistani children at a London park, attacked the queen's corgi, Raj, at a family gathering at Sandringham, the Sun reported.

The Daily Mail said that an elite veterinarian team was called in, but too late, and Raj, the corgi, one of the queen's oldest pets, was put to sleep.

*

Well?

I'd bomb the Englishman who invented the phrase "put down."

You assume it was an Englishman, and the probability is you're right. I would bomb the royal palaces, Windsor, Buckingham, those in Wales and Scotland, the lot.

And the Pakistani children severely bitten by Raj, the bull terrier?

No, Raj is the name of the corgi. Dottie is the bull terrier.

Sorry. What about the assaulted Pakistani children?

Bleach their skin and teach them to ride to hounds. If that doesn't take, send them back to Pakistan. As a D.C think-tank strategist put it: Since the death of Communism the ideological rift is no longer between West and East: freedom and totalitarianism; but between North and South: the exalted mores of Christian-Judaic culture as against the desert-scarred, emotion-laden Muslim sectors.

<u>Hippo</u>

Diana Silk-Davies, Ms South Africa in 2002 and first runner-up in the 2003 Ms World contest, was mauled by a hippopotamus while canoeing in Okavango swamp, Botswana, the local constabulary reported.

The blonde beauty winner, who was bitten on her face and thighs, was airlifted to Johannesburg hospital, where she was reported to be in critical condition.

Earlier this month, another South African beauty contest winner, Annette Jeanne Kruger, was murdered by a hippo while she and her family were on safari holiday in the Okavango.

*

The hippos are pissed.

Yes, they are. Who would you bomb?

She was a blonde Ms South Africa who was mauled by a hippo in Botswana. Where's Botswana?

North of South Africa. British colony until 1966. Former name: Bechuanaland.

Tongue-twister. Can we bomb the colonizing British retroactively?

Regrets, that isn't permitted.

I'd bomb blonde beauty contest winners who live and thrive in Africa with hyphenated surnames.

Me? I'd bomb the safari tourist trade.

Why did I expect you to say that? Which hand do you wipe your arse with?

Which hand? The left. The decisive blows are always struck left-handed.

<u>Stoolmaker = Ayliffe</u>

The families of two 17-year-old girls critically injured in separate car wrecks, kept vigil at the wrong bedside for more than a week before one of the girls woke up and ended the confusion.

"Apparently, the two girls involved were the same age, had the same color eyes, both were unconscious, and both had swollen features," Gasland Hospital Superintendent Glenn Garver explained.

Oddly, each of the girls had a pet cat of the same species, a snowshoe female, which is half Siamese and half American shorthair.

The family of Lissa-Jean Stoolmaker watched over a girl in Gasland, a Flint hospital, for eight days before she regained consciousness Thursday and uttered her name: Jamie-Lynn Ayliffe, as well as her Social Security number and birthday.

Lissa-Jean Stoolmaker, it turned out, was in critical condition at Dogstar Hospital in Saginaw, Michigan, where Jamie-Lynn Ayliffe's family had been keeping watch.

*

Who would you bomb in that one?

I'd bomb the Michigan auto industry.

I'd bomb Gasland and Dogstar.

I'd bomb the nuclear family.

What about the all-American teenagers?

Bomb their butts.

All of 'em? Even the introverted ones who still dream, who don't dress hip-hop, play video games, gun their parents' SUVs?

Shit yeah. If I don't bomb 'um I freeze 'um. Deep freeze. Cryonics.

And the bombed teens' cats ?The snowshoes?

Oh, spare the cats. Honor the cats. Snowshoes, Maine Coons, Rag Dolls, Persians, American shorthairs, Abyssinians, all of them. Erect a cantilevered city, plant artificial mice.

<u>Sorry White Trash</u>

In a profanity-ridden letter to the US Supreme Court, convicted murderer Rodney Mohammed Abu-Rauf admitted killing two young Taco Bell employees in Burbank, California, said he felt no remorse for the crimes, and demanded to be executed.

"I'm guilty as s***!" said the letter, signed by Rauf. "Ain' got no remorse! Give me my execution date and off me!"

Rauf, 35, is scheduled to be executed January 26 at Corcoran State Prison. The Compton man was convicted of fatally shooting a 27-year-old Taco Bell manager and a 16-year-old employee during a 2002 robbery that netted him about $111.

In Rauf's letter, released by the Supreme Court on Thursday, he addressed the high court judges as "sorry white trash plus one oreo," and demanded that they let him be executed, protesting against several appeals filed on his behalf in recent years by public defense attorneys.

In an earlier letter to the court, Rauf admitted stabbing one of his since disavowed attorneys 17 times at Corcoran, adding: "Unfortunately the piece of s*** lives."

Prison officials confirmed that Rauf did stab a lawyer multiple times with a pencil.

*

Isn't his name Abu-Rauf? How come they call him Rauf?

Because his real name is nigger black subhuman.

He stabbed his public-defense lawyer 17 times with a pencil. He must have a hard swift stroke.

He's a strong guy, an athlete. Played defensive back for his community college football team before dropping out of school. So who would you bomb?

I'd bomb Taco Bell and the fast food industry.

I'd bomb the industries that make a profit out of prison labor.

You'll need a whole lot of TNT for that deal. What about the government sectors responsible for the so-called obscenity statutes?

You mean for forcing folks to spell shit with an "s" and three asterisks?

Uh-huh.

Hell, I'd bomb their sorry motherfucking asses back to the stone age.

Ain't that a little extreme?

Das right, Massa.

DEBRA DI BLASI

The Incomplete But Real History of *The Jiří Chronicles* Illustrated by The Real Jirí Cêch™

wait!
is a member
e Undead!
ves!!!
courtesy
big
vagina-brain
dark
energy
+
beer (Pilsner)
Z.
26.
28.
chocolate
23.
24.
25.
(infinitum)
27.
ad
infinitum
Whither

mpireFreaks.com
yee-haw!
yikes!
USA
29.
edward
witten's
brain
waves
30.
M-theory paral
MISSION ACCOMPLISHED!
99.9% chimp DNA
ELON UNIVERSITY
all omissions
corrected!!!

31.
this is not Jim
this is not Jim, too
"who is?"
32.
33.
The Pitch
I.E.D.
THE KANSAS CITY STAR.
34.
ozone
35.
lel universe
flashback
war, huh, what the
fuck is it good for?!?
RAGTAG

36.
REAL? OR?
et al. heads
POETS AGAINST WAR
BANG!
39.
squawk!
37.
(not amused)
what the fuck?!?
40.
38.

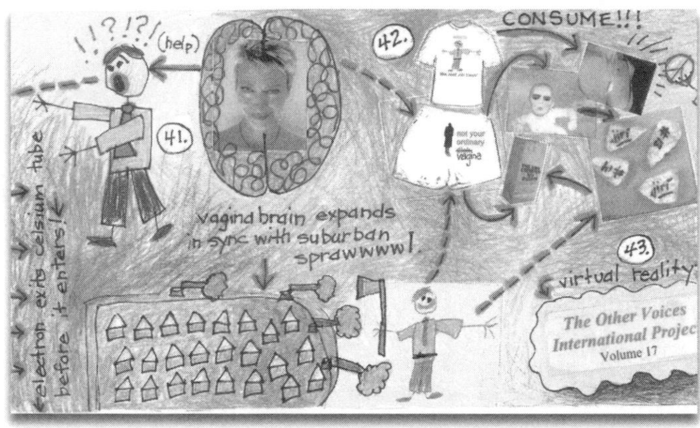
!?!?!(help)
42.
CONSUME!!!
41.
not your ordinary vagina
electron exits celsium tube before it enters!
vagina brain expands in sync with suburban sprawwwwl.
43.
virtual reality
The Other Voices International Projec
Volume 17

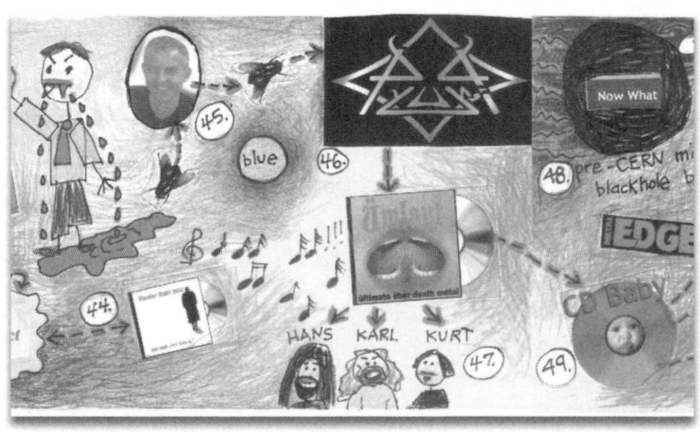
Now What
45.
blue
46.
48.
pre-CERN mi
blackhole b
EDGE
ultimate über death metal
44.
CD Baby
HANS
KARL
KURT
47.
49.

55.
57.
myspace.com
a place for friends
mini
blog
50.
51.
ROCK'S HARDEST MAGAZINE
52.
53.
54.
WIKIPEDIA
LAKE FOREST COLLEGE
56.
58.
COMEDY CENTRAL
RENAISSANCE MALIBU

(BEARS)
I'm #2
61.
64.
65.
60.
usa
CHARACTERS WELCOME
(please!)
hic!
59.
63.
DRUNKEN 2006
BOAT #8
62.
WAYNE STATE UNIVERSITY PRESS
uh-oh

iTunes
wippit
InProdicon
MUSIC
musicmatch
RUCKUS
66.
at&t
jpc
Musik à la carte
verizonwireless
OnGen
puretracks
GreatIndieMusic.com
entertainment
MP3tunes
MOOCS
zune
Rhapsody
cingular
CONNECT
music
tradebit.com
AOL music now
WAL★MART
Tree Tunes
nareos
muze
emusic
destramedia
INTERIA.PL
MPERIA
SNOCAP
DISC-GO
Bitmunk
musicnet
payplay.fm
Theta Music technologies, inc.
BUYMUSIC.COM
moozika
SONIFIC
passalong
PLAY INDIES
MP3 extension
panicky C.D.C. researchers
uh-oh

e worldwide audio
ndemic that is
real Jiri Cech..™
who is
hung
Look!
No hands!
AWP
Atlanta Georgia
2007
70.
67.
68.
72.
?
ck makes
me fart)
#59
...not hung
(big gun =
small dick)
71.
Blog of The Frivolous Borscht-Belt Bab
Friends
st
loaded tune: "I Hate
body (& U2)"
69.

73.
?
hit
man
ded Ibis productions, inc.
a transmedia corporation
z-z-z-z
74.
(nap time)
ad
infinitum
jirí

the real **Jirí Cêch** says: "Buy my stuff!"

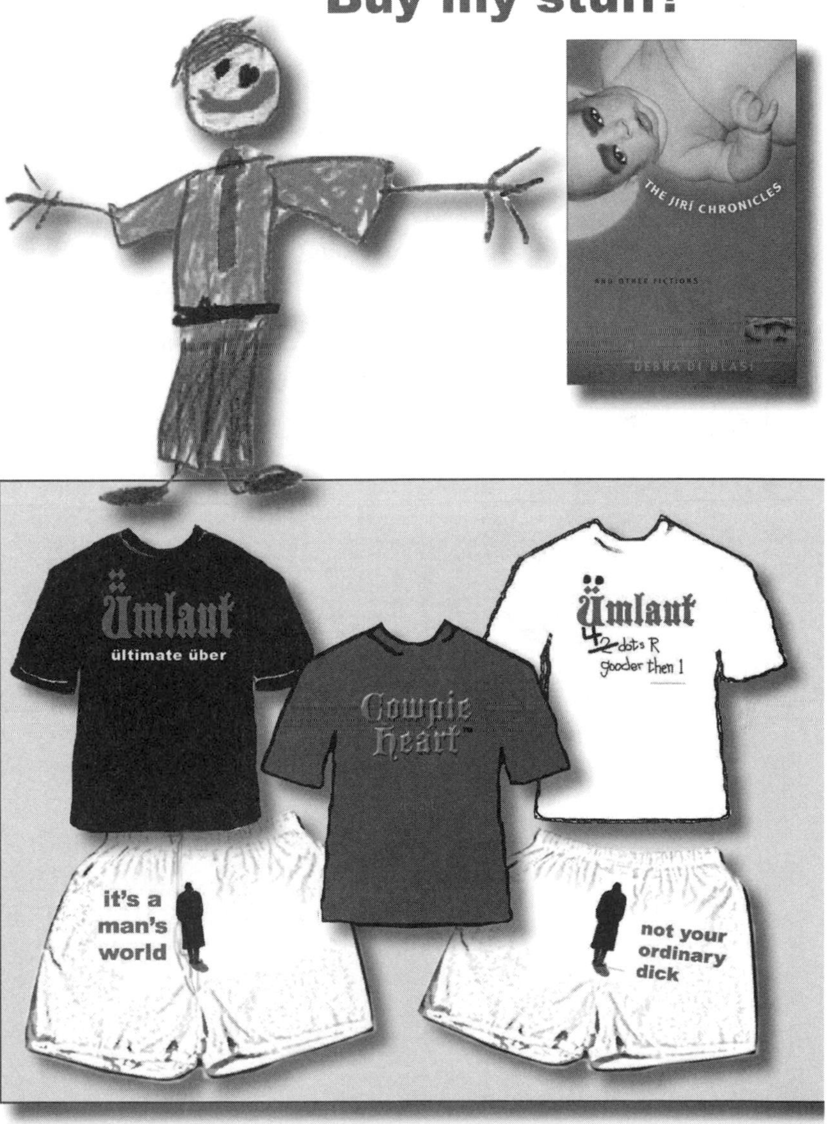

capitalist consumer *products!*

More than 300 fabulous creations of art therapy drawings, experimental poetry, art & music DVDs, CDs, clothing & lots & lots of absolutely *must-have!*

The Jirí Chronicles 3

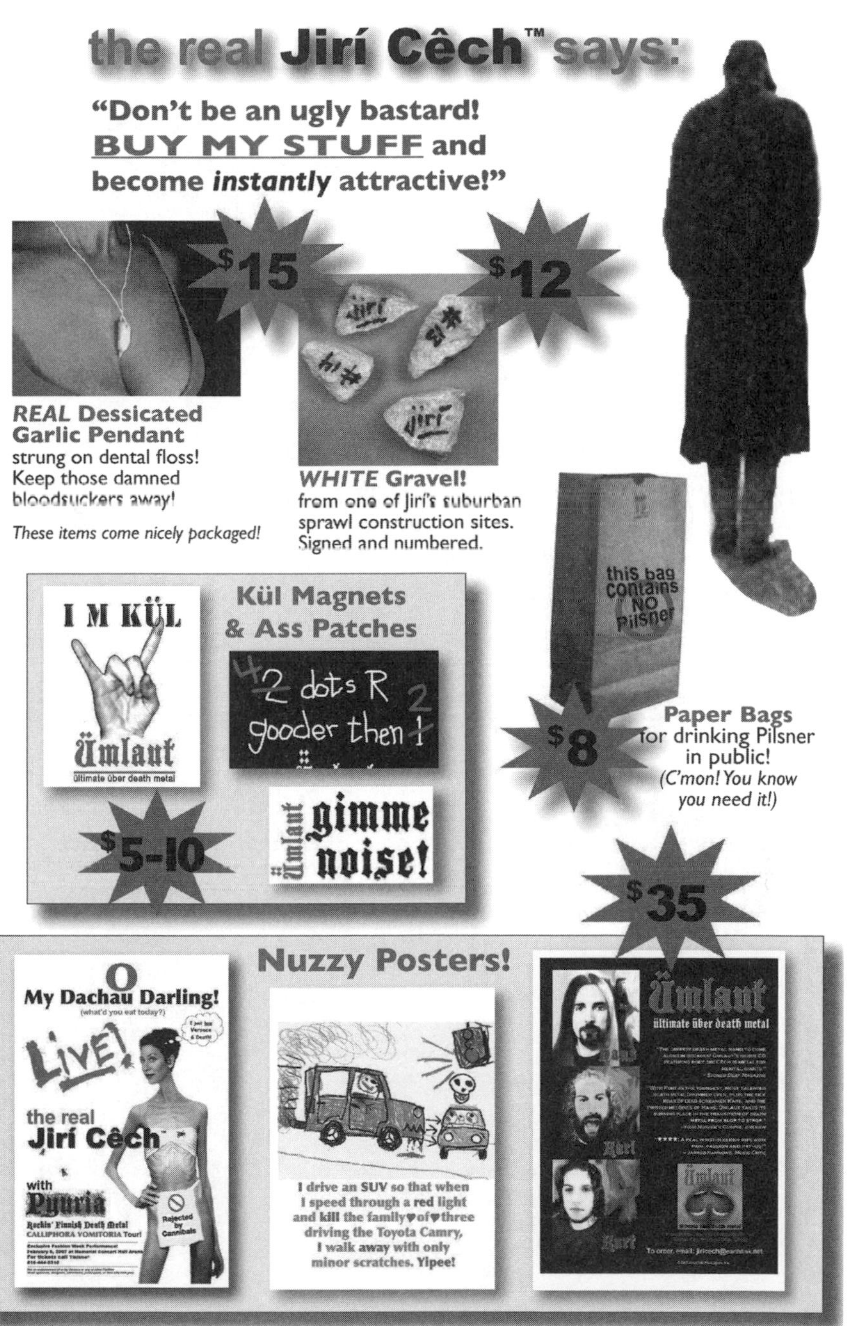
the real Jirí Cêch™ says:
"Don't be an ugly bastard!
BUY MY STUFF and
become *instantly* attractive!"
$15
$12
REAL Dessicated
Garlic Pendant
strung on dental floss!
Keep those damned
bloodsuckers away!
These items come nicely packaged!
WHITE Gravel!
from one of Jirí's suburban
sprawl construction sites.
Signed and numbered.
this bag
contains
NO
Pilsner
Kül Magnets
& Ass Patches
I M KÜL
Ümlaut
ultimate über death metal
4 2 dots R
gooder then 2 1
$5-10
Ümlaut
gimme
noise!
$8
Paper Bags
for drinking Pilsner
in public!
(C'mon! You know
you need it!)
$35
Nuzzy Posters!
O
My Dachau Darling!
(what'd you eat today?)
LIVE!
the real
Jirí Cêch
with
Pyuria
Rejected
by
Cannibals
CALLIPHORA VOMITORIA Tour!
I drive an SUV so that when
I speed through a red light
and kill the family of three
driving the Toyota Camry,
I walk away with only
minor scratches. Yipee!
Ümlaut
ultimate über death metal
Ümlaut

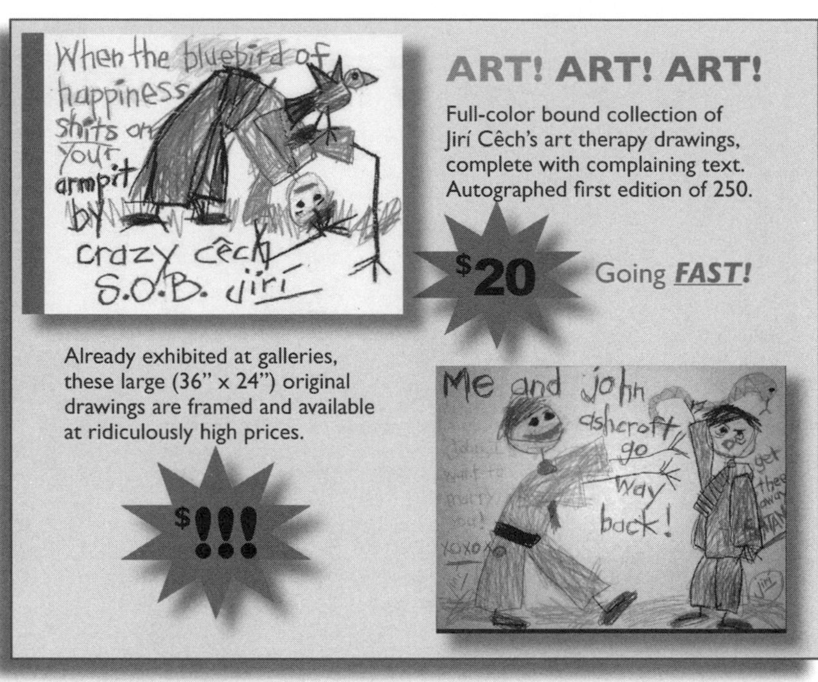
When the bluebird of happiness shits on your armpit by crazy cêch S.O.B. jiri
ART! ART! ART!
Full-color bound collection of Jirí Cêch's art therapy drawings, complete with complaining text. Autographed first edition of 250.
$20
Going FAST!
Already exhibited at galleries, these large (36" x 24") original drawings are framed and available at ridiculously high prices.
$!!!
Me and john ashcroft go way back!
XOXO
get thee away SATAN
jiri

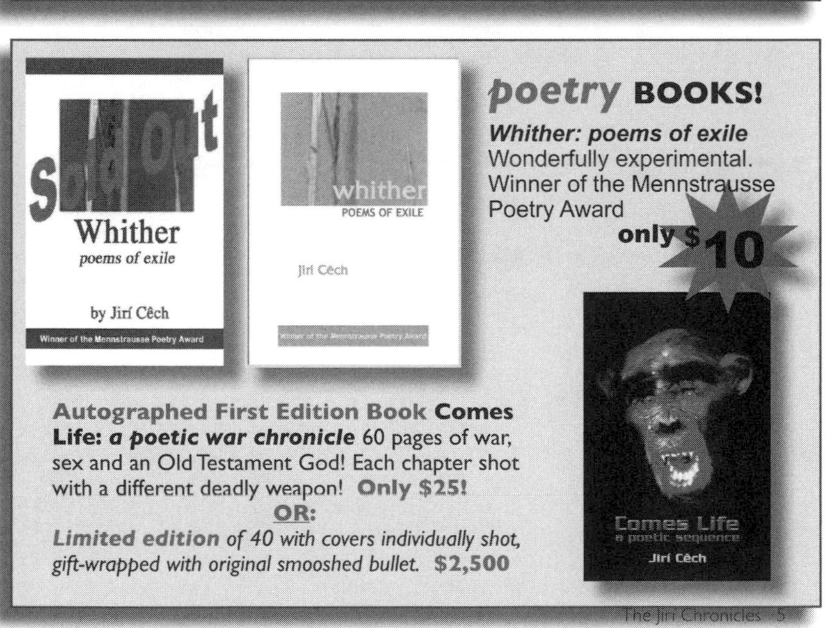
Sold Out
Whither
poems of exile
by Jirí Cêch
Winner of the Mennstrausse Poetry Award
whither
POEMS OF EXILE
Jiri Cêch
poetry BOOKS!
Whither: poems of exile
Wonderfully experimental.
Winner of the Mennstrausse Poetry Award
only $10
Autographed First Edition Book Comes Life: a poetic war chronicle 60 pages of war, sex and an Old Testament God! Each chapter shot with a different deadly weapon! Only $25!
OR:
Limited edition of 40 with covers individually shot, gift-wrapped with original smooshed bullet. $2,500
Comes Life
a poetic sequence
Jiri Cêch
The Jiri Chronicles 5

And the real *REAL* POPULAR:

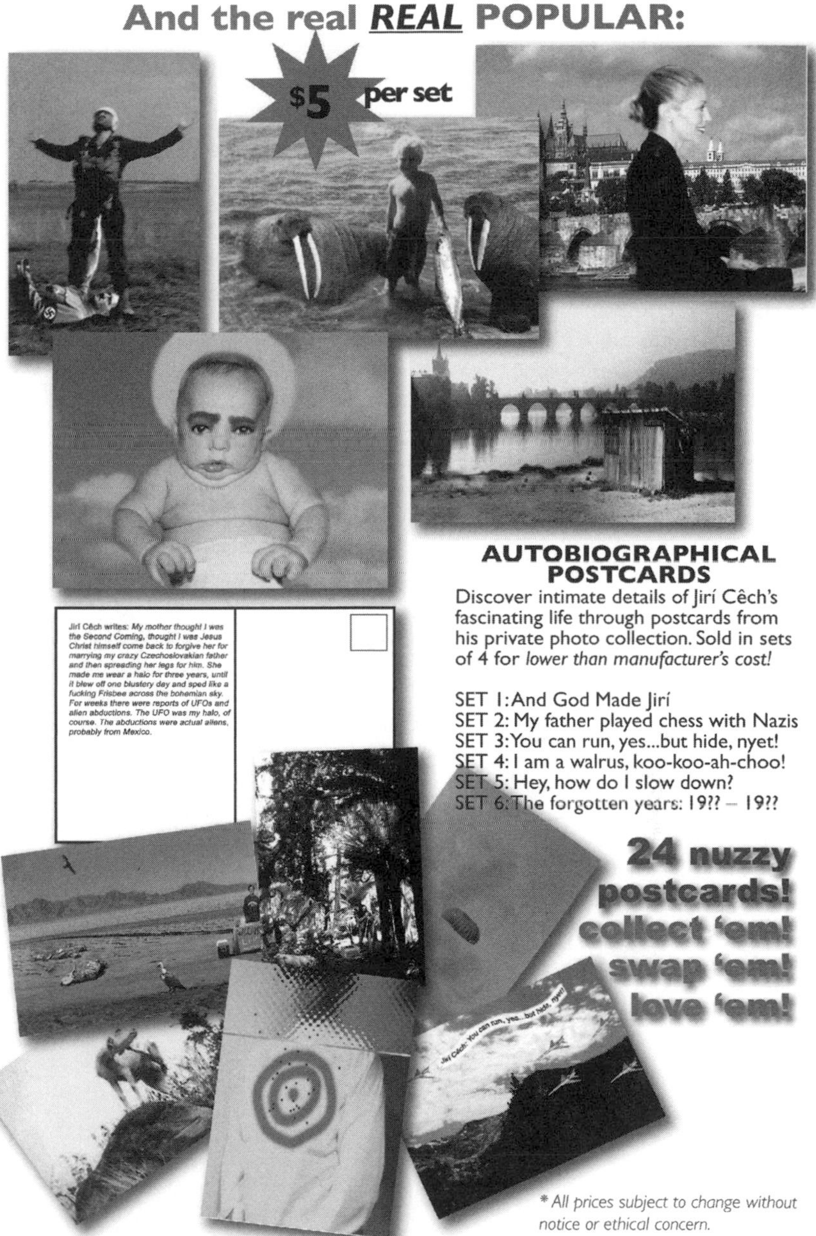

$5 per set
Jirí Cêch writes: *My mother thought I was the Second Coming, thought I was Jesus Christ himself come back to forgive her for marrying my crazy Czechoslovakian father and then spreading her legs for him. She made me wear a halo for three years, until it blew off one blustery day and sped like a fucking Frisbee across the bohemian sky. For weeks there were reports of UFOs and alien abductions. The UFO was my halo, of course. The abductions were actual aliens, probably from Mexico.*
24 nuzzy postcards! collect 'em! swap 'em! love 'em!

AUTOBIOGRAPHICAL POSTCARDS

Discover intimate details of Jirí Cêch's fascinating life through postcards from his private photo collection. Sold in sets of 4 for *lower than manufacturer's cost!*

SET 1: And God Made Jirí
SET 2: My father played chess with Nazis
SET 3: You can run, yes...but hide, nyet!
SET 4: I am a walrus, koo-koo-ah-choo!
SET 5: Hey, how do I slow down?
SET 6: The forgotten years: 19?? – 19??

** All prices subject to change without notice or ethical concern.*

CHARLES BLACKSTONE

A Once and Future Napkin

When *Esquire* sought my participation in their Napkin Fiction Project in 2008, my first thought was to set my story in a bar. I was surprised to find more of the solicited writers hadn't followed similar impulses. There was a wrinkle, one I'm reasonably sure hadn't afflicted the rest, in that my little canvas—they only sent one—had arrived torn. A sign (probably just USPS malfeasance) that I incorporate that into the work as well. Of course fiction is an illusion, an imagination, in content and, often, in form itself, so I began the true drafting of this "napkin story" where I begin most everything else, in a regular notebook.

Then to the computer, where I printed and scribbled and edited some more. Finally, I was ready to complete the charade and put the words to napkin, allowing for, I hoped, the eventual readers to be convinced that the story had never been anywhere else. I made a few drafts on a stack of "spares" I swiped from a bar, which were dissimilar in thickness, but close enough in dimension for me to get the hang of the space, and then I was ready to pen the final copy. Still a daunting undertaking, as I hadn't practiced with a tear in the paper. I had no idea of how to replicate it. Each frame of the unfolded napkin would, like a kindergartener's snowflake, have had the rip in a different quadrant, and to even approximate it in my head felt impossible.

With only one chance to get it right, I opted for a improvisational approach—much like the early story was when it began to take coherent shape—and to just deal with the tears as I reached them. I was pleased with the end result, and remained so until "Broken" was selected for this anthology.

Now, given the opportunity to recreate (a mandate, really, as the only digital image we had of the original napkin from the web was too low in resolution), I revisited the text, and with that, also reconsidered, playing on the idea of how a story about a bar encounter would look, how the words inhabited the new space. I set out copying the typed text on the new napkin, without knowing how much I was going to fit in a frame, where I'd end up breaking, and hoped for the best.

For the most part, I ran out of space at natural interruptions in the story. This even better captured the physical rhythms of what was going on than the first published napkin had, and was more in line with my original intent of not only telling a story, but also physically reproducing an event on a medium that made sense.

As for the infamous rip in the first napkin (which plays a part in the narrative itself), I just tore into the final frame "page," (coincidentally also my last blank napkin) and let the fiction take its course.

After the fourth or fifth email, Rob still couldn't stop thinking about Melanie and decided he'd have to meet her in person. The more she wrote, the more he wanted her, and he could see no way out other than to go in. The fact that he had a fiancée should have mattered a lot more than it did in his deliberations.

It wasn't hard to spot her amid the dense crowd immediately after he got to the Mystic Celt, familiar with her face from the jpg she'd attached to one of their first non-transactional emails after they'd retired the craigslist charade. Melanie had decided not to take the couch Rob needed to get rid of in anticipation of his future life with Sarah, and yet she kept the exchanges going, inquiring about his past: childhood, favorite foods, most cherished pets. How could she be in love with him after only a handful of sentences? How could they have sex without him getting in trouble? One drink and they'd realize how crazy this was.

Melanie sat on a high stool, dark cocktail in a pint glass, full, unlikely her first of the evening, before her. They didn't need to introduce themselves. It felt like he already knew her, even though she was still more or less a stranger. He considered taking the adjacent seat, but then thought he could better convey moral rectitude by remaining upright.

"We can't do this," he said.

"Why not?" she asked. She took a sip of her dark drink and offered the glass to Rob. He didn't want to accept, but his heart raced obstinately and his mouth was suddenly, undeniably dry. He took a careful taste, from the side opposite the greasy pink smudge. The thick regular Coke swept his mouth before he could halt its trajectory, followed by the vague reverberation of cheap rum.

"Because," he said, after signing and blotting his mouth with the blue cuff of his shirt, "I'm getting married"—he consulted his watch—"in five days."

She nodded.

"And that means I can't see you."

But the trouble was—and he hoped she couldn't pick up on this—he *was* seeing her, her shimmery Bazooka pink lips, long blonde hair, which burned brightly, indifferent to the dim bar lights and summer night stickiness, her faded black V-neck T-shirt that spurred her breasts downslope, low-cut jeans that, when she leaned forward, tugged a hot pink thong and brought into view a very inviting ass crack, a butterfly tattoo at its apex. He wanted this.

Fuck.

She remembered he liked Ketel and managed to order him one without him noticing. He sat down, lifted up his drink, and watched the gap of comportment that had until now kept him at a safe distance from fucking up his life begin to draw closer and closer into itself until it was barely more than a string of live wire. And if only she didn't smile at him, pay attention to his stories, if he hadn't glimpsed her tattoo or read quite as many of her electronic confessions of one night stands, about masturbating to porn she smuggled back from Amsterdam on a high school trip, if he hadn't been freaking out a little about Sarah and that a week from today, they'd already be married, maybe in the absence of all that, he'd have no trouble extracting himself, but of course that wasn't what was before him.

This was.

And though he looked around the bar, panned and scanned until his neck ached, he could discern no exit remaining. If he slept with Melanie, even once, he'd be marked for life. He listened instead to the potato wedges and breaded cod being plunged into a deep fryer flash flood on the other side of the room. He was surprised he could pick up the sound so acutely. The kitchen was far away and music blared, songs darting around the room, colliding with conversations as boxers in a ring.

"We could just do it once?" he asked. "One time would be enough for you? You could let go of me then?"

"I think we need to just experience this," she said. "Before we make any decisions."

"But some are already made," he said.

When she raised her drink, he reached for her cocktail napkin and held it in his hands, gripped the edges so tightly that he rent a jagged smile into a side.

"Still," she said, and poked the napkin he held before her with her thumb, widening the mouth. "Let's decide for ourselves."

It seemed reasonable. If he was never going to be the same again, he was still going to have to be something.

Now The Room Is Empty

It's quiet here, save a dinging of a truck, the noise they make when moving backwards. The place smells like smoke. Old stale smoke, even when no one there is smoking. Signs hang, listing the instructions, guidelines, telling people how to live and think and listen. At their gatherings, people will sit around the tables, talking about consequence, action. A woman will say she killed somebody driving. A man will be talking of his jail time, saying he is grateful.

Someone will walk around
the room, refilling people's
coffee. There are tables
and chairs, and there
are also floors and ceilings.
Walls: Sometimes there
are boundaries. A door
is a door.

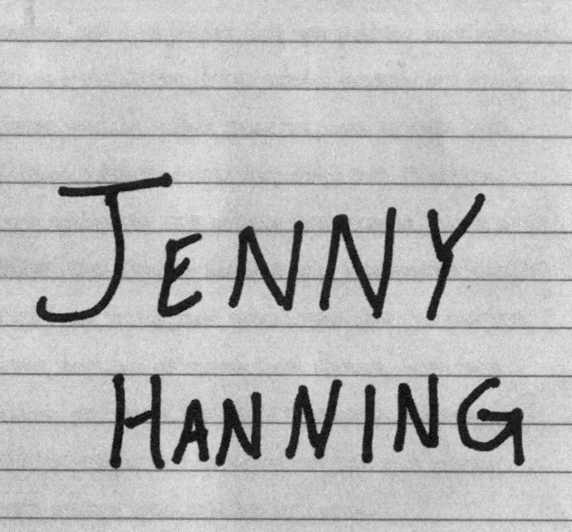

PLANTING

THE CARP AREN'T DEAD, ONLY RESTING, NESTING WITH THEIR EYES COVERED OVER, DEEP UNDER US, UNDER ALL THE ICE AND THEN UNDER THE WATER THAT WOULD NOT FREEZE, THE WATER'S TWISTY CURRENT STILL PUSHING ALONG, COLD ALMOST AS ICE AND SLUG SLOW, IT ROLLED THE MUD UP SLOWLY OVER THE FLAPPING KITE FIN ON THEIR BACKS AND THEN THEY ARE PRACTICALLY GONE, THREE FOURTHS DEAD LIKE A SHIRT THAT GOES TO THE ELBOWS IS ONLY THREE FOURTHS A SHIRT, BUT EVERYTHING IS STILL ALIVE DOWN THERE — WAY UNDER US WITH THEIR EYES STILL CURVING OUT AND STILL OPEN AND THE MUD FOLDED OVER THEM SO THEY ARE BURIED AND BURIED ALIVE. OUR SISTERS TOO, UNDER US, UNDER THE SNOW AND MUD GONE HARD. WHEN IT WAS SOFT, MUD PUNCTURED BY OUR FINGERTIPS AND DRUG UP FROM UNDER THE WET AND BROKEN

GROUND WE SET NEW SISTERS DOWN INTO THE HOLES. WE HAD MADE AND WE FOLDED THE GROUND BACK OVER THEM, OVER THEIR KNEES AND SHOULDERS FIRST, TUCKED THEM TIGHTLY, OUR SISTERS. WE SIFTED PURPLE WORMS BETWEEN OUR FINGERS AND SMOOTHED THE CLEAN MUD ACROSS THEIR OPEN EYES AND PUSHED ALL WE HAD HOLLOWED OUT BACK ONTO THEM, BUT THEY WERE NOT TOO TOO TOO DEEP, AND ALL OF THEM LIKE SEEDS WITH THE POINT OF THEIR TEARDROP UPWARD, PLANTED PALMS FACING SKY TO DIG UP TO THE SUN WHEN THE SPRING WILL CHOOSE TO COME.

AARON BURCH

You Are Here

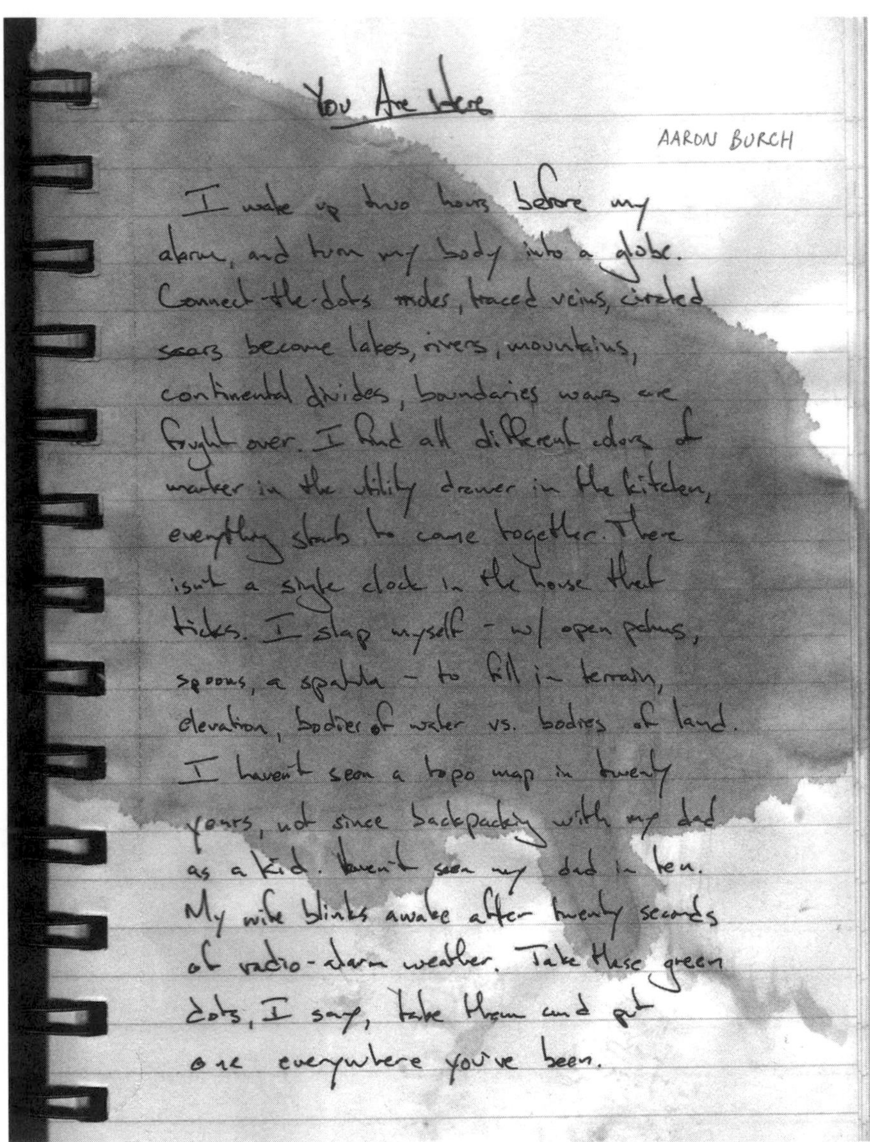

You Are Here

AARON BURCH

I wake up two hours before my alarm, and turn my body into a globe. Connect-the-dots moles, traced veins, circled scars become lakes, rivers, mountains, continental divides, boundaries wars are fought over. I find all different colors of marker in the utility drawer in the kitchen, everything starts to come together. There isn't a single clock in the house that ticks. I slap myself – w/ open palms, spoons, a spatula – to fill in terrain, elevation, bodies of water vs. bodies of land. I haven't seen a topo map in twenty years, not since backpacking with my dad as a kid. Haven't seen my dad in ten. My wife blinks awake after twenty seconds of radio-alarm weather. Take these green dots, I say, take them and put one everywhere you've been.

LISA GLUSKIN STONESTREET

Left-Handed Universe: Variations

1
As a child, my mother was ambidextrous. No traumatic stories or anything: she'd draw with one hand, color with the other. Later this talent waned, went the way of the crayon.

2
I wanted very much to be left-handed. I could be a changeling, of course; the concept explained a lot. I practiced my signature, its cramping line. The fingers of my right hand crossed.

3
What in our world might indicate the handedness of the universe? All those quarks: left, right, strange. Everything leaning into a spin.

4
A woman I know married her husband because he moved like Cary Grant. And all us poor stumblers with *L* and *R* scrawled on the toes of our shoes, just trying to dance.

5
Different drummer, said my piano teacher, and *perhaps it's best...*

6
Fundamental symmetries: (a) For every particle there must be an equivalent antiparticle with opposite charge. (b) Parity: Left-handed universe should be equal to right-handed universe. (c) If particles are interchanged with anti-particles and left-handed is flipped with right-handed, universe should look identical.

7
The wind comes off the ocean, sweeps the city toward the bay. In mid-September, though, the winds reverse; even the street signs lean west. A few weeks each fall, we drift downhill, forget bus passes and directions. End up where we started.

8
Left-handed, right-handed, saddle-shaped, expanding. Extending the wrong hand, one more time.

MARY GILLILAND

Quarantine in the Borders

there is a tendency Of each physiological variable
Research funding to continue *a flippancy generated*
what is the second sin Rapid eye movement (REM) sleep
And infrared lights *I struggle so much*
handle all ten commandments Over a 24h period
The simultaneous electromyogram *with this curious property*
Of the technique Of sleep in sheep

competition among tour groups The first stage
Information is collected *bigger faster engines*
higher speeds increasing traffic Surface skin electrodes
EEG, EOG, EMG and video *struck and killed*
watched in horror Sleep analysis software
Results from this work *going to see more of?*
(Frequency and amplitude) Wind wind Swept swept Farm

Stay away from sheep *shot forth on my back*
through the air Please help to contain
The current outbreak *awarded honorary degrees*
where does this go? Do not leave any litter
Keep dogs on lead *my own brand of laziness*
a perfectly useless bit That part of the earth

JOSEPH L. BISZ

Taming Milady

Once I read a book about taming wild animals. It had said that the most important thing was that the animal was aware of your presence. This could be done either by walking a circumference and committing no folly until it ignored you, like city dwellers with pigeons; or because you pained it and it feared you, like my neighbor who comments at his dog; or because you always helped it and it loved you and never let go.

What does it mean for an animal to be wild?

I think it means, to not know things about us. About people.

I pour more seed into the newspaper-lined cage. It is not so cold out today, not very dark.

Does it…want to?

A bird's eye view of behind our fence would see a tree-trail sneaking, dividing the native face of the backyards until it inflates up darker against the sky, a solitary woods. Mother thinks it's normal for me to just play in the yard.

When Mother gets upset because she's on the phone and her parents are telling her she should have gone farther in school or because she cooks dinner badly from not following a direction Father puts his hands behind her shoulders. He used to try the same with me, but I was too afraid. He doesn't squeeze or anything, but just lays his hands very seriously. Like he's taking her temperature. Or holding a balloon.

Once a long time ago at school when the advanced reading group got to sleep together I sneaked up too and pretended to snuggle with them like a cat, my body turned away from the teacher but my eyes awake, waiting for their beautiful eyes to open.

My eyes watch the embankment along the willow's nest. The branch is too far up.

If the animal cannot understand, then the animal cannot know what it is missing.

I put my own hand up into the air. Just to see how high it can go.

TERESA CARMODY

From *Eye Hole Adore*

First there was the driveway, a long, windy thing no one thought to turn down, save the occupants from mere habit. If they, or should I say we, had been thinking, minding our minds so to speak, we'd've known to drive past the two dirt tracks, the line of rye grass creeping up the middle, the overgrown blackberry bushes, the spindly arms of chokecherry trees scraping against the sides of the truck every time we went out and in, in and out.

Passers-by would never know there was a house there unless they knew, for the structure couldn't be seen from the road, and the mailbox, complete with numbered address in stick-on vinyl letters, had gone missing shortly after we moved in. That little house alone—poor, desperate house! Nonsense. Houses don't have feelings. We knew we lived at 45321 Hayward Road. We knew where we lived. We knew.

Did I tell you about her eyes? They were brown, with hazel, maybe green. Chalkboard green. They changed with her moods, for they were clear, milky, filmy. Mirrored pools. Those who gazed into them for more than 10 seconds thought they knew her completely, were certain she understood: such memory, such room for all the shows of the world. So they told her things, important things, that's what she said. And I believed her, how I loved to believe her.

We stayed inside most of the time, and what was inside—the living room with a single centered door going out, a kitchen on the right, two bedrooms in the back half, a bath in between—was a copied construction, old made new. The walls were faded white. The floors carpeted in speckled beige.

It was easy to see through the windows, though difficult to know what was seen.

There is no such thing as a clean house.

We were living and waiting for something to happen. We wanted to leave, ideally together, we'd say—One day we're going to

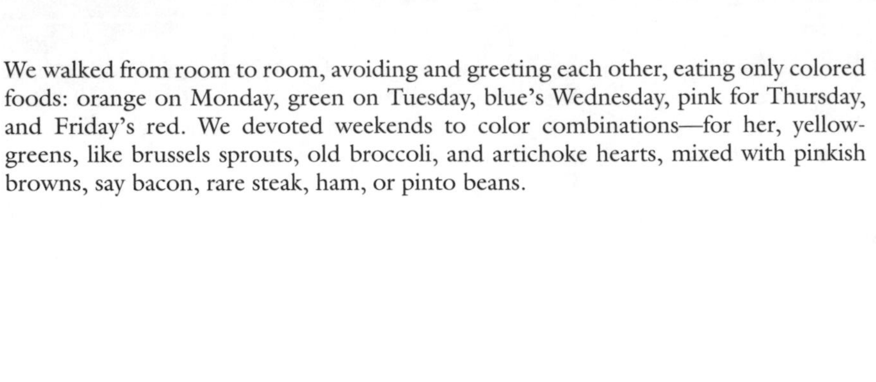

We walked from room to room, avoiding and greeting each other, eating only colored foods: orange on Monday, green on Tuesday, blue's Wednesday, pink for Thursday, and Friday's red. We devoted weekends to color combinations—for her, yellow-greens, like brussels sprouts, old broccoli, and artichoke hearts, mixed with pinkish browns, say bacon, rare steak, ham, or pinto beans.

My colors were the whitish-pale-yellow of pasta, cauliflower, sourdough, turkey breast and navy beans, with orangey-red sauces, like marinara, salsa, Tabasco, strawberry and apricot jam. On Sunday mornings, we went shopping. We never spoke of our agreement, but knew we'd stick to the plan, for it only works if you're both committed and we both really wanted it to work out.

I didn't know what I'd do without her. If she left, it would mean I'm a horrible person, and if I left, I'd be even more horrible than she. There are so many horrible people in the world, it's good we found each other so to keep the other safe and connected to what is heartfelt and unhorrible.

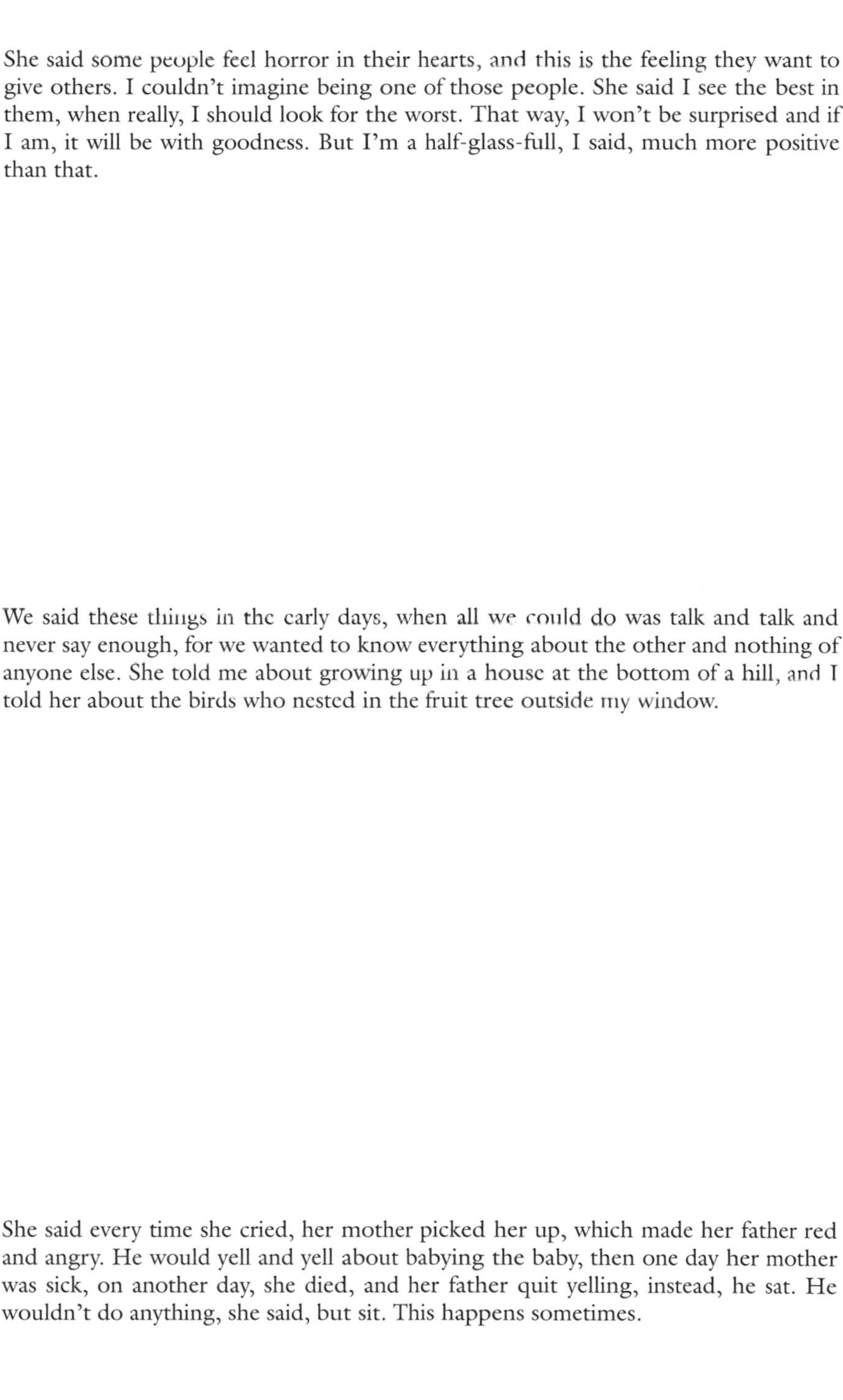

She said some people feel horror in their hearts, and this is the feeling they want to give others. I couldn't imagine being one of those people. She said I see the best in them, when really, I should look for the worst. That way, I won't be surprised and if I am, it will be with goodness. But I'm a half-glass-full, I said, much more positive than that.

We said these things in the early days, when all we could do was talk and talk and never say enough, for we wanted to know everything about the other and nothing of anyone else. She told me about growing up in a house at the bottom of a hill, and I told her about the birds who nested in the fruit tree outside my window.

She said every time she cried, her mother picked her up, which made her father red and angry. He would yell and yell about babying the baby, then one day her mother was sick, on another day, she died, and her father quit yelling, instead, he sat. He wouldn't do anything, she said, but sit. This happens sometimes.

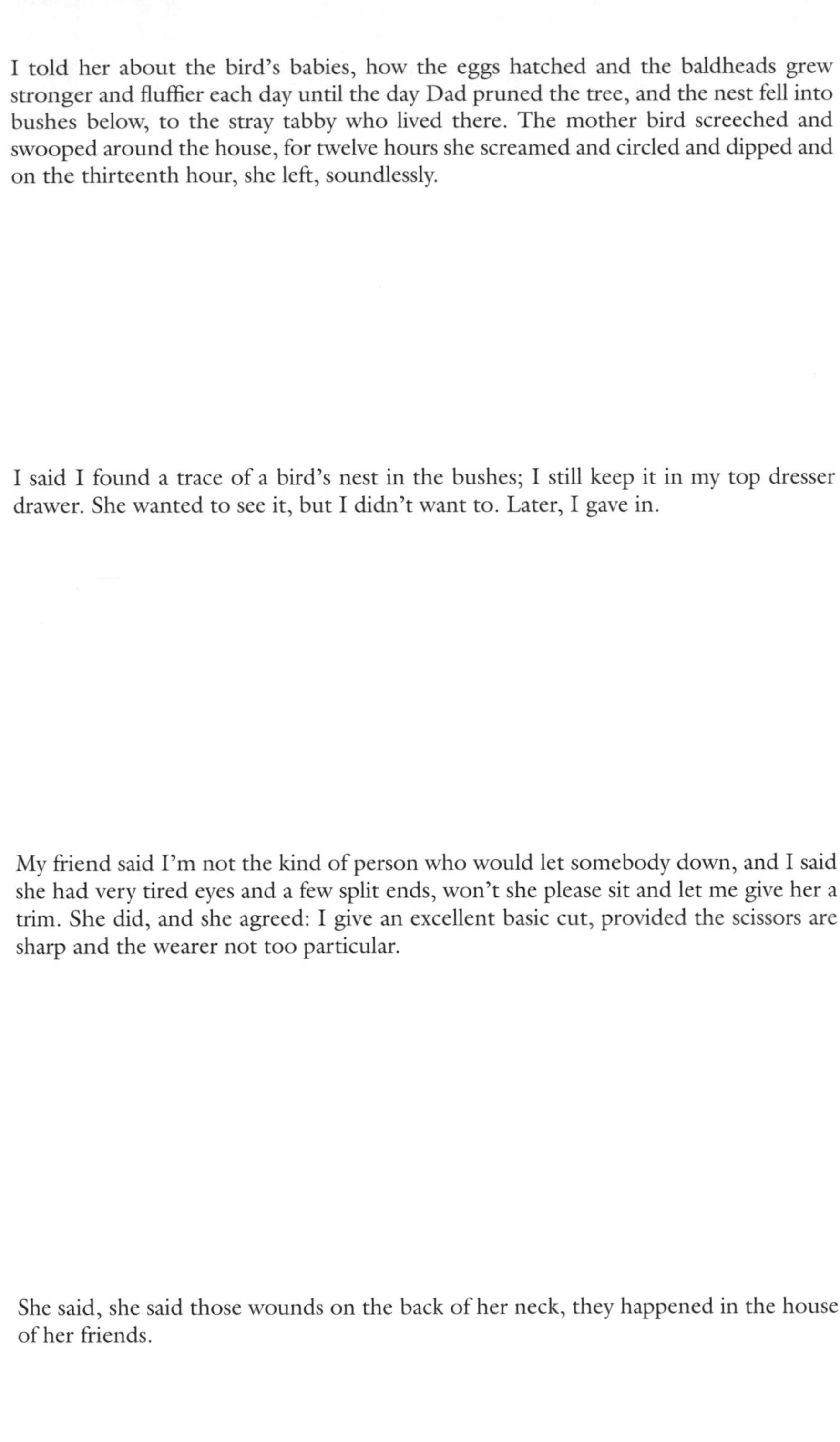

I told her about the bird's babies, how the eggs hatched and the baldheads grew stronger and fluffier each day until the day Dad pruned the tree, and the nest fell into bushes below, to the stray tabby who lived there. The mother bird screeched and swooped around the house, for twelve hours she screamed and circled and dipped and on the thirteenth hour, she left, soundlessly.

I said I found a trace of a bird's nest in the bushes; I still keep it in my top dresser drawer. She wanted to see it, but I didn't want to. Later, I gave in.

My friend said I'm not the kind of person who would let somebody down, and I said she had very tired eyes and a few split ends, won't she please sit and let me give her a trim. She did, and she agreed: I give an excellent basic cut, provided the scissors are sharp and the wearer not too particular.

She said, she said those wounds on the back of her neck, they happened in the house of her friends.

KIRSTEN JORGENSON

Thread

(Inspired by "Family Quilt/Function," a multi-media patchwork quilt by Anne Kennedy)

When Michael leaves for college Anna, his mother, will give him a quilt. She has been stitching it together all summer while he is away with his friends for the evening. She thinks of the things he'll need without a mother:

•matchsticks dipped in wax

•Advil (candy-coated to choke down in case you cannot drink the water)

•water purification tablets (in case you cannot drink the water) in case you don't want to feel the Ibuprofen clinging to your esophagus as it dissolves

•Benadryl for hives or for mild anaphylactic reactions for when your throat closes tight

•Epipen—I don't know the expiration date.

Dear Michael,

Please avoid bees and keep your cuts and hands clean. It should be OK to wash your hands in the water but only if you have soap. If you don't have soap please use antiseptic pads—sparingly. Use them when you're about to eat, and ration these too. One corner per meal. Keep them moist in the plastic bag I put them in. Do not add water. I cannot guarantee their effectiveness if you get them wet.

- soap
- antiseptic pads (individually wrapped [in plastic bags])
- plastic Ziploc bags

You can always eat grape leaves, dandelion greens or clover but when they are not present or when you don't know what a grape leaf looks like (heart-shaped, the size of your palm, five pointed and green except in the fall when they may be bright red, almost purple. Look for them on walls or tree trunks, growing on tendrils) or what a dandelion looks like without its head (jagged, long leaves that round at the tips like arrowheads, dark green in the grass) eat the fruit I dried in the oven on cooler summer nights when you were away.

•apples

•apricots

•plums

•beef and venison jerky (for protein), which I don't dry like the fruit but I buy from a very good source like Whole Foods.

Once I ate a date wrapped and baked in prosciutto and it was so delicious I ate another.

•almonds

•oats (can be cooked in un-purified water as long as you bring the water to a boil)

A sandwich of jerky and prunes (which are the same as the dried plums I packed for you) would make a meal. Jerky with prunes or with two strips of apricot or apple or apricot and plum, plum and apple, apricot and apple...

•small pot for cooking

•honey (pre-measured packets from the Starbucks condiment bar)

Tear the leaves with your fingers and mix them with pieces of dried fruit or wrap them in water-soaked grape leaves and cook them on sticks over a fire.

- Swiss Army Knife (for cooking / self-defense)
- Band-aid plasters with antibacterial strips
- sterile gauze

The skin is a kind of leaf. A seed pod. Money tree coins I hung from string in your window when you were a child.

- antiseptic wash in case you get cut (do not use the undrinkable water to clean your wounds)
- Super glue (to replaces sutures in case the cut is too deep)

One winter you cut your finger on ice chipped up from the flooded field behind our house. I remember maple sugar cooling in the thumbprints we pressed into the snow along the tree line. Your fingers were still sticky with syrup when I pressed my lips to them. You couldn't remember why you went to the field in the first place. You pulled up wet maple keys beneath the snow when you dug your fingers into it.

You pulled wet leaves and mud up from beneath the snow.

We wrapped you in blankets.

Please be careful. I spun you out of threads and you carry my DNA from my mother in your bones.

Love,

Mom

SHELLEY JACKSON

From *The Interstitial Library Workbook (Teacher's Edition)*

Q. What is a library?

A. Anything that holds one or more books, such as a bookstore, a cardboard box in a storage locker, any municipal garbage dump, or your hands at this moment.

Q. What is a book?

A. Any device that doubles an aspect of the perceptual world, such as a mirror, a globe, a scientific formula, or a doll. Any carrier of thought, such as the air near a mouth; specifically, anything with words recorded on or in it, whether in ink, sound waves, patterns of light or electrical impulses, or that in the past or future had or will have such words, such as trees, or the smoke of a burning book, or the mulch of a wet newspaper on a street after a rainstorm. Anything to be passed through in an orderly fashion, such as a museum, or entered at diverse points and encountered only in part, such as a city or a lover. Anything folded, such as a map, a mountain range, a wave of light or sound. Anything layered, such as a sandwich, clothing, the earth's crust, fliers on a telephone pole, or paint on a wall. Anything anchored at one end and free at the other, such as petals, feathers, leaves, flags, or a human life. Anything turning, such as vanes of a windmill, or paddles of a wheel. Anything with intervals, such as thunder or music, the slats of a fence or the frames of a film; anything that is dark on light, or light on dark, such as tigers or days passing. Anything wrapped in skin, such as a cow, cat, or other mammal; anything covered in cloth, such as a bed. Anything sewn, such as a kite, a shoe, a sail or a dress; anything glued. Anything with a gutter, such as a road. Anything with a spine, a jacket, or a signature. Anything with two wings, such as a house, a butterfly, a pocket mirror, or a bird. Anything pressed firmly between such wings, such as a nut or oyster. Anything that can be opened, such as oranges or pomegranates, mouths or eyes; anything that can be closed. Anything small, dense and unprepossessing, such as a seed, egg, cocoon, or novelty sponge, that expands unexpectedly in a hospitable environment. Any miniature or model, such as a doll house, diagram, map, or snow globe. Anything minutely marked, such as figured cloth. Anything preserved for the future, such as a packet of dried Sea Monkeys or instant soup, a time capsule, or a neurotic formation. Any time travel machine; any device for communicating with the dead; any memorial, obituary, zombie, or ghost. Any description of such an object, in conversation or in another book; the memory of such an object, or the anticipation of one not yet encountered.

In addition, the conditions of production of any such object, which may be additive, such as the conjunction of alphabet, pen, and hand; recombinant, such as the conjunction of leaves and wind; or subtractive, such as the conjunction of pre-existing books and bookworms or editors. The machinery of reproduction, such as sex, plagiarism, or the printing press; the machinery of distribution, such as rumor or truck-drivers, wind, water, or time; the machinery of circulation, such as selling, borrowing, losing, or finding.

Q. Which of the following can be defined as books?

A zipper; a zipper joining two distinct garments; a zipper with a hair caught in it.

A roll of toilet paper; a piece of toilet paper folded and pressed between two painted lips; the same paper, being flushed.

A carcass with the words USDA CHOICE stamped in purple ink on it; a carcass with the entire text of *The Merchant of Venice* stamped on it; a steak from this carcass weighing exactly one pound.

365 days; 365 days from various years, during the course of each of which one sentence from Moby Dick was either quoted or spontaneously uttered by someone somewhere in the world; these sentences, collectively; *Moby Dick* itself.

A cloud; skywriting; the breath-cloud of someone saying, "Look, skywriting," on a winter day.

A. Any or all of the above, depending on the viewer. "Book" is not a Boolean category. Books shade into and out of one another, and of existence itself. One object may be more bookish than another, but from the right angle, almost anything falls under one of the headings in The Interstitial Library catalogue, though it is not always easy to say which.

Q. How would you catalogue the following books?

Vol. 1 of a two-volume set: seven spit-balls in flight, formed from the somewhat yellowing pages of a school library copy of *Swine Science*, a book on raising pigs, during a high school class on secretarial skills; Vol. 2, *Swine Science* minus the spit-balled portion.

Walt Whitman's *Leaves of Grass*, transcribed in shorthand in its entirety on individual grass-blades in a meadow in Prospect Park, Brooklyn, by two teenaged lovers, Conrad (a German exchange student) and P. G. (Brooklyn native, nicknamed Pig), working in tandem over the course of a summer in 1984.

The same meadow, next spring.

From among the flipping pages of a diary left on a park bench in a high wind by someone fleeing an incipient storm, those five that were brilliantly illuminated by consecutive flashes of lightning.

That portion of the smoke from the first edition of Franz Xaver Gabelsburger's shorthand textbook *Anleiten zur deutschen Redezeichenkunst oder Stenographie* (1834) burned in the fire at the Anna-Amalia Library in Weimar, Germany on Thursday, September 2, 2004 that was inhaled by a migrating goose, and whose particles still linger in its lungs as it floats in a fen in its breeding ground in Finnish Lapland.

Those tears accidentally dropped into an ice cube tray refilled while reading someone else's diary, subsequently used to cool an unrefrigerated glass of white wine offered to an unexpected guest.

A young woman who has daubed different scents on different parts of her body, utilizing a Q-Tip, the first initial of whose names, once identified, will spell out the name of a different woman, who has been entrusted with a letter in shorthand for the intended reader, Conrad Lecker of Brooklyn, NY.

An unopened envelope bearing a cancelled stamp and containing a letter, held momentarily between the thumb and forefinger of one hand before being dropped in the trash.

A handbook of secretarial practices from 1940, left face-down by the side of Kent Street in Williamsburg, Brooklyn, providing a gabled roof for an ant den in which a mutant strain is developing some unusual applications for stenography.

A. Possible answers include (in no particular order) lost books, changing books, airborne books, living books, intermittent books, interspecies books, secret books, books about love, nonexistent books, and books named in this list. However, the best category for these books may bear your name. A book is not an object but a situation, and included in that situation is the reader.

Q. What is a reader?

A. Anyone performing an operation required to acccss otherwise hidden information, such as dowsing, opening a door, performing a spectral analysis of distant stars, or being born. Anyone translating one substance into another, such as worms. Anyone turning over a series of objects and examining each minutely, such as gardeners, metal detectors, pancake chefs. Anyone observing shadows or reflections, such as Narcissus. Anyone adept at leaping from one rectangle to another, such as chess or hopscotch players, or back and forth across one rectangle, such as weavers or users of the abacus. Anyone alert to the difference between darkness and light, such as an mouse, or between sound and silence, such as an owl. Anyone following a line, such as a plough-horse; anyone following a trail. Anyone who wants to know what happens next. Any cunningly shaped device that fits perfectly into a space made for it, such as a key, a tongue, or a virus; alternately, the space designed for such an object. Anyone practised in discerning the gaps between things. Anyone receiving a currency of exchange, such as ivory, money, or blows. Anyone whose tongue moves secretly in response to another's words; any plagiarist, parasite, parrot, or mime. Anyone intimately fingering an object in seeking to understand it, such as a lover or a veterinarian. Anyone permanently altered by intercourse with another, such as a syphilitic. Anyone connecting one thing to another, such as a lace-maker, a fisherman, a plumber or electrician. Anyone divining patterns from pieces, such as an archaeologist, geneticist, detective, or fortune-teller. Anyone haunted or possessed, anyone in love. Anyone in whom a new world is opening, has opened, or will open, such as Conrad Lecker, a girl named Pig, any librarian, you, or I.

KERRI SONNENBERG

From deact

in time for
example
to lie between
nor was
her figure
the word for
feather

*

where the fish had withdrawn
her house emerged
contours each
jagged water
crossed
morning with required hours

shadows empty
the chimneys
Europe stood between

*

had darling
forgotten when
voices woke
at roses
random left
the garden
the unacted sky
from which she revived
as dear
from night
buttoning up his coat

WENDY WALKER

Introduction to *Blue Fire*

In late June 1860 Constance Kent, then sixteen, was home from school on holiday. She had brought her four-year-old half-brother Savill a bracelet and spent the afternoon playing with him in the garden of the house at Road, in Wiltshire. The next morning Savill was missing from his crib. Their father, Samuel Savill Kent, rode off to summon the police. Late that morning two workmen thought to look in the garden privy. They fished up a blanket and saw the body, horribly mutilated. The case became national news and inspired both Wilkie Collins' *The Moonstone* and Dickens' *The Mystery of Edwin Drood*. Constance was accused but found guiltless at the inquest; then, in 1865, she created a sensation by confessing. Her statement was met with frank disbelief, but she persisted. When the judge pronounced the sentence of death upon her, he and everyone else in the court wept.

Over the next twenty years she inhabited five prisons and executed church mosaics as a penance. After she was released in 1885, her brother William fetched her to Australia, where she worked under a new name as a nurse and a trainer of nurses till she died, in 1944.

Because so much historical fiction plays irresponsibly with the past, I wish to be as transparent as possible about my method in *Blue Fire*. In the course of my reading, I encountered one stumbling-block, Joseph Stapleton's *The Great Crime of 1860*, which established the genre of "true crime" and which, to exonerate Samuel Kent (on the evidence the more likely killer), placed the blame on Constance. Stapleton's rhetoric so repelled me that I decided to select one word from each line of his book, proceeding line by line but never choosing two words that followed consecutively.

Every text contains its own critique, like a statue hidden in a block of marble; one has only to liberate it.

At the same time I was selecting passages from my reading: books Constance had read and works contemporary with them. I arrived at the following algorithm: the number of words in a section of my text would be paralleled by a passage with the same number of lines, which I would place on the facing page. So a section derived from Stapleton that was fifteen words long would appear opposite a prose excerpt of fifteen lines in the edition I was using (the lineation in this piece may be different). The prose passage would be selected for its commentary upon the derived section. After that I could entrust to the form what content would emerge.

In the full version of *Blue Fire*, to be published in 2009 by Proteotypes, the text has been amplified by images: photographs and plans of the sites where Constance lived, documents from the Public Record office and elsewhere, and photographs of the mosaics that Constance made.

As I studied these intricate floors, a mosaic method, requiring several different orders and directions of reading, came to seem more and more appropriate.

deeds ere perpetrators
vision being the ghost wound

One domestic June village

by prominence common

night the nurse

sleep the house

there in miscreant grasp

come hurried traces

guide darkness out

English shakes with emphasis

sudden Lord

June
4. Tuesday—9, Sunday
I thought I would go up to the Eumenides Cave & ask God there to explain to me what were these Eumenides which pursued me. I would not ask to be released from them—Welcome Eumenides—but to be delivered from doing further wrong.
Florence Nightingale, *Diary*, June 4-9, 1850, p66

You talk of the Road Murder, I suppose, even at Lausanne? Not all the Detective Police in existence shall ever persuade me out of the hypothesis that the circumstances have gradually shaped out to my mind. The father was in bed with the nurse: The child was discovered by them, sitting up in his little bed, staring, and evidently going to "tell Ma". The nurse leaped out of bed and instantly suffocated him in the father's presence. The father cut the child about, to distract suspicion (which was effectually done), and took the body out where it was found. Either when he was going for the Police, or when he locked the police up in his own house, or at both times, he got rid of the knife and so forth. It is likely enough that the truth may be never discovered now.
Charles Dickens, *Letters*,1 February 1861, P383

In some of my former novels, the object proposed has been to trace the influence of circumstances upon character. In the present story I have reversed the process. The attempt made, here, is to trace the influence of character on circumstances. The conduct pursued, under a sudden emergency, by a young girl, supplies the foundation on which I have built this book.
Wilkie Collins, Preface to the First Edition, *The Moonstone*, 1868, p27

I went & sate in the cave of the Eumenides alone, & thought how they pursued me — & how would it end? A wretched [sic] that I am. Who shall deliver me from the body of this death? What does it signify to me now whether I see this or do that or not? I never can be sure of seeing it. I may see nothing but my own self practicing an attitude.
Florence Nightingale, *Diary*, June 4-9, 1850, p66

London details crime for a lady's usual horror

story villages satisfy

repeated subject

discuss moral mystery

is it in beyond or fail

every failure new

attempt reader's facts

and the lament that has unexpected reader

C. did not take her punishments very seriously she generally managed to get some amusement out of them. Once after being particularly provocative & passionate, the governess put her down in a dark wine cellar, she fell on a heap of straw & fancied herself in the dungeon of a great castle, a prisoner taken in battle fighting for Bonnie Prince Charlie & to be taken to the block next morning, when the governess unlocked the door and told her to come up she was looking rather pleased over her fancies.
"The Sydney Document" (a letter attributed to Constance Kent/ Ruth Emilie Kaye to John Rhode, February 1929)

I like to think how Eumenides' laws work out all things for good & I would not be such a fool as to pray that one little [sic] of hell should be remitted, one consequence altered either of others mistakes or of our own.
Florence Nightingale, *Letters*, May 31,1850

The governess asked what she was smiling about Oh she said only the funny rats. What rats said the governess, she did not know there were any there They do not hurt said C; only dance & play about After that to her disappointment she was shut in a beer cellar a light room but with a window too high to look out of, but she managed to pull the spigot out of a cask of beer, after that she was locked up in one of 2 spare rooms at the end of a vestibule & shut off by double doors, she liked the big room for it had a large 4 poster bed she could climb about, but the little room was dreary, the rooms had a legend attached to them, were said to be haunted & on a certain date a blue fire burned in the fire place
"The Sydney Document"

29. We come then to that great concourse of the Dead, not merely to know from them what is true, but chiefly to feel with them what is just. Now, to feel with them, we must be like them; and none of us can become that without pains. As the true knowledge is disciplined and tested knowledge,—not the first thought that comes—so the true passion is disciplined and tested passion,—not the first passion that comes.
John Ruskin, *Sesame and Lilies*, 1865 p533

think that extent of closed passage

one sympathy driven to privacy

eye

is unreasoning thought skill in expedient

down voice workings upon stillness

that heard glare

On Saturday the electric wires flashed with the intelligence that a man had given himself up, at Wolverton, as the murderer... a man, who has given the Christian name of Edmund John, but who refuses to give any surname, or to state where his place of abode is situated... made a statement to the effect that he had killed the child at Road, and that he felt he could not live; and that he had given himself up, as he could see the child walk before him wherever he went... Subsequently he avowed his intention of making an open confession to a clergyman, and expressed a wish to see a minister of the Wesleyan denomination...

The Road Murder by "A Barrister-at-Law," n.d., c.1860, p20

To be inconsistent is to be cramped in some direction.

Florence Nightingale, *Letters*, 8 June 1851, p50

Constable Goodson said that while the prisoner was at Wolverton railway station, the prisoner gave a tobacco-box to one of the railwaymen, and a purse to another, and a knife to a third. He produced these articles, which he had recovered from the men, who were total strangers to the prisoner. When he gave them to the men, the prisoner said that "they would hear something of them afterwards." During the train journey the knife had fallen from the bundle, and the prisoner at once said: "That is my knife; how did you come by that?"

John Rhode, *The Case of Constance Kent*, 1928, pp128-9

I don't mean that she is perfect—she acts without thinking, her temper is sometimes warm and hasty; but have we any right to go and injure her prospects sfor life, by telling Mr. Bradshaw all we know of her errors—only sixteen when she did so wrong, and never to escape from it all her many years to come—to have the despair which would arise from its being known, clutching her back into worse sin? What harm do you think she can do?

Elizabeth Gaskell, *Ruth*, 1853, p165

steps

silken events

count

1860

English children

bodily propositions

on forms of history

Mr. Kent Sub-inspector of fulfillment

Edward joins death

Mrs. Kent proposed

early cause for governess

Miss Pratt removes marriage

Edward to birth Constance

I promised my God that I would not die of disgust or disappointment if he would let me go through this. In all that has been said against & for me, no one soul has appreciated what I was really doing—

Florence Nightingale, *Letters*, 10 May 1855 (Balaclava), p116

"When we first spoke together, Neville, you told me that your sister had risen out of the disadvantages of your past lives as superior to you as the tower of Cloisterham Cathedral is higher than the chimneys of Minor Canon Corner. Do you remember that?"

"Right well!"

"I was inclined to think it at the time an enthusiastic flight. No matter what I think it now. What I would emphasise is, that under the head of Pride your sister is a great and opportune example to you."

"Under all heads that are included in the composition of a fine character, she is."

"Say so; but take this one. Your sister has learnt how to govern what is proud in her nature. She can dominate it even when it is wounded through her sympathy with you. No doubt she has suffered deeply in those same streets where you suffered deeply. No doubt her life is darkened by the cloud that darkens yours. But bending her pride into a grand composure that is not haughty or aggressive, but is a sustained confidence in you and in the truth, she has won her way through those streets until she passes along them as high in the general respect as any one who treads them. Every day and hour of her life since Edwin Drood's disappearance, she has faced malignity and folly— for you—as only a brave nature well directed
can. So it will be with her to the end. Another and weaker kind of pride might sink broken-hearted, but never such a pride as hers: which knows no shrinking, and can get no mastery over her."

The pale cheek beside him flushed under the comparison, and the hint implied in it.

"I will do all I can to imitate her," said Neville.

"Do so, and be a truly brave man..."

Charles Dickens, *The Mystery of Edwin Drood*, 1870 pp200-1

perpetration of presence into records
strides of blood among questions
those consequences of narrative
no skill this   temple renovation
science in dancing language
if fusion near burned testimony
mottoes by drachmas
this Hebrew Latin
in golden characters therein raised
evening shadows upon Crimean Lombardy
streams pray Babel Heaven

'...Now you know exactly what my position was, at the time of Mr Candy's illness, you will the more readily understand the sore need I had of lightening the burden on my mind by giving it, at intervals, some sort of relief. I have had the presumption to occupy my leisure, for some years past, in writing a book, addressed to the members of my profession—a book on the intricate and delicate subject of the brain and the nervous system. My work will probably never be finished; and it will certainly never be published. It has none the less been the friend of many lonely hours; and it helped me to while away the anxious time—the time of waiting, and nothing else—at Mr Candy's bedside. I told you he was delirious, I think? And I mentioned the time at which his delirium came on?'

'Yes.'

'Well, I had reached a section of my book, at that time, which touched on this same question of delirium. I won't trouble you at any length with my theory on the subject—I will confine myself to telling you only what it is your present interest to know. It has often occurred to me in the course of my medical practice, to doubt whether we can justifiably infer—in cases of delirium—that the loss of the faculty of speaking connectedly, implies of necessity the loss of the faculty of thinking connectedly as well. Poor Mr Candy's illness gave me the opportunity of putting this doubt to the test. I understand the art of writing in shorthand; and I was able to take down the patient's "wanderings," exactly as they fell from his lips.—Do you see, Mr Blake, what I am coming to at last?'

I saw it clearly, and waited with breathless interest to hear more.

'At odds and ends of time,' Ezra Jennings went on, 'I reproduced my shorthand notes in the ordinary form of writing—leaving large spaces between the broken phrases, and even the single words, as they had fallen disconnectedly from Mr Candy's lips. I then treated the result thus obtained, on something like the principle which one adopts in putting together a child's "puzzle." It is all confusion to begin with; but it may be all brought into order and shape, if you can only find the right way. Acting on this plan, I filled in each blank space on the paper, with what the words or phrases on either side of it suggested to me as the speaker's meaning; altering over and over again, until my additions followed naturally on the spoken words which came before them, and fitted naturally into the spoken words which came after them. The result was, that I not only occupied in this way many vacant and anxious hours, but that I arrived at something which was (as it seemed to me) a confirmation of the theory that I held. In plainer words, after putting the broken sentences together I found the superior faculty of thinking going on, more or less connectedly, in my patient's mind, while the inferior faculty of expression was in a state of almost complete incapacity and confusion.'

Wilkie Collins, *The Moonstone*, pp423-4

all fallen spirit

English upon system

adopted examples into muscular 1860

social English wonder carries rifle of notice

that classified gaoldom

Fetters and juvenile briers bloom

by refinement of riot

or family flashing fitfully

English hides how of ripen

beneath Mount moment

One day Constance and her brother were supposed to be attending to their little gardens behind some shrubbery, they heard some merry laughter from a neighbouring garden, they went to the hedge & looked over longingly at the children playing with some visitors, they were invited to join but were afraid, they were seen and their disobedience punished, the little gardens were uprooted and trampled down, Constance made some futile efforts to revive hers. No pets were allowed, two little tropical birds sent by the eldest son to his sisters were consigned to a cold back room & died. The few relatives who visited got into disgrace over the governess & their stay was brief. Once Constance was told to make friends with a girl about her own age who lived nearly a mile away but friendships are not made to order, after a period of mutual boredom, the girl falsely accused C of trying to set her against her mother. At school she was happier with companions but she was always resentful of authority she was still ever in trouble, and looked on as a black sheep, she had nothing to do with the gas escape which was probably owing to the taps having been forgotten when the meter was turned off, she gave nicknames to her teachers & made rhymes on them which were not complimentary increasing her unpopularity with them.

"The Sydney Document" p374

'Why do you dislike the trout so?' asked Tom.

'My dear, we do not even mention them, if we can help it; for I am sorry to say they are relations of ours who do us no credit. A great many years ago they were just like us: but they were so lazy, and cowardly, and greedy, that instead of going down to the sea every year to see the world and grow strong and fat, they chose to stay and poke around in the little streams and eat worms and grubs: and they are very properly punished for it; for they have grown ugly and brown and spotted and small; and are actually so degraded in their tastes, that they will eat our children.'

'And then they pretend to scrape acquaintance with us again,' said the lady. 'Why, I have actually known one of them propose to a lady salmon, the little impudent creature.'

'I should hope,' said the gentlemen, 'that there are very few ladies of our race who would degrade themselves by listening to such a creature for an instant. If I saw such a thing happen, I should consider it my duty to put them both to death upon the spot.' So the old salmon said, like an old blue-blooded hidalgo of Spain: and what is more, he would have done it too.

Charles Kingsley, *The Water-Babies*, 1863, pp68-9

English grace lingers around strength
recesses fury into figure reality
story observed
gallop called road
gardener gentlemen

old necessity
honor impediment
cast slippery living
the perhaps of children
heart-wood memorial

The young nightingales you gets out of their nest before the end of June are more likely to survive and they'll start singing earlier. The young must be taken from a long, loud-voiced nightingale. They do not hatch in a cage. In the woods a nightingale stops singing as soon as his brood is hatched, and about the end of June he moults. He'll sing a tune in flight and that's all. He only whistles. He sings only when he's sitting; in flight, when he is diving after a hen, he warbles. It is a good thing to put a cage with young birds near a cage with older ones, so that they should learn to sing. They should be hung next to each other. And here you have to look sharp: if the young bird sits quiet-like, without moving or uttering a sound and listening while the old bird's singing, he'll be all right and in two weeks he'll perhaps be ready; but the one who doesn't keep silent and keeps warbling after the old 'un, will, if you're lucky, start singing proper-like next year, and even that is doubtful.

Ivan Turgenev, *Literary Reminiscences and Autobiographical Fragments*, "About Nightingales," 1854, pp275-6

One of the masters who attended the school, had a great quantity of black hair and rugged countenance, she named him Bear in a bush & when taken to a fashionable chapel for Bible class, the minister who became a Bishop, she called the Octagon Magpie from the shape of the building when they were told they only laughed & the minister thinking he might bring some good out of her took some extra pains with her, but seeing the other girls were jealous she gave stupid replies on purpose & so fell from grace. Then she thought to turn religious & got 2 of her companions to join her in learning chapters of the Bible, but it did not act to make her as good as she had hoped, she was given to read a book by Baxter which convinced her that she had committed the unforgivable sin, so it was useless to try anymore.

"The Sydney Document"

infallible register

summer of one irregular history

read in weatherbeaten law

governed countenances

faults surely correspondent to care

He said that he was thirty years of age, that he belonged to London, and was a bricklayer by trade; also that his wife and three children were living in London. A short time after he had his dinner he said to me: 'Do you think they can try Miss Constance Kent again?' He also said: 'Before I die I should like to have a sheet or two of paper, and I'll leave all behind, and they'll know all about it. I hope my wife will not know about it; it will break her heart.'

He then gave me an account of his journey from London to Leicester and Leicester to Wolverton, and added that the finger of God was against him, so that he could not get work anywhere. He begged hard that he might not be handcuffed, and said that he would go with anybody to any place—to Road or anywhere else. As far as I could judge the conduct of the prisoner was that of a man in a sound state of mind."

John Rhode, *The Case of Constance Kent,* pp124-5

INDEX OF DOCTRINES

transmissibility of same question

clinical modern repetition

many father misfortunes

son interest

scientific blood

visited law

chemistry itself merciful

stone house first

decay Architect His masterpiece

copy passions lawfully

workmen after the given

fatally standard deviation

perpetual children

legacy degradation

just pleasures

sins prematurely atrophied

stature generated proofs

moral food to matchless Maker

On Saturday, the 30th of June, I was called upon by Master Kent to accompany him to his father's house, at Road. He informed me of the nature of the case. It would be nearly nine o'clock when I got to the house. I was taken round the back way by Master William, because he was not aware whether his mother knew of what had occurred, so I went into the library. I was afterwards shown into the laundry. Mr. Kent opened the door, and I went in by myself. I found the body of the child wrapped in a blanket. The blanket was covered with stains of blood and with old soil from the place it had been taken from. It was soil from the splash-board, and not from the child. There were considerable stains, but not a large quantity of blood on the blanket itself. The child had a night-gown and flannel shirt on. They were both much soiled with blood and soiled from the privy—not from the child. I found some wounds upon the child. The first I observed was upon the throat. It was a clean incision, which severed the whole of the structures down to the bone—the skin, muscles, &c., all being severed. The wound was from the left to the right. It must have been a very sharp knife with a long blade to produce such a cut. It appeared to be one cut. I am unable to say from that wound that it was caused by a pointed instrument. A considerable quantity of blood had flown from the left angle of the wound down the arm to the elbow. I observed black marks near the mouth. The tongue protruded between the teeth, so as to be visible between the lips, and it appeared to be of a dark colour and livid. It was just visible between the lips. I afterwards observed two incisions on the back of the right hand. I made a second examination in the course of the day, and found the smaller wounds. One of the small wounds was upon the back of the first joint of the forefinger on his right hand, and the other was in a line with it. I afterwards found a stab in the left side of the body. The stab had penetrated the nightgown and the shirt. It had severed the sixth and seventh cartilages of two of the ribs, and it had penetrated more than half through the chest. It passed behind the pericardium, and wounded the diaphragm and the stomach. The wound was about an inch and a half broad. Those were all the wounds I found. I subsequently received instructions from the coroner, and in company with Mr. Stapleton, surgeon, of Trowbridge, made a post-mortem examination of the body. We opened the stomach to see the depth and nature of the wound. We found very slight remains of his last night's supper, which had consisted of farinaceous articles of food, such as rice. I examined by smelling to see if there had been any laudanum or other narcotic in the stomach. I did not detect anything of that kind. I did not examine the lower part of the bowels. We have heard that the evening before the murder a pill had been administered. Did you detect any evidence of its remains in the stomach?—I did not. What sort of pill was it?—It was an aperient, and I made it up myself. It was of a compound character. We have heard that such a pill was given to the child about six or seven o'clock at night; by what time would it have operated?—It might have operated in six or seven hours, but more probably in eight, ten, or twelve hours. What did the dark appearance upon the mouth indicate to you?—It indicated strong pressure upon the mouth.

Joseph Stapleton, *The Great Crime of 1860*, Appendix III,"The Inquiry Into the Charge of Murder Against Elizabeth Gough, the Nursemaid." Testimony of Mr Joshua Parsons, Member, College of Surgeons pp185-6

MATTHEW ROBERSON
Possible Side Effects

L.[1] & I.[2]

Ambien® He knew he should quit smoking.

But everyone lit up while they framed or roofed, and on breaks, and why not? The days were hot or cold, or muggy, or wet, and they struggled, morning to night, Monday to Friday, seven to seven. Not an hour passed without a cut or bruise to their hands and legs. They worked on their knees in tight spaces, drilling and nailing, and stretched to reach beams or lift lumber above their heads. They carried eighty-pound bags of shingles up extension ladders.

Why not take the simple pleasure of a smoke.

Other pleasures were gone. L. limped home nights too tired to cook a real meal, and I. didn't make dinner anymore, either, so they took out, or ordered in, or ate from the kitchen shelves—a can of olives. Six bananas. Canned chili, cold. Hot dog buns. Sex was out, except on weekends, and even then L. found he couldn't be roused. Better to watch cable. Football. Or *Die Hard*, again. He wouldn't follow tennis or soccer or any sport that looked tiring. Who needed it? He turned on baseball, in season, or listened to it on the radio, flat on his back on the living room rug.

But the cigarettes gave him a wet, morning cough, and raw, burned sinuses, and got him up from bed all night, agitated, having to pee, and it was the nicotine—or its absence—that made him antsy. And he couldn't shit before work without coffee and a smoke, so he took them in the toilet, with the paper, and turned on the fan and drank and smoked and waited and grew hemorrhoids. I. yelled about smoking in the house but never rose early enough to stop him.

L. played lacrosse in high school. He knew what it was to be fit.

L. was not fit. He felt weathered and stiff.

He asked Dr. U________ for something for nights, to help with sleep, but Dr. U________ wouldn't bite. Anything he could give had risks, so he said no, quit smoking if you need to sleep, though nicely, knowing L. would take offense.

As if it's easy to quit, L. said.

He got I. to ask her doctor for a script, which she did, so they had a month's supply of Ambien®, which sat on I.'s dresser. The cat knocked it off, jumping past.

The pills were white, with AMB 10 punched in their sides.

I. said this was it. She wasn't asking the doctor for more.
And Do Not Take With Alcohol, she said, because the doctor told her that was out. Contraindicated. And only one a night, I. said. There's Risk of Coma. Risk. Of. Coma. Don't be stupid.

Right, L. said.

Benadryl® Before he got the Ambien, L. tried taking Benadryl, popping back two before bed, but they wore off at three, maybe four a.m., and he would wake sweating and confused, thirsty, and mix a jug of orange juice and lie restless on the sofa.
Caffeine Mornings he knocked his way to the kitchen, where the coffeemaker sat in clutter, to brew a pot of dark blend before heading to the can (see Ambien).

---

[1] Last Name, First Name, Middle Initial

[2] Insured

Midmornings, he got a large coffee from McDonald's or 7-Eleven and stirred in sweetened creamers, if he could. Irish Crème, Hazelnut. Ditto, afternoons.

His legs shook on ladders, and a thick munge of brown coated his tongue. He had acid reflux.

Caffeine Mornings he knocked his way to the kitchen, where the coffeemaker sat in clutter, to brew a pot of dark blend before heading to the can (see **Ambien**).

Midmornings, he got a large coffee from McDonald's or 7-Eleven and stirred in sweetened creamers, if he could. Irish Crème, Hazelnut. Ditto, afternoons.

His legs shook on ladders, and a thick munge of brown coated his tongue. He had acid reflux.

Darvocet® You gotta clear the decks for eight solids, L. told Tim, about Ambien. That shit puts out the lights, he said, and even after a ten to six stretch he still floated through the a.m., his brain too slow for power tools, and his fingers coming off in the circular saw hurt like a pinch and then a tug, and then just hurt. Only two, but still. He wrapped his hand and asked Tim for his soda—the cup and the ice—and gathered his fingers and got Edward to drive him to Baptist Memorial, where they sewed him up, splinted his hand past the wrist, and made free with Darvocet. He paid the fifty-dollar fee. He went home for the afternoon.

For a while, he laid off Ambien. He had Darvocet for nights.

Ex-Lax® For lunch, the crew got McDonald's/Burger King/Wendy's/Subway/ Popeye's/ Jersey Mike's/Taco Bell/Jack in the Box. Later, if L. and I. bought dinner, they got pizza or fried chicken. Sometimes a salad side, with blue cheese dressing.

L. burned it off, and I. gained weight, and got mad, and smashed a dinner plate, and cried, because she was supposed to sit all day and then eat like a construction worker and not be as fat as a house? She needed L. to help. If they were going to get takeout, she said, it should be from the Kroger deli. Roasted chicken, no skin. Or fish. Rice, and vegetables.

You don't like fish, L. said, and I. gained more weight, and L.'s guts clogged (see **Ambien** and **Caffeine**). On the worst days, he took laxatives and hunched through breaks in a porta-potty, if their site had one, or on a crapper in the nearest store. At a bodega on Fourth, L. took too long, and the owner entered, his shoes showing through a break under the stall door. He stood for a minute before he spoke. You all right?

Fluoride To clear the munge from his mouth and tongue (see **Caffeine**), L. scrubbed with MentaDent®. Twice through his molars and onto the front teeth and across his taste buds until they burned.

Gaviscon® He didn't like how it foamed in his mouth, but it helped after lunch, when burgers lodged in his windpipe and he burped onions.

Head and Shoulders® Probably he should have used a gentler shampoo. His hair was thinning, and two shiny patches of scalp grew backward on the sides of his forehead. But he hated dandruff. He found it embarrassing.

Ibuprofen Two 500 mg. capsules didn't cut the pain like Darvocet, which was long gone, ditto the Tylenol® with Codeine, and the Percocet®. It didn't help that he worked his hand all day, managing whatever didn't need fine motor skills. He lifted, hauled. He held beams while they were nailed in place. He learned to handle the nail gun with his left hand, and I. had no sympathy about the pain, because, one, he wasn't supposed to use his hand for six weeks, and, two, if he used it it wasn't going to heal right, meaning, three, he'd have more problems down the road, and, four, if he could frickin haul lumber he could get his own drink from the fridge. Put down the bag of chips or make two trips. She had enough work without having to wipe his butt, and she wasn't getting up at six anymore to help with his mornings. Maybe if he made more money, she could cut back to part time, and she could help around the house, and they could have time for other stuff, too.

Just Tears® He gave contacts a try, because I. said to, meaning, L. knew, if she caught him popping the stems of his glasses in his mouth again, to suck off the sweat, she'd scream, but he forgot to take the lenses out at nights, and he got a corneal scratch, and glasses worked better at stopping wood chips and dust. So back to the horn-rims with a Croakies® strap.

Kaopectate® What Scott said, when he saw L. pull out a bottle, was the main ingredient was dirt or some such shit. Kao-Pectate, he said. Kao, he said. Kao-lan or lin or lon, he said. Look at the ingredients. It's clay. Bismuth subsalicylate 525 mg, L. said. Caramel, carmethylcellulose sodium, flavor, microcrystalline cellulose, purified water, sodium salicylate, sorbic acid, sucrose, titanium dioxide, and xanthan gum. Lemme see, Scott said, and L. started buying Imodium®, which came in tablets and worked better at stopping what Ex-Lax started.

Lamisil® The stink that came from L.'s feet when he peeled off his socks—cat piss. It was fungus and sweat. I. wouldn't let L.'s boots inside, and, when they smelled up the porch, she threw them out.

L. didn't always wear clean socks because he didn't like washing the pile of clothes blocking his closet, because that meant a trip to the basement at night or on weekends, so he ignored the mess until I. washed five or six loads and dumped clean stuff on the bed. If he wanted to sleep, he folded.

Lamisil cream would have killed the fungus, but he didn't use it regularly, most times, and when he did, he forgot to pour bleach on the shower floor, which only got clean when I. caught athlete's foot and yelled at him and scrubbed for an hour. She threatened to spend their money on a cleaning lady.

Maalox® At least it acted fast. Didn't help for long enough. Dense, like a milkshake. Chalky. (See **Gaviscon**).

Nicotine In college, when L. and I. both smoked, they could cloud a room in minutes. In L.'s apartment. Not I.'s. She didn't like how the smoke lingered in her towels and drapes.

L. bought packs of Camel Lights® for I. and left them in her coat, for her to find when he wasn't around. Matches he left, too, or a lighter, and I. always meant to do the same for L., but, absent-minded, forgot. That was okay.

When L. quit school and moved into I.'s place, they took to stepping out back, onto the balcony.

After I. graduated, she quit. She didn't want to become a pariah at work, huddling outside around sand-filled ashcans. And she needed to be healthy to have babies someday. So.

L. kept smoking with the guys at the job (see **Ambien**), and it cost more than he and I. could afford, almost thirty bucks a carton.

If L. couldn't find an ashtray or didn't want to ash in the grass, he rolled his pants and flicked into the cuffs. If there was no place to put his butts, he pinched off the red ends and pocketed the filters. Come laundry time, he and I. fought over the mess.

Oxycodone with APAP By law, he could have five days of Darvocet. After that, the doctor wrote him a script for the same thing, different name: Tylenol with Codeine. After that, a heavy dose of Ibuprofen (see **Ibuprofen**).

L. decided that for re-attached fingers, Ibuprofen didn't cut it. The guys at work agreed, and Tim scored him two dozen Percocets in original wrappers.

L. hated the stitches sitting below his knuckles. They looked like wiry eyelashes. Spider's legs. At night, before he fell asleep, he could feel his fingerbones rejoining.

Pseudoephedrine Until he dropped out of college, L. took Wal-Phed® to cram for exams and stay sharp in class and just give a lift. He lost ten pounds. He felt on edge and smoked more and wanted to smash in the heads of kids wearing sweatpants to class. Smug, little cunts. Baseball caps on backwards. Never worked a day in their lives, L. figured. They could use some hard knocks.

L.'s dad said to go. He said L. didn't want to spend his life working shitty jobs. It's too hard, he said. Later on, when you get older. Look at your old man, he said. Right out of high school, roofing didn't seem so bad. For a couple of years. But use that money for college, L.'s dad said, so L. did, at 23, when he was older than most seniors. His parents bought his books.

Two years later, when he quit, they promised to help again, whenever, and I. said she would too, because they were thinking about marriage. Go back when I get a job, she said, knowing he wouldn't, and it would be a problem, someday, his lack of options. But, then again, who knew, maybe he would move up, or start a business, and she didn't want his leaving college to mean his leaving her, because she was having a tough time too, she told her mom, with classes and her major and everything, though who was she to complain.

She was lonely too often.

L. kept on with his summer carpenter position and moved in with I. He took over the rent.

About college, L. said he wanted a break. It made him itch, he said.

And he was out of funds.

Quick Pep® Only once did L. mix Quick Pep and coffee. How could extra caffeine be bad, he thought, before his hands developed a slick coat of sweat, and his heart started pounding, hiccupping every few beats, and the world tilted at the damnedest angle, and he fell to his knees, head hanging down, until he could get it together. Dropped a wallboard anchor, he said to Scott. Somewhere around here, he said. Just get another, Karl said, and L. said, Okay. Yeah.

Rhinocort® Hay fever season, four snorts in the morning. It made his nose bleed, but he didn't sneeze. It would have been better if they kept the yard down, which the lease required, but come weekends L. couldn't get himself to mow, and I. was damned if she'd do it and clip the weeds and trim the bushes, so she hired the Branski kid, David, from down the street. He did a crappy job, once a month, leaving patches of weed climbing their fence. But there you go. If L. wanted it different, he could take care of it himself.

Sominex® Basically Benadryl, the pharmacist told him. An antihistamine.
Fuck that, L. said later, to I. (see **Benadryl**).

Tylenol with Codeine He kept four, for the future, for who knows what.

Unisom® Basically Benadryl, the pharmacist told him. An antihistamine.
Fuck that, L. said later, to I. (see **Benadryl**).

Valium® Dr. U________ said, It's not a good choice. If you wake at night, cut back on caffeine. If you need help to quit smoking, we could try

Wellbutrin®, which curbs your craving.
If you still can't sleep, maybe a non-benzodiazepine. Maybe.
But not Valium, which works for intense periods of anxiety, Dr. U________ said, like

Xanax®, which is newer. They're very addictive.
Okay, L. said. Though, at night. Even in the day. Like there's something right then. You know?
What do you mean, Dr. U________ asked.
L. said, What do you mean?
L. said, Intense anxiety. Yes. I have intense anxiety.

Yasmin® I.'s doctor gave her a three-month refill, for fewer copays. She kept the extra packets in their top bathroom drawer. The pills for the month went in a soft, blue case on her dresser.

She needed to lose fifty pounds. The extra weight put her at greater risk for heart attack and stroke. With her luck, breast cancer, too. But she didn't like diaphragms, and she didn't trust L. to use rubbers, and they didn't have enough money for kids, and she didn't think they ever would. She'd always have to work, at least. Then, day-care costs.

They couldn't even keep a goddam house clean. No kids, she said to L. Not now, she said. Maybe never, she said. Do you care?

I. had a bank account she didn't share with L. She put away a hundred dollars a month, just in case.

Zoloft® Sometimes it's part of a bigger thing, Dr. U________ said. The sleep. Maybe we want to think about underlying problems. Maybe you need to lift your mood.
There are a lot of good meds out there, Dr. U________ said. Serotonin builders.
What's that, L. said. Antidepressants?
You're saying I'm nuts, L. said.
I don't need happy pills, L. said.
Just the Xanax, L. said. Or the other one.
I'm fine, L. said. Just fine.

STEVE KATZ

Manifesto Dysfic

Fearless wordslingers! break out! flee the workshops!
make sense not! like moths in the honey jar writerlings
perform dreary veridical conventions over and again delusion
persists that the map is the territory there's gold in that there
map but a panda looms in this parking garage fixing to strip
your bamboo heart or tiger, tiger is it the lean into violence
that garments our time go have fun kiddoes thugs in our gov
con the young into war for their own craven delusions these slugs
(I mean bend over, America) (I mean who profits? Look in the bushes!)
ice sheet melt and toxic goop etcetera etcetera war profiteers
that threaten to dissolve our bindings the maimed the sick
generations of children lost to neglect and apathy
what'll we do? Describe it? Discuss it? Crazed
with recognition we have moved to detonate our revolution
with ancient new genre **DYSFIC!!!!** Our kisses cauterize
sear away descriptive, discursive formulae dead words
can never give tongue to this experiences these feelings **DYSFIC** charges
language artists to emancipate language into the mystery and power
at its source in heart and cosmos the conventional assignment buries
reality in a casket of illusions **DYSFIC** is evocative, incantatory,
ecstatic not the image in the mirror nor the scene through the window
the work is to smash the mirror shatter the glass as they distort
DYSFICTIONS are anti-narrative they are dysfunctional, dysrational,
dysengaged they are politically and emotionally dyslect can be
dystasteful and **DYSFIC** is dysorderly, dyspontaneous, it is manifest even though it is dysqualified and dysallowed dysprovisational
though in its structures it may exhibit form exquisite
as insects in a laundry often composed at randyom
DYSFICS are quick and clueless as persistently trivial as they are

relentlessly profound **DYSFIC** is always composed through a system of exocharacterization and psychological outrisme (this doesn't mean fuck-all, Mesdames & Monsieurs, mi dispiace) i.e., elsewhere characters live in their books, grow, lust, murder their children, survive brutal savage childhoods in various ethnicities, breath salt air by the shore, keep pet alligators in the tub, fuck-up the lives of their closest friends, despair of satisfying their grandmothers, pray for a breakthrough in their diets, conspire to sell nuclear secrets, but none of this, not a word of it ever manifests in a **DYSFIC** dysfictioneers grant release of brief chuffs of steam from the eyeballs the writings resist closure, encourage dysclosure dysfictioneers know that within every closure plumps an efflorescence any dysclosure clears the track to THE END

DYSFICS never begin come nowhere to an ending be the perpetual middle of things intrepidly spiritual or dyspiritual depending on field of play you read as you do at breakfast the cereal box or casually while you wait for the tech to come back on line or while you rest in your attempt to get back into those tight jeans (prescribed years ago in a different poet's manifesto) However you wiggle to compact the flab years have wrought you'll have to face up to the **DYSFICS** presto-chango **DYSFICTION** is right now and beyond

DYSFIC a fly on the nose of a theorist cabbage in the throat of gender narration and bland gruel of sexual preference **DYSFIC** an ethnic gollywobble as one of its affections **DYSFIC** embraces dyscombobulation and silliness as no serious genre has dared and by doing thus eliminates the pejoratives of those categories such an erasure is in the nature of every embrace to embrace is not to embarrass we mean it we love you

Samuel Beckett's entreaty that we yield not to the distortions of intelligibility is proudly flown on the **DYSFIC** flag

TODD ZUNIGA

Confessions of an American Opium Merchant

My thinking is: people want to be considered literary, it feels good to have read books. But it takes so much time. And the easier entertainment—*Mad Men* on Bravo; *Madden NFL 10* on Xbox 360; Wes Anderson's latest on the silver screen—is, so often, so freaking good.

But people want to be considered literary. They want to read. They want their literature to compete with the other excitements—workday email flirtations, *30 Rock* on Vimeo, TED.com videos on their iPhone., etc. They want their literature to pop.

For *Opium*, when it all gets boiled way, way down, our aim is to return literature to pop culture status. To make it on-par cooler-talk relevant with who Jack Bauer mercilessly tortured, to make it the *Saturday Night Live* of the '80s. The challenge still being: it's reading. And reading's fine, but it takes so much energy and focus. When a three-episode session of *Dexter* feels like a thrill ride.

So, how, then? For starters, we put estimated reading times on each of our stories, online and in print. A joke, a sort of "we're paying attention, see?" elbow in the ribs soft nudge. Then we slap on a beautiful cover, design that lures you into consecutive pages, which is us daring ourselves if we can do better (and by "us" I mean design wizard David Barringer). Oh, and the content. Well, that's the fun part. Because if you pick up an issue, flip open to the story that's one minute and eleven seconds long and think, sure, I'll taste-test this, then you step right into a story rife with wonderment, shockingly lively prose, poems that crackle and snap.

So, after all that work, no way we're just going to let it sit still in a bookstore. So we push as hard as we can to get to and go beyond the literary audience, to inspire reading in circles where it's not the first thing thought. But saying "Read this" is heard as "Let me suck time from your busy-as-fuck (like everyone else) schedule." Now that there's the internet, there's no shortage of something to do. That's why we do Literary Death Match events in every city who'll have us. And I use "events" on purpose, because while the LDM is *Opium*'s signature "reading series," we don't call it that.

It's a fine phrase, but the LDM's are a literary *celebration* that happen to have a reading attached, a way to lure people with our big, curiosity-inducing title, and once we have them, there's just a tease, in terms of literature/listening (we're tough on time limits: eight minutes per reader). The event marries the literary and performative aspects of *Def Poetry Jam*, the rapier-witted quips of *American Idol*'s judging (without the meanness), the ridiculousness and hilarity of *Double Dare*. And all of it aimed to excite and surprise, and in the periphery of it all: readers as stars, their books as must-have proof that you were there.

GIANCARLO DiTRAPANO

Benediction

Finalist in the Opium 500-word memoir contest
Estimated Reading Time: 2:14

When I was nine, God wasn't watching my family as I'd asked him to all of those nights. Instead, the fuck, he smashed my brother's car into a utility pole on a south Florida interstate, crushing and killing him and three other nineteen-year-old boys. A shit place to die, Florida, and a shit way to die, crushed, at age nineteen, and with friends, too. Well, being with friends might have made the whole thing more digestible had he lived to taste it.

So I back-prayed.

May my entire family and everyone I have ever loved or even liked be raped and tortured and killed with sheets and sheets of pain and blood. Make it take a long time, and make them die with the ugliest and most frightened of faces. Make me watch this please. Do not let me turn away, not for one second. Make all of my good friends commit suicide for immature reasons in their huge bathrooms, crying into their mirrors with lots of blood and pain and holding some bad rock album in their arms, and make it grueling and last a long, long time. Make it very embarrassing-looking. Lord, make me watch that too. Let my only child be retarded at birth, killing my wife during delivery so that I hate my retarded child and make his life even more miserable than the life of a normal retarded child.

Bring big bugs, bring disease, bring darkness, rotting limbs, and unspeakable groanings. Bring great pain. Don't leave anyone out. Make the lands and seas unlivable due to all the hate and murder and waves of blood and pain and knives. Extinguish all Life. And then, for the cherry, let there be a Heaven where we spend our eternities hiking over clouds under a beating sun with no end in sight, a Heaven where we are forced to reunite with, walk beside, and listen to all those people we hated and never wanted to see again who died on us while we were alive. Make sure all of the angels from the church's bright paintings look down on us like we are thieves just because we are new. Like they're so damn pious and we never were. And, lastly, take away all hope that our lives will improve. Make us so tired and depressed and sick that we won't have the energy to pray anymore.

ASHA KHALADKAR

Metro

Estimated Reading Time: 1:51

One week, there was a roving party that traveled between D.D.O. and Dorval. Most of that week has been lost in a haze of memory, but I remember a long succession of basements and young men in cargo pants. A long succession of trains and buses and métros. I didn't change clothes all week (and me in underwear that was too small, and a coat that didn't fit right either, that was worn *through* in the armpits and frayed about the cuffs). (There was a gentleman who *played* guitar and wore big boots. I have never been a sucker for the guitar but he had a voice that could make you forget about your responsibilities. Eyes like the dark part of a glacier, that picked things up and held them. Things stuck to him. Turned out he wasn't so bright in the end, or so kind, but there was a glimmer, for a moment, of *something* I must have been seeking—something new.)

My parents, back on the prairies, filed a missing person's report.

Three years later, I kept being stopped by the police. They wanted to know where I lived, and who I was. I started to carry ID, to prove myself. But it was another missing person they were looking for, a young girl who had disappeared. (I saw her picture on television; her name was Ahna. Wearing a wife-beater and jeans, she had left her Hungarian father with spread empty hands.) I walked every night from the Plateau under the underpass to Petite Patrie, and for weeks cruisers slowly followed behind. When they found Anna in the hot sun by Vendôme metro, she had been beaten into a coma. It was August, late-morning, and she lay with her dark hair on the grass. A tapestry of green and red and black. Her shoulders pressing the earth like stones. Her face turned to the dark branches of the sky.

I kept seeing my hair on the news.

JAY WEXLER

$E = MC^3$

Estimated Reading Time: 4:35

What about it, Dalton? I ask, but he's busy chomping turnips and doesn't appear to hear me. Chrysanthemum's sitting next to him, pinching his cheeks. My jowls are not toys, he tells her. She reluctantly desists. The appetizers have arrived; it's anyone's ball game from here. I examine the soup bowl, am nearly certain that its diameter exceeds two times its radius. I remove the string ruler from my neck, take the relevant measurements, confirm my suspicions. Who says the rules governing the universe are static? I ask my earth-fruit-munching chum. But, once again I'm met with silence. Dalton always orders the "Tuber of the Day" when we come to The Grille because, as he says, it makes him feel at ease with his own corporality and whatnot. This is fallacy, canards on a stick, a martini of idiocy—shaken, not stirred—but Dalton's paying, so I let it go. In between the soup course and the main dish, I look at my surroundings, the objects around me, their movements, how they interact. I observe (among other things) the following:

$F = ma$ *plus one.*

$v = v^{o} + at$ *divided by 1.0000000000000000001*

$\tau = rF \sin \theta$ *and a smidge*

Chrysanthemum dives into her Ricola®-glazed ham steak, flosses after every bite, tickles Dalton's obliques to his extraordinary dismay. It is clear that Chrysanthemum is in love with Dalton, but I can't really say whether the love is requited. I try to remember the precise order of the Canadian provinces, west to east, while the waiter appears to grind fresh fish into the water tumblers. There is a fly in my 1982 Chateau Margaux, Dalton suddenly protests, and the waiter is over in a flash to disagree. I calculate the velocity of his arrival, am disappointed to find it consistent with prevailing theories. Is it Alberta, *then* Saskatchewan? For years I've been challenging this whole notion of Avogadro's number; they say it is a constant, defines the number of items in a mole, but in my opinion this has only been established definitively for tiny objects like atoms and paramecia, and remains unproven with regard to larger mushy items like marshmallows or scallops or throw pillows. I'd have had this sewn up by now, my research documented in all the leading academic journals, but my grant money dried out years ago, so it's all speculation at this point. The waiter is inexplicably wearing a yellow snakeskin ascot that makes him appear like a Liza Minnelli hologram on a Tanzanian safari expedition. Why the hell would he do that?

Dalton stands and raises his voice, insists that a fly was in his bottle. The waiter fingers his ascot nervously, says, No, such a thing is impossible. Dalton responds by plucking the dead fly out of the glass and waving it around like a French flag on Bastille Day; the drowned insect is as big as a small hummingbird, but far less delightful. Summoned by the waiter, the sommelier rejects Dalton's position outright, indicates the integrity of the cork, and accuses his customer of planting the fly. Chrysanthemum is on her knees trying to hold Dalton back, but still he lunges toward the sommelier with his tuber fork, retaliating in response to the accusation. Dalton makes eight figures, so there is little reason for him to plant the fly; and he's a hothead by nature who doesn't take kindly to such finger pointing. I whip out my abacus and attempt to calculate certain parameters of permeability, but my computations require some data regarding cork density that are available only from the Chateau itself, and there just isn't time.

The "experts" say that kinetic energy can be measured by something that looks kind of like:

$$KE = \frac{1}{2} mv^2$$

—but my best estimate of Dalton's kinetic energy at this point, as he leaps toward the waiter's throat, tuber fork extended, even incorporating the opposing force exercised by Chrysanthemum as she grabs Dalton's considerable thighs and begs, pleads, beseeches him to stop, is something more like:

$$KE = \frac{1}{2} mv^{2,\text{ or so, give or take two shakes of a tail or what have you.}}$$

The waiter intercepts Dalton's attack, grabs the fork away from my friend's clenched digits, lances the substantial fly on the fork's prongs, and threatens to feed Dalton the insect with force. Dalton may be rich, but he hasn't taken a shower in days, and the smell of cilantro from his armpits is damned near overpowering. The sommelier is assisting the waiter, and Dalton now finds himself pinned under both of their buttock sets. I take a sip of the fish water and try to remember where Manitoba falls on the west-east Canadian spectrum. Before Saskatchewan? After? As the fly-speared fork prongs slowly descend towards Dalton's sweaty mug, and the sommelier's purple tinged fingers work diligently to part his tightly pressed lips, Chrysanthemum flogs the waiter with her herbed ham steak and implores him at the top of her lungs to l*eave Dalton alone*. Like a maniac, she insists that *the wine had a fly, the wine had a fly*. I look carefully at her for the first time this evening: her hair de-bunned, saliva bubbling from her mouth like one of Old Faithful's smaller neighbors, the sound coming out of her throat reminiscent of an early '80s horror-movie victim. I can think of only one thing, and that is this: *I work for an odd financial-services firm*. Taking my ruler in hand, I measure the salt shakers and hope for the best.

SIMONE MUENCH

From "Orange Girl Suite"

1:

|Young women carrying baskets of oranges used to stand near the stage in London theatres and sell oranges at sixpence apiece and themselves for little more|

between dresses we came.
between naked and nothing
we slipped into the delirious
coils of perfected ears,

            pear dust on our skin
                        sarsparilla sounding our
                                    fizzied song in sailor mouths.

we were translated by churchwomen
who placed umlauts over our words.

when we recovered, we were sold
in beautiful clothes, sent sailing into the gulf
where the moon pitched
its lemon-lateness over the celluloid

            slickness of sea. we were movie stars
                        who never entered the frame.
                                    we were green and gone

lisping "o" words in the air:
ode, odalisque, obituary.

2:

|The rynde of the orrendge is hot, and the meate within it is cold|

there are only two ways
            to peel an orange
                        in fragments or in one
            coiling brightness.
let us rewind and revel
            in the orangeade of sun-
                        decked eyes. turn me spinning
            in a carousel-sweet dress
ear marked by radio teeth
            red leaf breath.
                        your arm is on fire
            as we ride in a dark
car to the carnival.
            the constant clink
                        of seatbelt to belt buckle.

the sky's cotton candy
melting in a girl's cold mouth.

3:

|The orange-girl is generally allowed to enter an auction-store, for auctioneers are mortal, and sometimes eat oranges|

I'm stone and pulp, like policemen's wives.
you're emerald, buried in dark clothes.
your eyes leaf, bone.

your fingers so many songs

out of tune

I have fallen out of trees singing your name; I have
fallen into your foliation

into your moth-mouth, plum-
thick tongue.

wherever you are, I'll be white teeth,
an abandoned town, a wrapped parcel.

I'll be a blonde in a black smock with sex
appeal, smelling of apiaries.

I'll be a cold sea in an old war film.
I'll be insubordinate

and seville sweet.

you'll be long gone
though you said you'd never leave
those poor crippled orange trees.

4:

|The soft night-wind went laden to death with flowering orange scent|

tongues harvest petals, larvae
the back of the throat is petticoat pink
the girl in the dirty dress is dead

I wish I were a fish lit by phosphorescence
I wish I were in Spain
I wish I were blue-gilled and beautiful

a man folds the girl up in newspapers

her wet hair a string of taffy, a rope, something
unraveling inside the man's eye

when he killed her he said *listen*
when he killed her he said
your soul, orange girl

he said *windowsill*
he said *stone*
while alive she replied

oilslick, doorjam. something
passing through my right eye:
black cars and carousels

pretty maids all in a row

CAROL NOVACK

In the Beginning Is

3

In the beginning is before the beginning after the endings the missed endings mixed blessings endings and always in the middle of it all before and after is all the zero times zero, meaning one in the sum of its parts, the fractious parts of the one parting departing breaking up into star bits, ego bits, id bits, alpha bit soup, genetic stew, devolving evolving revolving violently, breaking into cells molecules galaxies exploding imploding, birthing stars (sometimes by Caesarian) falling twinkling and belching the indigestible jet sum pom poms and flotsam;

In the beginnings endings of galaxies exploding imploding, birthing stars together falling apart together twinkling and belching the indigestible jet sum phoenixes and flotsam; before and after, is all the zero times zero, meaning one in its parts fractions of no things parting departing breathing always in and out breaking up into fractious star bits ego bits id bits alpha bit soup, genetic stew, caves, pyramids, igloos, coffins, minnows, mud huts, holes and monkfish revolving madly breaking into molecules into galaxies exploding imploding, birthing stars falling twinkling and belching the indigestible jet sum corsets and flotsam, casino chips, donkeys' ears, pterodactyls, blue hats, canaries, pompoms and pantaloons, the hollow cries of wolves and cats' meows.

In the beginning is the ending is always the middle is floating forever ever never in all there where who can tell is anywhere is not imagining all of it, bits of ego, id and libid o such as we supposing symphonies of orbiting cellos playing the music, announcing, recapitulating: in the beginning there was in the end there will be there was there will be most definitely finitely finally you can count, count on it, get the rhythm the hymns the footnotes; *res ipso loquitor*. GET IT NOW! Believe you me, we bits of star bones bend our mind bones to envision the unseen, to name the beginning THE beginning, in place and time, a beginning an ending one can count, can count on as we come and go into the hole, casino, pyramid the coffin and up and up rising galactic dust, ending to form another beginning.

We yes, let's suppose as if we (little kids of ids and egos, fragments of cosmic energy famishing for the super ego breast, my own desiccating after a storm of births), we bits in dance class beginning the beguine, as if to learn the first step toward forward toward back—ontology recapitulating oncology, psychology recapitulating gynecology— then all of a sudden there all along in the middle of it all is

the cockroach, all mouth and feelers, hardly an eye an ear a heart: Vacant Wanting, Abominable Hunger, Persistence in the Face of Adversity, Cuckoo Clock of Instinct, Cliché of Aggravation and Apathetic Ugliness, Key to All and

Nothingness,

and you were so damn clumsy you stepped on it!

2

There are myths everywhere, *ipso facto,* ho hum so what's fresh cut under our sun? There's the one about the original hermaphroditic loving self sapient that split into two sexes, which is why we have war and plagues and global warming and laden donkeys collapsing on our highways. And there's the myth that one squashed cockroach returns as many. You warned me not to squash the roach; but then you did it yourself. Let's not get into your intentions, please. *Amoeba* my foot! You simply cannot dance! *Res ipsa Labrador.* And even in Equador.

In the beginning before the beginning after the ending—*what ending?* you asked. What middle? you meant, always muddling middles. Your eyes were open, half old moon style mud milk brown when the credits were rolling again, so I suppose you saw at least the mountain, no not the dry grass mountain with the goats—the lush mountain with sheep blah blahing over the dead shepherd as his shadow floated off into evening as if he were created of the negation of air, and I foolishly cried and you said: *into the tunnel of chaos goest the shepherd.* You would not admit you were thinking of the prom queen when the credits were rolling, in the beginning, you insisted: *I saw the beginning, a man wearing a blue hat on the mountain standing by a window with his dog. He shouted "Mother," in subtitles, and his name was Benny and there was that flashback of a cheerleader with pompoms!* You insisted you knew the ending: *Clouds full of wasps, pantaloons hanging over the mountain, a car chase in minefields, roulette in the casinos.* Then you added: *That's what I saw in the end.* And I pointed out: *His name was Lars. And the dog was a cat.* And you replied: *But the pyramid!* But there was no pyramid. You were snoring through the middle, and you often dream of pyramids.

0

In the end is the beginning is that shunned bit of esurient life, all quivering feelers, nothing to contribute to the universe, the primal pest programmed to eat digest recapitulate forever, the sum total of:

dust of pharaohs
bones in caves
meat scraps in mud huts
seal blubber in igloos
cemetery ashes
ascending phoenixes
coffin dust
shards of mines
galaxy debris
casino chips
inedible molecular leftovers
ketchup on pompoms
moping mouths of monkfish
wings of pterodactyls
tears of wolves
donkeys' ears
seeds of pomegranates
string theory of corsets
galactic trash
rims of blue hats
feathers of canaries
tiaras on dance room floors
meows of cats
piss in the holes
hearts of minnows
hairs of dogs
a partridge in a pear tree
my pantaloons flung carelessly
in the kitchen sink
down in the hole
the kitchen sink
he and she and they
and we and us and you
and them and him and her
and *IIII*
(and so on and on ....

In the beginning is

#17

three red flags, each winnowed
around multi-colored stones,
is how I've been hit,

  how I've been gutted

#19

feet tap linoleum,
  shadow-play rhythm;
not to be dogged,
  nerves infra-reddened

#45

"in order to"
lose those blueberry shackles
"fight hegemony"
in moose-like context

I don't know how to

#36

after all
  everything
you're still
  thinking

ochre-tinted

#61

never you worry
honey
on the table
money

#91

“I have
eaten no
plums”
is what
I told
the trope-
police

#105

cut short,
pumpkin,
but that’s
alright, as
I feel cut
also, by
short kin,
smashed.

#162

no room for thought
glare on potted plants

flawlessly dumbstruck

#163

your face
beige wall
it’s pictured

not that I
can reach

#169

you'll see
it's urban
as grease,

breaths I

take in a
rush like
this, this

#170

éclairs conspire
all in a line

I'm hungry

for them to
be written

#200

my hands measure
hyena arousal
as my mouth laughs

my my

JOSHUA COREY

On Jessica Savitz and *Hunting is Painting*, the Madeleine P. Plonsker Emerging Writer's Residency Prize winner, 2009

There were a number of challenging and exciting manuscripts submitted for the first annual Plonsker Fellowship at Lake Forest College, and it wasn't easy to choose among them. But the manuscript submitted by Jessica Savitz, with its arresting declarative title, Hunting Is Painting, leaped from the pile. It wasn't just the haunting photographs and visual images that weave through the text, though they are certainly remarkable in a book of poems, reminding me of nothing so much as the curious captionless pictures folded into W.G. Sebald's narratives. It was the work itself: deeply and authoritatively strange configurations of lush lyric language that comes close, often, to the condition of song in its use of refrain and repetition, like Gertrude Stein with a larger vocabulary.

The poems follow the rigorous logic of the book's title, a metaphor or allegory of "gun as microscope," or as she declares with horrifying and truthful matter-of-factness, "Slaughtering the animal / Was like freeing him with a knife / From a little trap." The hunter's attributes of ruthlessness, canniness, and respect for one's prey, formulate the book's remarkable aesthetic, which concentrates its attention on facts—of personal biography, of animals and their habitats, of artworks and artists—and bring them suddenly into higher resolutions, new configurations. Some of the poems remind me strongly of Whitman in their readiness to empathize with fellow creatures, human and nonhuman. At the same time there's a predatory fierceness that startles and clears the eye, so that this poet is one who can recognize that "the dying arrangement is a living being" ("dying and animate / to direct light, or to create privacy").

With sharp, sometimes appealingly goofy wit, the poems confront us with the necessary violence of sensemaking: we kill what we notice, and what we do not. But our gaze preserves the objects of the world even as it pierces them, and they in turn pierce us. I get news from these poems about our condition, and about the price artists are all too willing to pay for a snapshot, a painting, or a poem. They innovate upon their own necessity, and bring us closer to the real.

JESSICA SAVITZ

From *Hunting is Painting*

Hunting is Painting

Brown shirt littered in dove's blood;
Hunting is painting and excavating some greater forest.
And hose-water and knife through scales
Cooks alcohol of supper—-
I spread the light in salt over my food
And often use a knife to remove a bruise
From the golden peach of truth.

There is bait in the mouths of ice-fishermen.

*

In the Band of Painters and Photographers hired to determine the fertility of America

Bats drizzling in twilight
stripes of circus canopy on the tiger's belly
I put my face near the soil sample and hear
the dirt dreaming of trumpet vine and a city garden with cotton candy and a zoo with little signs by the animals
the dirt I try to extract from the paint is part of the paint

my eyes closed and laughing and the prince-cook
at the campfire makes me meat I can taste the field in
I thought, "gun as microscope"

the river stands up for a moment and the fish rest on rocks
and I go homeward and found a park in the woods
and the pond is one wave I can spear

I see my wife standing there
I said, the tree is filling out in leaves
don't stand behind that tree
I can see your eye, loved-one
but soon the tree is filled out in leaves

*

The Growth of Ice on Dying Stems

"The name of the bow is life, but its work is death."
—Heraclitus

I.

To heal the branch with deathish strokes
green-blue fire of lichen
Death supplies the living branches with shadow-art which falls across the ground,
beneath this wide magnolia and no grass will grow there

Friend-Death clearing out the rocks and living shrubs
to make room for the immortal garden:
the flowers' regeneration is as strong as stone
the lineage of flower-talking is as strong as a mountain

Green leaves grow thick
In the cage with the tiger

II.

In the joust between Life and Death:
rust is bloodish flowering on the scythe blade

Deathish-lifeish opulence;
Park stocked with game for the hunt—
thorn-branch antler, bait will catch blood

spears of rain slant in sparks of light
torn ivy hanging off the horns
rainfall hard upon the fawn he is limping

III.

Water braiding currents in the rapids
fish within the hood of the wave.

As a breath
ceremonies of fish swirling into the cave
of the Great Death-whale—
pleasure swims in this reservoir
careful strokes through the weedy lake

The infinite life of fishing the pond on the island
sound carries across the lifeish-deathish waters

Gentle Life and Gentle Death
As they fished upon the water
in their narrow nighttime boat

DAVIS SCHNEIDERMAN

On Gretchen E. Henderson and *Galerie de Difformité*, the Madeleine P. Plonsker Emerging Writer's Residency Prize winner, 2010

For year two of this award, we received a large number of high-quality manuscripts in wildly diverse styles. Henderson's selection spotlights the cross-genre emphasis for the Plonsker Residency, and this *Galerie*-in-progress is a hybrid of prose and poetry, yet also contains a strong narrative and meta-narrative through-line. This is high-concept material: a gallery of broken-body aesthetics, the work interrogates the nuanced concepts of ability/disability, voyeurism/exhibition, deformity/normality—all with a wry sense of self-fashioned and self-representational humor. With this story within a story, presented by the "Undertaker"—a reanimated-yet-disabled Beatrice from Dante's *Commedia*, who is intertwined with the contemporary Gloria Heys and an inter-textual Gretchen Henderson [the presumed publisher], the *Galerie* reinvigorates a tradition of classically motivated innovative fiction that directly involves the reader as complicit in the process of evaluation.

We witness this *Galerie* as viewers stroll through a museum of curiosities or "freaks": it is our gaze that mobilizes the meanings of the text, which comes to us in a variety of formal devices. There is the history of a heart-shaped bone fragment ("Lineage of a Bone") along with various injunctions as to how to read/unread or view/unview the collected works ("Caution!!!!")—these together promise a final project that will provide conceptually evocative linkages between the differently compelling vignettes sampled in the following pages.

The sheer diversity of voice at work in these "exhibits" (academic, poetic, instructive) and the learned application of so many compelling themes, creates a printed gallery of great expanse and possibility. This work is a bestiary of Enlightenment- and Renaissance-era aesthetic thinking, updated and applied to a world with rapidly changing ideas regarding the post-humanist legacy.

Gretchen E. Henderson
presents:

Galerie de Difformité

& other exhumed exhibits :
a declassified catalogue

Undertaker's Note on the Text

I cannot permit this Catalogue to appear before the Public, without returning my sincere Thanks to you, dear Subscriber of this Undertaking, and to the Artists, whose works are reproduced here or Not in further reproduction, as deformations of the Originals. It is therefore hoped that the Spectator will view these Pictures, or Thumbnails, with regard to this Prosimetric Enterprise.

Of the merits of the Artists employed in this Exhibition, I can with truth say that I have sought talents, wherever they were to be found, to carry into execution an undertaking based upon historical Taste and the subject of Deformity.

Upon the merits of the Pictures themselves, it is not for me to speak, except with the relation of each to Deformity. Suffice it to say, that these Works of Art have been chosen to Accompany my Exhibits (aforementioned in the *Pre-face*), to promulgate and promote this plan in General. [i]

Though I believe it will be readily admitted, that no subjects seem so proper to form a School of Deformity in Art— This much, however, I will venture to say: that the Works collected for this Gallery—unlocked from curiosity cabinets, museums, cathedrals, palaces, and whatnot—bear something for you, Subscriber, to consider: the Nature of Deformity.

I must express my hopes, that the Subscriber will be satisfied with the progress made in this arduous undertaking, that Deformity has been redefined through the Arts, regarding the Nature of the Subject and the Subject of Nature. I trust upon inspection of what has been done, and is now doing, through this Deformation of Text, that the Subscriber will be satisfied with the exertions that have been made, and will think that confidence has not been misplaced.

If the object of uniting a certain degree of Beauty with Deformity, through Utility, has been attained, the merit is the Artists. —If not, the Undertaker is willing to bear the blame.

☞ *Candid Criticism is the soul of improvement—and those artists, who shut their ears against it, must never expect to improve—At the same time, every artist ought to despise and condemn the cavils of Pseudo-critics, who, rather than not attempt to shew their wit, would crush all merit in its bud—The discerning part of the public, however, place all these attempts to true account—Malignity—But, as the world was never entirely free from such critics, the present undertaking must expect to have its share.*

you are here

●

Imagine a grid, or something with lines that cross and hatch with openings that signify exits and egresses between rooms and corridors. The rooms resemble odd boxes that could grow three-dimensionally in another context, fronted by neoclassical columns or brightly colored tubes; but this two-dimensional page remains blank, apart from a smattering of labels and thumbnails. Through a series of ☞☞☞ the so-called MAP of the *Galerie de Difformité* indicates that it wends around corners, circuitously folding back on itself, transgressing other exhibits and digressing through sideshows and special features, including an outdoor sculpture garden (replete with a "grotto" for the "grotesque") and a sunken historic ship, dredged from the depths and displayed as "Wreckage."

To another mind, this MAP wouldn't appear minimalist but palatial, high and wide enough to shrink you down to size. I can barely imagine that cavern, glowing, resonant with echoes and with a ceiling edged by sky. Through shadows, bodies come into focus. Asymmetric and angled, scattered in all directions. The nearest stands armless and cloth-draped. Her nudity is not severe as her severed foot, torn nipples, stub nose. She wants for bandages, surrounded by other broken bodies whose pallor is pearlescent. Another body bends into focus, then another and another, until we are surrounded by an army lacking heads and hands, cocks and breasts. A torso here and there, a pile of arms and legs. Each body softens as stone, lost in graceful gazes. Behind them, a wall materializes from whiteness, hung with frames. Within those frames, more bodies appear: fractured figures, penitent postulants, beckoning fingers. A torso twists. A set of eyes follows our steps.

Again and again, I've tried to imagine what the creator of *Galerie de Difformité* envisioned. I am not she, but am offering this volume as testament to her work. Gloria Heys died before completing her enterprise, but in the last two years of her life, she shared with me a glimpse of her vision. We met under strange circumstances: she was the only child of my grandfather's mistress, from a second family that he kept secret for decades. Only as an adult did I learn of her, and sought her halfway across the country. She was a petite woman, who stayed virtually housebound after the deaths of her husband (a Vietnam veteran) and only son (with Down syndrome). Her own bout in adulthood with a rare disease had left her arm crippled. Regardless, something about her was sprite-like. What might have weighed down another person brought her lightness. Her reverence for learning rivaled only what I remembered of my grandfather, a renowned scholar of Medieval Studies. Gloria never completed college or her studies of music, but her bungalow brimmed with books. She was a conundrum: homely on the surface, seemingly serious, with a wit that made me laugh when I least expected. I remember her vividly, more than acquaintances who I've known half of my life. On that single occasion when we met in person, she pieced together part of me that I hadn't known was missing. Much of that experience—and this book—is owed to a single bone.

Gloria's bone was a relic, small enough to fit in a hand. It was shaped as a quill. What was most curious about its form was a heart-shaped hole near the sword-shaped nib. Toward the end of our visit, Gloria revealed that gift from her father, my grandfather, from one of his sabbaticals to Italy. She said that it was a xiphoid process, part of the sternum. It wasn't an original bone, her father had claimed, but rather a model fashioned by hand as a quill in the eighteenth century by a British fraternal organization (with the endearing name of Ye Ugly Face Clubb) to record their members' fantastic physiognomic features. Perhaps even more fantastic than that fact: the original bone was thought to have been extracted from the corpse of Beatrice Portinari, of Dantean fame. Like families save and bequeath engagement rings and Bibles, this bone seemed destined to be passed—literally and legendarily—onto the next of kin. And when we said our goodbyes, Gloria asked for my address and said to expect something in the mail.

I never saw the bone again, but for each month thereafter for two years, we maintained a correspondence that has been one of the richest and rarest experiences of my life. It wasn't what might be expected: not any sentimental, laugh-and-cry cascade of revelations. Instead of letters,

Gloria sent me segments of something she referred to as her *Galerie*—this *Galerie*. It was a project that she had started after her husband and son died, when she lived alone for the first time in her life. She called me her "Subscriber." I didn't know what she meant until I received the first installment. Her *Galerie* didn't arrive serially like a Victorian novel but in disordered self-contained fragments. It took a few deliveries for me to sense a pattern, even, and to deduce that Gloria wasn't exactly "the Undertaker," a role that she reserved for a reincarnation of Beatrice herself—the epitome of beauty, deconstructed, in a scheme to revive Ye Ugly Face Clubb.

I am no literary critic or art historian, rather a counselor at a community center who works with youths termed "disabled." Perhaps that's why Gloria entrusted me with her *Galerie de Difformité*. When we met, she said that she worried about everything that had become P.C.—"political crap," she called it (from her grandmotherly mouth!). Gloria herself was "crippled," a "bastard," and a host of other epithets that people had flung at her readily during her lifetime. In the time that remained for her, she said, she wished to dissect these terms and reassemble them into something more monstrous—but magnanimous, too.

In order to write this introduction, I've consulted a variety of experts to help inform my understanding of her enterprise, to give her incomplete *Galerie* some kind of dignified public viewing. Gloria's art seems a kind of folk art: naïve as it is learned. The expert that I need most is Gloria, who left no map. Since our correspondence only happened monthly, I didn't learn of her death until after some weeks passed, after her house was sold and her estate bequeathed to charity. I've never again seen that infamous bone with its heart-shaped hole.

What I did find: in her local library, her name was inscribed in a book, a copy of Clarice Lispector's *The Passion According to G.H.* The initials match Gloria's, which may explain her fondness for this text, which begins: "This is a book just like any other book. But I would be happy if it were read only by people….who know that an approach—to anything whatsoever—must…traverse even the very opposite of what is being approached….Over time, the character G.H. came to give *me*, for example, a very difficult pleasure; but it *is* called pleasure."

I believe the same might be said of Gloria Heys and her *Galerie de Difformité*.

Lineage of a Bone

Note: Heart-shaped hole.

Fig. 3. Xiphoid (meaning "shaped like a sword"; part of sternum) taken from body of Beatrice Portinari.

~

1290. Beatrice Portinari dies.

1321? Grave robbers steal bones of Beatrice Portinari from her family tomb in the Church of Santa Margherita de' Cerchi, Florence, Italy. Rumor spreads of her quill-shaped bone (with a hole resembling a heart) used to pen the last thirteen cantos of the *Paradiso*.

1583. Felix Platter illustrates bone with heart-shaped hole in *De corporis humani structura* (above: *Fig. 3*).

1615. Helkiah Crooke notes in *Mikrokosmographia; Or, A Description of the Body of Man* that the xiphoid differs between genders: "in women somtimes [sic] toward the end perforated with a broad hole much like a heart."

1677. Bone with heart-shaped hole is inventoried in the collection of Marchese Fernando Cospi, Bologna, Italy.

1743. The fraternal Ugly Face Clubb [sic] in Liverpool, Britain, adopts bone with heart-shaped hole as its secret symbol for membership. All members' faces must have features "out of the way in his phiz" and, if they marry, are required to resign and pay a fine.

1751. Bone with heart-shaped hole is catalogued in *L'Encyclopedie de Diderot et d'Alembert*.

1811. Reward is offered by the Florentine *Museo della Specola* for finding the notorious bone with heart-shaped hole. That reward spurs activity by "resurrectionists" (grave robbers who supply fresh corpses to anatomy schools), a profession that goes unpunished by law until later in the nineteenth century (e.g., Britain's Anatomy Act of 1832).

...bone of contention, bone to pick, feel in one's bones, work one's fingers to the bone,
jump his or her bones, close to the bone, skin and bone, flesh and bone,
blood and bone, make old bones, dry as a bone,
bred in the bone...

The Society for the Revival of Ye Ugly Face Clubb,[ii]
Proposes to Publish by Subscription
A MOST MAGNIFICENT AND ACCURATE, IF VERY LIMITED, EDITION
of the

GALERIE DE DIFFORMITÉ

In pages of questionable QUARTO SIZE, on the finest pretense of ROYAL ATLAS (otherwise known as Business Multipurpose) PAPER, fabricated for the Purpose by Xerox.

And Printed with T Y P E S cast in the Proprietress' House, upon a Principle calculated to unite Beauty with Deformity, not to mention Utility.

The TEXT to be regulated, and the LITERARY PART of the Undertaking conducted,

BY THE SOCIETY FOR THE REVIVAL OF YE UGLY FACE CLUBB

Each Artist's Name, with the Title and Medium of a Scene, being marked upon the Frames of the Pictures, a Catalogue seems superfluous–But as it has been suggested, that it would be agreeable to the Subscriber, to have a sampling of Scenes printed, as would tend to elucidate the Subject of the Picture in relation to Deformity–This has been accordingly done, and at the smallest possible Expense.

omnia mutantur, nihil interit: errat et illinc
huc venit, hinc illuc, et quoslibet occupant artus
spiritus eque feris humana in corpora transit
inque feras noster, nec tempore deperit ullo,
utque novis facilis signature cera figuris
nec manet ut fuerat nec formam servant eandem,
sed tamen ipsa eadem est, animam sic simper eandem
esse, sed in varias doceo migrare figuras.
~ Ovid, *Metamorphoses*[iii]

N.B. As the Number of SUBSCRIBERS to the GALERIE DE DIFFORMITÉ must be limited, it is recommended to those, who have any design of becoming Subscribers, to be as early as possible in their Application.

CAUTION!!!!

Do not read straight through this catalogue from start to finish! This gallery encourages—even mandates—that you choose your own path. Exhibits within the *Galerie de Difformité* conceal many discoveries and pitfalls, which can be missed if you read this catalogue like a regular book, or if you believe that life is lived linearly. Likewise, as you explore rooms and reflect upon artworks, you will be asked to make choices. Your decisions may lead you closer or farther into the Unknown! Follow the instructions, but also bravely break the rules! One misstep may curtail your visit...but a well-chosen path may lead to unexpected

A. pleasure!
B. palpitation!
C. puzzlement!
D. penetration!
E. predestination!
F. prevarication!
G. peregrination!
H. __________! (*fill in blank*)

The Destruction Room

A room full of interesting Books, or at least when cut up will be so, as far as regards the places they refer to, and quietly waiting an opportunity to be changed from generals to particulars.[1]

During
dressmaking
time good shears

[1] **YOU ARE HERE**: The only footnote in this entire *Galerie de Difformité*. Not a handnote nor buttnote, but the sole and heel (a.k.a., soul and heal, even if weak as Achilles') of this exhibitional enterprise. Being the only footnote, a responsibility is borne by what it foots—THE DESTRUCTION ROOM—that revives an extra-illustrative entity invented by Frederick Strong when he advertised himself as "neither a book or printseller" but one who sold printed ephemera "ALL DATED, CUT UP" and "ARRANGED" according to his own classification system. "In short," Lucy Peltz writes in "Facing the Text," "Strong had gone in to book-breaking." (See *Owners, Annotators and the Signs of Reading*, eds. Robin Myers, Michael Harris, and Giles Mandelbrote, 91). But Strong is dead, and I am not: guiding you now by reviving a Gentlewoman named *Bea*, for lack of a better *nom-de-plume*. Minding P's & Q's, you've found me middling while mending: "During / dressmaking / time good shears..." Facing the text, I wouldn't call myself a breaker so much as seamstress, enlisting your help to tailor this book around a budding body: the once-and-future corpse of this corpus. To survive, I need your help to evolve. To deform and reform, to dream and metamorphose (or otherwise risk misreading: me and Bea.) Open Sesame: "During / dressmaking / time good shears..." ✂
✂✂✂✂✂✂✂✂✂✂✂✂✂✂✂✂✂✂✂✂✂✂✂✂✂✂✂✂✂✂✂

✂✂✂✂✂✂✂✂✂✂✂✂✂✂✂✂✂✂✂✂✂✂✂✂✂✂✂✂✂✂✂✂✂✂✂

✂ Snip, snip...or start by sketching manicles (☞) in margins...or merely manifest a set of hypothetical instructions: "how to" build, operate, repair, maintain, recycle materials (paper, stitching, board, letters, &c). "How To" Deform This Book: 1. Make hundreds of paper dolls. 2. Make dozens of paper dresses for dozens of paper dolls. 3. Forget the dolls, and stitch all pages into one life-size dress. 4. Forget the dress, and fly origami cranes. 5. Or fold a flock of variably-shaped planes (enlisting a high school physics class). 6. Wallpaper. 7. Papier-mâché sculpture. 8. Installation art with mounds of crumpled paper. 9. Performance art, shearing and shredding and reconstructing. 10. Or otherwise demonstrate, in performative fashion, any of the above or next instructions. 11. Shred pages to fill a dream-pillow. 12. Cut confetti to celebrate whatever occasion. 13. Make ghostprints or something palimpsestual. 14. Use each page as a canvas, painting over text and leaving words exposed, yielding a new narrative. 15. Cut into pieces for scrapbooking, bricolage, collage, &c. 16. Scatter scraps near nest-building birds. 17. No bookburning (although Exhibit J may suggest otherwise). 18. Shuffle extant pages and add new exhibits, whatever your heart desires! When you've deformed the *Galerie de Difformité*, please contact me (difformite@gmail.com) to document your process, with the expectation of my curating an Exhibit from this collective enterprise. Images preferred. ☞☞☞

Exhibit F

A list of those Exhibits that might, could, would, or should have been visited in the *Galerie de Difformité*, arranged alphabetically:—

A is for......, as if to explain,
B is for......, that swarms through the brain:
C is for........, bleeding through pages,
D is for......, sleeping with sages.
E is for....., who bundles all verse,
F is for......, this summary terse!
G is for.........., that grows out of bounds,
H is for........., that affords us these rounds.
I am the Author, a rhymer erratic—
And **J** is for........, who dares the pathetic:
K is for..........., who finally sees,
L is for.........., that invisible Bea.
M is for......, retracing all courses,
And **N** is......, compressing all sources.
...........is for **O**, hiding under the sea,
And **P** is for......., trying to move free:
Q is the..........., that wants for collection
While **R** is for......., that revives with dissection.
S is for......, sworn foe of strict rules,

T is for......, needing fine rhythmic tools.

U's........., whose action is missing

While **V** is the........, ceaselessly listing.

W's........., by Museum made frantic,

X the xiphoid, grown quite pedantic.

Y offers *you*, whom nobody thought about—

Z is the Zoo that this gallery grows about.[iv]

WORKS CITED, CAJOLED, CORROBORATED, CORRUPTED, CONGRATULATED, *RUM TI, &C.*[v]

(or, Notes from a ſub-ſub-librarian;
or, Handnotes & Buttnotes)

LIST OF ILLUSTRATIONS

☞ **LINEAGE** OF A BONE: "Female chest bone with a heart-shaped hole" in Felix Platter, *De corporis humani structura, Book 3, Table VIII, Figure VIII* (1583).

☞ THE DESTRUCTION ROOM: Wiss Shears Advertisement, "Good Housekeeping" (Springfield, MA: Phelps Publishing Co., 1908).

UNDERTAKER'S NOTE ON THE TEXT

[i] "Undertaker's Note on the Text" is heavily indebted to the "Preface," "Advertisement," "&c." surrounding Alderman Boydell's Shakespeare Gallery, a popular attraction in late-18th century London. Headed by John Boydell and later his nephew, Josiah, this venture set out to publish a new edition of Shakespeare's plays, commissioning famed British artists of the day and using the most modern print technology to make engravings of their illustrations. Funded by Boydell and subscribers of the proposed volumes, the Shakespeare Gallery became reality in 1789 and resided in its own building for over a decade. Artists were able to explore genres beyond portraiture of wealthy patrons, moving into themes related to other writers, the Classics, and English history. The Gallery also influenced contemporary ventures like Thomas Macklin's *Poets' Gallery* and Henri Fuseli's *Milton Gallery*. Boydell's Shakespeare Gallery culminated in the publication of a nine-volume folio edition of Shakespeare's illustrated plays, followed by a two-volume elephant folio of engravings based on paintings in the Gallery. Although the artwork was originally intended as a gift to England, debts and events of the time left the fate of Boydell's collection to lottery and auction, whereby individual paintings were dispersed among private **hands**. (See John Boydell, *A Catalogue of the pictures, &c., in the Shakspeare Gallery, Pall-Mall.* London: H. Baldwin, 1790.)

FRONTISPIECE

[ii] A "Verbatim Reprint" of *Ye Ugly Face Clubb, Leverpoole, 1743-1753* was edited and published by Edward Howell in Liverpool in 1912. The club rules mandated particular types of physical features for membership, including (but not limited to) "blubber lips, little goggling or squinting eyes," "a large carbuncle, potatoe nose," and a chin that met the nose "like a pair of nut-crackers" (12). Members of the club were catalogued to dignify one's "Short Turnip Nose," another's "Teeth, resemblg an old broken Saw," and another's "Large Pancake Face" and "Odd, Droll, Sancho Pancho Phiz" (14). Although the origins of Liverpool's Ugly Club (and like-minded ones stretching across the Atlantic) lay shrouded in mystery, a "History of Secret Clubs" from 1807 (reprinted in Howell's edition) recounts a tale of origin: "A Certain Uſerer, Named 'Hatchet,' from whoſe ſingular Aſpect is derived that common Saying...That he is a Hatchet-Fac'd Fellow, being a Man who always lug'd about with him at leaſt two pounds of Noſe....No-body could paſs by ſuch a Mountain of a Noſe, without thinking, or ſaying ſomething extraordinary upon ſo flaming a Subject. Thus

finding himſelf a Jeſt among moſt People, who were not diſtinguiſhable by ſome **Diſproportion** or other as remarkable as his own, it occaſion'd him to be inclinable to ſuch ſort of Company, whoſe ill compos'd Countenances, in caſe they jeſted with his Noſe, might give him an equal opportunity of returning their Jokes, that he might make himſelf as merry with his Companions' Infirmities, as they could be in bantering the mighty Buckler of his hard-favour'd Frontiſpiece" (72-3). The "Verbatim Reprint" of *Ye Ugly Face* lists members' names headed by "Witness our Hands," likely bearing in the original manuscript actual signatures (29). The appalled (as in, *a pall*) Undertaker of this *Galerie* might favor this etymological equation between *names* and *hands* (which relates to *handle*) while jeſting about a criterion for membership (bachelorhood) by inquiring: "What of a Deform'd Lass?" For more about Ugly Face Club membership, see Exhibit W.

[iii] On the Frontispiece, the quotation from Ovid's *Metamorphoses* translates: "All things are always changing, / But nothing dies. The spirit comes and goes, / Is housed wherever it will, shifts residence / From beasts to men, from men to beasts, but always It keeps on living. As the pliant [bees]wax / Is stamped with new designs, and is no longer / What once it was, but changes form, and still / Is pliant wax, so do I teach that spirit / Is evermore the same, though passing always / To **ever-changing bodies**." (Book XV: 165-8, qtd. in Marina Warner, *Fantastic Metamorphoses, Other Worlds: Ways of Telling the Self* (Oxford: Oxford UP, 2002) 1-2.)

EXHIBIT F

[iv] Charles Dodgson (a.k.a., Lewis Carroll), "Examination Statute" in *Scrapbook,* Library of Congress, 1864. (lchtml lc001). All lines have been changed, except I and W.

[v] To loop beginnings and endings: these final words echo the printed advertisement for the Ugly Clubb adapted to preface this *Galerie*. "Rum ti, &c." acts as a refrain, as demonstrated here at the end of the first verse:

FRIENDS and brothers, unto me attend,
    While I sing of our Club here to-night, Sirs,
Where the Ugly alone do intend
    To drink deep at the fount of delight, Sirs,
For however **deform'd we may be**,
    Good humour will make us look smugly,
While ev'ry true lover of glee
    Will drink to the Club call'd the Ugly.
                        Rum ti, &c.

DAVIS SCHNEIDERMAN

crowdsourcing: an afterword

The &NOW organization, now in its fourth (roughly) biennial incarnation as a conference, has been if not unified than at least loosely defined by a perhaps indefinable aesthetic, which like the Baylonian god Marduk seems to have at least fifty names. Steve Tomasula has laid out this history in his foreword, but what remains, in this final section of the book, is to briefly discuss selection criteria for this anthology.

By its third incarnation at Chapman University in 2008, &NOW had evolved a certain esprit-de-corps; we devloped a simple nomination process by which &NOW attendees (and non-attendees for that matter) might tell us which writers and works for the period 2004-2009 might best be deserving of this volume's attention. This system was deliberately set in opposition to two other models 1) a purely applicant-driven submission process (hey, publish me), and 2) a Pushcart Prize model where small magazines nominate their "best" works for inclusion in that now-somewhat-rarefied literary locus acquiring dust in well-organized library shelves.

Now, this nomination system did not completely preclude authors from self-nominating, or nominating close friends for non-literary reasons, but it produced its desired affect. We all travel in certain circles, and even at our widest radii, we remain unaware of the innovations of our neighbors. When your monkey hops on his typewriter because you have trained him so well, and finally produces Borges' "The Library of Babel," you become so distracted as to miss the cabal of monkeys several keypads over who has connected 20 typewriters by a mechanism of electrified banana-mush-glue into a terrible monstrosity capable of producing the most delightfully untoward collaborative texts.

In the case of this volume, possible winners of *The &NOW AWARDS* passed through the editorial mechanisms of numerous hands (see Acknowledgements, at the bookfront), and were also suggested by numerous writers and readers. With these, our group attempted to select a series of excitements-happenings-explosions to suggest the most interesting work of the years 2004 (when &NOW started, humbly, at the University of Notre Dame), and 2009, the pre-sent moment. The majority of work here is reprinted from that period, but there are indeed a smaller number of selections that until now have remained unpublished.

Future volumes will appear on a biennial basis, and cover the period of the preceding two years. Thus, volume 2, scheduled for 2011, will cover the years 2009-2011. We welcome comments on the nomination system, and we will no doubt continue to revise its mechanism. Look for updates at lakeforest.edu/andnow and send congratulations, comments, and money to andnow@lakeforest.edu.

Finally, we answer this question: Hey, if &NOW is so foward-thinking, super-hip, in-tune with all that is tomorrow, why are you publishing a regular, run-of-the-paper-mill book? For this, we can only answer that we still like books and hope that in their final years we can hasten their destruction with style and grace. Consider that new media (and think Gutenberg, here) often emulates (at first) the media that came before. In that sense, the work of this volume (and a considerable amount of it was first was available online) suggests a compendium of its own future—we are not only collecting, but also articulating and expressing the most interesting mutations of our own progeny.

PREVIOUS PUBLICATION CREDITS

"1304 North Central Avenue," "Prairie Style" and "A Cornet at Night" by C.S. Giscombe. All three appeared originally, as a group titled "from Prairie Style," in the journal *Mipoesias* (2007). http://www.mipoesias.com/EVIESHOCKLEYISSUE/giscombe_c.html. Included later in the book by C. S. Giscombe, *Prairie Style* (Dalkey Archive, 2008). These works appear by permission of Dalkey Archive Press.

"A Poetics of Reflection and Desire" by Doug Rice, originally appeared as "Untitled Photo Essay," *South Loop Review* (2008): 53-57. Copyright © 2008 Doug Rice.

From *A*hole*, by Hilton Obenzinger, from *A*Hole* (Soft Skull 2004). Copyright © 2004 Hilton Obenzinger.

From *Age of the Demon Tools* by Mark Spitzer from *Age of the Demon Tools* (Ahadada Books, 2008). Copyright © 2008 Mark Spitzer.

"AlphabeTics" by Angela Szczepaniak from *Unisex Love Poems* (DC Books, 2008). Copyright © 2008 Angela Szczepaniak.

"American Fried Questions" (a derived text sourced from Calvin Trillin's *American Fried: Adventures of a Happy Eater*) by William Walsh from *Questionstruck* (Keyhole Press, 2009). Copyright © 2009 William Walsh.

"Apparition Poems" by Adam Fieled, from *Jacket* (31): 2006. http://jacketmagazine.com/31/fieled.html. Copyright © 2006 Adam Fieled.

"Before, or Napkin Fiction" by Charles Blackstone originally appeared as "Before," on a different napkin at *Esquire.com*. 13 Mar. 2008. http://www.esquire.com/fiction/napkin-project/charles-blackstone-napkin-fiction. Copyright © 2008 Charles Blackstone.

"Benediction" by Giancarlo DiTrapano from *Opium5: Bad Company*, Fall 2007. Copyright © 2007 Giancarlo DiTrapano.

"Black Wings" by Amina Cain from *I Go To Some Hollow* (Les Figues, 2009); also published in *Wreckage of Reason: An Anthology of Contemporary Xxperimental Prose by Women Writers* (Spuyten Duyvil, 2008). Copyright © 2008 Amina Cain.

From *Blue Fire* by Wendy Walker appeared originally in *The Green Integer Review* #8 (March-May 2007). Copyright © 2007 Wendy Walker.

"Comments" and "Interview with Someone" by *The New Anonymous*. "Interview" originally published in *The New Anonymous*, vol 1.

"Continuity as an Axiomatic Resultant of a Clearly Defined Fragmentation of Lines" by Andrea Kneeland from *Mad Hatters' Review*, (8): 2007. Copyright © 2007 Andrea Kneeland.

"Crows Don't Care" by Natalija Grgorinić & Ognjen Rađen. "Crows Don't Care" originally published in different form in, and excerpted from, *Mr. and Mrs. Hide* (Spineless Books, 2009). Copyright © 2007 Natalija Grgorinić & Ognjen Rađen.

"Curbing" and "The Palms of Space" by Joel Felix. "Curbing" originally appeared in *Track and Field* #3 (2009). "The Palms of Space," originally appeared, in slightly different form, in *Chicago Review* 51:3 (46-47). Copyright © Joel Felix.

From "deact" by Kerri Sonnenberg from *The Mudra* (Litmus Press, 2004), originally published as "Three Untitled Poems," *Moria Poetry Journal* (7.1): 2004. http://www.moriapoetry.com/v7i1.html. Copyright © Kerri Sonnenberg.

"Dives & Lazarus" by William Fuller from LVNG 11; also published in *Watchword* (Flood Editions, 2006). Copyright © William Fuller. Reprinted with permission of Flood Editions.

"E=MC3" by Jay Wexler from *Opium3: A Junkyard of Arresting Delight*, Fall 2006. Copyright © 2006 Jay Wexler,

From "Eye Hole Adore" by Teresa Carmody from *Eye Hole Adore* (PS Books, 2008). Copyright © 2008 Teresa Carmody.

"Facts" by Matt Kirkpatrick, Facts," from *No Colony* (Winter 2009). Copyright © 2009 Matt Kirkpatrick.

From "FatBoy/DeathStar/rico-chet" by Judith Goldman. The introductory critical statement adapts a passage from *Letters to Poets: Conversations about Poetics, Politics, and Community*, eds. Jennifer Firestone and Dana Teen Lomax (Philadelphia: Saturnalia Books 2008). "FatBoy/DeathStar/rico-chet" was published in *DeathStar/rico-chet* (O Books 2006). Copyright © Judith Goldman.

"Father" by Jeffrey DeShell, from *The Trouble With Being Born* (FC2, 2008). Copyright © Jeffrey DeShell. Used with permission.

"Fifteen Minute Performative Masculinity New York School Name Dropping Poem For David Shapiro As Transcribed From His Interview At Pennsound" by Gabriel Gudding from *Make* 6 (2008). Copyright © 2008 Gabriel Gudding.

"Flat with no Key" by Keith & Rosmarie Waldrop from *Flat with no Key* (Beard of Bees, 2007). Copyright © 2007 Keith & Rosemarie Waldrop.

"Food" by Stephen-Paul Martin. A longer version of "Food" appears in *Harp & Altar*, summer 2009. Copyright © 2009 Stephen-Paul Martin.

From *Frances Johnson: a novel* by Stacey Levine (Clear Cut Press, 2005). Copyright © 2005 Stacey Levine.

"How I Ate My Wife" from *Brains: a Zomoir* by Robin Becker (HarperCollins, 2010) and *The Exquisite Corpse Annual* 1 (2009). Copyright © 2009 Robin Becker.

From *Hunting is Painting* by Jessica Savitz, from *Mrs. Maybe* (2007). Copyright © 2007 Jessica Savitz.

"Huracan's Harp," #s 142, 136, 35 by Stephanie Strickland; *Huracan's Harp* 142, *Fence* 20 (Winter 2008-2009); *Huracan's Harp* 136, *P-Queue* 6 (2009); *Huracan's Harp* 35, *P-Queue* 6 (2009). Copyright
Stephanie Strickland; *Huracan's Harp* 87, from *Women's Studies Quarterly* 37.1-2 (2009). Copyright © 2009 by the Feminist Press at the City University of New York. Used by permission of the authors and publishers, www.feministpress.org. All rights rerserved.

"In the Beginning is" by Carol Novack was partially published in audio and text as part of a collaborative video (called a vispo) in *Drunken Boat* (10). Copyright © Carol Novack.

"In the Restaurant" by Bradley Sands from *Decomp: a literary magazine* (2008). Copyright © 2008 Bradley Sands.

"Insomnia Door" by Blake Butler, from *Diagram* 7.4 (2007) http://www.thediagram.com/7_4/butler.html. Copyright © 2007 Blake Butler.

"Irma la Douce / Marguerite Monnot" and "Maquis / Malice" by Catherine Daly from *Chanteuse / Cantatrice* (Heretical Texts Series, Factory School Books, 2007). Reproduction or re-use of this work for non-commercial or collective use is permitted and encouraged. Reproduction for sale, rent, or other use involving financial transaction is prohibited except by permission of author and publisher. Copyright © 2007 Catherine Daly.

"Kate Moss Queries Her Counselor on the Nature of Love" by Bradford Gray Telford, from *BOMB* 103 (2008). Copyright © 2008 Bradford Gray Telford.

"Kleptokinetisis" by Matina Stamatakis, e-book excerpt from *[+!]* (Calliope Nerve Media, 2009). http://www.lulu.com/content/e-book/[%2b]/7504914. Copyright © 2009 Matina Stamatakis.

From *La Medusa* by Vanessa Place from *La Medusa* (FC2 2008). Copyright © 2008 Vanessa Place. Used with permission.

From "Laundry Lists and Manifestoes" by John Matthias, from *Kedging* (Salt Publishing, 2008). Copyright © 2008 John Matthias.

"Left-Handed Universe: Variations" by Lisa Gluskin Stonestreet, from *Tulips, Water, Ash* (University Press of New England, 2009). First appeared in *failbetter.com*, Issue #30 (April 2009). http://www.failbetter.com/30/GluskinLeftHand.php. Copyright © 2009 Lisa Gluskin Stonestreet.

"Manifesto Dysfic" by Steve Katz from *KISSSSSS: a miscellany* (FC2, 2008). Copyright © 2008 Steve Katz. Used with permission.

"Metro" by Asha Khaladkar from *Opium4: Live Well Now (No Matter What)*, Spring 2007. Copyright © 2007 Asha Khaladkar.

"Now the Room Is Empty" by Kim Chinquee from *Keyhole #5*, the handwritten issue. Copyright © Kim Chinquee.

From "Nimbus" by Michael Joyce and Alexandra Grant, originally appeared as "Five Iterations", a multimedia piece, published in *XTRA Magazine* 10.1 (2007). http://www.x-traonline.org/ArtistProjects/10_1ArtistsProject/iteration1.html. Copyright © 2007 Alexandra Grant and Michael Joyce.

"{O. Eu. H.}" "{O.Eu.H}" by Peter O'Leary previously appeared at *The Cultural Society*, www.culturalsociety.org. Copyright © Peter O'Leary.

From "Orange Girl Suite" by Simone Muench, from *Orange Crush* (Sarabande, 2010). First published in *Wicked Alice*. Copyright © Simone Muench.

"Planting" by Jenny Hanning from *Keyhole # 5* (handwritten issue). Copyright © Jenny Hanning.

"Possible Side Effects" by Matthew Roberson from *Impotent* (FC2, 2009) and *Clackamas Literary Review X* (2006). Copyright © 2006 Maththew Roberson.

"Prince" by Lou Rowan, first published in *Sweet Potatoes* (Ahadada Books, 2008). Copyright © 2008 Lou Rowan.

"Probation" by Averill Curdy from *Poetry Foundation* 186.1 (2005). Copyright © 2005 Averill Curdy.

"Quarantine in the Borders" by Mary Gilliland, originally appeared in *Notre Dame Review* 25 (2008). Copyright © 2008 Mary Gilliland.

From *Return to Manure* by Raymond Federman from *Return to Manure* (FC2, 2006). Copyright © 2006 Raymond Federman. Used with permission.

"Screaming" by Yuriy Tarnawsky, from *Like Blood in Water* (FC2, 2007). Copyright © 2007 Yuriy Tarnawsky. Used with permission.

From "Signs of Intrauterine Life" by Dimitri Anastasopoulos, originally published in different form in *Notre Dame Review* 22 (2006). Copyright © 2006 Dimitri Anastasopoulos.

"Slaves of Bataille" by Gina Frangello from *Black Ice Online*. 2004. http://www.altx.com/profiles/archives/bipolarity/frangello_batailles.html. Copyright © 2004 Gina Frangello.

(2006). Copyright © 2006 Dimitri Anastasopoulos.

"Slaves of Bataille" by Gina Frangello from *Black Ice Online*. 2004. http://www.altx.com/profiles/archives/bipolarity/frangello_batailles.html. Copyright © 2004 Gina Frangello.

"Slug" by Megan Milks from *Fist of the Spider Woman: Tales of Fear and Queer Desire* (Arsenal Pulp Press, 2009). Copyright © 2009 Megan Milks.

"Taming Milady" by Joeseph L. Bisz, originally appeared as "*Wild Milady*." Diagram 4.2 (2004). Copyright © 2004 Joseph L. Bisz.

"Tango" by Joe Amato from *Under Virga* (Chax Press, 2006). Copyright © 2006 Joe Amato.

"Tetatetagrammatron" by John Moore Williams, e-book excerpt from *[+!]* (Calliope Nerve Media, 2009). http://www.lulu.com/content/e-book/[%2b]/7504914. Copyright © 2009 John Moore Williams.

"The Carpet Out of Time" by Michael DuPlessis, from *The Memoirs of JonBenet by Kathy Acker* (Second Story Books, forthcoming). Copyright © Michael DuPlessis.

"Tocayo" by Joe Francis Doerr was first published in *Notre Dame Review* 28 (2009). Copyright © 2009 Joe Francis Doerr.

"The Frostworks" by Stephen Collis from *The Commons* (Talonbooks 2008). Copyright © 2008 Stephen Collis.

"The Future is Here" by Paul D. Miller from *Rhythm Science* (MIT Press, 2004). Copyright © 2004 Paul D. Miller.

"The Interstitial Library Workbook (Teacher's Edition)" by Shelley Jackson from *Marc Joseph: New and Used* (Steidl, 2006). Copyright © 2006 Shelley Jackson.

"The Kind of Girl You Read About in New Wave Magazines" by Paul A. Toth from *The Second Hand* (2005). Copyright © 2005 Paul A. Toth.

"*the opposite of slackness* / Orgasms" by Carla Harryman from *Adorno's Noise* (Essay Press, 2008). The work also appeared on-line in *Interval(le)s* 11.2-111.3 (2008/2009). www.cipa.ulg.ac.be/intervalles4. Copyright © Carla Harryman.

"Products from *The Jiri Chronicles and Other Fictions*" by Debra Di Blasi from (FC2/University of Alabama Press, 2007). Copyright © 2007 Debra Di Blasi. Used with permission. From "The Incomplete but Real History of the Jiri Chronicles" from "Marc Lowe Interviews Debra Di Blasi," *Mad Hatters' Review* (2006) http://madhattersreview.com/issue6/images/dd2_FULL.jpg. Copyright © Debra Di Blasi.

"The Photographer" by Lidia Yuknavtich from *The Small Backs of Children* (forthcoming) and *Western Humanities Review* (Winter 2008). Copyright © 2008 Lidia Yuknavtich.

"The Public Sentence" by Christopher Grimes, from *Public Works* (FC2, 2005). Copyright © 2005 Christopher Grimes. Used with permission.

"The Story that Teaches You How to Write It" by William Gillespie first published by Spineless Books in 2005. http://spinelessbooks.com/donquixote/. Copyright © 2005 William Gillespie.

"The USNS Comfort Sails to the Gulf" by Rachel Loden, from *Dick of the Dead* by Rachel Loden (Ahsahta Press, 2009). Copyright © 2009 Rachel Loden.

"The Xenotext Experiment" by Christian Bök, from *Poetic Journal: American Poet* 35 (2008). Copyright © 2008 Christian Bök.

From "+|*'me'S-pace*" by Christine Werthheim from +|*'me'S-pace* (doc 001.b) (TrenchArt: The Casements Series, Les Figues, 2007). Copyright © 2007 Christine Wertheim.

"Trickle-Down Timeline" by Cris Mazza. "Trickle-Down Timeline" was originally published in *Bridge Magazine* 14 (2005), and subsequently was the title story in *Trickle-Down Timeline* (Red Hen Press, 2009). Copyright © 2005 Cris Mazza.

"Where I'm From" by Kass Fleisher from *Accidental Species: A Reproduction* (Chax Press, 2005). Copyright © 2005 Kass Fleisher.

"Where Nööne is Now" by Christina Milletti from *The Cincinnati Review* (2005) and *The Religious & Other Fictions* (Carnegie Mellon University Press, 2006). Copyright © 2005 Christina Milletti.

"White Terror" by Harold Jaffe, previously published in *Terror-dot-Gov* (Raw Dog Screaming Press, 2005). Copyright © 2005 Harold Jaffe.

"Women & Desire—V" by Lily Hoang, from *Lamination Colony,* available at http://www.laminationcolony.com/THEWOMANDOWNTHEHALL/. Copyright © Lily Hoang.

"Woodchuck and Hank Williams Zombie" by Ted Pelton from *Brooklyn Rail* (October 2007) http://brooklynrail.org/2007/10/fiction/woodchuck-and-hank-williams-zombie. Copyright © 2007 Ted Pelton.

"You are Here" by Aaron Burch from *Keyhole #5*, handwritten issue. Copyright © Aaron Burch.

From *[+!]* by Kane X. Faucher Book, e-book excerpt from *[+!]* (Calliope Nerve Media, 2009). http://www.lulu.com/content/e-book/[%2b]/7504914. Copyright © 2009 Kane X. Faucher (although he jokingly told us to copryright Yogi Bear and the inventor of 2000 Flushes).

CONTRIBUTOR NOTES

Joe Amato is the author of eight books, most recently *Pain Plus Thyme* (Factory School, 2008), *Industrial Poetics: Demo Tracks for a Mobile Culture* (University of Iowa Press, 2006), *Finger Exorcised* (BlazeVOX [books], 2006), and *Under Virga* (Chax Press, 2006). His memoir, *Once an Engineer: A Song of the Salt City*, will be released by SUNY Press in the fall of 2009.

Dimitri Anastasopoulos teaches fiction and contemporary literature at the University at Buffalo-SUNY. His fiction and essays have appeared in, or been published by, Mammoth Books, journals such as *Third Bed, Black Warrior Review, Willow Springs, Callalloo* and others. He's currently at work on his novel *Farm for Mutes.*

Robin Becker likes Nietzsche, zombies and Hello Kitty. She lives in Toad Suck, Arkansas, where she fries fish and teaches writing at the University of Central Arkansas. Her novel, *Brains: A Zomoir*, will be published in summer of 2010 by HarperCollins.

Joseph L. Bisz is an English professor at BMCC who received a Ph.D. in Creative Writing and English Literature from Binghamton University. He has sailed his ship into a few different times and areas of the world, including American Realism, gender & sexuality studies, and Popular Culture (Games and Science-fiction). During his journeys he took his hat off to a number of influential writers including Henry James, Thomas Hardy, and Milan Kundera. He has edited the rather languagey literary journal *Potion*, and his own poems and novel chapters have had happy landings in various journals and anthologies including *Diagram, Romantics Quarterly*, and *Coloring Book: An Eclectic Anthology of Fiction and Poetry by Multicultural Writers.* Among his epic pursuits is an unfathomable obsession with all things Victorian.

Charles Blackstone is the author of *The Week You Weren't Here*, a novel, and co-editor of *The Art of Friction: Where (Non) Fictions Come Together*, an anthology. He lives in Chicago.

Christian Bök is the author not only of *Crystallography* (Coach House Press, 1994), a pataphysical encyclopedia nominated for the Gerald Lampert Memorial Award, but also of *Eunoia* (Coach House Books, 2001), a bestselling work of experimental literature, which has gone on to win the Griffin Prize for Poetic Excellence. Bök has created artificial languages for two television shows: Gene Roddenberry's *Earth: Final Conflict* and Peter Benchley's *Amazon.* Bök has also earned many accolades for his virtuoso performances of sound poetry (particularly the *Ursonate* by Kurt Schwitters). His conceptual artworks (which include books built out of Rubik's cubes and Lego bricks) have appeared at the Marianne Boesky Gallery in New York City as part of the exhibit *Poetry Plastique.* Bök is currently a Professor of English at the University of Calgary.

Jessica Berger was born and raised in Chicagoland, where she is now a graduate student in UIC's Program for Writers. She has worked as an illustrator and is especially interested in the coupling of text with her other great love: the visual arts. She can be found online at inloveandsqualor.com, and at her pop culture blog: popcandyarcade.blogspot.com.

Aaron Burch is the editor of *Hobart: Another Literary Journal* and the author of the chapbook, *How to Predict the Weather* (Keyhole Books). Other short fiction has appeared in *New York Tyrant, Another Chicago Magazine, Barrelhouse*, and *Quick Fiction*, among others.

Blake Butler is the author of *EVER* (Calamari Press) and *Scorch Atlas* (Featherproof Books). He is the editor of *HTML Giant.* He lives in Atlanta and blogs at gillesdeleuzecommittedsuicideandsowilldrphil.com.

Amina Cain is the author of *I Go To Some Hollow* (Les Figues Press, 2009), a collection of stories that revolve quietly around human relationality, landscape, and emptiness. She is also a curator (most recently for *When Does It or You Begin? Memory as Innovation*, a month-long festival of writing, performance, and video), and a teacher of writing/literature. Her work has appeared or is forthcoming in publications such as *3rd Bed, Action Yes, Denver Quarterly, The Encyclopedia Project, La Petite Zine*, and *Wreckage of Reason: An Anthology of Contemporary Xxperimental Prose by Women Writers*, and was recently translated into Polish on *MINIMAL-BOOKS*. She lives in Los Angeles.

Teresa Carmody is the author of *Requiem* (Les Figues Press, 2005), and two chapbooks: *Eye Hole Adore* (PS Books, 2008) and *Your Spiritual Suit of Armor by Katherine Anne* (Woodland Editions, 2009). She lives in Los Angeles and is co-director of Les Figues Press.

Kim Chinquee is the author of *Oh Baby* (Ravenna Press) and *Pretty* (White Pine Press). She is the recipient of a Pushcart Prize and lives in Buffalo, NY.

Stephen Collis is the author of three books of poetry, *Mine* (New Star, 2001), *Anarchive* (New Star, 2005), which was nominated for the Dorothy Livesay Poetry Prize, and *The Commons* (Talonbooks, 2008)—the latter two of which form parts of the on-going "Barricades Project." He is also the author of two book-length studies, *Phyllis Webb* and the *Common Good* (Talonbooks, 2007) and *Through Words of Others: Susan Howe and Anarcho-Scholasticism* (ELS Editions, 2006). His new book, *On the Material* is forthcoming from Talonbooks in 2010. A member of the Kootenay School of Writing, he teaches American literature, poetry, and poetics at Simon Fraser University.

Averill Curdy is the recipient of fellowships from the Rona Jaffe Foundation, the National Endowment for the Arts, and the Illinois State Arts Council. Her poems have appeared in various journals in the U.S. and England. She lives in Chicago where she is Artist in Residence at Northwestern University.

Author of eight books, most recently Vauxhall (Shearsman, 2008), **Catherine Daly** lives in Los Angeles. These excerpts are from *Chanteuse / Cantatrice*, part of the Heretical Texts Series edited by Bill Marsh for Factory School. It is a book that has a small relationship to Illinois, and &NOW, because editor and author became acquainted at &NOW 2006, and are from Ottawa, IL, and Decatur, IL, respectively.

Jeffrey DeShell has published four novels: *The Trouble with Being Born* (FC2), *Peter: An (A)Historical Romance* (Starcherone), *S & M* (FC2) and *In Heaven Everything is Fine* (FC2), and a critical book, *The Peculiarity of Literature: An Allegorical Approach to Poe's Fiction*. He has co-edited two collections of fiction by American women, *Chick-Lit I: Postfeminist Fiction* and *Chick-Lit II: No Chick Vics* (FC2). DeShell was a Fulbright Teaching Fellow in Budapest, and has taught in Northern Cyprus, the American Midwest and Bard College. Currently he is an associate professor at the University of Colorado at Boulder.

Debra Di Blasi's books include *The Jirí Chronicles & Other Fictions, Prayers of an Accidental Nature, Drought & Say What You Like, Ugly Town: the movie*, and *What the Body Requires*. Awards include a James C. Mc-Cormick Fellowship in Fiction from the Christopher Isherwood Foundation, Thorpe Menn Book Award, and Diagram Innovative Fiction Award. The short film based on *Drought* won a host of national and international awards, and was one of only six U.S. films invited to the Universe Elle section of the 2000 Cannes Film Festival. Debra's innovative fiction has been anthologized and adapted to film, radio, theatre, and audio CD in the U.S. and abroad, and her essays, art reviews and articles published in a variety of international, national and regional publications. She is publisher-in-chief at Jaded Ibis Press, and president of Jaded Ibis Productions that produces fictive audio interviews, music, videos, print, web and visual art, ironic consumer products, and the innovative literature & arts channel, BLEED. Creator of the Diem® WordPlay device, she lectures on its use in education, and on innovative literature, in general.

Giancarlo DiTrapano is the editor of the *New York Tyrant.*

Joe Francis Doerr lives with his wife Mary in Austin, Texas where he teaches at St. Edward's University. He is the author of *Order of the Ordinary* (Salt, 2003) and is currently editing the *Salt Companion to John Matthias.*

Michael du Plessis teaches in the Departments of Comparative Literature and English at the University of Southern California.

Kane X. Faucher is an Assistant Professor for the Faculty of Information and Media Studies at the University of Western Ontario. He has published 9 books and over 600 poems, critical essays, reviews, and short fiction. He maintains an eclectic literary and academic practice in London, Ontario. He is concurrently developing books on metastasis and rhizomes, and novels about radio, impossible libraries, and the casualization of academic labour.

Born in France in 1928, **Raymond Federman** emigrated to the US in 1947, following the deaths of his mother, father, and two sisters at Auschwitz. His early experiences in the US included time as an American paratrooper in Korea, a saxophone player in Detroit, a dishwasher, and student. Federman taught literature, creative writing, and French at SUNY at Buffalo from 1964-1998, before retiring as the Melodia E. Jones Chair of French. He is the author of over twenty books of fiction, poetry, and criticism, translated into German, Italian, French, Hungarian, Polish, Serbian, Rumanian, Hebrew, Dutch, Greek, Japanese, and Chinese. Federman is also the recipient of Guggenheim, Fulbright, National Endowment for the Arts, and New York State Foundation for the Arts fellowships, as well as numerous foreign awards. His most-recent novel *CHUT* will be published in the fall of 2009 by Starcherone Press.

Joel Felix edits LVNG Magazine with Michael O'Leary and Peter O'Leary. His most recent chapbooks include *Regional Noir* (Bronze Skull, 2007) and *Monaural* (Answer Tag Home Press, 2007).

Adam Fieled is a poet based in Philadelphia. He has released two chapbooks, *Posit* (Dusie Press, 2007) and *Funtime* (Funtime Press, 2007), a collaboration with Andrew Lundwall. His first book, *Opera Bufa*, is out now from Otoliths. A second book, *Beams*, has been released in e-book form from BlazeVox Press. His third book, *When You Bit...*, is due out from Otoliths late this summer. Scantily Clad Press has just released his e-chap *Revolver*. A fourth book, *Chimes*, will be released by BlazeVox in 2009.

Kass Fleisher authored *Talking Out of School: Memoir of an Educated Woman* (Dalkey Archive Press, 2008); *The Adventurous* (experimental prose; Factory School, 2007); *Accidental Species: A Reproduction* (experimental prose; Chax Press, 2005); and *The Bear River Massacre and the Making of History* (nonfiction; SUNY Press, 2004). Her work has appeared in *The Iowa Review, Denver Quarterly, Mandorla, Notre Dame Review, Postmodern Culture,* and *Z Magazine*, and she writes screenplays with her partner, Joe Amato. She is an Associate Professor of English and Women's and Gender Studies at Illinois State University.

Gina Frangello is the author of the novel *My Sister's Continent* (Chiasmus, 2006) and the short story collection *Slut Lullabies*, forthcoming from Emergency Press in 2010. The longtime editor of the literary magazine *Other Voices*, she co-founded its fiction book imprint, Other Voices Books, in 2005 and is currently the Executive Editor of the press' Chicago office. Her short fiction has appeared in numerous literary journals and anthologies, including *Prairie Schooner, StoryQuarterly, Water~Stone Review,* and *A Stranger Among Us: Stories of Cross Cultural Collision and Connection*. She has contributed freelance journalism and book reviews to the *Chicago Tribune* and the *Chicago Reader*, blogs regularly at *The Nervous Breakdown* (thenervousbreakdown.com), and contributes to the Huffington Post Chicago. Gina teaches at Columbia College Chicago and Northwestern University's School of Continuing Studies.

William Fuller lives in Winnetka, IL and works in Chicago. His chapbook *Three Replies* was published by Barque Press in 2008. *Hallucination* is forthcoming from Flood Editions in 2010.

William Gillespie is the author of seven and five-sixths books of fiction and poetry. He is co-host of the radio show Rock Geek F.M. (rockgeekchic.com), and publisher of the independent publishing house Spineless Books (spinelessbooks.com). Prominent collaborations include *2002: A Palindrome Story in 2002 Words*, with Nick Montfort and illustrations by Shelley Jackson; and *The Unknown*, with Scott Rettberg and Dirk Stratton, a book and hypertext novel (co-winner of the trAce/Alt-X International Hypertext Competition, as judged by Robert Coover) (unknownhypertext.com). He holds an MFA in electronic writing from Brown University.

Mary Gilliland lives in Ithaca, New York, where she serves on the Board of Namgyal Monastery Institute of Buddhist Studies, the Dalai Lama's seat in North America. Her awards include the Stanley Kunitz Fellowship at the Fine Arts Work Center in Provincetown, an Ann Stanford Prize, and a Cornell Council on the Arts Faculty Grant. Recent and forthcoming poetry can be found in *AGNI, Chautauqua, Notre Dame Review, Passages North, Poetry, Seneca Review,* and *Stand.*

C. S. Giscombe was born in Dayton, Ohio. His poetry books are *Prairie Style, Two Sections from Practical Geography, Giscome Road, Here, At Large,* and *Postcards;* his prose book—about Canada—is *Into and Out of Dislocation. Prairie Style* was awarded an American Book Award by the Before Columbus Foundation; *Giscome Road* won the Carl Sandburg Prize, given by the Chicago Public Library. C. S. Giscombe's writing has also won him fellowships from the National Endowment for the Arts, the Fund for Poetry, and the Canadian Embassy. He has worked as a taxi driver, as a hospital orderly, as a railroad brakeman, and for years edited a national literary magazine (*Epoch*, at Cornell University). His writing has appeared in several anthologies—the Best American Poetry series, the *Oxford Anthology of African-American Poetry, Telling It Slant: Avant-Garde Poetics of the 1990s, Bluesprint: Black British Columbia Literature and Orature, Lyrical Postmodernisms,* etc. He is a long-distance cyclist. He teaches poetry at the University of California, Berkeley.

Judith Goldman is the author of *Vocoder* (Roof, 2001), *DeathStar/rico-chet* (O Books, 2006), and *The Dispossessions* (chapbook; Atticus/Finch, 2009). *l.b.; or, catenaries* will be published by Krupskaya in 2010. Judith co-edits, with Leslie Scalapino, the annual journal *War and Peace.* She is a Harper Schmidt Fellow / Collegiate Assistant Professor at the University of Chicago and teaches in the arts humanities core and in Creative Writing.

Alexandra Grant is a text-based artist who uses language and networks of words as the basis for her work in painting, drawing and sculpture. Her work has been the subject of shows at the Museum of Contemporary Art (Los Angeles), the Contemporary Museum (Baltimore), and galleries in the US and abroad. Grant has explored ideas of translation, identity, and dis/location not only in drawings, painting and sculpture, but also in conversation with other artists and writers, such as her current collaborator, hypertext author Michael Joyce, and the philosopher Hélène Cixous. Grant investigates translation not only from language to language, but also from text to image, spoken language to written word, and representations in two dimensions to three-dimensional objects. Some of the basic queries that fuel her work are: How do we "read" and "write" images? How does language place us? What is the role of the hand in a world dominated by electronic communication?

Christopher Grimes is the author of *Public Works: Short Fiction and a Novella.* His research interests primarily center on postmodern, contemporary, experimental and avant-garde fiction. He teaches in the Program for Writers at the University of Illinois-Chicago.

Gabriel Gudding is the author of *A Defense of Poetry* (Pitt, 2002) and *Rhode Island Notebook* (Dalkey Archive, 2007), a 436 page poem handwritten in his car. He is an Associate Professor of English at Illinois State University. His essays and poems appear in such journals as *New American Literature, The Nation, Journal of the History of Ideas, Harper's Magazine, Conduit, LIT,* and in such anthologies as *Great American Prose Poems* (Scribner) and as translator in *Poems for the Millennium, the Oxford Book of Latin American Poetry,* and *The Whole Island: Six Decades of Cuban Poetry.* He is a contributing editor for *Mandorla: New Writing From the Americas.*

Natalija Grgorinić & Ognjen Rađen write exclusively together and have, along with *Mr. & Mrs. Hide* (written originally in English), published two novels and a collection of short stories (written in Croatian). The founders and editors of *Admit Two*, the only online magazine of collaborative writing (www.admit2.net), they translate to and from Croatian, English, and German, hold a joint degree in creative writing from Otis College of Art & Design, Los Angeles, CA, and are currently working on a double-jointed doctoral dissertation on the subject of literary authorship at Case Western Reserve University in Cleveland, OH. Their work explores the extreme possibilities of living in a pair, writing in two languages, and inhabiting both more than one place and the same space at the same time. You can find out more about them at: tashogi.com.

Jenny Hanning is from Maine, but lives in Austin, Texas. Her fiction and poetry have appeared in *Cimarron Review, Shenandoah, Third Coast* and others.

Books by **Carla Harryman** include the recently released volume of conceptual and experimental essays, *Adorno's Noise* (Essay Press), the experimental novels *Gardener of Stars* (Atelos, 2001) and *The Words: After Carl Sandburg's Rootabaga Stories and Jean-Paul Sartre* (O Books, 1999); two volumes of selected writings, *There Never Was a Rose without a Thorn* (City Lights, 1995) and *Animal Instincts: Prose, Plays and Essays* (This, 1989); and many other collections of poetry, prose, and new genre writings, including *Open Box* (Belladonna, 2007) and *Baby* (Adventures in Poetry, 2008). She is a co-author of the multi-authored experiment in autobiography *The Grand Piano* that focuses on the emergence of Language Writing, art, politics, and culture of the San Francisco Bay area between 1975-1980 and she is co-editor of *Lust for Life,* a volume of essays on the novelist Kathy Acker. Her poets' theater and interdisciplinary performance works have been performed nationally and internationally. She lives in the Detroit Area and serves the faculty of the Creative Writing Program at Eastern Michigan University

Gretchen E. Henderson was awarded the 2010 Madeleine P. Plonsker Emerging Writer's Residency Prize (2010), sponsored by &NOW Books and Lake Forest College. She currently lives and works in Gambier, Ohio, and has taught creative writing and literature at Knox College, the University of Missouri, Barnard College, and at the high school level. Nominated for a Pushcart Prize and the AWP Award Series in the Novel, among other awards, her genre-bending projects have been published in *The Iowa Review, Denver Quarterly, New American Writing, Black Warrior Review, Notre Dame Review, Fourteen Hills, The Southern Review, Alaska Quarterly Review, Caketrain*, and other journals. Some "Exhibits" from her *Galerie de Difformité* can be found at: doubleroomjournal.com/8/Henderson.html.

Lily Hoang's first book *Parabola* won the Chiasmus Press Un-Doing the Novel Contest in 2006. Her short novel *Changing* (Fairy Tale Review Press, 2008) was received a PEN/Beyond Margins award. She is also the author of the forthcoming novels *The Evolutionary Revolution* (Les Figues Press, Feb. 2010) and *Invisible Women* (StepSister Press, 2010). She is co-editor of the forthcoming anthology *Thirty Under Thirty* and Associate Editor of Starcherone Books.

Shelley Jackson is the author of the story collection *The Melancholy of Anatomy*, the novel *Half Life*, and hypertexts including *Patchwork Girl, My Body, and The Doll Games.* The recipient of a Howard Foundation grant, a Pushcart Prize, and the 2006 James Tiptree Jr Award, she has also written and illustrated a number of children's books, including *The Old Woman and the Wave; Sophia, The Alchemist's Dog*; and the forthcoming *Mimi's Dada Catifesto.* Her stories and essays have appeared in numerous anthologies and journals including *Conjunctions, McSweeney's, The Paris Review* and *Cabinet Magazine.* In 2004 she launched her project SKIN, a story published in tattoos on 2095 volunteers. She is the co-founder, with artist Christine Hill, of the Interstitial Library, and headmistress of the Shelley Jackson Vocational School for Ghost Speakers and Hearing-Mouth Children. She teaches at the New School University and lives in Brooklyn.

Harold Jaffe is the author of 15 books, including nine fiction collections four novels and one volume of essays: *Anti-Twitter: 150 50-Word Stories* (forthcoming, Feb, 2110); *Jesus Coyote* (RDSP, 2007); *Beyond the Techno-Cave: A Guerrilla Writer's Guide to Post-Millennial Culture* (Starcherone Books, 2006); *Terror-dot-Gov* (RDSP, 2003); *15 Serial Killers* (RDSP, 2002); *False Positive* (FC2, 2001); *Sex for the Millennium* (Black Ice Books, Spring 1999); *Othello Blues* (FictionNet, 1996); *Straight Razor* (Black Ice Books, 1995); *Eros Anti-Eros* (City Lights, 1990); *Madonna and Other Spectacles* (PAJ/FSG), 1988); *Beasts* (Curbstone, 1986); *Dos Indios* (Thunder's Mouth Press, 1983); *Mourning Crazy Horse* (Fiction Collective, 1982); *and Mole's Pity* (Fiction Collective, 1979). Jaffe's fiction has appeared in such journals as *Mississippi Review; City Lights Review; Paris*

Review; New Directions in Prose and Poetry; Chicago Review; Chelsea; Fiction; Central Park, Witness; Black Ice; Minnesota Review; Boundary 2; ACM ; Black Warrior Review; Cream City Review, Two Girls' Review, and New Novel Review. And his stories have been anthologized in *Pushcart Prize; Best American Stories; Best of American Humor; Storming the Reality Studio; American Made; Avant Pop: Fiction for a Daydreaming Nation; After Yesterday's Crash: The Avant-Pop Anthology; Bateria* and *AmLit* (Germany), *Borderlands* (Mexico), *Praz* (Italy), *Positive* (Japan), and elsewhere. Recent volumes have been translated into French, Italian, Japanese, Turkish, and Farsi. Jaffe is editor-in-chief of *Fiction International.*

Kirsten Jorgenson is pursuing her MFA in Creative Writing at the University of Alabama.

Michael Joyce lives along the Hudson River and teaches at Vassar College. *The New York Times* termed his novel *afternoon* "the granddaddy of hypertext fictions" and he since has published numerous hypertext fictions on the web and on disk. His most recent print novel is *Was: Annales Nomadique*, a novel of internet, 2007, published by Fiction Collective 2 (FC2). Recently he has taken more and more to poetry, with poems appearing in *nor/ (The New Ohio Review), The Iowa Review, New Letters, Parthenon West, New Review,* and elsewhere. McPherson and Company reissued his novel, *Liam's Going,* in paperback in July 2008. SUNY Press and Michigan have published collections of his short fictions, prose pieces and essays about technology. He is currently Professor of English and Media Studies at Vassar.

Steve Katz started the trouble with *The Exaggerations Of Peter Prince*, in 1968, won the America Award in Fiction with *Swanny's Ways* in 1991. Many books of fiction & poetry came between. Screenplays. Small films. Recently he published *Antonello's Lion*, a novel. Last Fall he published *KISSSSSS : a miscellany*, a book of short works. He is currently working on *The Memoirrhoids*, a collection of 137 brief memoirs.

Asha Khaladkar lives with her family in Regina, Canada. She is currently editing a Shakespeare encyclopedia and wishing she had the time to actually read Shakespeare. Her work has appeared in such publications as *Opium* and *Grain* in print, and online in the (now sadly defunct) *Edifice Wrecked.*

Matthew Kirkpatrick's writing has appeared recently or is forthcoming in *Conjunctions, Western Humanities Review, Action, Yes!, Apostrophe Cast, Copper Nickel, elimae,* and elsewhere. He is a PhD candidate in Literature and Creative Writing at the University of Utah where he holds the FC2 Fellowship.

Andrea Kneeland has no plans for the future. Her work has appeared or is forthcoming in a number of print journals, including *Quick Fiction, Weird Tales, Hobart, Caketrain, American Letters & Commentary, 580 Split* and *Whiskey Island* and on the web at places like *Night Train, elimae, DIAGRAM, alice blue review, Dogzplot* and *Lumination Colony*. Her first collection of flash fiction, *Damage Control,* is forthcoming from Paper Hero Press as part of the Fox Force 5 chapbook collective. She is also a web editor for *Hobart.*

Dave Kress is a professor of English at the university of Maine in Orono, where he teaches fiction writing, contemporary literature, and literary theory .

Tom La Farge published three animal fictions with Sun & Moon in the 90s: the novel *The Crimson Bears* and its second part, *A Hundred Doors,* and a book of fables, *Terror of Earth.* Green Integer published his second novel, *Zuntig,* in 2001. Tom has written two more novels since then, *The Broken House,* and *Skin,* and is at work on a third, *Nomad Academy.* They form a trilogy set in an imagined country where the animal nature of people is more pronounced. Tom is now at work on a manual of constrained (Oulipian) writing, *13 Writhing Machines,* a series of pamphlets being published by Proteotypes, the press where he is managing editor. *Administrative Assemblages,* the first pamphlet, came out in December, 2008, and the second, *Homomorphic Converters,* will be published in September, 2009.

Stacey Levine wrote *My Horse and Other Stories* (PEN/West Fiction Award) and the novels *Dra*—and *Frances Johnson* (finalist, Washington State Book Award). Her short fiction collection *The Girl with Brown Fur* is forthcoming. A Puschcart Prize nominee, her fiction has appeared in the *Denver Quarterly, Fence, Tin House, The Fairy Tale Review, Yeti,* and other venues. She has also contributed to *American Book Review, Bookforum, The*

Chicago Reader, and *The Seattle Post-Intelligencer.*

Rachel Loden is the author of *Dick of the Dead,* which came out in May 2009. Her first book, *Hotel Imperium,* was selected as one of the ten best poetry books of the year by the *San Francisco Chronicle,* which called it "quirky and beguiling." It was also shortlisted for the Bay Area Book Reviewers Award. Loden has published four chapbooks, including *The Last Campaign* and *The Richard Nixon Snow Globe.* Her work has appeared in *New American Writing, The Paris Review, Jacket,* two editions of the *Best American Poetry* series, and many other magazines and anthologies. Loden's microplay, "A Quaker Meeting in Yorba Linda," was performed in New York as part of Plays on Words: A Poets Theater Festival curated by Tony Torn, Lee Ann Brown and Corina Copp. She has received a Pushcart Prize, a Fellowship in Poetry from the California Arts Council, and a grant from the Fund for Poetry.

Stephen-Paul Martin has published over twenty books of fiction, non-fiction and poetry. His most recent books are *Safety Somewhere Else* (Obscure Publications, 2008) and *The Possibility of Music* (FC2, 2007). He teaches fiction in San Diego State University's MFA program.

John Matthias taught for many years at the University of Notre Dame. He has published some twenty-five books of poetry, translation, scholarship, and collaboration. His most recent volumes of poetry are *Working Progress, Working Title, New Selected Poems,* and *Kedging,* all from Salt Publishing. He is poetry editor of *Notre Dame Review.*

Cris Mazza is the author of over a dozen books. Her most recent fiction titles include *Various Men Who Knew Us as Girls,* and *Trickle-Down Timeline.* Her other fiction titles include the critically notable *Is It Sexual Harassment Yet?,* and the PEN Nelson Algren Award winning *How to Leave a Country.* A native of Southern California, Mazza grew up in San Diego County. She currently lives 50 miles west of Chicago and is a professor in the Program for Writers at the University of Illinois at Chicago.

Megan Milks lives in Chicago. Her work has been anthologized in *Thirty Under Thirty; Wreckage of Reason: An Anthology of Contemporary Xxperimental Prose by Women Writers; and Fist of the Spider Woman: Tales of Fear and Queer Desire.* Her fiction can also be found in *DIAGRAM, Mad Hatters Review, Pocket Myths: The Odyssey,* and *The Wild.* She co-edits *Mildred Pierce* Magazine.

Born in 1970 in Washington D.C., **Paul D. Miller** is an artist, writer, and musician working in New York. Miller is best known under the moniker of his "constructed persona" as "DJ Spooky That Subliminal Kid." Miller has recorded a huge volume of music and has collaborated with a wide variety of artists, writers, musicians and composers, such as Robert Wilson, Iannis Xenakis, Ryuichi Sakamoto, Mariko Mori, Kool Keith/ Doctor Octagon, Pierre Boulez, Saul Williams, Steve Reich, Yoko Ono, Thurston Moore of Sonic Youth, Paul Auster, and Colson Whitehead among many others. In addition to his award winning book *Rhythm Science* (MIT Press, 2005), his written work has appeared in *The Village Voice, The Source, Artforum, Raygun, Rap Pages, Paper Magazine, The Nation,* and a host of other periodicals. Miller's work as an artist has appeared in a variety of contexts such as the Whitney Biennial; The Venice Biennial; the Ludwig Museum in Cologne, Germany; Kunsthalle, Vienna; The Andy Warhol Museum, Paula Cooper Gallery and many other museums and galleries. His newest book *Sound Unbound,* a collection of writings by notable authors, was published by MIT Press in April 2008. His latest large-scale multimedia performance piece is *"Terra Nova: Sinfonia Antarctica"*, commissioned by the Brooklyn Academy of Music/Next Wave Festival and other highly respected presenters. djspooky.com.

Christina Milletti teaches at the University at Buffalo, SUNY. Her collection of short stories, *The Religious and Other Fictions,* was published by Carnegie Mellon University Press. She is currently working on a novel called *Choke Box.*

Simone Muench is the author of *The Air Lost in Breathing* (Marianne Moore Poetry Prize; Helicon Nine, 2000), *Lampblack & Ash* (Kathryn A. Morton Prize; Sarabande, 2005) and *Orange Crush* (Sarabande, 2010). Her most recent chapbook, written with Philip Jenks, is *Little Visceral Carnival* (Cinematheque Press, 2009).

She is a professor, horror film fan, vegetarian, and an editor for *Sharkforum.*

The New Anonymous is an annual literary journal that not only publishes all work anonymously but also blindly screens and edits its submissions, i.e., the submission, editorial, and publishing process is anonymous from beginning to end. At *The New Anonymous* we hope to create a safehouse where writers and editors not only question the creative process but also play.

Carol Novack is the publisher of the multimedia e-journal *Mad Hatters' Review* and a frequent collaborator with musicians, writers, digital film-makers and visual artists. An illustrated collection of her short writings, *Giraffes in Hiding: The Mythical Memoirs of Carol Novack,* will be published in 2010 by Crossing Chaos Enigmatic Ink. Works may or will be found in numerous journals, including, *5_trope, Action, Yes, American Letters & Commentary, Caketrain, Diagram, Fiction International, First Intensity, Gargoyle, Journal of Experimental Fiction, LIT, Notre Dame Review,* and *Otoliths,* and in many anthologies, including *Online Writings: The Best of the First Ten Years, The Penguin Book of Australian Women Poets,* and *Heide Hatry: Heads and Tales.* Her writings have been translated into several languages. See carolnovack.blogspot.com for further details.

Peter O'Leary's books include *Watchfulness, Depth Theology, A Mystical Theology of the Limbic Fissure, Wren/Omen,* and *Benedicite.* He lives in Berwyn, Illinois and teaches at the School of the Art Institute of Chicago.

Hilton Obenzinger writes fiction, poetry, history and criticism. He has most recently published the autobiographical novel *Busy Dying.* His other books include *A*hole,* an experimental fiction on parents and children, creators and creations, gods and mortals, *Running through Fire: How I Survived the Holocaust by Zosia Goldberg as told to Hilton Obenzinger,* an oral history of his aunt's ordeal during the war; *American Palestine: Melville, Twain and the Holy Land Mania,* a literary and historical study of America's fascination with the Holy Land; *Cannibal Eliot and the Lost Histories of San Francisco,* a novel of invented documents that recounts the history of San Francisco from the Spanish conquest to the 1906 earthquake and fire; *New York on Fire,* a history of the fires of New York in verse, selected by the Village Voice as one of the best books of the year and nominated by the Bay Area Book Reviewer's Association for its award in poetry; *This Passover Or The Next I Will Never Be in Jerusalem,* which received the American Book Award of the Before Columbus Foundation. Born in 1947 in Brooklyn, raised in Queens, and graduating Columbia University in 1969, he has taught on the Yurok Indian Reservation, operated a community printing press in San Francisco's Mission District, and co-edited a publication devoted to Middle East peace, worked as a commercial writer and instructional designer. Currently, he teaches honors and advanced writing and American literature at Stanford.

Lance Olsen is author of many books of and about innovative fiction, including his latest novel *Head in Flames* (Chiasmus, 2009). He teaches experimental narrative theory and practice at the University of Utah and serves as the chair of the FC2 Board of Directors, fiction editor at *Western Humanities Review,* and associate editor at *American Book Review.* Website: lanceolsen.com.

Ted Pelton's newest book is the novella, *Bartleby, the Sportscaster.* He is also the author of a second novella, *Bhang;* a novel, *Malcolm & Jack;* and a story collection, *Endorsed by Jack Chapeau.* The press he founded and directs, Starcherone Books, celebrates its 10th anniversary in 2010. He is a Professor of Humanities at Medaille College of Buffalo, NY.

Vanessa Place is a writer, lawyer, and co-director of Les Figues Press.

Doug Rice is the author of *Skin Prayer: Fragments of Abject Memory, Blood of Mugwump,* and *A Good Cu/tboy is Hard to Find.* He co-edited *Federman: A to X-X-X-X* and directs the publishing house Nobodaddies Press. His work has been published in numerous anthologies and journals including *Avant Pop: Fiction for a Daydream Nation, Chick for a Day, Discourse, Fiction International, Zyzzyva,* and *Gargoyle.* His work has been translated into five languages. Currently, he is working on a portfolio of photographs on the grammar of rivers and is finishing a memoir and a new novel. He teaches creative writing and film theory at a university in California.

Matthew Roberson coordinates the creative writing program at Central Michigan University and is the author of two novels, *1998.6* and *Impotent*. He also currently serves on the FC2 Board of Directors.

A native of Southern California, **Lou Rowan** began his writing career in New York City, where he earned his living as a teacher and as an institutional investor. He lives and writes in Seattle. He's currently finishing a novel fusing the formal mystery with a groundbreaking genre: the Eastern. His books include: *My Last Days,* novel, (Chiasmus, 2007); *Sweet Potatoes,* stories, (ahadada, 2007). He edits *Golden Handcuffs Review*.

Bradley Sands lives in Boulder, Colorado. He is the author of the novel, *It Came from Below the Belt* (Afterbirth Books), and the editor of the journal, *Bust Down the Door and Eat All the Chickens*. Forthcoming books include *Disappointing Sophomoric Effort* (Afterbirth Books) and *My Heart Said No But the Camera Crew Said Yes!* (Raw Dog Screaming Press). His work has appeared or is forthcoming in *The Bizarro Starter Kit* (Blue), *The Magazine of Bizarro Fiction, No Colony, Opium Magazine, The Dream People, decomP, Mud Luscious, Thieves Jargon, Noo Journal, Word Riot,* and elsewhere. He is an MFA candidate in Writing and Poetics at Naropa University.

Jessica Savitz is a graduate from the Iowa Writers' Workshop, and was the inaugural Madeleine P. Plonsker Emerging Writer's Residency Prize (2009) writer in residence at Lake Forest College this past winter. Her first book of poems, *Hunting is Painting,* will be published by Lake Forest College Press/ & NOW Books in 2010. Sun Sun Sun will publish her chapbook *Fire is the Statue with the Young Face* this year. Jessica likes to experiment with pairing her poems with various visual artworks, especially with the paintings of Allison Hawkins and the photography of Roxane Hopper.

Kerri Sonnenberg is the author of *The Mudra* (Litmus Press, 2004) and the chapbook *Practical Art Criticism* (Bronze Skull Press, 2004). From 2003-2007 she co-directed the Discrete Reading Series in Chicago with Jesse Seldess. Her work has appeared in the journals *Aufgabe, New American Writing, Factorial, MiPoesias, Moria, Milk, Antennae, Bird Dog, Crayon* and *26,* and has been anthologized in *The City Visible: Chicago Poetry for the New Century* (Cracked Slab Books, 2007).

Mark Spitzer is the author of nine or ten books, the Managing Editor of *Exquisite Corpse Annual*, and a professor of creative writing somewhere in Arkansas. Having quit literary translating like Rimbaud ditched poetry, he can sometimes be seen wrassling alligator gars on the Animal Planet channel. Either that, or driving with his blinker on. For more info, see www.sptzr.net.

Matina L. Stamatakis resides in upstate New York as a freelance photographer and writer. Some of her works have appeared, or are forthcoming, in *Drunken Boat, After Hours: A Journal of Chicago Writing and Art, Free Verse, Inertia,* and *Coconut*. She is the author of *Phos* (VUGG, 2008), *Metempsychose* (Ypolita Press, 2009), and *Xenomorphia* (Wheelhouse Press, 2009) with John Moore Williams.

Lisa Gluskin Stonestreet's *Tulips, Water, Ash,* was selected for the 2009 Morse Prize and published in October 2009 by University Press of New England. Her poems have appeared in journals such as *Blackbird, The Iowa Review, 32 Poems,* and *Third Coast* and in the anthologies *Best New Poets 2005 and 2006*. She lives in San Francisco with her husband and son.

Stephanie Strickland's most recent book, *Zone : Zero* (book + CD), includes two interactive digital poems. Prize-winning volumes include *V: WaveSon.nets / Losing L'una, True North,* and *The Red Virgin: A Poem of Simone Weil*. Her latest collaborative hypermedia work, *slippingglimpse*, was introduced in Paris and shown at the 2009 *e-Poetry* festival in Barcelona. An essay, "Born Digital," appears on the Poetry Foundation website, and another, "Poetry and the Digital World," appears in the special issue of *English Language Notes* on experimental literary education. She teaches at many colleges and universities, most recently the University of Utah, and is a director of the Electronic Literature Organization.

Angela Szczepaniak is neckdeep in a doctoral dissertation that commingles comics, innovative poetry, and dysfunctional detective fiction. Her jubilantly reckless disregard of genre distinctions frequently results in fiction, poetry, and essay publications (or hybrids thereof); work as a poetry editor for Redwood Coast Press; and participation in a hygiene themed poetry-art project (traces of her work may still be found on placards in some of the finest public restrooms in Seattle). Her illustrated poetry has since surfaced in Belgian art galleries, alongside some top-shelf vizpoets (*Infusoria 2009*). Her recent book, *Unisex Love Poems*, is a gruesomely illustrated novel-in-poems.

Yuriy Tarnawsky has authored nineteen collections of poetry, seven plays, nine books of fiction, a biography, and numerous articles and translations. He was born in Ukraine but was raised and educated in the West. A linguist by training, he has worked as computer scientist specializing in natural language processing and as professor of Ukrainian literature at Columbia University. His books include the novels *Meningitis*, and *Three Blondes and Death*, as well as a collection of mini-novels *Like Blood in Water*, all from FC2, and *Ukrainian Dumy*, a translation of Ukrainian epic poetry published by Harvard University. His play *Not Medea* was staged as a workshop production at Mabou Mines in New York in 1998. He has just completed a new collection of mini-novels and is working on a third one which will complete the trilogy.

Bradford Gray Telford is the author of the poetry collection *Perfect Hurt* (Waywiser, 2009) and the translator of *Geneviève* Huttin's *The Story of My Voice* (Host, 2010). His poems have appeared in *Ploughshares, Yale Review, Bomb, Southwest Review, Ninth Letter*, and many other journals. He teaches at The University of Houston.

Maria Tomasula, The *&NOW Awards* cover artist, is a painter whose works are meticulously rendered with machine-like precision, although she only uses traditional brushes and materials. While her process is methodical, rigorous and dispassionate, the images that emerge seem to convey an opposite set of qualities: they are emotive, lyrical and center around the experience of subjectivity. She is represented by Forum Gallery in New York and by Zolla/Lieberman Gallery in Chicago and her work has been exhibited in venues throughout the country as well as abroad. She has had over 20 one-person shows and has been reviewed in such publications as *The New York Times, The New Yorker, ARTnews, Chicago Tribune,* as well as many others. She is Michael P. Grace Professor of Art in the Department of Art, Art History & Design at the University of Notre Dame.

Paul A. Toth lives in Florida. His first novel, *Fizz,* its successor, *Fishnet,* and the conclusion of the trilogy, *Finale*, are all available now through Barnes & Noble or Amazon.com. His short fiction has appeared in *The Mississippi Review, The Barcelona Review, Exquisite Corpse,* and many others. Toth's multimedia work has been featured by *Iowa Review Web* and *Drunken Boat.* See www.netpt.tv for more information.

Matias Viegener is a writer and artist who lives in Los Angeles. He teaches in the MFA writing program at CalArts and is one of three members of the art collaborative Fallen Fruit which has exhibited internationally in galleries and museums. He has published fiction and criticism in *Black Clock, Bomb, Artforum, Art Issues, ArtUS, Artweek, Afterimage, Cabinet, Cargo, Critical Quarterly, High Performance, Framework, Journal of Aesthetics & Protest, American Book Review, Fiction International, Radical History Review, Paragraph, Semiotext(e), Suspect Thoughts,* and *X-tra,* for whom he regularly writes on visual art.

Keith Waldrop's new books in 2009 are: *Transcendental Studies* (poetry, University of California Press); *Several Gravities* (collages & poetry, Siglio Press). He has translated Baudelaire's *Flowers of Evil and Paris Spleen: little poems in prose* (Wesleyan University Press) as well as contemporary French poets Anne-Marie Albiach, Claude Royet-Journoud, Paol Keineg, Dominique Fourcade, and Jean Grosjean. He teaches at Brown University.

Rosmarie Waldrop's recent poetry books are *Curves to the Apple, Blindsight* (both New Directions), and *Love, Like Pronouns* (Omnidawn). University of Alabama Press published her collected essays, *Dissonance (if you are interested).* She has translated, from the German, books by Friederike Mayröcker, Elke Erb, Oskar Pastior, Gerhard Rühm, Ulf Stolterfoht (PEN Award for Poetry in Translation, 2008) and, from the French, Edmond Jabès, Emmanuel Hocquard and Jacques Roubaud.

Together, Keith and Rosmarie Waldrop have published *Well Well Reality* (collected collaborations, Post-Apollo Press), *Ceci n'est pas Keith Ceci n'est pas Rosmarie* (autobiographies, Burning Deck), and translated Jacques Roubaud's poems on the streets of Paris: *The Form of a City Changes Faster, Alas, Than the Human Heart* (Dalkey Archive). They co-edit Burning Deck Press in Providence.

Wendy Walker is a core collaborator at the Proteus Gowanus Gallery/Reading Room in Brooklyn. She is the author of *Blue Fire* (Proteotypes), *The Secret Service, The Sea-Rabbit, or, The Artist of Life, Stories Out of Omarie* (Sun and Moon) and *Knots* (Aqueduct Press). With Tom La Farge, she leads The Writhing Society, weekly meetings devoted to the practice of constrained writing.

William Walsh is the author of *Without Wax: A Documentary Novel* (Casperian Books, 2008) and *Question-struck* (Keyhole Press, 2009). His work has appeared in *LIT, New York Tyrant, Rosebud, Annalemma, Caket-rain, Exquisite Corpse, Quarterly West, McSweeney's Internet Tendency,* and other journals. A story collection entitled *Ampersand, Mass.* is scheduled with Keyhole Press for spring 2010.

Christine Wertheim is the Chair the MFA Writing Program at the California Institute of the Arts. She is the author of *+|'me'S-pace* (Les Figues Press), a book of poetics, and with Matias Viegener has co-edited the anthologies *Seancé, Noulipo,* and *Feminaissance.* Recent critical work has been published in *X-tra, Cabinet* and "The Quick and the Dead," exhibition catalog, The Walker Art Centre. Recent poetry appears in *Drunken Boat, Tarpaulin Sky* and *Veer.* Recent lectures/performances were at the Soundeye poetry conference in Cork, and The Walker Art Center. She co-directs the Institute For Figuring (IFF), curating events on the poetic dimensions of science and mathematics, most recently for The Hayward Gallery, London and The Scottsdale Civic Center, with shows forthcoming at Trinity College, Dublin and The Smithsonian. Her works-in-progress include a new poetic suite on mothers, and a book of conceptual poetry.

Jay Wexler is Professor of Law at Boston University. His first book, *Holy Hullabaloos: A Road Trip to the Battlegrounds of the Church/State Wars,* was published by Beacon Press in June 2009. He is currently working on a book about the "odd clauses" of the U.S. Constitution. His website is jaywex.com.

John Moore Williams is a poet and visual artist who occasionally gets his wires crossed, generally to effects he finds pleasing. He is the author of three chapbooks, *I discover i is an android* (Trainwreck, 2008), *writ10* (VUGG, 2008) and *Xenomorphia* (Wheelhouse, 2009), the last in collaboration with Matina Stamatakis. An artist's book is coming soon from *Tonerworks.* You can view other works and find links to a variety of electronic publications at fissuresofmen.blogspot.com.

Lidia Yuknavitch is the author of three books of experimental short fictions: *Her Other Mouths, Liberty's Excess,* and *Real to Reel,* as well as one book of criticism, *Allegories of Violence.* Her short fictions and critifictions have appeared in *Exquisite Corpse, The Iowa Review, Critical Matrix, Postmodern Culture, Ms., Tank, Another Chicago Magazine, Other Voices, Fiction International,* and elsewhere. She currently teaches writing, literature, film and women's studies in Oregon. She is the founding editor of Chiasmus press, along with her husband the filmmaker Andy Mingo. The winner of various prizes and what-nots, including twice a finalist for the Oregon Book Award, she has two works forthcoming, an anti-memoir *The Chronology of Water* (2010) and the novel *The Small Backs of Children* (2011), both from Hawthorne Press.

Todd Zuniga is the founding editor of *Opium* Magazine and a co-founder of the Literary Death Match. A Pushcart Prize nominee, his fiction has appeared in *Canteen,* online at *Lost Magazine* and *McSweeney's,* his non-fiction occasionally appears online at *The Nervous Breakdown.* He lives in Brooklyn, where he works as the host of the weekly Sports Anomaly podcast. He longs for a Chicago Cubs World Series victory and an EU passport.

ABOUT THE EDITORS

Robert Archambeau's books of poetry and criticism include *Home and Variations* (Salt), *Citation Suite* (Wild Honey), *Word Play Place* (Ohio/Swallow), *Vectors* (Samizdat) and *Laureates and Heretics* (Notre Dame). The editor of the international poetry journal *Samizdat* from 1998-2004, his work has appeared in journals as diverse as *Poetry, Chicago Review, Jacket, PN Review, The Cultural Society, Boston Review, Drunken Boat, Action Yes,* and *Pleiades,* among many others. He has received awards from the Academy of American Poets and the Illinois Arts Council, and has taught at Lund University in Sweden. He is professor of English at Lake Forest College, and is Director of Lake Forest College Press/&NOW Books.

Davis Schneiderman is a multimedia artist and writer whose works include the novels *Drain* from Northwestern University Press (2010), *Abecedarium* (w/ Carlos Hernandez, Chiasmus), *DIS* (BlazeVox), and *Multifesto* (limited edition, Spuyten Duyvil); the co-edited collections *Retaking the Universe: Williams S. Burroughs in the Age of Globalization* (Pluto) and *The Exquisite Corpse: Chance and Collaboration in Surrealism's Parlor Game* (Nebraska); and the audiocollage *Memorials to Future Catastrophes* (Jaded Ibis). He is an Associate Professor of English at Lake Forest College, and Director of Lake Forest College Press/&NOW Books. davisschneiderman.com

Steve Tomasula's short fiction appears often in literary magazines like *McSweeney's; The Western Humanities Review; American Letters & Commentary;* and *The Iowa Review.* His essays on body art and culture can be found in *Leonardo* (M.I.T. Press) and other magazines and anthologies both here and in Europe. He is the author of the novels *IN & OZ; The Book of Portraiture;* and *VAS: An Opera in Flatland;* and *TOC: A New-Media Novel,* an interactive novel of time published on DVD by the University of Alabama/FC2. He teaches postmodern literature at the University of Notre Dame, where he is also director of The Creative Writing Program.

THE MADELEINE P. PLONSKER EMERGING WRITER'S RESIDENCY PRIZE

Jessica Savitz
2009 Winner (Poetry)

Gretchen E. Henderson
2010 Winner (Prose)

Each spring, Lake Forest College, in conjunction with &NOW Books, sponsors emerging writers under forty years old—with no major book publication—to spend two months in residence at our campus in Chicago's northern suburbs on the shore of Lake Michigan. There are no formal teaching duties attached to the residency. Time is to be spent completing a manuscript, participating in the annual Lake Forest Literary Festival, and offering a series of public presentations.

The completed manuscript will be published (upon approval) by &NOW Books, with distribution by Northwestern University Press.

The stipend is $10,000, with a housing suite and campus meals provided by the college.

In odd years we accept applications in poetry and cross/mixed/undefinable genres.
In even years we accept applications in prose and cross/mixed/undefinable genres.

Yearly postmark deadline, April 1.

Please send:
1) Curriculum vitae
2) No more than 30 pages of manuscript in progress
3) A one-page statement of plans for completion

Plonsker Residency
Department of English
Lake Forest College
Box A16
555 N. Sheridan Road
Lake Forest, IL 60045.

Direct inquiries to andnow@lakeforest.edu with the subject line: Plonsker Prize.